Thomas J. Bennett, C.D.

Skill At Arms

A History of Canadian Army Trades
Including their Badges
& Parachute Wings

Bunker to Bunker Books
Magic Mouse Enterprises

© Copyright Thomas J. Bennett 2005

All rights reserved. No part of this publication my be reproduced, stored in a retrieval system, or transmitted in any form or by any means, electronic, mechanical, photocopy, recording or any other method without the prior written permission of the author.

Researched and written by
Thomas J. Bennett, C.D.

ISBN 1-894255-52-6

Library and Archives Canada Cataloguing in Publication

Bennett, Thomas J., 1946-

**Skill at Arms: A History of Canadian Army Trades
Including their Badges & Parachute Wings / Thomas J. Bennett**

**Includes index.
ISBN 1-894255-52-6**

1. Canada. Canadian Armed Forces - - Medals, badges, decorations,
2. Etc. - - History. I. Title

UC535.C3B458 2005   355.1'342   C2005-905475-1

Published by
Bunker to Bunker Books, Calgary, AB
& Magic Mouse Enterprises, Stony Plain AB

Cover: The Canadian Army Crest (top left)
is copyrighted and used with permission of DND

Printed in Canada

This book is dedicated to all the soldiers of the Canadian Army who are no longer alive to read it.

ACKNOWLEDGEMENTS

Many people helped me with the research for this book. I can't possibly list them all by name. However, I would be remiss if I did not thank some of the people who went out of their way to gather information for me or to loan me books or photographs.

Ken Holmes - RCE
CWO Wayne Shields - CE Section Edmonton
Paul Tulk RCASC
CWO Gino Morretti - ATWO course
Sam Moore - RCASC
WO White - Ammo Tech
MWO Blier - Court Reporter
WO Ed Story - Geomatics
Archie Beare   - RCA
Shawn Hodges - Saftey Systems Tech and Pathfinder
George Hennecke - assisted with checking for errors.
People who gave me the use of their photographs are named near the photo they contributed.

I would like to express my gratitude to the staff of the Directorate of History and Heritage, Ottawa who gave me access to their archives and an assistant to find publications for me. They continued to send material by mail when I was no longer in Ottawa. Without their help, this book would not have been possible.

Also, I would like to thank the curators of the following museums. All of them went out of their way to assist me in my research.

The Communications and Electronics Museum, Kingston
The Royal Canadian Artillery Museum, Shilo
The Royal Canadian Regiment Museum, London
The Military Museum, CFB Petawawa
The Loyal Edmonton Regiment Museum, Edmonton
The Provincial Museum of Alberta, Edmonton
The Museum of the Regiments, Calgary

Major General (retired) Herb Pitts has been very supportive. Not only did he read the manuscript and write the forward, but he took it upon himself to correct my grammar and typing mistakes, of which there were quite a few. He also supplied some of the information about the Infantry and the Canadian Airborne Regiment. I really appreciate it sir. Thank you very much.

Finally, too numerous to mention individually, my thanks to the many soldiers of CFB Edmonton who gave their time and knowledge in numerous interviews. Every single person that I asked for assistance, went out of their way to find the information that I was seeking.

FORWARD

It has been my very great pleasure to review **SKILL AT ARMS** prior to its publication. The author has done a tremendous service to the preservation of the story of the evolution of the Canadian Army, and by extension, the Canadian Armed Forces. The material presented in the book assists in tracing the transformation of the Army from its beginnings as a "horse and buggy" force into a modern, technologically sophisticated fighting force, including changes currently underway as the book goes to print.

Some the Trades researched and presented in this book appear in the very earliest phases of Army records. The Artillery Trades for example, in one form or another, are a common thread throughout the book and through he development of the Army. The vehicles used in training and in combat are visualized by studying the Trades that were needed to keep them in serviceable condition. Weapon Technicians give glimpses into the weapons that have been used over the last century. The Parachute Badge Section will have great appeal to the many Canadians "who have soldiered under the silk" and are branded and bonded as "Jumpers".

This book will prove invaluable to collectors and Museums interested in gathering information and materials to assist in the preparation and presentation of displays for the public. Students of Military History will find this to be yet another indicator of our growth as a sovereign nation, whose Armed Forces have been a vital contributor to our well-being and security.

Thomas Bennett is to be congratulated on gathering this information and collating it into a unique reference book. It is evident that this publication has been a "labour of love" and has needed an enormous amount of time and dedicated research to complete. To my knowledge there is no other Canadian book which brings the story of our badges, representing our **SKILL AT ARMS**, under one cover. **"Well Done, Jumper"**.

"My very Best Wishes to Tom,

his Contributors and Collaborators

and finally, to you his Readers.

"Have a Good One".

Major General (Retired) Herb Pitts, M.C., C.D.

Former CO, 1st Bn The Queen's Own Rifles of Canada
Regimental Commander, Canadian Airborne Regiment
Colonel of the Regiment, Princess Patricia's Canadian Light Infantry
Colonel Commandant, Canadian Infantry Corps.

TABLE OF CONTENTS

Part One 9

    Skill-At-Arms Badges   10
    Instructors' Badges   15
    Trades and Badges before 1942   18

Part Two 73

    T Badges   74
    Trades 1942 to 1945   76
    Trades 1946 to 1955   97

Part Three 125

    Trades and Badges 1956 to date   126

Part Four 219

    Parachute Badges   220
    Pathfinder Badges   234
    Rigger Badges   236
    Search and Rescue Badges   239

Part Five 245

    Service Chevrons   246
    General Service Badge   248
    Trained Soldier Badge   248
    Good Conduct Badges   248
    Wound Stripes   249
    Corps Insignia   250
    Marksmanship Badges   252

Appendix A
Acronyms, Abbreviations and Definitions   253

Appendix B
    Bibliography   254

Appendix C
    Notes   255

Index 257

PREFACE

This book is intended to be a guide for both militaria collectors and historians. It covers the subjects of trade badges, skill-at-arms badges, instructors' badges and parachute badges for the Canadian Army other ranks (not officers) from 1900 to date. For the military historian, I have attempted to write a brief job description of each trade. This information should be of interest to the collector as well. I believe that a badge is of more interest and value to the current owner if he or she has some information about its background, and who would have worn the badge in a certain time period.

Another reason for writing this book was to keep alive the memory of Canadian soldiers who toiled and sometimes gave their lives while working in now obsolete trades. I found it disturbing that trades such as the loftman, the carriage and wagon repairer, the edgerman, the bomber and many others seem to have vanished without a trace. History books provide accounts of battles and corps but seldom mention individual trades.

I am not aware of any book of this type in existence. There are many publications on hat badges, uniforms and weapons, but none on cloth arm badges and job descriptions that I could find.

The book does not go into great detail about the history of any corps. That is not the purpose of this book. Rather, the aim is to give the reader at a glance: a photo of the badge, the name of the trade or trades who wore it, the different colours that were available for wear on different uniforms, the levels of expertise in which each badge existed and a brief job description. For each trade, I have also named the corps the soldier would have belonged to at the time. For example, a concretor, was a member of the Corps of Royal Canadian Engineers.

Trade badges were made in different coloured backgrounds to match several different uniforms. Khaki (worsted drab was the official term) for the battledress and tropical worsted uniforms in use from 1939 to 1968. These badges were worn by most soldiers but there were exceptions. The rifle regiments wore badges that were black on a red background. The Royal Winnipeg Rifles wore badges that were green on black. Badges for the Canadian Women's Army Corps were drab on beech brown. With the change of uniforms in 1968, trade badges were abolished for a while. When they made a comeback in 1985, they were gold on a black background. Badges for the short-lived garrison dress were gold on a green background.

Most trade badges existed in four levels of expertise, showing not only the trade of the wearer but his skill level from beginner to expert. Some of the badges were not made in all four levels. This will be indicated for each badge.

The book is divided into five parts:

1. Skill-at-arms and trade badges before 1942.
2. The "T" badges 1942 to 1955.
3. Modern trade badges 1956 to date.
4. Parachute badges.
5. Miscellaneous badges such as service chevrons, good conduct, and other badges

These time periods match the various issues of trade badges used by the Canadian Army. The current type of trade badge worn by the army today, was first introduced in 1956. Since then, there have been many changes, but the basic style and levels of badges remain the same.

Also covered in this book, are skill-at-arms badges. These badges are often confused with trade badges, as to the novice, that is what they appear to be. To set the matter straight, an explanation, with photographs, will be the first subject of the book.

There is some information on the proper wearing of the badges. Mostly, they were worn on the lower portion of the right sleeve, but there were exceptions to this rule. Also, the proper location of wear for a badge sometimes changed from year to year.

Military acronyms are used throughout the book. That is because it takes so little space to write RCASC as compared to writing "Royal Canadian Army Service Corps" over and over again. It is assumed that the vast majority of collectors and historians who read this book will be familiar with this terminology. For those who are unfamiliar with them, there is a list in appendix "A" at the back of the book.

The trades are listed in alphabetical order by section heading. For example, all the artillery trades are grouped together. Therefore, you will find "gun layer" listed under "A" for "Artillery." Another reason for doing this, is that some trades have changed their names over the years. An Accounting Clerk was later renamed to a Finance Clerk. Years later, the Finance Clerk was merged with the Administrative Clerk to create a Resource Management Support Clerk. All of these trades are found in one place under the common heading of "Clerks." If you can't find a certain trade, an index can be found at the back of the book.

The book does not contain information on badges of rank, shoulder titles, formation patches or hat badges, except where this information is required to explain some other badge.

Although years of research have gone into the making of this book, I know that it is not complete. A few badges have been left out because insufficient documentation could be found to write about them. No doubt there are some errors that have crept into my work. To make the book 100 percent accurate would take a lifetime of research and the book would never get published. Therefore, I decided to go to print with what I have. The intent is to share the information that is currently available, while still searching for the answers to some of my questions. If you have any information to add, please contact the author via his web site (see back of the book). Hopefully, I will be able to release an updated edition sometime in the future.

Finally, it is my wish that you enjoy this book, as much as I did writing it. Collecting trade badges is, in my opinion, an excellent hobby. It leads to a greater understanding of our military history. Not many collectors are content just to own the badge to fill a hole in their collection. Most will want to know a little bit of information about the history of its previous owner. Have fun.

A note on abbreviations

Although a complete list of abbreviations is given in Appendix A, a short list is provided here of those that are used most frequently throughout the book. Abbreviations are used in the military in daily conversation and not only on paper. When vehicle repairs are required a soldier would ask for a "Vehicle Tech", not a Vehicle Technician.

Tech	Technician
Mech	Mechanic
Op	Operator
Recce	Reconnaissance
Veh	Vehicle
Admin	Administrative

Skill-At-Arms Badges, Instructors' Badges and Trade Badges before 1942

Part One

**Skill-At-Arms Badges
Instructors' Badges
and Trade Badges
before 1942**

SKILL AT ARMS
to be skilful at a military profession

SKILL-AT-ARMS BADGES

By 1900, many different trade and skill at arms (SAA) badges were in use. What is the difference between a trade badge and a skill-at-arms badge, you are probably asking? The trade badge, as it is named, shows the trade, or occupation, of the wearer. Was he an armourer, a pioneer, or a musician. The badge will tell you.

Skill-at-arms badges also indicate the profession of the wearer, but that is not their purpose. They were created to encourage a higher level of skill at one's profession. Soldiers who wore a skill-at-arms badge were "good at their job". A soldier was required to pass a comprehensive test in order to qualify for a skill-at-arms badge. They were worn with pride, and the hope was that they would encourage less skilled tradesman to improve their abilities, until they too, could qualify for the badge.

I used the word "profession" to distinguish skill badge from trade badges because some skill badges were awarded to soldiers whose job was not considered to be a trade. This subject comes up several times throughout the book. Just because a soldier worked at a job for many years does not mean that it was a recognized army trade. None of the combat arms soldiers were considered tradesman until recent years.

Most skill-at-arms badges were oval and featured a letter (or letters) surrounded by a laurel wreath, the letter indicating the occupation. Most, but not all badges followed this pattern. Some, like the marksmanship badge, consisted of cross rifles, and a skill-at-arms badge for a signaller was a set of cross flags. One, the tank driver, was star shaped. Many of them were produced in both cloth and metal.

Skill-at-arms badges of the United Kingdom are often confused with Canadian badges as many of them look alike. Some were used by the UK only and were not worn officially by Canadians. Only the SAA badges for which I have written or photographic proof that the badge was worn by Canadians are included in this book.

Two types of Skill-at-Arms badges

There were two categories of SAA badges. Some were issued to all members of a certain profession up to establishment levels. These were worn permanently by the qualifying soldiers. The second category of SAA badges were those issued as a prize in the annual competitions. These badges could be worn for one year only. After one year, if he wanted to retain the badge, the soldier would have to pass the test again.

Most skill-at-arms badges were worn on the lower left arm. If no other badges were worn, then the SAA badge would be 6 ½ inches from the bottom of the sleeve. Many other badges were worn during and before the Second World War including good conduct badges, long service chevrons, general service badges, wound badges, etc. The SAA badges were to be worn above all other badges on the forearm, which might result in the badge being worn higher than the normal 6½ inches. They were not to be worn on shirts, work cloths or great coats. [1]

Permanent issue SAA badges were worn on the upper right arm. "Permanent" meant as long as the soldier remained qualified and was covering an authorized unit position. Should he fail to meet these conditions the badge would have to be removed.

Permanent Issue Skill-at-Arms Badges

L All qualified Gun Layers (up to establishment)

A Gun Layer is an artillery profession. A layer's job is to operate the sighting device and lay it on target. The gun has a elevating gear to raise the barrel. A device called a "sight clinometer" indicates the angle. For direct fire a foresight and backsight is provided. For more information see "Gun Number" in Part Three.

The colour of the wreath and lettering on this badge is grey. It is noticeably darker than the other badges shown below. You can see that the badge on the soldier in the photo is also dark. The other badges shown below have white lettering.

Skill-At-Arms Badges, Instructors' Badges and Trade Badges before 1942

A version of this badge exists with white lettering but without the word "Canada" at the top. This may be a British badge as I have not seen any photographs of a Canadian soldier wearing it.

Photo courtesy of the LER museum

Each unit was allowed to have a certain number of soldiers employed at each profession. The term "up to establishment" means the maximum number of soldiers of a certain profession that the unit is allowed to have. Soldiers in excess of establishment were not allowed to wear these badges.

These badges were worn on the upper right arm nine inches from the top of the sleeve on privates, or above rank chevrons on NCO's.

O All qualified Observers (up to establishment)

The Observer was a member of an artillery unit. He would hide himself in a position where he could see enemy targets. He would observe the results of artillery fire and report effectiveness back to the unit. If the shell missed the target, he would  give instructions as to how to correct the fire by aiming more to the left or right or up or down. During the First World War, Observers sometimes worked from observation balloons. This badge was obsolete by the mid 1920's. [2]

P All qualified Plotters (up to establishment)

The Plotter was an artillery profession. The Plotter's job was to determine the map coordinates of the target, given the bearing and the distance. [1]

R All qualified Rangetakers (up to establishment)

Rangetaker was an artillery profession. The Rangetaker's job was to determine the distance to the target. He would use a piece of equipment called a "rangefinder", which, with skilled use, can give distances of 5000 yards within 100 yards of accuracy, or 3000 yards within 40 yards of accuracy. In the 1930's, this badge became obsolete as a permanent SAA badge but still existed as a prize badge. [1]

All of the above badges were awarded to all personnel in their profession, up the establishment levels. Note that all of these badges were awarded to artillery personnel. (notes 1-3)

Prize Badges

Prize badges were awarded at the annual competitions in the summer. They were accompanied by a small cash prize of about $2.00 to $5.00 (the amount varied from year to year and from competition to competition). Badges could be awarded "up to establishment" levels. However, the maximum number of badges would probably not be given out. This would happen only if all personnel on establishment qualified as first class in the annual qualifications.

Prize badges could be worn for a period of one year. If the badge was awarded after 1 July, however, it could be worn until December of the following year. [4]

SAA badges in this category were worn on the lower left arm 6 ½ inches from the bottom or above any other badges worn on the lower arm.

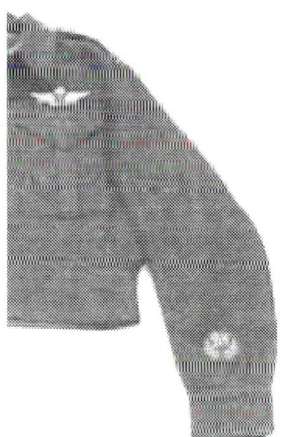

Photo courtesy of the Petawawa Military Museum

DM Driver Mechanic

A Driver Mechanic was not a vehicle mechanic by trade. They were, nevertheless, highly skilled in vehicle maintenance and repairs. Those that wore this badge would have been even more skilled than the average Driver Mechanic.

The photo at left shows the badge being worn on the battledress of the 1st Canadian Parachute Battalion.

G 1st class Gunner - tank (up to establishment)

Worn by those who could pass the 1st class gunner competition. Unless otherwise mentioned, all of these skill-at-arms badges were worn on the left forearm. Without giving any reason, orders state that the "G" badge was to be worn on the right forearm instead of the ususal left. [1]

In spite of the above regulation, photographic evidence shows that the badge was worn on the left forearm like the other badges in this category.

The soldier in the photo is also wearing a wireless telegraphy badge. See the Communications section for details.

Photo of Tpr Ralph Cole RCAC (later of 1CACR) courtesy of his daughter Mrs. Debbie MacRae.

H 1st class Height Taker (up to establishment)

The Height Taker was an artillery profession. A Height Taker determines the height above sea level of a given target. This information is needed for an accurate shoot. [1]

MG 1st class Machine Gunner
(up to establishment)

1st class Machine Gunner - tank crew (up to establishment)

This skill-at-arms badge was awarded to marksmen with the Vickers machine gun and to 1st class machine gunners in a tank crew. [1]

LG 1st class Lewis Gunner (up to establishment)
Light Machine Gun (after 1921)

This badge was awarded to marksman with the Lewis Machine Gun. In 1921, "LG" was changed to stand for "Light Machine Gun" and was awarded to all machine gun marksmen, including Lewis, Bren and Hotchkiss Gunners. (I have no record that the "HG" badge was ever worn by Canadians.) [1]

12

Skill-At Arms Badges Instructors' Badges and Trade Badges before 1942

At right is the LG badge in metal. Skill-at-arms and trade badges were produced in both metal and cloth before and during the First World War. After the war the SAA badges were produced in worsted (cloth) only. Trade badges were still produced in metal until the Second World War.

Changes to the Above Regulations

Some of the regulations for these badges changed over the years as follows:

• According to 1926 regulations, the Rangetaker badge was in the permanent category and was awarded to all qualified Rangetakers. [3]

Regulations in 1941 state that the badge had moved to the prize category and instead of "all qualified" Rangetakers. It was now described as **"1st Class Rangetaker in an Artillery battery or a Machine Gun squadron"**. The location was changed from the upper right arm to the lower left. [1]

• The 1941 regulations also state that all SAA badges are to be of worsted (the metal versions became obsolete after the First World War). [1]

• By the time of the Second World War, many SAA badges had become obsolete. The only authorized skill badges (oval with wreath) in 1941 were G, H, LG, MG, P, and R. The "G" refers to a tank gunner; not an artillery gun layer. [1]

• The description for LG was changed from "First Class" in 1926 to "Marksman" by 1941. (I don't have the exact year of this change in terminology.) The letters, formerly standing for "Lewis Gun" was changed to mean "Light Machine Gun" in 1921.

MG was changed to mean Heavy Machine Gun Marksman instead of 1st class shot. It was still called 1st class in tank units. These were minor changes in terminology. The basic purpose of the badge remained unchanged.

More Prize Badges

G Best six gunners in a battery

This prize badge was awarded to the best six gunners in each battery of artillery. They were tested for proficiency in gun practice, gun laying and signalling. Winners of this badge also received a small cash prize and had their names listed in the Artillery Association Annual Report. [5]

The term "Gunner" refers to any member of the artillery. Therefore this badge could be worn by a signaller, whose rank would be Gunner (see the description of rank below).

The badge shown is blue for the dress blue uniform but was normally issued in khaki. Note that this is a different shape "G" than that of the tank gunner.

This badge was issued in three levels as follows:

G	Third Class
G with wreath	Second Class
G with wreath with crown	First Class

Completions for SAA badges were not held during the war. [4]

Private, Gunner, Signalman, Sapper

These terms refer to the rank of the soldier and not his job. They are all equal to the rank of Private but have different names in different corps. All privates in the Engineers were referred to as Sappers. All privates in the Signal Corps were referred to as Signalman. The artillery also had signallers who were not members of the Signal Corps. In this case his rank would be Gunner and his job would be signaller. In the Signal Corps, the rank would be Signalman and his job could be radio operator or despatch rider. I have read some books where the trade of a solder was referred to as Signalman. You must keep in mind that these are ranks and not trades.

SKILL AT ARMS

In addition to the oval SAA badges, the following other shapes were also awarded:

 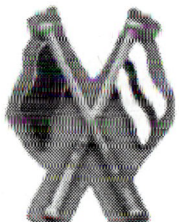 

Crossed flags
all qualified signallers up to establishment

The crossed flags is one of the Canadian Army's oldest badges. It was first authorized for wear in 1908 but was in use before that date and is still in use on a trade badge today. It has been produced in different colours of cloth, metal, and even enamel. It was worn by signallers of both RC SIGS and other corps. In addition to being used as a skill-at-arms badge, it was worn as an instructors badge and a trade badge. It was worn in different locations, depending on its purpose. (See instructors' badges and the communications section in this part of the book.) [1 and 2]

Crossed cannons
best battery in a regiment
NCO who has passed gunnery staff course
(up to establishment)

This was originally an artillery award, given to every man and NCO in the best battery in an artillery regiment to wear for a period of one year. It was not worn by instructors until sometime in the 1920's or 1930's. The badge was eventually discontinued as an award badge, but continued to be used by artillery instructors. As a skill badge it was worn on the lower left arm. (See instructor badges.) [1]

First Class Shot
I don't know the score needed to qualify for this badge. It was worn on the lower left arm 6.5 inches from the bottom. If a soldier qualified as first class with both rifle and a machine gun, this badge would be worn above the LG or MG badge. [3]

Crossed rifles   Marksman
This badge was issued for marksmanship. It was also worn by instructors at the School of Musketry. This is the only skill-at-arms badge that is still in use today. The crossed cannons and crossed flags are still in use, but not as skill badges. They are used as instructor and trade badges respectively. This badge was worn on the lower left arm. See Part Five of the book for information on the current use of this badge. [1]

Star   1st class driver - tank
The star badge was awarded to first class drivers in a tank unit.

There are other skill-at-arms badges that were probably worn by Canadians, but some of them were worn by the British army only. I have included only those badges for which I have some evidence that they were worn by Canadians. I hope to include more SAA badges in a future edition of the book. If you have photographs or other evidence of SAA badges worn by Canadians other than those shown here, please contact the author.

Remember, just because a profession has a skill

Skill-At-Arms Badges, Instructors' Badges and Trade Badges before 1942

badge does not mean that this profession is a recognized army trade. The armoured, artillery and infantry badges shown in this section are skill badges only. They did not become trades until after the Second World War.

INSTRUCTORS' BADGES

Assistant Instructor in Gunnery

The Assistant Instructor in Gunnery badge was worn by Artillery NCOs who had completed the staff course in Gunnery. This badge was worn directly on top of the rank chevrons. For example, the rank badge of a Sergeant-Major during the First World War was four inverted stripes with a crown above. All artillery NCOs above the rank of Corporal wore a small gun above their stripes. Therefore this soldier's sleeve would have, starting from the elbow and working upward, four inverted stripes with the AIG badge sewn on top, an artillery gun above that and a crown above that. The grenade was slightly different than the other two grenade badges in use during this time frame. The Engineer grenade has nine flames; seven in the back and two in the front centre overtop of the others (see Part Five for a picture). The Bomber badge does not have any flames in the front; only the seven rear flames (see infantry bomber in Part One for a picture). The artillery grenade has a single flame in the front centre and seven in the rear.

The photo shows the badge being worn over the rank of Sergeant.

I don't have the exact date, but sometime in the 1920's or 1930's the grenade was dropped from the badge. There are two versions of the badge after the grenade was removed; one with a crown above the guns and one without a crown. The badge with the crown was worn by Warrant Officers and without a crown if the soldier was of a lower rank. The crossed cannon badge shown previously as a skill badge eventually replaced this badge for instructors.[2]

Gymnastics Instructor

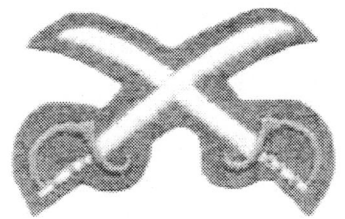

This badge was originally worn by cavalry units. It was awarded annually to the best swordsman in a troop of cavalry in the British army and probably Canadian as well but I have not researched this. Sometime before the First World War, it was adopted as the badge of the physical training staff. It was no longer used by the cavalry. Gymnastics, as it was called at the time, consisted of a combination of physical training (PT), fencing (swordsmanship), bayonet drill and sports. Some gymnastics instructors were sent to Canadian military hospitals to conduct remedial PT. This job was taken over by medical corps personnel in 1946. The fencing and bayonet drill was eventually dropped and the name changed to Physical Training Instructor. The badge was worn on the upper right arm of both sleeves above the rank badge, except for WO who wore it on the lower sleeve. Cloth and metal versions are shown.

The photo at right shows a gymnastics instructor of the 54th Battalion CEF.
He wears the crossed swords badge below his WO1 rank badge.
Photo at left and above right: Bennett collection
Photo at lower right courtesy of Ron Beamish

15

School of Gymnastics

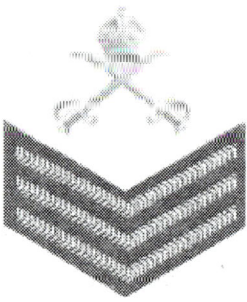

A crossed swords with crown was worn by instructors at the School of Gymnastics. For NCOs this badge was worn above their rank chevrons. Warrant Officers wore crossed swords with a larger crown which was the badge worn by them as a rank badge. These instructors were members of the Army Gymnastics Staff.

Unit Gymnastics instructors wore the crossed swords badge without the crown as previously described. They were not members of the Army Gymnastics Staff, but they had to be in possession of an Army Physical Training Certificate.

The badge at right with the large crown would be worn by a Warrant Officer; the others with the smaller crown by NCOs of the School of Gymnastics. [2]

Assistant Instructor

In the 1930's, several corps began requesting their own instructors badge. NDHQ decided against giving each corps its own distinctive badge. Instead, in 1940, instructors who worked at schools and training centres, were given a badge with the letters "AI" for "Assistant Instructor" This badge was oval when issued (as shown in the illustration) but soldiers often trimmed off the excess material on the left and right of the figure, creating a badge that was flat on the bottom and somewhat of an hourglass shape.

The badges were to be worn on the right arm only. For Warrant Officers, it was to be worn below the rank badge, but above all other badges. For NCO's, it was to be above all badges, including rank badges. This badge was in use until 1947.

Instructional Cadre

Soldiers who were permanent instructors wore a badge with the letters "IC" for "Instructional Cadre". The term "Permanent Instructor" refers to members of the Permanent Active Militia, as the regular force was called before the Second World War, who were sent out to instruct members of the Non Permanent Active Militia, or part time reserve forces as we would call them today. This badge had been in use since 1928. [3]

In 1940 the names Permanent and Non Permanent Militia were changed to Canadian Army (Regular) and Canadian Army (Reserve). The "IC" badge continued to be used until 1956.

Photo courtesy of Museum of the Regiments

Some skill-at-arms badges doubled as instructor badges.

Signals Instructor

A skill badge, when worn above the rank badge, was used as an instructor's badge for the particular skill designated by the badge. The same badge, when used as a skill badge, would be worn on

Skill-At-Arms Badges, Instructors' Badges and Trade Badges before 1942

the lower sleeve. The photo on the right is a Signals instructor. The badge was worn on both arms except for privates who wore it on the right army only. [2 and 6] (See Signaller in the Communications section for more information on the wearing of this badge.)

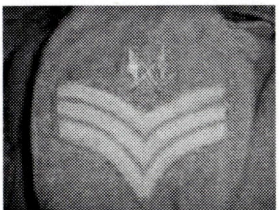

Photo courtesy of Mike Stewart

Lewis Gun Instructor

This Sergeant of the 3rd Canadian Division was an instructor with the Lewis Gun. The service chevrons on the forearm show how long the soldier had been overseas.
(See service chevrons in Part Five for details.)

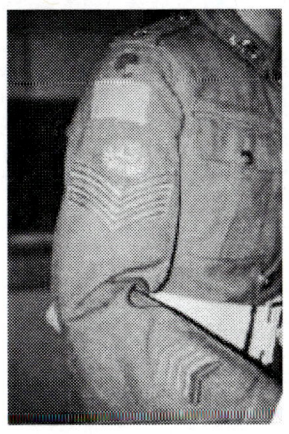

Photo by author

Machine Gun Instructor

Sgt Wally Bennett was a machine gun instructor with the 10th Battalion CEF. This unit was equipped with the U.S. made Colt machine gun.

Photo courtesy of the Calgary Highlanders Museum and Archives

A badge showing the colt machine gun exists. However, photographic evidence and documentation show that the MG badge was worn by this unit. Perhaps the colt machine gun badge was worn unofficially by some personnel but I have not found any evidence of this.

Instructor in Musketry

This Sergeant in the 2nd Canadian Division CEF was an instructor in musketry. This same badge when worn on the forearm represents a skill-at-arms badge for a marksman.

The same badge was worn by unit instructors and those employed a the School of Musketry. I found no mention of a crown being worn above this badge as was the case with the crossed swords.[2]

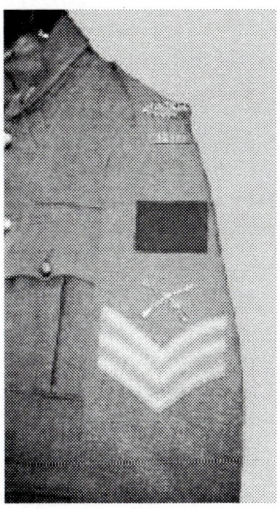

Photo by author. Uniform courtesy of Allan Kerr.

These instructor badges were worn on both arms.

Badges with the letters "L", "O", "P", or "R" worn above the chevrons do not indicate an instructor. That is the normal place of wear for these badges. See permanently issued SAA badges in this section.

Pre 1942 Trades and Badges

The purpose of trade badges are to designate a soldier who has some unique or special trade that others are not qualified to do.

At this point, the main problem is how to tell a trade badge from a skill-at-arms badge. With a few exceptions, skill-at-arms badges are oval, while trade badges were odd shaped. The skill-at-arms badges that are exceptions to the rule are either crossed weapons of some type, crossed flags, or a star. All other odd shapes are trade badges. The only trade badge that is oval is the "S" for the Artillery Surveyor. The medical badge is round.

Skill-at-arms Badges
mostly oval
crossed weapons or flags
made of cloth or metal

Trade Badges
odd shaped
the only oval badge crossed is "S"
mostly cloth, some are metal

　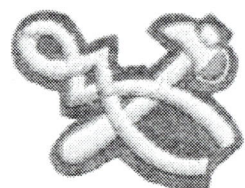

What Constitutes a Trade?

In the modern Canadian Army, all non-commissioned members are considered to have a trade. Prior to 1952, this was not the case. Some members, such as armourers, smiths, despatch riders, linemen, surveyors, pioneers, and many more were considered tradesmen. Others such as infantryman, runners, etc., were considered to be just soldiers and not tradesmen.

During the many interviews that I conducted in the writing of this book, I found that there is quite a bit of confusion as to which jobs are a trade and which ones are not. Even soldiers with many years in the military were unsure. Today, all soldiers have a trade so they may find it difficult to relate to the days when this was not so. Many soldiers were simply that, soldiers only, and not a tradesman. Combat troops did not receive any special recognition until 1952. Other jobs were phased out without ever becoming a trade. The army once had chimney sweepers, gardeners, packers and helpers, cleaners and batmen. None of these were trades and are therefore not described in this book. They existed in the army as jobs only. (There is a list of these non-trade soldiers at the end of Part One.)

I have found that jobs and trades are easily confused. Before unification, it was common to find soldiers who were misemployed. The Royal 22nd Regiment had a tailor for many years. Or did they? They had a soldier who worked in the tailor shop, but working for many years in a tailor shop did not make him a tailor. He would still be an infantryman, no matter how he was employed. In another example, during the Second World War, most infantry units had soldiers who drove around on motorcycles and delivered messages. They were known as "despatch riders." Despatch Riders could be found only in the Royal Canadian Corps of Signals. A soldier in the infantry who happened to be doing the exact same job did not qualify as a despatch rider. Even though he might be doing the job, his classification would remain that of infantryman, unless he was to remuster (to officially change trades.)

The word "trade" in this book refers to the official military occupations used in the army, and not necessarily the job at which a soldier may have been employed. For this reason, the reader will find little information on the combat troops before 1952 as they were not considered to be trades. (From 1952 until 1968 the combat troops received trade badges and trades pay, but not full recognition as an official trade. For more information on this see the article in Part Two dated 1951).

Being a tradesman got a soldier more than just a nice badge. Along with the badge came trades pay. Each trade was placed into a group according to its degree of skill required to perform the duties of that trade. Some trades were spread over more than one group but this was unusual. Most trades existed in one group only during this time period. (After 1942 most trades were spread over three groups as explained in part two.) Within the group, each trade was divided into three classes. This was not indicated on the badge (except for the "S" surveyor badge which was produced in three levels). The following chart shows the different levels and the corresponding trades pay for a private in 1928. [7]

Skill-At-Arms Badges, Instructors' Badges and Trade Badges before 1942

Daily Pay (Pte)
$1.20

GROUP C
class 3   class 2   class 1
$1.20 $1.25 $1.30

GROUP B
class 3   class 2   class 1
$1.35 $1.40 $1.45

GROUP A
class 3   class 2   class 1
$1.50 $1.55 $1.60

The above chart dated 1928 shows a private's pay of $1.20 per day. This would increase with promotion in rank. If he was a tradesman he could receive an additional amount ranging from $1.20 to $1.60 per day. This was known as trades pay and did not increase with rank.

A soldier could increase his pay by changing to another related trade. For example, a Lineman Field, which was a Group C trade, could aspire to become a Lineman Permanent Line or a Switchboard Operator, which were Group B trades.

As you can see, each advancement brought with it a five-cent raise in pay. To advance to the next class, the tradesman had to improve his skills. For a Signalman, this could be an increase in typing speed or learning to install a switchboard, etc. This advancement could bring in as much as 40 cents per day in extra pay, over basic trades pay. This was a worthwhile amount in 1928. Even the lowest grade of trades pay would double a soldier's income. If one was not a tradesman, then he did not receive trades pay.

It is interesting to note that most tradesmen did not have a trade badge. A skill-at-arms badge could be worn by any soldier who could pass the test. Thus, a machine gun badge could be worn by a marksman with the machine gun, even though this was not a trade. Some badges, like the crossed flags badge was used as both a trade badge and a skill badge and was worn by members of several corps.

Note that in the pay chart below, each group was divided into three classes. In 1938 or 39, the classes within groups were done away with. Instead, trades pay increased with rank. In the previous system above, the daily pay increased with rank but the trades pay was the same for all ranks.

Trades pay was restricted to unit establishments. For example, a soldier who was a skilled carpenter, may not receive trades pay if the authorized number of carpenters in the unit had already been reached. So, if a soldier became qualified for an advancement in trade, he would not be able to do so, until there was a vacancy. If a soldier was posted to another unit, he may lose his trades pay if the gaining unit had already reached their established limit of personnel for that particular trade.

Also, trades pay would be forfeited if the solder was not employed at his trade for a period of more than 30 days. For example, if a tradesman was sick in the hospital for a period of 35 days, he would lose five days trades pay. He would continue to

1940

Rank	Daily Pay	GROUP C	GROUP B	GROUP A
WO1*	$4.20	$4.45	$4.70	$4.95
WO1	3.90	3.35	4.40	4.65
Qsgt**	3.10	3.35	3.60	3.85
WO2	3.00	3.25	3.50	3.75
WO3	2.75	3.00	3.25	3.50
S/Sgt	2.50	2.75	3.00	3.25
Sgt	2.20	2.45	2.70	2.95
L/Sgt	1.90	2.15	2.40	2.65
Cpl	1.70	1.95	2.20	2.45
L/Cpl	1.50	1.75	2.00	2.25
Pte	1.30	1.55	1.80	2.05 [8]

*WO1 with appointments such as RSM, Foreman of Works, or Foreman of Sigs.
**Quartermaster Sergeant was a rank that is now obsolete.

SKILL AT ARMS

receive his daily pay for his rank.

Many tradesmen had helpers (aka learners, apprentices). A helper in a Group A or B trade received trades pay at the next lower rate than the trade they were learning. For example, a Millwright, which was a Group A trade might have a helper who would be paid at the Group B rate. Helpers of Group C trades did not receive trades pay. To advance from helper to tradesman, the soldier would have to pass a test. There were separate tests for each class within the group.

Advancement in trade was also linked to rank. Group C tradesmen were privates, Group B were Corporals, and Group A were Sergeants or above.

Following is the list of trades that existed from 1900 to 1942. This does not mean that all of these trades existed for that entire period. Some became obsolete, while some were combined with others to create a new trade. Some of them were dissolved after the First World War only to be reactivated for the Second World War. Some were new trades near the end of this time period.

TRADES AS THEY EXISTED BEFORE 1942

AMMUNITION

Ammunition Examiner

This was a new trade in 1935 and has been in existence ever since. The duties of this tradesman are the care and custody of ammunition and explosives. They checked ammunition for cracks, dents, corrosion or any other kind of damage. They would supervise the storage of ammunition to ensure that it was properly housed. Defective ammunition would be destroyed by members of this trade. They had to know the proper method of handling and storage of chemical weapons. Before 1935 the job was done by officers of the RCOC. Prospective members were selected from clerks or storeman in the RCOC. There was no direct entry. Candidates for training were sent to a British military school as no such course was taught in Canada until 1947. There was no trade badge for the Ammo Examiner until 1956. Group B.

ARTIFICERS and ARMOURERS

An Artificer was a tradesman who was more skilled than other technicians or mechanics. In 1919 the armament artificers and the armourers became the Artificer Branch of the RCOC. (This was later renamed the Engineering Branch.) At first the artificers and armourers were mainly involved with the repair of weapons but later they began to repair vehicles and wireless equipment (as two-way radios were originally named) as these items came into use. The RCOC was divided into two basic branches called Ordnance and Engineering. The abbreviations for these branches were RCOC(O) and RCOC(E). The Engineering Branch became RCEME when it was formed in 1944. The term artificer is no longer used in the military but was still in use as late as the 1960's.

Some trivia. Artificers were affectionately known as "tiffies". If a mechanic was unable to repair an item, he would send for the tiffy.

Armament Artificer (Fitter)

This soldier had to create weapon parts on a machine lathe. The course was taken at the Military College of Science in Woolwich, England. Upon successful completion of the course, he would be promoted to the rank of "Armament Staff Sergeant." His job in the 1800's was the repair of weapons, but when motorized vehicles began to appear in the military, it was the fitter who was given the duty of repairing them. After the creation of the weapon and vehicle repair artificers, the fitter returned to his original job of creating replacement parts for weapons, vehicles, and other mechanical items. This trade became obsolete in 1942 or 1943 when it was merged with the Armament Artificer Anti-Aircraft or Field. This was a Group A trade.

Armament Artificer (Instruments)

This tradesman repaired instruments such as sighting devices, elevating and transversing mechanisms on artillery weapons, range finders, binoculars, anti-aircraft plotters and

Skill-At-Arms Badges, Instructors' Badges and Trade Badges before 1942

other optical instruments. The trade would be split in 1942 or 1943 into three as follows: Armament Artificer Anti-Aircraft, Armament Artificer Coastal Defence and Armament Artificer Field Artillery. Group A.

Armament Artificer (Wireless)

This was a short-lived trade. It was instituted in 1941 to repair wireless radio equipment. They were members of the RCOC Engineering Branch. RCEME was not formed until 1944 and the Signals Radio Mechanic trade did not exist until the late 1940's. From 1944 to 1946 this trade and the RCEME Telecommunications Mechanic existed simultaneously. The Armament Artificer (Wireless) was considered to be of greater skill than the Telecommunications Mechanic. In 1946 these two trades were combined. Group A.

Artificer RCA

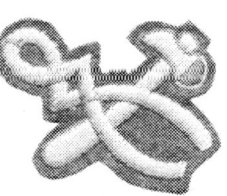

In addition to artillery repairs, such as overhauling the breech mechanism, repairing elevating, traversing and brake gears, pumps, and hydraulic jacks, the Artificer Artillery also had to repair unit vehicles. He was expected to be able to dismantle and overhaul an engine, adjust bearings, maintain wiring, clean magnetos, grind valves and much more. This was a very old trade. The task of repairing vehicles was added to their duties in the early 1900's. About 1943, they were relieved of this task by the Armament Artificer MV so that they could concentrate on the repair of artillery weapons. Today's Weapon Tech repairs all types of weapons but not vehicles. See Weapon Tech in Part Three. This trade was moved from Group B to Group A in 1941. Most of the trades in this section were members of RCOC. This artificer was a member of RCA.

Engine Artificer

The Engine Artificer was a new trade about 1938 or 1939. The Engine Artificer repaired and rebuilt engines, but not motor vehicle engines. They repaired engines on pumps, compressors, cement mixers (a cement mixer was not a truck in this time period but was a separate piece of machinery usually mounted on a trailer) and other equipment used in the construction of buildings. They could do a complete engine overhaul and repair or replace valves, ignition systems, carburetors, pistons, crank shafts, rods, bearings, gears, etc. The Engine Artificer must first have been qualified as a Fitter. This was a Group B trade. Most of the trades in this section were members of RCOC. This artificer was a member of RCE. For vehicle engine repairs see the Vehicle Mechanic section.

Armourer

This tradesman repaired small arms including machine guns and small artillery weapons up to two pounders. He also test fired weapons for accuracy. As strange as it may seem, they were also responsible for unit repairs of bicycles, helmets, respirators and other miscellaneous equipment that was not repaired by any other tradesman. He had to have a fair knowledge of drilling, forging, welding, brazing, soldering, fitting, lapping, polishing, browning, woodworking, leather working, hardening, tempering, blueing and manufacture of small springs of steel and bronze. See Weapon Tech in Part Three. They must have previously been a Fitter. The Armourer did not rate as high as an artificer and was therefore included in Group B. Most artificers were Group A trades.

Armourer IC RCOC Workshop

The Armourer IC (in charge) would be basically the same as the regular armourer described above. The difference is that this armourer would have more seniority (and probably a higher rank) and would be placed in charge of a RCOC workshop. Why it was necessary to make him a separate trade seems strange today, but you will see as you read the book, this was done many times. (In the 1960s the highest level of the cook trade had to change to a different trade called a Master Cook.)

SKILL AT ARMS

The dress regulations for the CEF (1916) state that the hammer and pincer badge was worn by artificers, armourers, fitters, machinery gunners and smiths. No exact list of trades is given. Even if I had a list, I am sure that it would be correct for that year and incorrect for other years before and after. Therefore the author has used his own judgement as to which trades this may be. If anyone has such a list I would appreciate hearing from them.

I have shown the badge beside most artificers and fitters that were Group A trades. No badge is shown for the Fitter IC Tank (below) because this was a Group B trade and may not have qualified for the badge. I will continue to seek confirmation of this for future editions of the book.

This badge was not worn by members of the RCE. They wore the Engineer grenade badge instead.

ARMOURED

Fitter IC Tank

This fitter made replacement parts for tanks and made repairs. This was the first tradesman in the Canadian Armoured Corps. It was very short lived however. This trade was new in 1941 and was obsolete by 1943. Group B.

ARTILLERY

There were very few artillery trades in this time period. Combat soldiers were not considered to be tradesmen.

Master Gunner

The Master Gunner was an expert in artillery weapons and ballistics. See Artillery in Part Three for complete job description. They also supervised the accounting and storage of all  ammunition and small arms in their district. They would be responsible for the care and preservation of all artillery weapons. The class one and class two Master Gunner were in Group A, while the class three Master Gunner was in Group B. Class one and two Master Gunners would have been a WO1 while the class three Master Gunner would have been a WO2.

Fitter Gun

This was a new trade in 1941. It was instituted to make repairs to artillery weapons. They could overhaul and reassemble breech mechanism, sights, recuperators, elevating and traversing gears and hydraulics. They also repaired other  weapons in artillery, armoured and infantry units. This trade was found in all three of these combat arm units. This was a Group B trade. Complicated repairs would be made by the Artificer RCA.

Surveyor RCA

Basically, the job of the artillery regimental surveyor was to determine and record the positions of the guns and the targets. This is an oversimplified job description as this was a very complicated and detailed process. As this was the only type of artillery surveyor in those days, they also did sound ranging, plotting using a plane table, and other jobs that were later split into separate trades. For a detailed job description of this and similar artillery trades see artillery surveyor and artillery technical assistant in Part Three. Note that this is the only trade badge that looks like a skill-at-arms badge. The Surveyor RCA had to have previously qualified as a Driver IC and have completed the basic course for a gun number.

The class one Surveyor RCA is shown on the left with the crown above. Class two and three Surveyor RCA wore the badge without a crown. There are two versions of this badge with different wreaths. This was a Group A trade

Battery Surveyor

The Battery Surveyor was an artillery surveyor who worked at the battery level instead of the regimental level. This was a Group C trade. It was abolished about 1940 and merged with the Surveyor RCA

Photo courtesy of the LER museum

Until the 1930s, artillery was pulled by horses. These teams of horses were controlled by a soldier known as the artillery driver. This was not an trade; it was simply a profession like the gun layer and most other jobs in the artillery in those days. The only trades in the artillery before 1942 are those listed in this section.

Photo courtesy of the RCA museum

The gun layer became a specialty in 1952 and a full trade in 1968. This photo was taken in 1937 in Petawawa.

Artillery units had other trades that were not exclusive to the artillery. For example, an artillery regiment would have clerks, cooks, butchers and electricians, to name a few. Although the butcher would be in the artillery, he would be the same trade and would have taken the same qualifying course as an butcher in another corps. The courses for some trades, such as cook, were run by the individual unit (before 1942). More complicated courses, such as electrician were run by a technical training school in Hamilton and a typical class might have students from several different corps.

CLERKS

There were many different types of clerks between 1900 and 1942. They were tradesmen but did not have a trade badge. Most clerks were Group C but a few specialized clerks were Group B.

Clerk Accommodation
Did accounting for the barracks, bedding and furniture used therein.

Clerk Artillery
An office clerk in an artillery unit.

Clerk Engineers
An office clerk in an engineer unit.

Engineer Store Accountant
Did accounting for Engineer stores.

Clerk RCAPC, later renamed Clerk Pay
Looked after pay records.

Clerk Signals
An clerk in a Signals message centre.

Clerk Stores RC SIGS
Did accounting for equipment in a Signals unit.

Clerk Stenographer Signals
A stenographer in a Signals unit.

Clerk Typist Signals
An office clerk in a Signals unit.

Clerk RCASC
An office clerk in a RCASC office.

Military Staff Clerk
The Military Staff Clerk performed the same duties as the regular clerk but at a higher degree of skill. The typing test for a Military Staff Clerk, for example, was based on a 800 word test whereas the regular clerks had to take only a 150 to 300 word test. A longer test created more room for errors and a greater chance of failure. The test would also be graded for irregularities in line spacing and indentation. The Military Staff Clerk would be employed at Brigade and higher formation headquarters. Group B.

Scrutineer
This clerk was involved with the paperwork done in a automotive workshop. He had to be able to type and take shorthand like other clerks, but he also had to be familiar with the workings on the internal combustion engine. He did filing and accounting of paperwork for the ordering of automotive parts. He had to draft letters using technical automotive terminology. Group B.

Veterinary Clerk
This was a clerk that worked for a veterinary. He did all the necessary paperwork for the care of animals required by the army, such as ordering replacement horses when one died.

Clerk RCOC
An office clerk in an RCOC office.

Clerk Dental Records
A clerk in a dental office.

Clerk Fuel and Light Accountant
Did accounting for fuel and electricity used.

Clerk Medical Records
A clerk in a medical office.

Clerk MT Accountant
Did accounting for parts in a transportation unit.

Clerk Movement Control
Looked after paperwork involved with the movement of personnel and equipment.

Clerk Personal Selection
A clerk in the personal selection office.

Clerk Radiographer
Looked after the filing of X-rays.

Clerk Records
Looked after the filing of base records.

Clerk Statistical
Compiled statistics of activity on the base.

Clerk Stores and Equipment
Did accounting for a QM store.

Clerk Supply Accountant
Did accounting for supplies in a warehouse.

Clerk TMT
Unknown duties.

Clerk Tactical Scales
Unknown duties.

Clerk Transport
Looked after despatch of vehicles.

Clerk Transport and Freight
Unknown duties.

Clerk Shorthand Writer
Took dictation using shorthand.

All of the above clerks existed between 1900 and 1938. (This does not mean that all of them existed for that entire period. Some of them may have existed for only a few years.) Their duties varied slightly depending on their place of employment. They could be placed into three basic types:

- office clerks
- equipment and stores accountants
- financial accountants

About 1938, all of the above clerks were combined into a single trade called "Clerk". Two new trades were created called Clerk Superintending and Clerk Departmental.

Clerk
Called simply "Clerk," this tradesman was a

general clerk that did common office work. He had to file documents and maintain the filing system, amend publications and register and despatch mail, He had to able to type 150, 250, or 300 words in ten minutes, with not more than 2% errors, to qualify for class three, two or one respectively. He also had to be able to take shorthand starting at 50 wpm for a class three. They were normally employed in a unit orderly room. He could be a member of any corps.

This trade was a combination of many of the trades listed above. Although just one trade, the Clerk could not possibly learn all of the duties of the many previously separate trades. Some of these clerks specialized in pay office duties while other concentrated on increasing their shorthand speed. Most of the previous clerks probably kept doing their same job, only now they all belonged to a common trade. They could be in Group C or B depending on their skills. The shorthand writer would be Group B whereas a regular orderly room clerk would be Group C.

Clerk Departmental

In addition to the duties of the regular clerk, the Clerk Departmental could run an office without supervision. He was also trained in the proper handling of classified material. In order to became a Clerk Departmental, the soldier must have served for at least three months as a regular clerk described above. This was a Group B trade whereas most of the regular clerks were Group C.

Clerk Superintending

The Clerk Superintending was a chief clerk who was in charge of a large office. He would be employed in branch or department headquarters where a large number of office clerks would be working. In addition to supervision of the Clerk's duties, he would be responsible for military discipline and dress. He had to be familiar with the regulations, orders and the work being performed by the department or directorate with which he was employed. The Clerk Superintending could be a member of any corps. Group A.

Court Reporter

The Court Reporter attends courts-martial and records the proceedings using shorthand at a rate of at least 140 w.p.m. They must have a good understanding of the rules governing courts-martial. For more information see Court Reporter in Part Three. Group A.

This is the hat badge of the Corps of Military Staff Clerks. This corps existed from 1912 until 1946. These clerks were employed at Division and Corps Headquarters during the First World War and at District and National Headquarters in Canada. Unit clerks did not belong to this corps. They were members of the same corps as other soldiers in the unit, such as Signals, Artillery or Engineers.

COMMUNICATIONS

During the First World War, communication duties were shared by the Canadian Signalling Corps and the Corps of Royal Canadian Engineers. Both of these corps were formed in 1903. The Engineers were responsible for wireless and line communications between units, brigades and higher formations. Signals was responsible for communications within a unit. Signals was also responsible for the training of unit signallers, except for the Engineers who had their own signalling school in England and trained their own personnel.

Being responsible for communications within a unit did not mean that the work was done by CSC personnel. Unit signallers could be of any corps, but were mostly infantry and artillery. Being responsible might mean that the CSC would attach one Signals officer to the unit to supervise and to send signallers on courses at CSC run schools. (See Signaller in this section.)

CSC communications were carried out using morse telephony, heliographs (mirrors), lamps, flags and despatch riders. Messenger pigeons and even messenger dogs were also utilized. The Engineers concentrated on formation level communications using wireless and line as the main methods.

There was one Signal Company per Division in the Canadian Expeditionary Force. This did not mean that they were all CSC personnel. The 1st Div Sig Coy was commanded by a Sig Officer but was made up of men from CSC, RCE, and from cavalry and infantry. The 2nd, 3rd and 4th Div Sig Coys were all RCE personnel. These were called "Signal Companies, Canadian Engineers". The Chief Signalling Officer was from the CSC. At the beginning of the war he reported to the Chief Engineer RCE, but by the end of the war the CSC had become an independent entity reporting to the division commander. [9]

At the Battle of the Somme in 1916 the main methods of communication, in order of use, were: line, runners, visual (flags, heliographs and lamps) and messenger pigeons. The use of radio was negligible in 1916 but by the end of the war, wireless, which was somewhat of a novelty in 1914, had become the primary means of communications.

In 1917 the CSC became responsible for installing line for electric light at corps and division headquarters.

After the war, all communication duties were gradually transferred to the CSC. The Engineer Telegraph and Wireless units were disbanded in April 1920.

In 1920, the Canadian Signalling Corps was renamed the Canadian Permanent Signalling Corps. (This refers to their status in the permanent force. The CSC originally existed in the reserve force only.) In 1921, this was changed again to Royal Canadian Corps of Signals. The acronym for the corps was RCCS. This was later changed to RC SIGS.

The Royal Canadian Corps of Signals had a great variety of trades that are not associated with comminations today. They had their own mechanics, carpenters, clerks and draughtsmen. The RCCS clerks are listed with the others in the clerk section.

Cable Joiner   Cable Splicer

The job of this tradesman was to join (or splice) large multiple conductor telephone cables. They waterproofed the splice by wrapping it with muslin (a bandage-like material), then covered it with lead. They tested cables for continuity. The Cable Joiner was later renamed the Cable Splicer. I have found that the Cable Joiner trade existed in 1928. After that date, I found no record of the trade until 1944 when it reappeared on the list of trades under the new name. Lists that I have between 1928 and 1944 show no record of this trade. The Cable Joiner was a Group A trade. The Lineman and the Switchboard Operator, which were Group B trades, could become a Cable Joiner.

Carpenter Signals

The Carpenter Signals was simply a Carpenter who was a member of the Signal Corps. This trade became obsolete in the 1930's. Group C.

Cabinet Maker Signals

This was a higher skilled tradesman than the ordinary Carpenter. See Cabinet Maker in the Fortress Section. This trade became obsolete in the 1930's. Group B.

Despatch Rider

The job of the DR was to deliver messages by motorcycle.

This was an RC SIGS trade. However, other soldiers such as infantrymen were also employed as Despatch Riders. In this instance, it would be a temporary job. An Infantryman employed as a DR would still be an Infantryman by trade. Working as a DR did not change his trade. A soldier who was a DR by trade would receive trades pay. A soldier who was temporarily working as a DR would not. This was a Group C trade for RC SIGS personnel only.

The photo at right shows a Signals DR (note the Signals armband) during the

Photo courtesy of the Communications and Electronics Museum

First World War. He is delivering a box of homing pigeons to the troops at the front.

Photo by author. Uniform courtesy of Victor Taboika

Despatch Riders of the RCCS did more than just deliver messages or pigeons. They also had to be qualified in traffic control, map reading and reconnaissance. They could use cars or bicycles as well as a motorcycle to deliver messages over all types of road or across country by day or night. They did not have jeeps in the First World War. They were also trained to make minor repairs to telephone line if they saw any that were damaged while en route. If they were unable to repair the line, they would report it to the signal centre at their next stop. They also had to be knowledgeable of RCCS organization and security regulations.

Many soldiers, such as the infantryman, were not considered to be tradesmen until after the Second World War. There was also a soldier known as a motorcyclist, who could be of any corps. His job was similar, but not as detailed, as the Despatch Rider. He did not repair telephone lines. The motorcyclist, like the infantryman, was considered to be only a soldier and not a tradesman.

Despatch Riders wore an armband in the white and blue colours of the RCCS. Since the First World War they have also worn a winged wheel trade badge with the letters "DR" above. The wings were added to the wheel sometimes after the war. Sometimes the crossed flags badge was also worn. During the First World War this trade badge was worn on the right arm only. I have seen uniforms dating from the Second World War with the winged wheel on both arms above the rank badge. The armband was supposed to be worn only on the right arm, but I have seen several examples of the armband being worn on both arms. It seems that regulations were not strictly followed. Group C.

The Signalling manual of 1916 states that the DR must be careful of where to leave his bicycle so that it would not be damaged by horses. This manual covers visual signalling with flags, signal station work, DR duties, line laying and map reading. There is no mention of radios.

Draughtsman RC Signals

The Signals draughtsman had to prepare detailed circuit or wiring diagrams, and drawings for the construction of parts. They also had to operate mimeograph and hectograph machines for making copies of their work. Group B.

Driver MT RC Signals   Driver Mechanic

This was the equivalent of the Driver Mechanic in the Signal Corps. (MT stands for Motor Transport.) He had to drive and maintain vehicles used by the Royal Canadian Corps of Signals. In 1938 this trade was renamed Driver Mechanic and became part of the trade that was common to all corps. See the Driver section. Group B.

Driver Operator

The Driver Operator was a driver who could also set up and operate wireless radio and telegraphy equipment. He had to receive messages at a minimum of ten w.p.m. while stationary and six w.p.m. while mobile. Before becoming a Driver Operator, they would first have been a Driver I.C. (See driver section.) At this point in time the Driver Operator was an RC SIGS trade, but as you will see, in later years the trade became common to most corps. Group C.

Electrician Signals

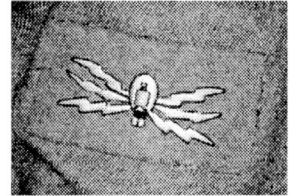

The Signal Corps had their own electricians. In the 1920's this trade was known as the Electrician Signals. They repaired all types of electrical equipment including generators, converters, transformers, switchboards, electric motors, telephone and telegraph equipment, cable terminals and wireless radio. They were also good mechanics and could clean spark plugs and carburetors and make other minor engine repairs. This tradesman would also look after the charging of batteries used to operate radio equipment. They did installation of battery banks into vehicles. The Electrician Signals could make minor repairs to devices such as voltmeters, gauges, relays, thermostats and starters. They could test and repair wiring in vehicles

SKILL AT ARMS

or generators for faults. A member of this trade could be placed in charge of a power plant. Like all members of the Signal Corps, they had to know corps organization and security measures. Later in the book you will find these same jobs being done by other Signals trades after the Electrician Signals became obsolete. Group A.

The name of this trade does not fully illustrate the Electrician Signals' abilities. In the 1930's, this was the tradesman that would be called to repair radios. Although the name was not used, this was the "radio technician" of the day.

Fitter Signals

Several corps had their own fitters but they were all members of the same trade except for those in the Signal Corps. In other corps the name of the trade was simply "Fitter." (See Electrical and Mechanical section.) The Fitter Signals could dismantle, repair, or overhaul and reassemble an internal combustion engine. Using drills, taps and dies, they could make or repair metal parts to replace broken ones. They also made repairs and splices in metal cables. They made major repairs to motorcycles, motor vehicles, cable layers, generators and chargers. They could repair worn or broken valves, brakes, ignition systems, starters, coils and wiring. They would grind worn parts if possible or make new replacement parts. This required very precise measurements using micrometers and other measuring tools. This trade was in pay Group A. They would previously have been a Driver Mechanic.

Fitter Machine
Machinist Signals

These trades were similar to the Fitter Signals. They could create metal parts from scratch on a metal lathe. These tradesman however, did not take the next step and make the actual repairs themselves, leaving that to the Fitter Signals. The Fitter Machine worked at the Group C level and the Machinist at the Group B level. These trades became obsolete in the 1930's and were included with the Fitter Signals.

Foreman of Signals

This was a supervisor for the RC SIGS technical trades. He would supervise and instruct electricians, fitters, and instrument mechanics in first line repairs. He would perform very difficult or unusual repairs himself. The F of S, as he was known, would supervise the keeping of repair records and the ordering of supplies and tools. He would have to be good at electrical theory, algebra, trigonometry and logarithms. This tradesman would formerly have been a Group A in a RC SIGS trade such as fitter or electrician. Group A.

Instrument Maker W/T
Instrument Maker L/T
Instrument Mechanic Signals

In the 1920's there were two trades called Instrument Maker Wireless Telegraphy and Instrument Maker Line Telegraphy. These two trades were combined in the early 1930's to create the Instrument Mechanic Signals.

This tradesman made repairs to a variety of electrical instruments. Using a wavemeter, he would calibrate wireless radios to ensure that they were on the correct frequency. He could also measure the inductance and capacity of a circuit. He would create grounds for vehicles to eliminate static charges. They could make repairs to electric motors, generators, converters, transformers, wireless radio, telephones and telegraph equipment. The Instrument Mechanic Signals could build replacement parts if they were not available. They installed wireless equipment into vehicles and made repairs or splices to the radio installation wiring. They could find faults in A.C. and D.C. power supplies. They could repair their own testing equipment such as voltmeters, gauges, frequency metres and other devices. The duties of this trade also required them to make all types of repairs to teleprinters. Group A

There were several other types of Instrument Mechanics (non-RC SIGS trades). The Instrument Mechanic is in the Electrical and Mechanical section. The Instrument Mechanic RCE can be found in the Fortress section, and the Instrument Mechanic Surgical is described in the Medical section.

Lineman Field

The job of the Lineman Field was to lay telephone cable between locations in the field in a tactical situation. He also had to recover the line if possible to be used again. They also repaired telephone line. The repairs that this lineman did were minor compared to the Cable Splicer who repaired large, multiple conductor cables. This tradesman's course included horsemanship and short-rein riding. See Communications in Part Three. Group C.

Lineman Permanent Line

This Lineman laid permanent overhead and underground telephone line between buildings and the switchboard on an army base. See Communications in Part Three. A Lineman Field, which was a Group C trade, could become a Lineman Permanent Line or a Switchboard Operator which were Group B trades. The Lineman Permanent Line could aspire to become a Cable Splicer which was a Group A trade.

Photo courtesy of the Communications and Electronics Museum

This photo shows a horse drawn telephone cable layer. This job was done by the Engineers during the First World War. This photo was taken in 1919 and shows linemen of the Canadian Signalling Corps. The soldier riding on the carriage and at least three of those on horseback in the rear are wearing the Signals armband. Probably others are wearing it also, but it cannot be seen as it was worn on the right arm. All communications duties were taken over by the CSC by 1920. This photo was probably taken when the unit was newly acquired from the Engineers.

Lineman Signals

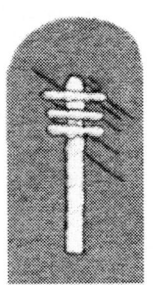

In the 1930's the two types of linemen were combined to create a single trade called the Lineman Signals. They laid both field and permanent line and erected telephone poles. They climbed poles to install cross arms, insulators and lightening arresters, as well as telephone line. They could find faults in telephone line and make the necessary repairs. They could set up field switchboards and hook all telephone lines into it. The trade would be split into two trades once again in 1949. Group B.

Switchboard Installer
Lineman Mechanic

The Lineman Mechanic did not repair telephone lines as one might think. That was the job of the Lineman Field, Lineman Permanent Line, and the Cable Splicer. This tradesman's job was the installation and maintenance of telephone and telegraph equipment such as field telephones, telegraph repeaters, teleprinters and switchboards. This trade had previously been called the Switchboard Installer. That trade became obsolete in the 1930's and the job was taken over by the linemen. That decision was reversed and the Lineman Mechanic was created in the early 1940's. This was a Group A trade.

Loftman

The Loftman breeds, trains, and cares for a loft of homing pigeons. Pigeons were used to deliver messages during the First World War and until after the Second World War. Pigeons would be sent to forward units by DR where they would be released and would return home carrying a message. There were six loftmen per battalion. They received about 100 messages by pigeon per day. Group C.

SKILL AT ARMS

The photo above shows a mobile pigeon loft. The picture on the right shows a pigeon being released from a trench at the front. It will carry a message back to the loft.

Mechanic MT RC Signals

This soldier was a vehicle mechanic in the Signal Corps. This trade became obsolete in 1938, but vehicle repairs could still be made by the Fitter Signals Group A.

Operator RC Signals

The crossed flags badge was authorized for wear in 1908, but had actually been in use since before 1900. It is our second oldest badge still in use after the crossed rifles. The job of the Operator Signals was to send and receive messages. However, when this trade existed in the early 1900's, the method of communications was not by radio. They used semaphore (flags), heliographs (mirrors), morse code by telegraph wire and even messenger pigeons. They could also be employed in a Signals message centre. The Operator Signals trade existed in all three trade groups depending on the tradesman's abilities.

Photos courtesy of the Communications and Electronics Museum

Photo courtesy of the Communications and Electronics Museum

The above photograph shows a Signal Troop from the First World War era. Their equipment consists of heliographs and flags. Heliographs were used to send Morse code signals by reflecting sunlight with mirrors. They also had telescopes for use by the receiver.

Note the use of the crossed flag badge. The third soldier from the right is wearing the badge on the lower left arm. This is a skill-at-arms badge indicating that he is a highly skilled Operator Signals. This badge was worn by members of the CSC (RCCS after 1921) and also by other corps. The Sergeant beside him is wearing the same badge above his rank badge on the right arm. In this case, it is being used as an instructor's badge. [2]

On the right is the original hat badge of the "Canadian Signalling Corps."

The CSC is one of the oldest military signal corps in the world; it was formed in 1903. The oldest is believed to be the signal corps of the Confederate States of America. The British Royal Signals was created in 1920. During the First World War, their communications service was run entirely by the Royal Engineers. In the Canadian army it was run mostly but not entirely by the Engineers. The CSC and the Engineers were both formed in 1903.

The Use of Flags

Flags were used in two ways to send messages. Using one flag in each hand, there was a position of the arms for each letter of the alphabet. Moving one's arms to a new position created a new letter.

Using a single flag, the signaller could send morse code. Certain short movements of the flag represented a dot, while another type of movement sent a dash.

H   O   T

Each letter of the alphabet was represented by holding the flags in a certain position. Holding the flags as shown above spell out the word "hot". This is known as "semaphore".

By holding the flags in a certain position, the receiver would understand that the sender was switching from letters to numbers. After doing this, some letters would become numbers. The letter H as shown above is also the number eight. Another unique position of the flags would indicate that the sender is changing back to letters.

There was also a position to indicate that the sender wished to erase the previous letter if he had made an error.

Dot   Dash

Using a single flag, the signaller could send morse code. Holding the flag as shown above represented a dot and a dash respectively. A dot followed by a dash is the letter "A" in morse code. After each letter the flag would be held in front of the body to separate it from the next letter.

The flags were produced in two sizes. Large flags, three foot square, were used for distances of five to seven miles. Small flags, two foot square, were used for distances of three to four miles. The receiving signaller would observe through a telescope and call out the letters for another soldier to write down.

The flags were produced in two colours, but they were not used with one of each colour as is shown on the badge and is commonly assumed. Light coloured flags were used with dark backgrounds and the dark flags were used in conjunction with light backgrounds. [9]

Operator Radio RC Signals

This trade sent and received communications using radio. They took over this job from the Engineers in 1919. They also had to maintain their own power supply such as a gas generator.

Operator Wireless and Line

In 1941, the Operator Signals and the Operator Radio were combined. This new trade was named

SKILL AT ARMS

Operator Wireless and Line. With radio (or wireless as it was often called in those days) becoming the main method of communications after the First World War, this tradesman concentrated on communications by radio.

They sent and received messages by wireless and by line telegraphy. They were still required to send and receive messages by lamp at a rate of six w.p.m. The OWL (as the Op Wireless and Line was called) had to set up antennas and tune radio equipment to the correct frequency. Another duty was to set up and operate field switchboards with a maximum of 20 lines. Charging their batteries was another responsibility.

The OWL could also be employed as a clerk in a signal centre. This was not an office clerk job. The duties at a signal centre involved the reception and despatch of messages. Each message had to be recorded as to its method of being sent (by radio, teletype, DR, pigeon, etc.). The signal centre clerk would decide which method to use based on the priority of the message and the means available. If the message was sent by DR, they would be sure to get a signature for it. Incoming messages were also logged.

In the photo on the right, a Signals DR delivers messages and picks up new ones from a message centre. (Note that the DR is wearing two Signals armbands. The proper dress was one armband only, worn on the right arm.) Group B.

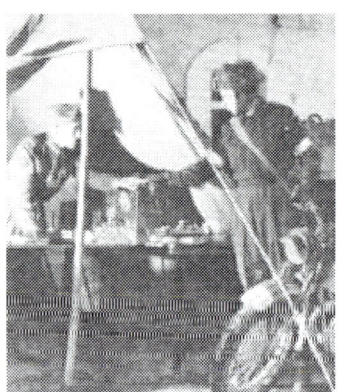

Photo courtesy Communications and Electronics Museum

This new set of badges was introduced in the 1930s. They were worn on the lower left arm by RC SIGS (see photo left); and on the upper left arm by members of other corps (see photo of tank gunner in the SAA section). They were not replaced by the "T" badges in 1942. Nor did they replace the crossed flags which were still in use. I have been unable to find documentation that gives an official explanation of their purpose.

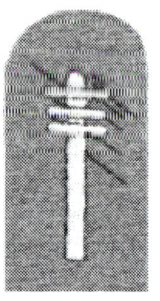

Photo of Gordon Dobson courtesy of Mike Dobson

Signaller

The signaller was a soldier who was employed at communications duties but was not a member of the Canadian Signalling Corps (or RCCS after 1921). Members of the Signalling Corps were called "Operators." He could be a member of any corps but was mostly infantry or artillery.

During the First World War each infantry battalion had a signals platoon of about 30 to 35 signallers. The infantry signaller was as highly skilled as any member of the Canadian Signalling Corps. They sent and received messages using heliographs, lamps, flags, flares, and smoke shells. They were proficient in morse code as well as line laying and repair. Before the use of radio, they even communicated with aircraft by arranging panels on the ground. Signallers were also employed as despatch riders, delivering messages on a bicycle, and provided guiding services for officers and troops travelling in their

Skill-At-Arms Badges, Instructors' Badges and Trade Badges before 1942

area.

Signallers wore the same crossed flags badge as Operators. Dress regulations for the CEF describe only two uses of the crossed flags badge. They were to be worn on the upper arm above the rank badge by instructors and on the lower left arm by members of both the CSC and other corps.

When the new wireless technology became available infantry and artillery signallers would take a course on its use. During the First World War, signallers and others were often pulled out of the front lines to attend short courses in new technology. Signaller Dobson probably took a course on communication equipment repair as well. Signallers were expected to repair their own equipment when problems arose. There were only two options for equipment repair in those days. One could fix the equipment himself or send it to the rear for repairs which was a lengthy process. There were no unit technicians.

The role of the Canadian Signalling Corps during the First World War was one of instruction. They set up schools in France, back from the enemy lines, and ran courses for unit signallers like Lance Corporal Dobson. Units were expected to provide their own signallers.

Unit signallers were also employed in observation balloons. A signaller and an observer would be raised in a balloon to spy on the enemy. The signaller would pass the information down to an artillery signaller on the ground via telephone line. The information would be used to fire on the enemy position. Enemy aircraft often shot down these observation balloons. When this happened, the observer and the signaller would parachute out of the basket hanging from the balloon, making them the first operational parachutists in the Canadian army. There was no extra pay for this dangerous job. However, all soldiers received ten cents per day for being in the field on top of the $1.00 per day pay for privates.

There were many dangerous jobs during the First World War. One of the most dangerous was that of the signaller who was often sent out to repair telephone lines or man a forward observation point to send information on enemy activity back to battalion headquarters. Sending messages using flags also exposed the soldier to danger. Of course, life was extremely dangerous for all infantrymen when a battle was taking place and the signallers would be in the thick of it. They would be just a few steps behind the front lines and many were killed. Some were lucky and would be employed at battalion headquarters during the battle, but could be in the front for the next one.

Infantry signallers were as capable as any rifleman in engaging the enemy. They could fight hand to hand or with bayonets like any other rifleman.

L/Cpl Dobson was killed at the Battle of Passchendaele in November 1917. He has no known grave.

Unlike the infantry signaller, the artillery signaller was not trained in combat and was often not even issued with a weapon. Many of them acquired a weapon by one means or another. They could be taken from dead soldiers, purchased, or even sent by family from home. (Can you imagine mailing a pistol from Canada to France these days.)

The crossed flags badge was worn by instructors on both arms if an NCO but only on the upper right arm if a private. In order to wear the crossed flags badge on the upper arm, the wearer must hold an assistant instructor's certificate in signalling. L/Cpl Dobson must have been qualified as an instructor. Signallers who were not qualified as

Photo courtesy of Steve Chambers

instructors wore the badge on the lower left arm as shown in the photograph on the previous page.

This rule applied to members of the Signalling Corps and to members of other corps equally. See the group photo of Signal Corps personnel under "Operator RC Signals".

In spite of this skill, the infantry and artillery signallers were not considered tradesman during this time frame. They were finally made trades in the 1940's with the names of Signaller Infantry and Signaller Artillery (see Part Two).

The term "Signalman" is the rank of a soldier in the Signal Corps, equal to Private. It is not a profession. Their trade was called Operator in the Signal Corps and Signaller in other corps.

Signaller Qualification

Personal wearing the crossed flags badge were tested annually in order to remain qualified as signallers. There were three separate types of signallers. They could be qualified in Visual Telegraphy (VT), Line Telegraphy (LT) or Wireless Telegraphy (WT). There was also a qualification known as Special Visual. During the First World War most line and radio work was performed by the RCE. After the war, LT and WT qualifications were reserved for RCCS personnel only. Infantry and artillery signallers could become qualified in VT only. Personnel holding a WT certificate will not be allowed to have a LT certificate as WT was considered to be a higher qualification than LT. A bonus was given to those who passed the test ranging from $5.00 to $15.00 depending on their score.

Visual Telegraphy (VT)

The requirements to pass the VT test were as follows:

- Read to morse code messages of 100 letters each with the small flag at five w.p.m.
- Read two messages of 100 letters each with the heliograph lamp at six w.p.m.

(The best message in each category would count, the other being discarded.)

- A map reading test.
- Three tests based on the training manual "Signal Training All Arms (1928).

(These tests could be oral or written. See more information on this two paragraphs further down.)
A test on electrical instruments.
(Semaphore was not required.)

If four or more signallers were to be tested, they would be testing collectively. Two messages of 200 letters each would be passed from one signaller to the next in a cross-country chain. The first message would be sent using the small flag and the second by lamp. The signallers involved would all pass or all fail as a group. Testing of less than four signallers would be conducted individually. A maximum of 12 soldiers would be tested collectively.

To obtain a third class signaller certificate, a soldier required to get at least 95 percent in sending and receiving plus at least 60 percent on an oral exam. For second class, a score of at least 95 percent in sending and receiving was required plus at least 60 percent on a written exam. For the first class certificate, candidates were required to receive an extra message (for a total of three) with 98 percent accuracy on two of them and at least 95 percent on the third message. They also had to obtain an accuracy of 98 percent on messages sent and at least 75 percent on a written exam.

Line Telegraphy (LT)

After the war, line telegraphy was open to members of the Signal Corps only. A first class qualification in VT was a prerequisite. The requirements to pass were as follows:

- Read and write plain language morse code from a buzzer at a rate of 24 messages per hour for a period of 15 minutes.
- Read and write cipher in five letter groups from a buzzer at a rate of 20 messages per hour for a period of 15 minutes.
- A map reading test.
- Three different electrical instrument tests.
- One test based on the training manual.

The scores need to qualify were 96 percent for first class and 90 percent for second class. There was no third class category in LT.

Wireless Telegraphy (WT)

After the war, wireless telegraphy was open to members of the Signal Corps only. A first class certificate in LT was a prerequisite. The requirements

to pass were as follows:
- Receive voice messages at a rate of 18 five-letter cipher groups per minute.
- Set up and adjust a wireless radio set for operation.
- Determine the condition of a bank of batteries using a hydrometer and voltmeter.
- Pack up a wireless radio set for moving.
- Answer five oral questions based on the training manual. Five questions must be answered correctly in order to pass. Should a solider answer a question incorrectly, he may be given a second chance with a different question up to a maximum of eight questions.

The scores needed to qualify were the same as for VT above.

Permanent Force Signallers

The above regulations applied to members of the militia which made up the bulk of the military forces during peacetime. Signallers in the small permanent force were not divided into the three categories of VT, LT and WT but were required to pass a test consisting of combination of the three categories as follows:

- Morse code at ten w.p.m.
- Small flag morse code messages at six w.p.m.
- Heliograph messages at eight w.p.m.
- Semaphore at ten w.p.m.

(The soldier being tested would be required to receive two messages of 200 letters each, in each of the above methods plus send one 200 word message in each of the four methods.)

Special VT

An advanced competition in VT was held annually. The course and subsequent test was open to members of cavalry, artillery, infantry, and machine gun units who already possessed a first class VT certificate. The requirements to pass were as follows:

- Receive two 100 letter morse code messages on each of small flag and lamp at six w.p.m.
- Receive two 100 letter messages in semaphore at eight w.p.m.

(Semaphore was not required on the regular VT test.)
- Receive two 100 letter morse code message on a buzzer at ten w.p.m.
- Send one 50 letter message on each of small flag and lamp at six w.p.m.
- Send one 50 letter message in semaphore at eight w.p.m.
- Pass three written tests on elementary electricity and magnetism, care and adjustment of wireless equipment, signals organization, signal centre duties and map reading.
- Pass an oral and practical exam of five questions; three questions on signal service instruments and two questions on line laying and testing and repairing. If an incorrect answer is given, the solider may have one additional question.

In order to qualify, candidates needed a score of least 96 percent in sending and receiving and at least 60 percent on each of three written exams and at least three out of five on the oral and practical tests.

Specialist Pay

Soldiers qualified as a signaller, although not a trade, would be entitled to specialist pay if a member of the permanent force. Signallers in the militia were not entitled to specialist pay. The qualification was good for a period of one year, after which the soldier must be re-tested.

Operator Keyboard

This was the original name for a teletype operator. He sent and received messages by teletype at speeds of 20 to 25 five-letter groups in 15 minutes. Some of the duties of the Op Keyboard overlapped that of the OWL. Both of these trades were required to set up and operate field switchboards. Some members of the Op Keyboard and the OWL trades were trained to operate the new high speed teletype machines using messages on previously prepared perforated tape that could be sent at a speed of 300 w.p.m. This was a Group B trade.

Operator Airways RC Signals

When air mail was introduced in Canada in 1927, RC SIGS was tasked with setting up a nationwide system of radio beacons to guide the aircraft. A radio beacon is a signal that is sent out to help aircraft find the runway when visibility is poor. Members of this trade maintained the radio beacon equipment, made by the Canadian Marconi Company, and the Royal Air Mail arrived safely at its destination. Obsolete 1936.

SKILL AT ARMS

Switchboard Operator

The Switchboard Operator operated large permanent base switchboards. They were also required to operate the small mobile switchboards that were used in the field, although these were more commonly operated by the Operator Wireless and Line. They had to send and receive phonograms (voice messages by telephone). The trade became obsolete in the 1930's. Switchboard operation was included with the duties of Operator RC Signals, later named Operator Wireless and Line. Group B.

Permanent and field switchboards.

Photos courtesy of the Communications and Electronics Museum.

Electrician Wireless

This trade was formed to make repairs to wireless radio and telephony equipment. This was a Group A trade.

Wireless Mechanic

This trade, like the Electrician Wireless, made repairs to wireless radio and telephony equipment. The Wireless Mechanic was not as skilled as an Electrician Wireless and therefore was in pay Group B.

Operator B2 RC Signals

The duties of this tradesman are unknown to me. The trade existed in the 1930's. If you have any information about the Operator B2 please contact the author via his web site. (See back of book.)

On 31 March 1929 the Corps of Guides was disbanded and the personnel absorbed into the Royal Canadian Corps of Signals. The Corps of Guides was formed in 1903 and was responsible for reconnaissance and scout duties as well as some security and military intelligence. The old Corps of Guides hat badge was adopted as the badge of the Canadian Intelligence Corps.

COOKS

Cook

There was no actual cook trade until about 1938 (other than those working in hospitals). Cooking was simply a job that someone had to do, like guard duty. Cooks were selected by their Commanding Officer based mostly on their lack of ability to do anything else. As you can imagine, the meals were not great! Starting in 1938 cooks became recognized as a trade and began to receive trades pay at the Group C level. They could be members of any corps. A course was run by each corps in their own kitchens at the corps school. There was no army standard. (There had been a Canadian "School of Cookery" in England during the First World War.) The course probably consisted mostly of on-the-job training. In 1942, all cooks became members of the RCASC and were sent on a specially designed course to properly learn their trade.

Baker

This is a very ancient trade. When armies were first formed, came the requirement to feed them, and bread was the main staple of existence. They baked bread, pastry, etc. in a building or in the field. The Baker could be a member of any corps. Group B.

Butcher

Today the army does not have to kill their

food; they simply buy it from a grocery wholesaler. When we think of a butcher today, we think of the guy at the grocery store who cuts up meat. An army Butcher before the Second World War had to have a thorough knowledge of killing and dressing cattle and sheep, and preparing the meat for issue. They had to know the time required between the slaughter of animals and consumption. They had to identify signs of deterioration in meat. Senior Butchers had to be able to construct and run a field abattoir. This trade existed in Group B and Group C. The senior members of the trade who could supervise an abattoir were in Group B. The Butcher could be a member of any corps.

Cook Hospital

This tradesman had to prepare meals for patients in a hospital. Class one of this trade was Group A, while class two was in Group B. Members in Group A could supervise the operation of a hospital kitchen in a 1,200 bed hospital. They also planed menus, requisitioned food and supplies, and instructed trade members at the Group B level. They had to prepare food for different diets. Hospital patients could be on one of the following diets: ordinary, soft, liquid or reducing.

DENTAL

Dental Chair Assistant
Dental Assistant

This tradesman assisted the dentist with dental work. They also performed some office duties. They arranged appointments and kept records of treatment given. Part of their duties was similar to that of a storeman; they had to maintain stock of dental supplies. When a patient arrived, they would lay out the dental tools, and prepare anaesthetic solutions. Another aspect of their trade was the making of dental moulds. After making an impression of the patient's mouth, they would pour wax around the impression, then pour plaster into it. After removing the other materials, a plaster cast of the patient's mouth would remain. This was forwarded to the Dental Tech to be made into false teeth. When the patient left, the Dental Chair Assistant would sterilize the tools for the next use. When the dental clinic moved to the field, all the dental equipment had to be packed and loaded into the dental van. This tradesman also maintained the X-ray equipment and prepared developing and fixing solutions and then processed the dental film. In 1940, the word "chair" was removed and the name shortened to Dental Assistant. Group B.

Dental Tech

This tradesman manufactured and made repairs to false teeth. See Dental in Part Three for more information. Group A

Dental Instrument Repairer

As the name implies, this person made repairs to dental equipment. See Dental in Part Three for more information. Group B.

DRIVERS

Driver IC (Tank)
Driver IC (Wheeled)
Driver IC (Tracked)
Driver IC (Semi-Tracked)

IC stands for "Internal Combustion" which refers to the motor vehicle as compared to a driver of horse drawn vehicles. He had to drive and maintain an internal combustion motor lorry or car, wheeled or tracked. In June 1939, this trade was reduced to non-trade status. This means that the qualification of Driver IC still existed after that date, but not as a trade. It could be a soldier's non-trade job, or it could be just a course that was a prerequisite for some other trade such as Driver Mechanic or Driver Operator. After June 1939, soldiers employed as a Driver IC would not receive trades pay. It had been a Group C trade.

Driver Mechanic

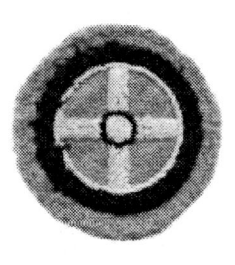

Although not a vehicle mechanic, this person had to be very knowledgeable in vehicle maintenance and repairs. He had to be able to read maps, find faults in generator, fuel and cooling systems, make tire and track repairs, and supervise recovery and towing operations. To be a Driver Mechanic, a soldier had to first be qualified as a Driver IC. This trade badge was worn by all drivers, both wheeled and tracked. This trade could be found in almost all corps. In the Signal Corps this trade was called "Driver MT RC Signals." It was a Group C trade.

Driver Steam Lorry and Steam Tractor

This driver had to drive and maintain a steam lorry or a steam tractor. He had to grease and oil the vehicle and have a good working knowledge of steam boilers. Obsolete late 1930's.

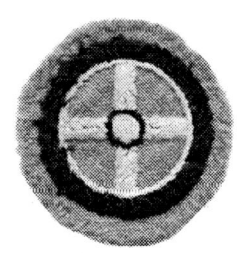

Driver Transportation Plant

This tradesman operated all types of vehicles and equipment including cranes, pile-drivers, excavators and even railway locomotives. The vehicles could be diesel, electric, gasoline or steam powered. He was required to do maintenance on his vehicle such as cleaning, oiling and checking for defects. He was also responsible for the safety of everyone near his vehicle.

They had to be qualified Fireman Stationary Engine if operating steam powered vehicles, or Engine Hand if operating gasoline or diesel powered vehicles. They would have to be qualified Engine Driver Railway if employed as a locomotive driver.

Not all members of the trade had to be qualified in all of these jobs. Each trade was divided into three classes for different skill levels. However, in this time period most trades existed in one pay group only (there were some exceptions). After reaching the class one level, a tradesman could advance further only by remustering to another trade. After 1942 most trades were split over two or three pay groups. A tradesman could then advance to the higher pay group as he increased his skills without changing his trade. The Driver Transportation Plant could be found in RCOC, RCASC and RCE.

Fireman Stationary Engine
Engine Driver Steam

This tradesman was not really a driver. "Steam equipment operator" would be a more accurate description for this trade. This tradesman was involved with the operation of steam powered engines other than trucks and tractors. Engines such as pumping plants, boilers, cranes, pile drivers, etc. Although steam powered engines are no longer used today, some construction equipment is often still referred to as "steam shovels," "steam rollers," etc. In the 1930's the trade was renamed Engine Driver Steam. It became obsolete by 1939.

Engine Driver IC
Engine Hand IC

This tradesman was not really a driver. "Equipment operator" would be a more accurate description for this trade. This tradesman had the same job as the Engine Driver Steam except with internal combustion engines instead of steam powered engines. In the late 1930's the trade was renamed Engine Hand. This was a Group C trade in RCA and RCE.

For Driver Operator see the Communications section.

ELECTRICAL AND MECHANICAL

RCEME did not exist until 1944. Most of these trades were members of the RCOC Engineering Branch.

Coppersmith

The Coppersmith worked with more than just copper. They made repairs and created objects with tin, brass, zinc, iron and sheet metal as well as copper. They could bend copper pipes to any shape. They did a lot of work that you might not associate with the name. For example, they could rebuild radiators. The Coppersmith cut and bent sheet metal into any desired shape including rolling it or bolting or welding pieces together. They were skilled at soldering, welding, brazing and rivetting. Coppersmiths were found in the RCASC as well as the RCOC. Group B.

Draughtsman Mechanical

The Draughtsman Mechanical made detailed and accurate drawings of machinery and parts such as gears or parts for automobiles or weapons. This trade could be found in CAC, RCA, RCE, and RCASC in addition to RCOC. Group A

Skill-At-Arms Badges, Instructors' Badges and Trade Badges before 1942

Electrician Fitter

The Electrician Fitter made repairs to all types of electrical equipment except radios. They repaired remote control equipment, generators, starters, electric motors and switchboards. Group A.

Fitter

The Fitter worked with metal objects to make them into a certain size or thickness. The workmanship had to be very accurate. For example, using a micrometer, he could create a piece of metal that was exactly .002 inches thick. His job was to make replacement parts for machinery and motors. They also made repairs using purchased parts. Their main duties were the repair of power trains, gears and valves. They could also repair artillery weapons but were mostly involved with major engine repairs and overhauls. He could advance to Armament Artificer (Fitter). The Fitter trade existed in CAC, RCA, RCE, RC SIGS and RCASC as well as RCOC. All Fitters were the same trade except those in the Signal Corps who belonged to a different trade called Fitter Signals (see Communications). Group A.

Grinder Precision

This tradesman used a grinding machine to grind both the inside and the outside of items such as crankshafts, cylinders and cutting tools. He had to work to precise measurements in both standard and metric measurements, using a micrometer and gauges. Group B.

Instrument Maker
Instrument Mechanic

The Instrument Maker was renamed the Instrument Mechanic in 1938. This tradesman carried out a variety of duties including making small springs of steel or bronze. They performed light fitting and turning such as cutting screw threads into a pipe. They could calibrate electrical or mechanical instruments such as voltmeters, ammeters, speedometers, pressure gauges, micrometers, theodolites and compasses, therefore they needed a good knowledge of electricity, magnetism and optics. The Instrument Mechanic was skilled at using a wide variety of tools for cutting, soldering, brazing, drilling, grinding and polishing. This was an RCOC trade. (There was also an Instrument Mechanic RCE, an Instrument Mechanic Signals and an Instrument Mechanic Surgical.) All Instrument Mechanics were in Group A.

Machinist Metal

The Machinist Metal was engaged in metal work such as sharpening and repairing tools, planing a flat surface, cutting threads, making axles for wagons, boring out pistons and much more. They made parts and tools from metal castings. This tradesman worked on all types of metal machines for slotting, shaping and milling as well as power hacksaws and drill presses. They worked with iron, steel, bronze, copper, lead and aluminum. The Machinist Metal was skilled at using micrometer and vernier gauges, and in using fraction and decimal arithmetic. They would be employed in an army machine shop. This Group B trade existed in the RCASC and RCE as well as RCOC.

Mechanist

The Mechanist was in charge of repairs and maintenance of all types of metal machinery found in an army workshop. Don't confuse this trade with the previous one. The Machinist Metal used the machinery to create or repair things. The Mechanist did not use the machines. He looked after them to ensure that they were in good working condition. He could take the machines apart and rebuild them if necessary. They needed a good knowledge of mathematics, draughting and internal combustion engines. The Mechanist would be the supervisor of the Machinist Metal and would give instruction in the proper use of the machinery. This was a Group A trade in the RCASC and CAC as well as RCOC.

Millwright

The Millwright would be called upon when a new machine shop was being set up. He would plan the layout of the machinery, and supervise the unpacking, erection and installation of equipment. If machinery is being moved, he would supervise dismantling and packing. The machines could belong to a metal or wood workshop. Once everything is set up, the Millwright would lubricate all machines and do other maintenance such as making pulleys. He would ensure that the machines are level, and the floor provides sufficient support. He could supervise the construction of large machines such as cranes and power plants. The Millwright could be found in the Forestry Corps and the Engineers in addition to RCOC. Group A.

Moulder

Using a furnace and foundry, the Moulder made moulds for the production of iron or brass parts such as pulleys, gear wheels, tools, manifolds and cylinders for steam and internal combustion engines. After making the mould, he would pour molten metal into it to create a metal part. They had to know the temperatures for casting various types of metal. When a part turned out to be less than perfect, they had to know the cause of the imperfections. This was a Group B trade. It existed in RCE as well as RCOC.

Tinsmith

This tradesman made or repaired items of tin such as cookers, steamers, funnels, buckets, lanterns, gasoline cans, water cans, stove pipes, etc. He joined seams by soldering, welding or rivetting. The Tinsmith could also remove stains from tinplate. He was required to use oxyacetylene welding equipment. Group B.

Tinsmith and Whitesmith

In addition to the duties of the Tinsmith, this tradesman could make or repair more complicated items using a wider variety of metals. He was able to repair lead, brass, and copper pipes, lamps and kettles. This tradesman could repair some automobile parts such as radiators, gasoline tanks, exhaust pipes and manifolds. He would sometimes be put to work at beating out dents or patching holes in automobiles. Group B.

Toolmaker

As the name implies, this tradesman had to be able to create tools. Starting with simple tools at the class three level, he would gradually build up his skills until, at the class one level, he could design and make all types of cutters, reamers, dies, cutting tools, jigs and gauges. He had to be skilled at working with grinding and milling machines, woodworking machines, and many other machine shop tools. Using micrometers, calipers and other instruments, he had to be very accurate in his calculations. The Tool Maker had to be familiar with geometry and trigonometry. Group A. It existed in RCE as well as RCOC.

Turner

The Turner was a combination of several trades. Although not as skilled as these trades, he had some of the abilities of the Grinder Precision, the Machinist Metal and the Toolmaker. He worked with a metal lathe and the metal machines such as the power hacksaw to cut metal for the creation of tools, jigs or other pieces of equipment. The Turner could also grind any tool to the required tolerance. He could turn, bore, thread or grind any metal object. He cut threads onto a pipe, both inside and outside. The work was very precise and he had to be able to use gauges, callipers and micrometers as well as fractional and decimal arithmetic. This was a Group B trade. It existed in RCASC and RCE as well as RCOC.

Typewriter Mechanic

This person's main job was to repair typewriters, but they also repaired adding machines and other small office equipment. Group B. It existed in RCASC as well as RCOC.

Watchmaker

This is a misnomer. This tradesman repaired watches; he did not make them from scratch. Most men carried pocket watches in the First World War and later. It was not until after the second world war that wrist watches became common. If a soldier required a watch for the fulfilment of his duties, and did not have one, he would be issued one. After the watchmaker trade was obsolete, the army continued to issue watches, but they no longer repaired them. Repairs were contracted out to a civilian jeweller. To qualify for this trade, the soldier had to be able to strip down, clean and assemble a general issue military watch in less than three hours. At the class two level, he had to replace winding stems and springs.

They would also repair some other instruments such as ammeters, voltmeters, barometers,

Skill-At-Arms Badges, Instructors' Badges and Trade Badges before 1942

binoculars, compasses and clinometers. During the First World War there were two Watchmakers at each division armourer's shop. The trade would later be combined with the Instrument Mechanic, then in 1947 made a separate trade once again. This was a Group B trade.

Welder Acetylene

This tradesman cut and welded metal of steel or aluminum using an acetylene welder. This was a Group B trade.

Welder Electric

This welder's job was to cut and weld various metal items using an electric welder. The two types of welders would later be merged into one trade. Group B.

EQUESTRIAN

In 1918 the Canadian army had more than 24,000 horses and mules with its overseas forces. Horses were used by the Canadian Army until the mid 1940's. The artillery switched from horse-drawn guns to vehicle-drawn in 1930.

Rough Rider

The job of the Rough Rider was to break in new horses and train soldiers to ride. This trade became obsolete in the 1930's.

Farrier

This tradesman worked with horses. He kept the horses feet in good condition by removing old horseshoes and nailing on new ones. Before putting on the new shoe, he would clean the hoof by rasping it with a file. The Farrier had a good knowledge of the structure of a horse's foot and of accidents and diseases that affect horses feet. He would shape the shoe to fit the horse by heating it in a forge and hammering it into the desired shape. They were also required to make repairs to the metal tyre portion of wooden wagon wheels. The Farrier also made their own forged tools, horseshoes and saddle and wagon parts. Group B

The photo following is of Harry Louden. The rank is that of Farrier Quartermaster Sergeant. Louden became a farrier when he was with the British army in South Africa during the Boar War. He later emigrated to Canada. He joined the 12th Canadian Mounted Rifles at Calgary when the First World War broke out, but after arriving in Europe he was transferred to the Fort Garry Horse. He served with distinction and was awarded the Meritorious Service Medal for gallant conduct and devotion to duty in a theatre of war.

His badge consists of (starting from the cuff and working up) four stripes pointing upward, a Fort Gary Horse crest, a horseshoe and a crown. (See Bandmaster for information about First World War ranks.)

My thanks to the Louden family and Harry Abbink for this photograph and information.

Shoeing Smith
Carriage Smith

The carriage smith made repairs to the metal parts of wooden wagons. They repaired or replaced the metal tyres on wooden wheels. The carriage smith was not a trade but was a job performed by the Farrier. In other words, a Farrier could be employed as a carriage smith or a shoeing smith. This did not change his trade.

Veterinary

In addition to caring for sick animals, mainly horses, the Veterinary had to be able to manage animals while on the march. He needed to know how to dispose of dead animals, either by cremation or burial, and to find the cause of their death. He had to consider sanitary requirements both at piquet lines and in the stable. He also had to oversee the selection of forage. Class three personnel had to do the menial work of cleaning stables, grooming, clipping, entraining and detraining. He was a member of the Canadian Army Veterinary Service. Although this tradesman cared for sick animals, he was not a veterinarian. A Veterinarian was a animal doctor with a university degree and would have officer status. Obsolete 1938.

Although they had motor vehicles, horses and mules were in wide-spread use in the Canadian military during the First World War. The cavalry still rode horses. The artillery used horses to pull their guns until 1930. Signals used horses for line laying. Just about every corps had them. Both horse-drawn and motorized ambulances were in use.

This photo shows a mule being used to bring artillery shells up to the guns.

Photo courtesy of the RCA Museum

FIELD ENGINEERS

Operator Special Engineering Equipment

This tradesman drove many different types of engineering vehicles such as bulldozers, graders, steam engines, steam shovels, cranes, etc. This trade had members in Group A and C. Those in Group C operated smaller vehicles such as concrete mixers and hoists.

Members of the Royal Canadian Engineers did not wear trade badges. Instead, Sergeants and Staff Sergeants wore a flaming grenade badge. (See March 1943 in Part Two for more information.) [3]

FORESTRY

The Canadian Forestry Corps was employed to operate sawmills in Scotland and France to produce lumber that was needed by the army. During the First World War, wood was needed to shore up trenches, build flooring in trenches, build ammunition boxes and shipping crates and many other uses. Wooden gun platforms were needed by the artillery to prevent the guns from sinking into the mud. Wood was also needed in the construction of railway tracks. It was disbanded after the war only to be re-formed during the Second World War and disbanded again in 1945.

The Forestry Corps was divided into two main parts. There were those who did the logging and those who worked at the sawmill. Hand saws and axes were the main tools; there were no power saws in those days. The logs were attached to sulkies (a small two wheel cart) and dragged to the road with horses. The trades listed here are those that worked at the sawmill plus those that operated or repaired tractors or repaired saws. The actual loggers were not considered to be tradesmen.

During the First World War, members of the Forestry Corps were not combat troops. This was changed for the Second World War and they received two months infantry training before being employed in logging duties. After that, they worked five days per week at logging and one day per week at infantry training. During the First World War the Forestry troops numbered 31,447 all ranks. In the Second World War there were 224 officers and 6,385 other ranks divided into 30 companies.

Driver IC Tractor Forestry

This tradesman drove bulldozers and graders with internal combustion engines (compared to steam powered). He also operated vehicles with winches to uproot trees and move boulders. The object of his work was to create and grade roads. He had to maintain and lubricate his vehicle. This was a Group B trade.

Edgerman Forestry

The Edgerman operated sawmill equipment, called an edger, that took the bark off of trees and then cut the timber into rough lumber. He had to keep the saw blades in good working condition. Teeth on the saws could be changed individually. Group B.

Engine Artificer Forestry

The Engine Artificer Forestry had the same duties as the Engine Artificer except that he was employed with the Forestry troops. The "engine" that they repaired does not refer to vehicle engines. They made repairs to stand-alone equipment such as generators, water pumps, compressors, cement mixers, etc. The Engine Artificer must have previously been a Fitter. This was a Group B trade.

Fitter Tractor Forestry

Like other fitters, this tradesman was mainly occupied with making metal parts for various machines. In the case of the Fitter Forestry, he made parts and did repairs to all vehicles used in the Forestry Corps including gas and diesel tractors. This included everything from minor jobs such as lubrication, battery charging, adjusting brakes and clutches, and greasing wheel bearings to major engine overhauls and repairing cracked cylinder blocks. If manufactured parts were not available, they would build their own. Also, like most other fitters, this trade was in Group A.

Foreman Departmental Forestry

This trade was similar to a storeman accountant. In fact, he would have been an ordinary storeman before being promoted into this position. He looked after the stores for a logging camp. He would be in charge of all receipts and issues including the shipping of lumber. This trade was new in 1941 and only lasted a couple of years. It was dissolved and the duties included with that of the Foreman of Works trades described below. The trade had existed at two pay levels. Class two personnel were in Group B, while class three personnel were in Group C.

Foreman of Works Bush Forestry

This person was the supervisor for the soldiers who were working on logging operations such as the loading and transport of logs. He directed and supervised road construction including building of bridges and logging camps. He would also take forest surveys and estimate the quantity of timber available. This tradesman would also supervise the use of forestry vehicles such as tractors, sulkies, donkeys, skidders, loaders and trucks. Group A.

Foreman of Works Mill Forestry

This person was the supervisor for a sawmill. He would supervise the installation and maintenance of all equipment. He would also be in charge of the lumber yard, ensuring that the lumber is properly stacked and graded. He would direct and supervise all shipments. The Foreman of Works Mill Forestry had to identify different species of trees and know which ones to use to fill orders. Group A.

Log Canter Forestry

This person was in charge of loading logs from the vehicles into the sawmill in the proper manner. The Edgerman would then cut off the bark. The Log Canter then had to rotate the log in order to obtain the maximum lumber. This tradesman would use a tool called a "cant hook" to manipulate the logs. He had to be highly skilled with the cant hook and an axe. In modern sawmills this job is done by a machine called a "log canter." Group C.

Motor Mechanic Forestry

This mechanic made repairs to the vehicles used by the forestry troops. The class one Motor Mechanic Forestry was in Group A. The class two Motor Mechanic Forestry was in Group B. They repaired all wheeled and tracked vehicles and power plants. The Motor Mechanic Forestry could do all mechanical repairs including major engine overhauls, replacement of transmissions, differentials, axles and steering systems. They also made repairs to tires. Personnel working at the Group B level would do the less complicated repairs. Unlike the Fitter Tractor Forestry, they did not manufacture their own parts.

Sawdoctor

As the name implies, the Sawdoctor repaired and sharpened all types of saws. This tradesman worked on large saws used in logging and saw mills as well as band saws and circular saws in a woodworking shop. They could replace broken teeth, remove dents or twists and kinks. This trade existed in RCOC and RCE (and RCEME after 1944) as well as the Forestry Corps. Group A.

Sawfiler Forestry

This tradesman maintained crosscut and web saws in a Forestry Company. He was not as skilled as the Sawdoctor. He was employed only in the woods at logging camps and made only minor repairs. Most of their work consisted of sharpening. Group C.

Sawyer Forestry

The Sawyer Forestry operated the saws in a sawmill. He would be required to cut timber to given specifications with a minimum of waste. They used circular saws and band saws. This was a Group A trade. There was also a Sawyer trade in the Fortress Company but it was not the same trade as this one.

Storeman Technical Forestry

This tradesman was a storeman accountant. They would keep track of the lumber in a lumber yard and file paperwork to keep track of shipments. This was a Group C trade. The Foreman Departmental Forestry would have been his boss. Both of these trades were new in 1941 and obsolete within a couple of years. Storeman duties at a lumber camp were probably taken over by a regular army storeman. (See Supply in this part of the book.)

Forestry units had other trades that were not exclusive to their corps. For example, they would have cooks, clerks and a millwright, to name a few. Although the millwright would be in the Forestry Corps, he would be the same trade and would have taken the same qualifying course as an millwright in the RCOC. See Millwright in the Electrical and Mechanical Section.

FORTRESS COMPANY

The Fortress Company consisted mostly of trades that made repairs to buildings. In Part Three of the book the name was changed to Construction Engineers. These tradesmen were members of the Corps of Royal Canadian Engineers but some of them also existed in other corps. If this is the case, it will be indicated after the job description.

Blacksmith

The Blacksmith made metal parts such as vehicle springs, chains, and tools, etc. The metal was heated on a bed of coke or coal and fanned with a bellows. When the metal is red hot, it can be twisted or pounded into the desired shape. The Blacksmith also had to be qualified as a welder. This trade existed in the RCASC, RCOC, and infantry as well as RCE. Group B.

Blacksmith's striker (aka Hammerman)

This person was a Blacksmith's helper. He must be able to prepare the Blacksmith's fire and be familiar with the Blacksmith's tools and duties. He could remuster to Blacksmith class three after passing the prescribed test. All helpers of Group B trades received trades pay at the Group C rate.

Boilermaker

A Boilermaker builds and maintains boilers. He cut the metal into the desired size, then shaped it, then rivetted or welded the pieces together. Then, he would caulk the seams and attach the pipes for the flow of water into and out of the boiler. The Boilermaker would inspect existing boilers and make a report as to their state of repair. Group B.

Bricklayer

The Bricklayer builds walls, chimneys, fireplaces, arches, etc. This trade also existed in the Forestry Corps, the infantry, and the RCAMC. (See Workshop Foreman Field Hygiene in the Medical section of Part Two to find out why they needed bricklayers in the Medical Corps.) Group B.

Cabinet Maker

The Cabinet Maker built wooden boxes and furniture including cupboards, book cases, tables and chests of drawers. They were capable of building fine quality furniture suitable for the officer's mess. The Cabinet Maker might have worn the same trade badge as the Carpenter but I have no documentation on this. Obsolete 1938.

Skill-At-Arms Badges, Instructors' Badges and Trade Badges before 1942

Carpenter

The Carpenter built and repaired walls and trim. They also installed flooring, windows and doors. This tradesman worked mostly on wooden buildings but they also planned and built just about anything the army needed that could be made of wood. The metal version of the badge is shown. The Carpenter existed in almost all corps. This was a Group B trade.

Carpenter and Joiner

This tradesman was more skilled than the ordinary Carpenter. He could make all types of joints, identify different species of timber, make complicated repairs to automobile bodies. In short, he was required to do any carpentry work that was needed. The Carpenter and Joiner could be required to supervise operations in a RCOC woodworking shop and to instruct Carpenters who worked there. (This was an RCOC trade but was later combined with the Carpenter which existed in several corps but was eventually limited to RCE.) The Carpenter and Joiner was a Group B trade.

Carpenter and Wheeler

The Carpenter and Wheeler would be an assistant to either the Carpenter or the Wheeler. This was a learner trade and could not advance past Group C. To advance he would remuster to Carpenter or Wheeler.

In 1938 the Cabinet Maker and the three different types of Carpenters were combined into a single trade called "Carpenter and Joiner". This trade badge was also worn by the Wheeler. (You will find Wheeler under Vehicle Mechanics where you can see a picture of the cloth version of this badge.)

Trade badges were not worn by RCE personnel. The Carpenter existed in most corps until after the Second World War. The trade is listed here because it was eventually eliminated in all corps except RCE. (See March 1943 in part two for more information on RCE badges.) [3]

Concrete Worker   Concretor

The Concrete Worker was renamed Concretor in 1938. This tradesman mixed, poured, and levelled concrete to build products from floors to runways. They could determine the mix depending on the strength of the work required. The Concretor could operate several different types of mixers. They were knowledgeable in curing the concrete and protecting it from frost. They were required to estimate the time and materials required by studying drawings. Group B.

Diver

The Diver performed underwater inspection, repairs, and salvage and construction in harbours and other waterways. These were not SCUBA divers. This was the old-fashioned diver that had to wear a special suit with a helmet and air lines connected to a boat. They made minor underwater repairs to ships and cleaned ship bottoms and propellers. The Diver could also make repairs to locks, docks, and canals.

The Diver had to know the safety rules for diving. He had to know the time limits for working in deep water. He knew the symptoms and treatment of compressed air illness and must be able to assist other Divers who were in trouble or incapacitated. They had to repair and maintain diving suits and equipment. This was a Group A trade.

Draughtsman Architectural

This tradesman made drawings for the construction of buildings. Group A.

Draughtsman Engineering

The Draughtsman Engineering had to prepare and work with drawings for engineering projects such as bridges, ditches, etc. The Draughtsman Architectural and the Draughtsman Engineering were later combined into a single trade known as the Draughtsman Architectural and Engineering (or Draughtsman A&E for short). This was a Group A trade.

Draughtsman Topographical

This tradesman prepared topographical maps. They took data from several different sources such as surveyor's notes, aerial photographs and other maps.

They could copy, enlarge or reduce existing maps. The Draughtsman Topographical also had to mark things on maps so he had to be very skilled at lettering and drawing map symbols. His drawings had to be very accurate and to scale. Group A.

Electrician

The Electrician repaired and installed electric wiring. They worked mostly in buildings on electric light systems, circuit boxes and alarm systems but also repaired wiring on generators, transformers, switchboards and electric motors. The Electrician needed a thorough knowledge of both A.C. and D.C. systems. He could be required to maintain a small electric power plant. This was a Group A trade. Besides RCE, this trade also existed in CAC, RCOC and RCASC. RCCS had a separate trade called Electrician Signals.

Fireman

This was not a fire fighter. His job was to start fires, not put them out. He made and maintained fires in furnaces for hot water heating systems. Obsolete 1938.

Foreman of Works

This was a supervisor for the construction Engineer trades. He needed to have a working knowledge of as many construction trades as possible, and should be capable of effecting repairs in carpentry, plumbing, or electrical wiring. The Foreman of Works supervised the construction or repair of buildings, roads, bridges, drainage systems, runways and waterworks. He was required to estimate the time and material needed for a project. Group A.

Engineer Works Foreman

The Engineer Works Foreman did the same job as the Foreman of Works. However, he was less skilled than the Foreman of Works and would not be given as much responsibility. These two trades were later combined. In the 1950s they would be known as Group three and Group four of the same trade. The Engineer Works Foreman was a Group B trade. The Foreman of Works was a Group A trade.

Gas Fitter

This Tradesman had to cut, screw and join pipes on a hot water or gas installation. To advance to the class one level, he must also qualify as a skilled plumber. This trade became obsolete in 1938.

Instrument Repairer
Instrument Mechanic RCE

The Instrument Repairer used a vise and lathe to repair small electrical instruments such as lamps. This trade was renamed in 1938 to Instrument Mechanic RCE.

There was already a trade called Instrument Mechanic which can be found in the Electrical and Mechanical section. There were also an Instrument Mechanic Signals and an Instrument Mechanic Surgical. All Instrument Mechanics were in Group A.

Mechanist Instrument Repairer

The duties of this tradesman are unknown to me. Perhaps he repaired the instruments used by the Instrument Mechanic. This trade was obsolete by 1938.

Mason

Have you read the job description for the Bricklayer? He built walls, fireplaces, chimneys, arches, etc. out of brick. The Mason built the same objects, but out of stone instead of brick. He also cut stone to desired shapes and joined stones at corners. The Mason could also make stone window sills and moulding. This Group B trade existed in several corps.

Mechanist Electrician
Mechanist Electrical RCE

The Mechanist Electrician was renamed the Mechanist Electrical RCE about 1940. His job was the installation, maintenance and repair of electrical machinery such as generators, convertors, rectifiers, transformers and other electrical devices. They could operate a power plant or repair wiring in buildings or vehicles. They could estimate the cost of a new electrical installation. The Mechanist Electrical RCE could also erect power lines. To qualify for this trade, he would have previously been a qualified Electrician. This trade was in pay Group A.

Mechanist Machinery RCE

This tradesman was a master mechanic. He could be placed in charge of all mechanical equipment in the corps. He would make regular visits to workshops to check on operating conditions. The

Mechanist Machinery RCE would draw plans for any new installations of workshops, generating stations, pumping stations, heating systems and refrigeration plants. He had to be knowledgeable in mathematics, draughting, engineer stores procedures, heating units, internal combustion engines, ignition systems, carburetion, fuel injection systems, pumping equipment, steam boilers, refrigeration, transmission of power, water purification, electricity, field bakeries, laundries, steam and oil cooking equipment, disinfectors and water distillation. He must have previously been a Group A of any RCE trade. Obviously, this was a Group A trade.

Although the above two trades would qualify to wear the hammer and pincer badge, trade badges were not worn by RCE personnel. See March 1943 in part two for details.[3]

Miner

A Miner's job was to drill underground to extract ore. They had to operate and maintain large miner's drills. They also made openings using explosives. The Miner must also be able to construct walls or roofing in the mine to prevent cave-ins. They had to know mine safety precautions and mine ventilation methods.

In wartime, Miners were also used to excavate tunnels under enemy territory. Group B.

Minor Diamond Setter

The Minor, as described above, used a large drill to excavate tunnels for the extraction of ore. These drills were often set with diamonds. Diamonds, being extremely hard, could be used to drill into solid rock. The Minor Diamond Setter reset these diamonds and made other repairs to drilling equipment. With drilling, the diamonds become worn, chipped or lost.

The Minor Diamond Setter was also a very good mechanic. They made repairs to internal combustion engines. Mining equipment consisted of many engines to power the drills, lights, conveyor belts, pumps and other equipment. This was a new trade in 1941. Group A.

Minor Mechanic or Driller

This tradesman was the mechanic for a mining operation. They made repairs to the many types of internal combustion engine equipment that was used at a mining site. The trade was new in 1941. The Minor Mechanic or Driller set up and maintained diamond or rotary drills. They made the power connection from the drill to the internal combustion engine. A pump needed to be set up to supply water to the drill hole. This tradesman set up that pump but still his work was not done. Next, a diamond studded steel drill bit had to be attached to the drilling rod. When everything was ready, another responsibility of this tradesman was to start the power supply and control the speed of the drill. As the hole gets deeper, additional lengths of rod would need to be attached. The Minor Mechanic or Driller made repairs to several other machines and equipment that were used at the mine. They also had to be a capable pipefitter. Finally, they had to disassemble and reassemble the equipment for transport. Group B.

In 1940 and 1941 two Canadian tunnelling companies of minors built a subterranean hospital on the island of Gibralter.

Paperhanger

You may have guessed this tradesman's job; he hangs wallpaper. In the 1920's and 1930's it was unusual to see a wall in an office or home that was simply painted and not covered with wallpaper. To advance to class one, he must also be a skilled painter. Note that the Painter and the Paperhanger must learn each others trade at the higher levels. Only the class three tradesman would have no knowledge of the other trade. This trade was obsolete by 1939 and the duties were included with that of the Painter and Decorator.

Painter

The Painter had to prepare surfaces for painting; then he must be able to paint or varnish the surface. He also had to do lettering. That was the extent of his knowledge. He was not required to mix colours or hang wallpaper. That was the job of the Painter and Decorator and the Paperhanger. Both the Painter and the Painter and Decorator were Group B trades.

Painter & Decorator

The Painter and Decorator needed a good knowledge of mixing and matching colours. He knew how to preserve brushes and paint after use. They were also skilled at lettering for sign making. This trade included the use of varnish and stain as well as paint. He could prepare any surface for painting, including walls and glass. He must also be able to hang wallpaper. At the class one level, he must also be able to estimate the quantities of paint required for a job and have a good knowledge of spray painting. Group B. The Painter and Decorator existed in several different corps.

Helper Engineers   Pioneer RCE
In 1938 or '39 the Helper Engineers was renamed Pioneer RCE. Be careful not to confuse this trade with the Infantry Pioneer. During this time period, the Pioneer RCE was a tradesman's helper. They would be an assistant to any trade in the Royal Canadian Engineers. They would be paid at the Group C level, regardless of the pay level for the trade. He would eventually become a member of the trade to which he was assigned as a helper. (The role of the Pioneer RCE would later change to become more like the Infantry Pioneer. See this trade in the 1946 to 1955 time period.)

Plasterer
This tradesman plastered walls and ceilings. He also repaired brick walls and worked with stucco. This trade was obsolete by 1939.

Plumber   Plumber and Pipe Fitter
This tradesman made all types of plumbing repairs and installations. This included cutting and threading pipe, cutting holes in walls for pipes to pass through, caulking and soldering and the installation of fixtures such as sinks and toilets. In the 1930's the name was changed from simply Plumber to Plumber and Pipe Fitter. This trade also existed in RCOC and RCAMC. It is surprising which trades were members of the medical corps. They also had Bricklayers. Group B.

Quarryman
The Quarryman, as you may have guessed, worked in a quarry. They produced stone or crushed rock from stone quarries. The Quarryman was qualified to drill holes into rock walls and insert explosives in order to break up the rock. Group B.

Rigger
This trade is not to be confused with the Parachute Rigger which was an RCOC trade and did not exist before 1942. The Rigger's job was to erect derricks to lift heavy equipment. For example, a heavy object may need to be moved across a gap. The Rigger was knowledgeable in the use of various types of hemp and wire rope and chains and could determine if they were strong enough for the job at hand. This was a Group B trade.

Riveter
The Riveter's job was to fasten together metal parts using rivets. He would first drill a hole, then insert a heated rivet, then form a head on the opposite side using an air hammer. The Riveter had to work from blueprints and sketches. This trade was later renamed the Structural Steel Worker. It also existed in RCOC. Group B.

Roofer
The Roofer layed tar, gravel, shingle, or tile roofing, or make repairs to them. This trade was obsolete by 1939.

Sawyer
This was not the same trade as the Sawyer Forestry who worked in a saw mill. This Sawyer operated band, chain, circular and ribbon saws in a woodworking shop. They had to maintain the saws by lubricating the machinery and cleaning the belts.

Steamfitter
The Steamfitter cut, thread and connected pipes in steam and hot water heating systems. Many of his duties were the same as that of the plumber with a few exceptions. The Steamfitter connected pipes to boilers and bent pipes using a hand or power pipe-bending machine. He also had to make repairs to burst steam pipes, whereas the plumber repaired burst water pipes. The Steamfitter needed a thorough knowledge of hot water heating systems. Group B.

Stoker Stationary Engine
The Stoker Stationary Engine operated a steam-driven plant, supplying heat to buildings or steam to power equipment. He stoked the fire by shovelling fuel (probably coal) into the firebox. He would adjust the fuel supply to keep the engine operating at the required level. This tradesman would also make minor repairs to the equipment. Group C.

Surveyor Engineering
This tradesman surveyed an area for

construction of building, roads, dams, bridges, etc. He would then draw up a plan for the site using triangulation, slide rule, trigonometry and logarithms. The drawing had to be to scale. Group A.

Surveyor Topographical

This tradesman's job was to survey the ground and produce sufficient data for the production of maps. He would compute angles, distances, elevations, latitude and longitude. To acquire this data, the Surveyor Topographical used transits, theodolites and aerial photographs. This was a Group A trade.

Wellborer

The Wellborer set up and operated well-drilling equipment to drill for water. If water was found, the Wellborer would connect a pump. Group B.

Several of the trades listed in the Electrical and Mechanical section also existed in the RCE.

GEOMATICS

The term "Geomatics" was not used in this period. This is a modern term. It refers to trades that deal with map making. It is used here to maintain consistency with this group of trades throughout the book. These tradesmen were members of the RCE.

Computer Trigonometrical

This person was a computer! This sounds strange today when the word "computer" means a machine. Before the modern age of computers, a computer was a person who computes. He was, in other words, a mathematician. The Computer Trigonometrical used the data created by the Surveyor Trigonometrical (see below) to calculate distances between points. Group A.

Surveyor Cadastral & Engineering

This tradesman surveyed land boundaries for legal purposes. Property boundaries had to be surveyed in order to obtain a Certificate of Title before a property could be sold or subdivided. Group A.

Surveyor Trigonometrical

This person conducted surveys using the trigonometrical method. In this process a survey was done by measuring a line which became the base of a triangle. Using equilateral triangles, the other two sides of the triangle would be measured. Then connecting the triangle with various points surveyed, he created a pattern of interlocking triangles. Points and distances of all corners of all the triangles could be computed from the data. Group A.

Two other trades that were involved with surveying and mapmaking were the Surveyor Topographical and the Draughtsman Topographical. These trades were part of the Fortress Company. There were also surveyors in the railway troops and the artillery.

INFANTRY

Bomber

A Bomber was a soldier who specialized in throwing grenades. In the Second World War, all infantrymen were trained in grenade throwing, but during the First World War it was a trade that required special training. In the trench warfare of this era it was extremely difficult to make any gains against an enemy in a well dug-in trench system. Attacking infantry would be shot down by machine gunners. The job of the Bomber was to sneak up to within throwing distance of the enemy trench and lob a grenade into it. He would continue to throw grenades while his troops advanced. The enemy was forced to keep their heads down and not shoot at the attacking soldiers. When the infantry got close enough to make a run for the enemy trench, the Bomber would stop throwing grenades. The riflemen would then engage the enemy with rifles and bayonets and the Bomber would join them in the battle.

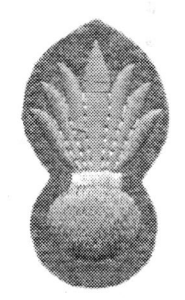

The most common type of grenade in the First World War was known as a Mills Bomb. It was invented by a person by the name of William Mills in 1915. The Mills Bomb was the first of the modern type grenades that, when thrown with the safety pin removed, would release a lever and initiate a fuse. At first, the fuses were set for seven seconds but this was reduced to four seconds when it was discovered that the enemy had time to pick up the grenade and throw it back.

Before the invention of the Mills Bomb, a

grenade was simply a tin can filled with gunpowder and a fuse. They would often explode prematurely and were almost as dangerous to the thrower as they were to the enemy.

The photograph shows a Lance Corporal Bomber being presented with a medal. The badge for the Bomber can easily be confused with that of the Field Engineer. They are almost the same except that the Engineer badge has two additional flames in front of the seven flames in the rear. (See March 1943 in Part Two for a photo of the Engineer badge.)

Although the Bomber's main job was the throwing of grenades, this privilege was not reserved for them alone. Many other soldiers also used bombs regularly. Mills bombs were carried and used by Scouts, signallers and riflemen on a regular basis. The difference was that these soldiers had no particular role concerning the bomb or a specific time to throw it. They used them whenever they saw fit. It was not their main occupation.

This trade became obsolete after the First World War.

The photo at right shows Infantry Bombers in the trenches. Note the bomber vest that they are wearing. This vest is actually just a bunch of pockets with straps around the neck and back. Each pocket holds a mills bomb. Additional bombs were carried in pouches. The soldier on the right has two of them under his bomber vest. Still more bombs could be carried in a large canvas bag as carried by the soldier on the left. (This photo is of British soldiers but the equipment used by Canadians was the same.)

Photo: Bennett collection.

Pioneer

The Infantry Pioneer trade has existed since long before the First World War. In the field, this tradesman built obstacles and traps to hinder the enemy. When in barracks they were basically carpenters and would be tasked with the building of cabinets or any other wooden items required by the infantry. They had to pass the same test as the Carpenter to qualify for this trade.

The Pioneer became obsolete in the infantry after the First World War. They were replaced by Carpenters and Bricklayers until the trade was revived in 1950.

In fusilier regiments a grenade badge was worn above the crossed hatchets. In light infantry and rifle regiments a bugle badge was added. All other units wore the crossed hatches without another badge above.

There were pioneers other than the Infantry Pioneer. There was a trade called Pioneer RCE. He was not engaged in traditional pioneer duties (see Fortress section). He worked on building construction and machinery.

The photo following shows Cpl John McKay at work. He was a pioneer in one of the several pioneer battalions in the CEF. Note that he is wearing the crossed hatchet badge on the lower left arm. This position indicates that this is not a trade. Infantry Pioneers wore the badge on

Skill-At-Arms Badges, Instructors' Badges and Trade Badges before 1942

the upper right arm. Pioneers in the pioneer battalions were considered to be more like labourers than tradesmen.

In the Engineers, pioneer work was carried out by the Field Engineer, not the Pioneer RCE. The Field Engineer was not a trade during this time period.

The photo at right is John Bennett who was an Infantry Pioneer in the 200th Battalion. He was a carpenter before the war (and is the author's grandfather). Note the badge on the upper right arm.

Photo on right and above: Bennett collection

Scout

In the First World War, each infantry battalion had an intelligence section. This section, which was led by an intelligence officer, included air photo interpreters, scouts, observers and snipers. The infantry observer was not a trade and did not have a badge. The "O" badge mentioned in the Skill At Arms section was for the artillery observer.

The infantry observer would spy on the enemy with a telescope and report back to the intelligence officer with his findings. The information could be used to deploy snipers if they decided to kill some of the enemy. Sometimes Scouts were sent out to gather more data.

A small group of three or four Scouts would crawl out of their trench into the no-man's-land under cover of darkness to approach the enemy trenches. The Scout's main duty was to gather information about the enemy. They often decided to kill a few of them while they were there. Scouts were trained and equipped with Mills Bombs. (See Bomber trade above.)

When a raid was planned on the enemy trenches, the artillery would first pound the position in an attempt to break up the large quantity of barbed wire that protected the trench system on both sides. After the barrage, Scouts would be sent out to look for gaps in the wire.

Sometimes Scouts were sent to capture prisoners in an attempt to discover the enemy's plans. If the Scouts found regular routes used by the enemy this information would be passed to the artillery. If a well-used route was found between the enemy trenches and their observation or guard post in no-man's-land, the Scouts would bring a machine gun crew with them on patrol in hopes of killing the enemy.

*Pte Archie Lethbridge of the 43rd Battalion CEF
My thanks to G. Tyler for this rare photo.*

Before going on these patrols, Scouts would change into what they called their "crawling suit." Most of their time on patrol was spent crawling around in the mud so one uniform was set aside for this purpose. This crawling uniform would have no badges or insignia of any type,

The Scout badge was the fleur-de-lys. Scout Sergeants and 1st class Scouts had a bar across the bottom of the badge. CEF dress regulations state that the badge was to be worn in brass on the upper right arm and above any rank badges if applicable. Yet the photograph of Pte Archie Lethbridge of the 43rd Battalion CEF clearly shows the badge being worn in cloth on the lower left arm.

This trade became obsolete after the First World War.

The Scout badge was also worn by cavalry units. In the infantry, the badge was worn by Scout Sergeants and first class Scouts only. The cavalry also had a lower-ranking version of the badge for all trained scouts. This version of the badge is lacking the horizontal bar across the bottom.

MATERIALS

Equipment Repairer

The Equipment Repairer repaired military items such as webbing, tents, tarpaulins, blankets and other canvas and leather goods. They made repairs by hand using awls, chisels, hammers, planes, pliers, punches, rulers, scissors, screwdrivers, shears and all types and sizes of needles. They also used sewing machines and other machinery. Some of their work included recovering seats, making canvas bags, installing or replacing buckles, grommets, rivets and eyelets for rope attachments. This trade could be found in all corps except RCOC, CDC, CPC, C Pro C and RCAMC. Group C.

Textile Refitter

This tradesman was very similar to the Equipment Repairer but was more skilled. Like the Equipment Repairer, he made repairs to canvas and leather goods. The Textile Refitter also did waterproofing and treated fabric for preservation. They also whipped ends of ropes to keep them from fraying. Both of these trades made repairs to webbing but the Textile Refitter also repaired or replaced the metal portions such as metal buckles. Both trades re-covered upholstery in automobiles but the Textile Refitter could also replace the springs in a seat. The Textile Refitter repaired several parts of automobiles including leather parts and fabric roofs. Because the Textile Refitter was more skilled than the Equipment Repairer, this trade was in Group B. These two trades were never found in the same unit. While the Equipment Repairer could be found in most corps, this trade was RCOC only.

Saddle and Harness Maker
Saddler

In 1938 the Saddle and Harness Maker was renamed Saddler. His main job was to repair or rebuild regulation pattern saddlery, using both machine and hand sewing. They formed the leather into shape using a frame called a saddle tree. They also made harnesses and many other leather items such as tool bags and straps. This trade could be found in RCOC and RCASC. It was a Group B trade.

Saddle Tree Maker

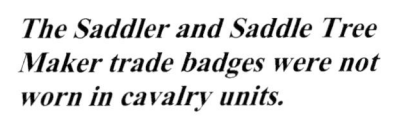

The Saddle Tree Maker made wooden frames around which saddles were formed. This was an RCOC Group B trade.

The Saddler and Saddle Tree Maker trade badges were not worn in cavalry units.

Shoemaker

The Shoemaker repaired both uppers and bottoms of boots and shoes. At the class two level, he must be able to decide if a boot or shoe is fit for repair or should be destroyed. At the class one level, he must have a thorough knowledge of leather and know which type is suitable for different kinds of work. This was an RCOC Group B trade.

Tailor

The Tailor made alterations and repairs to army uniforms. He would be proficient in the use of sewing machines and would sew badges and insignia on uniforms. He must be able to attach a new collar, pocket or epaulette to a uniform. At the class two level, he must be able to make any garment from scratch except tunics. At the class one level, he must be able to make any garment, including tunics. The Tailor also made curtains, flags and other items. This was an RCOC Group B trade.

Workshop Supervisor

This tradesman supervised the operation and personnel in a RCOC Returned Stores Depot. Saddlers, Tailors, Textile Refitters and other trades would be employed there. The Workshop Supervisor inspected the workmanship of people using sewing machines and other machinery, and ensured that proper maintenance was done on the machines. He would make estimates of time and material required for any given job. He made monthly reports on the work that was done. The Workshop Supervisor required a good knowledge of workshop accounting procedures and all RCOC trades under his supervision. Group B.

MEDICAL

Instrument Mechanic Surgical

This tradesman made repairs to surgical instruments. This was a new trade in 1939. It was in Group A.

Laboratory Assistant

The Lab Assistant was involved with the analysis of biological samples (urine, blood, etc.) to check for diseases. He could also determine a blood group from a drop of blood. He could determine the quantities of blood-sugar, urea, bile chloride and protein in a sample. Group A.

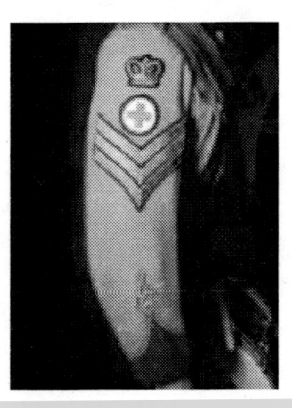

Photo courtesy of the RCR museum

The medical trade badge, a Geneva cross, was worn by all personnel in the Canadian Army Medical Corps, whether they were tradesmen or not. This included officers and non trade personnel such as stretcher bearers (but does not include stretcher bearers in other corps). It was worn above any rank badges. [2]

Before 1903, rank badges were worn on the right arm only. After 1903 they were worn on both arms but this was not implemented by all units and corps until after the First World War. If rank was worn on both arms, then this badge would be worn on both arms also.

For Warrant Officers, the badge was worn on the lower arm. For Sergeants-Major the badge was worn on the lower arm between the four stripes and the crown.

Masseur

The army had masseurs in the 1930's and 1940's to rub muscles of soldiers when there was a medical problem. This was intended to improve circulation and reduce swelling and to stretch contracted tendons. The Masseur also gave hot baths and instructed patients in methods of exercise to improve movement of muscles and joints. Group A.

Operating Room Assistant

This tradesman would prepare an operating room for surgery by sterilizing the equipment and the room. He would bring the patient to the operating room and ensure that they were properly positioned on the operating table. During the operation, he could assist the surgeon and the anaesthetist and would have to be familiar with the operation of anaesthetic equipment. The Operating Room Assistant could also administer some medical procedures such as applying plaster casts, tourniquets, hypodermic and intravenous needles. This was a Group B trade.

Pharmacist and Dispenser

Like your neighbourhood pharmacist, this person gave out drugs when requested by a doctor. They also mixed and measured ingredients to make up the necessary drugs. They had to take inventory and maintain the supply of drugs. The Pharmacist and Dispenser had to be licensed by one of the provinces of Canada to practice as a pharmacist. Group A.

Radiographer

Known today as an X-ray Tech, this person operated X-ray equipment. He would prepare the patient for the X-ray, take the exposure, develop the film and make minor repairs to the X-ray equipment. Group A.

X-Ray Maintenance Tech

This tradesman maintained and made repairs to X-ray equipment. He would also advise on the installation of X-ray equipment. He must have previously been a Radiographer. This was a Group A trade.

Sanitary Assistant

The Sanitary Assistant was responsible for the cleanliness of the kitchen area and latrines. His purpose was the prevention of diseases. In the kitchen he would inspect for the proper method of storage and preservation of food, disposal of waste and general cleanliness. If necessary, he would disinfect clothing and blankets if there was an infestation of vermin. The Sanitary Assistant would also assist in rodent control and the quarantine of patients with communicable diseases. This trade is known today as the Preventive Medicine Tech. See Medical in Part Three. Group B.

Wardmaster

The Wardmaster was responsible for the daily operation of a hospital ward. They would take pulse, temperature and respiration rates and apply dressings. The Wardmaster would administer all types of treatments, some of which are no longer used. Some of these included administering mustard plasters and poultices, throat and bladder irrigations, inhalers, catheters, enemas and hypodermics. He would also be required to make the beds and clean the rooms and washrooms. He would sterilize any equipment necessary, such as thermometers. If a patient had to go for surgery, the Wardmaster would make any necessary preparations. You might have recognized all of these duties. These jobs are done today by a person called a "nurse." Group B.

Some Wardmasters would be appointed as hospital administrator. See Hospital Sergeant at the end of this section.

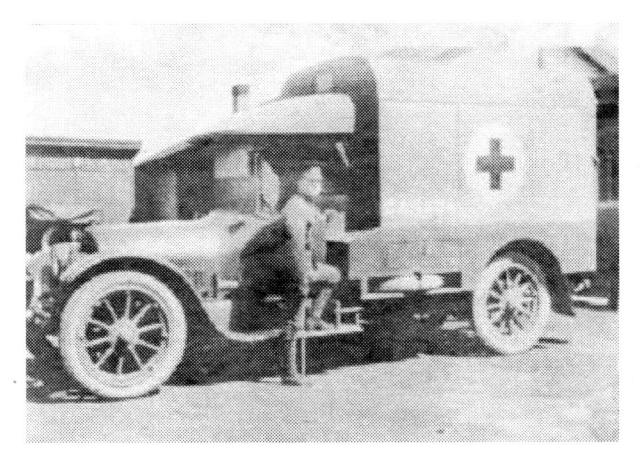

The photo of the soldier with the ambulance is courtesy of the Canadian Letters and Images Project. The other photo shows a soldier wearing a goatskin vest. He could be a member of any of the above trades or perhaps a medical orderly which was not a trade at this time. As mentioned earlier, the Geneva cross badge was worn by all ranks of the Medical Corps, regardless of trade or profession.

This photo is courtesy of Dave King.

Skill-At-Arms Badges, Instructors' Badges and Trade Badges before 1942

Medical Orderly

One important profession in the medical field is missing from the above trades. As incredible as it may seem, the medic was not a trade until the 1940's. There were nursing sisters to look after patients once they reached a medical facility but they did not go to the battlefields. During the First World War, the medic was known as the Medical Orderly. There was only one per unit.

Wearing of Trade Badges on Greatcoats

Trade badges were not usually worn on greatcoats. When they were worn on coats, they were placed on the lower sleeve even though they were worn on the upper sleeve on the service dress. The medical badge was one of the few that were authorized for wear on the greatcoat.

photo: Bennett collection

Stretcher Bearers

The stretcher bearer was not a trade but they did have a unique badge, so I have decided to include them here. Stretcher bearers in the Medical Corps would have first aid training and wore the Geneva cross badge. Other stretcher bearers would have little or no medical training and could be a member of any corps. Bandsmen were often employed as stretcher bearers during a battle.

Before the First World War, stretcher bearers wore a Maltese cross on the upper right arm. [11]

During the First World War, the Maltese cross was replaced with an brassard (armband) with the letters SB on it.

The photo above shows Pte Thomas Beckett as a stretcher bearer in the 226th Bn.
photo: Bennett collection

Reminder: These badges were worn by stretcher bearers in all corps except the medical corps which wore the Geneva cross badge.

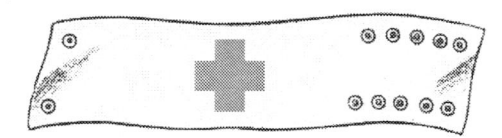

During the Second World War, the letters "SB" on the brassard were replaced with a Geneva cross. These soldiers were trained in first aid.

Only a limited number of soldiers were allowed to be permanently employed as stretcher bearers. Extra stretcher bearers could be assigned at any time on a temporary basis but they would not receive the "SB" armband. The allocated number of stretcher bearers was as follows:

Cavalry	6 per regiment
Artillery	2 per battery
Division Ammo Column	2
Engineers	2 per company

Cyclists   2 per company
Infantry   9 per battalion
Signals   2 per company
Division Train   2

The above list is in addition to medical corps personnel. [3]

There were five personal per unit for water detail. These soldiers were not tradesmen; nor were they members of the medical corps. They were trained by the unit MO in the sterilisation and testing of the water supply.

The photo above shows wounded soldiers being picked up by a horse-drawn ambulance after a battle at Cambrai.
Photo: Bennett collection

The Hospital Sergeant

The Geneva cross badge was worn by all members of the Medical Corps whether they were tradesmen or not. The badge was also worn by members of other corps if they were engaged in medical work.

Ernest Clendening was not a member of the Medical Corps; he was an RCR. His rank was "Hospital Sergeant" which was an appointment equal to the rank of "Colour Sergeant" which was one rank above that of "Sergeant".

Some of the duties of a hospital sergeant were:

- Be responsible for the personal belongings of patients which were left in his care.
- Ensure that all patients are aware of the regulations of the hospital.
- Visit the hospital wards frequently to ensure that the regulations were being obeyed. Some of these rules included no gambling, no liquor, etc.
- No soldier or relative could visit a patient or give anything to a patient without the permission of the hospital sergeant. [11]

Photo courtesy of the RCR museum.

At the time this photo was taken, rank badges were worn on the right arm only. The Geneva cross badge was also worn on the right arm only. Rank badges were worn on both arms starting 1903. After that, the Geneva cross badge was also worn on both arms above the rank badges.

Today, the hospital sergeant might be thought of as the RSM of the hospital. The appointment of hospital sergeant became obsolete by the time of the First World War. Before the formation of the Medical Corps, military hospitals were controlled by an Infantry Battalion Medical Officer. By 1914, all hospitals came under the control of the Army Medical Corps and the hospital sergeant was replaced by the Wardmaster, which was a Medical Corps trade. The Permanent Active Militia Medical Corps was formed in 1904. It was renamed The Canadian

Army Medical Corps in 1909.

The hospital sergeant was an appointment, not a trade.

The duties of the Wardmaster were similar to the modern day nurse. (See job description in this section.) However, one Wardmaster in each hospital was appointed administrator to take over the duties of the hospital sergeant. [10 and 11]

For those who may be unfamiliar with the duties of an RSM I will briefly describe them here. The Regimental Sergeant-Major is the highest ranking soldier in a unit except for the officers. He is in charge of discipline, dress, regimental parades and defaulters among other things. He is the advisor to the Commanding Officer on matters concerning the well-being and deportment of the soldiers from Private to Chief Warrant Officer.

In modern times, a military hospital would be controlled by a Medical Assistant with the rank of Chief Warrant Officer.

MILITARY POLICE

The Canadian Military Police Corps was formed in September 1917 and disbanded in December 1920. They did not have a trade badge but they did wear a unique armband with the letters "MP" on it. The armband was worn just above the wrist.

There were no military police in the Canadian Army from 1920 until 1940 when a new Military Police Corps was formed. They did not have a trade badge until 1956. (See Part Three.)

In the period between 1920 and 1940 each unit appointed a few soldiers to police duties. They were called regimental police and sometimes wore an armband with the letters "RP" on it. They could be members of any trade but were mostly infantry.

MUSICIANS

Photo: Bennett collection

Bandsman

The bandsman was not a trade in this time period even thought they did have a special badge that most people think of as a trade badge. The badge was more like a rank badge than a trade badge. Actually, it was an appointment. If the bandsman was a Corporal or a Sergeant, the badge would be worn above the rank badge. The instrument on the badge is a lyre. A metal or bullion version was worn on their ceremonial uniform. These badges have maple leaves around the lower portion of the lyre. The bullion version was produced with a red or dark blue background and has six maple leaves. The metal version has eight maple leaves. This badge was worn on the upper right arm only. The bandsman could be a member of any corps. There was no band corps or branch of the army.

Bullion and metal versions of the bandsman badge.

Bandmaster

The bandmaster is the person in charge of a military band. He is responsible only to the Commanding Officer of a unit. In this time period bands were unit property and not a separate entity. The bandmaster is responsible for all aspects of the band including uniforms, instruments and training.

The bandmaster badge was a lyre with a crown above if he was a warrant officer. This was a combination of the band badge (a lyre) and a WO rank badge (a crown).

Usually the bandmaster would be a Warrant Officer but it was possible that the Band Sergeant could fill this position if a WO was not available. In this case the normal bandsman badge would be worn. He could not wear the bandmaster badge, even though he might be one, unless he was a WO. A Bandmaster could also be a civilian if no suitable soldier could be found to fill the position. In this case, the civilian would wear a uniform without any rank badges.

Photo of the Bandmaster of the 37th Bn CEF courtesy of the LER museum.

Keep in mind that the rank structure in the early 1900's was not the same as it is today. In 1914 there were three ranks between that of Sergeant and WO. After Sergeant, the next highest rank was Colour Sergeant. The next highest was Quarter-Master Sergeant, then Sergeant-Major, then Warrant Officer. There was only one class of WO.

According to The Guide (1914) and other publications that I have, the Sergeant-Major was both an appointment and a rank. As a rank, a Sergeant-Major could be appointed to Regimental Sergeant-Major or Battalion Sergeant-Major. The rank badge was four inverted stripes and a crown. A Warrant Officer could be appointed to Regimental Sergeant-Major or bandmaster. The appointment of Regimental Sergeant-Major was the most senior in the unit except for officers. The badge was a crown only with no stripes. When appointed to bandmaster the badge was as shown above. This was simply the soldier's rank badge combined with the band badge. This was normal for all ranks in a band. For example, a Corporal would wear two stripes and a lyre.

Rank	Appointment	Badge
Warrant Officer	Regimental Sergeant-Major	Crown
Warrant Officer	Bandmaster	Lyre and Crown
Sergeant-Major	Regimental Sergeant-Major	Four stripes and a crown
Sergeant-Major	Battalion Sergeant-Major	Four stripes and a crown
Sergeant	Band	Three stripes and a lyre
Corporal	Band	Two stripes and a lyre
Private	Band	Lyre

As you can see, the Regimental Sergeant Major could be of Warrant Officer or Sergeant-Major rank. Therefore, if you see an old photo of a soldier titled "RSM" and his rank badge consists of four inverted stripes and a crown, he would be of Sergeant-Major rank and not a Warrant Officer. Although this has nothing to do with the band, it seemed necessary to explain the rank structure in order to explain the bandmaster badge which, as stated previously, was a combination of job and rank in one badge. To remind the reader once again, bandsman or bandmaster was not a trade in this time period; it was an appointment.

The bandmaster would have an assistant who would be a Sergeant. In the absence of a bandmaster, it would normally be this Sergeant who would be appointed to bandmaster and not someone of a Colour Sergeant, Quarter-Master Sergeant, or Sergeant-Major rank. They had other duties and would be unfamiliar with the daily operation of a band. A Sergeant appointed to bandmaster would be a temporary measure until a WO bandmaster could be found. He would not wear the bandmaster badge.

Skill-At-Arms Badges, Instructors' Badges and Trade Badges before 1942

In 1915, a second level of Warrant Officer rank was created. Now, instead of one Warrant Officer, there was a WO first class (WO1) and a WO second class (WO2). The badge of the WO2 was a crown. This was the rank badge of the previous WO. The badge of WO1 was a crown with a wreath around it. This new rank structure created the need for a new bandmaster badge.

This is the badge of a bandmaster who was a WO1 in rank. If a bandmaster was a WO2 he would wear the badge of the previous bandmaster. (A lyre with a crown above and no maple leaves).

This badge was worn on the lower portion of both arms where a Warrant Officer would normally wear his rank badge. The regular bandsman badge was worn on only one arm like a trade badge. The previous bandmaster badge was also worn on only one arm as shown in the photo on the previous page.

This badge is often confused with the British equivalent. The British badge consists of a lyre surrounded by oak leaves. The Canadian badge has maple leaves instead.

Band badges were not worn in the cavalry or foot guards. A bandmaster in these units would wear the same badge as other Warrant Officer first class which was a crown surrounded by a wreath (No lyre).

The above photo is the artillery band in the early 1940s. The bandmaster is seated in the front row at the right. Members of a band would wear the hat badge of their corps. There was no band branch until after unification in 1968. Photo: Bennett collection

Drummer Fifer Cymbal Player

These musicians were not necessarily part of a band. Not all units had a band but all units would have at least a bugler and a drummer. The drum badge was also worn by the fifer and the cymbal player if not part of a band. If they were members of a band, they would wear the bandsman badge. In the above photo, the cymbal player and two of the drummers wear the bandsman badge. The third drummer is wearing the drum badge. He is probably not an official member of the band. His job would be playing the drum when soldiers are doing drill on the parade square. These positions were not trades in this time period.

Bugler

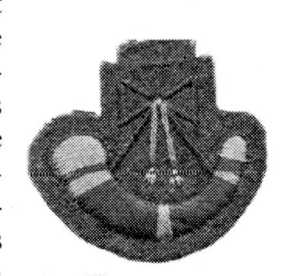

The bugler was not usually a part of the band. He played a bugle solo for ceremonies such as funeral parades or flag lowering when the playing of a bugle was required. In the early 1900's buglers played several tunes known as bugle calls to inform the soldiers of events that were happening on the base as follows:

Photo of bugler courtesy of the LER museum

bulge call	meaning
Reveille	Get out of bed.
Flourish	March past.
Stand Fast	This bugle call cancels any previous bugle call.
Defaulters call	Assemble the defaulters for drill or role call.

SKILL AT ARMS

Defaulters are soldiers being punished.

Rations	Orderly Corporals draw rations for their section.
Pioneers	Assemble the Pioneers.
Men's mess call 1	1/4 hour till Mealtime.
Men's mess call 2	Mealtime.
Fatigue	Assemble the fatigue party (soldiers on work detail).
Guard call	Assemble the guard.
Dress call	Assemble for parade.

This call to be played by all buglers. Most of these calls could be played by a solo bugler who was designated the orderly bugler of the day.

Sgt and Cpl call	Assemble all Sergeants and Corporals
NCO's call	Assemble all NCO's (Corporal to Sergeant-Major).
Officer's call	Assemble all officers.

Bugle calls would normally be played from the parade square. The Officer's call would be played in front of the officer's quarters.

Band call	Assemble the band.
Fall in	Fall in for parade.
Sgt's mess call	Mealtime at the senior NCO's mess.
Orders	Assemble the Orderly Sergeants for daily orders.
Officer's mess call 1	1/2 hour till mealtime (played at officer's quarters).
Officer's mess call 2	Mealtime (played at both officer's quarters and mess).
Picquet Call	Assemble picquet at other than the normal time.

A picquet is a sentry. He would watch for fires and any unusual activity.

Buglers and Drummer's call	Assemble the buglers and drummers.

These would be buglers and drummers who were not members of the band.

Retreat	Sunset.

At the playing of retreat, soldiers must return to camp.

Tattoo 1st post	The end of the working day.

Drummers and fifers play for a half hour while marching up and down the parade square, followed by God Save the King.

Tattoo last post	Prepare for bed. Usually 2200 (10 p.m.).

Tattoos would be played by all buglers.

Lights out	All fires and lights must be out.

This call would be played by the duty bugler. Other buglers would have the evening off.

Sick call	Assemble for sick parade.

The sick call would be played in the morning after breakfast. Soldiers who were ill would assemble to be marched to the base hospital.

Salute for the guard	The guard is to salute a general officer.
Alarm	Assemble all soldiers with weapons.
Fire alarm	Assemble for fire fighting.
Dismiss	Fall out after parade.
Recruits parade	Assemble recruits for training.
Advance	Advance.
Double time	Run.
Signaller's call	Assemble all signallers.
Colour Sergeant's call	Assembler all Colour Sergeants.
Stable call	Soldiers with horses march to the stables to tend to their mounts. Played half hour before breakfast and lunch and again after the evening meal.

In addition to all of the above bugle calls, each battalion would have a distinct call. If battalions became mixed, this call could be used to separate them.

The buglers, drummers and fifers together made up a sub-unit called the corps of drums. The name is misleading as the corps of drums was not a corps, but was a small sub-unit of an infantry battalion. The corps of drums would accompany the battalion into battle whereas the band would not. The bugler would play the advance or retreat to control the movement of the battalion on the battlefield.

"The band would not go into battle" means that they would not go into battle as a band. Band members were often used as stretcher bearers or work parties. In the 50th Battalion CEF, the band was ordered to turn in their instruments and they were employed as stretcher bearers, burial parties and other duties. Most of them were killed. Many of their instruments were buried and were never

recovered. *They were found by French civilians in the 1920's who gave them to their town band.*

Trumpeter

The trumpeter plays a trumpet in a band. Trumpets are also used in a fanfare which is an announcement of an important event or the arrival of an important person. This was not a trade in this time period.

Although none of these musicians were considered to be tradesmen during this time period, they are included here because they wore a special badge which most observers would think to be a trade badge.
(note that the names of tradesmen such as the Wardmaster are capitalized and non-trade jobs and appointments such as the hospital sgt, stretcher bearer, bandsman, bandsmaster and other band appointments are not.)

PHOTOGRAPHY

Photographer Wet Plate

This photographer made photographs using the wet plate procedure. This procedure involved making a negative impression on glass. The steps were as follows:

- Begin with a clean, polished piece of glass.
- Prepare a solution by mixing cotton, nitric acid, sulphuric acid, alcohol, either, cadmium iodide, ammonium iodide, cadmium bromide, chloride and iodine. This mixture was called collodion.
- Pour the collodion over the glass plate until it is fully coated. The excess collodion can be put back in the bottle and reused.
- The glass plate would then be put into a bath of acidified silver nitrate.
- Before the collodion could dry, the plate had to be inserted into the camera and exposed. Therefore, the camera had to be all set up and focussed beforehand. If a person was being photographed, they would have to be positioned and ready and waiting before the collodion was applied to the glass.
- Take the picture. The exposure would normally be about five to ten seconds in bright sunlight.
- The glass then had to be developed before the solution dried. It would be put into a solution of acidified ferrous sulphate.
- Rinse in water.
- The glass negative then had to be "fixed" to prevent the image from fading. This was done by putting it into yet another solution. This time potassium cyanide was used.
- The glass would be throughly washed in water.
- It would then be throughly dried over a low flame.
- Finally, the glass would be varnished to protect it.

This job was very dangerous as the chemicals were both poisonous and highly explosive. After making the glass negative, the photographer then had to get the picture onto paper. This was accomplished using the following method:

- The paper would be floated on a solution of egg whites and chloride.
- The paper would be left to dry.
- When dry, it would be floated on another solution, this time of silver nitrate.
- The paper would be left to dry again. When dry, it would have the required coating to turn it into photographic paper. It was not possible in the early 1900's to simply purchase photographic paper at a store.
- The paper, once properly coated, would be placed on the glass in a wooden frame and placed in direct sunlight. The image would be transferred to the paper.
- The paper then needed to be "fixed" to prevent it from fading. This was accomplished by bathing it in a solution of sodium thiosulphate.
- Finally, the paper would be throughly washed in water and hung to dry.

The result of all this would be a photograph. Quite a procedure. As this job was both complicated and dangerous, this tradesman was in Group A.

Photographer Dry Plate

This photographer used a different method than the wet plate photographer to achieve the same results. Instead of using all the different chemical solutions used by the wet plate method, the glass plate was simply coated with a special gelatin that already contained all the necessary chemicals. The plate was not really "dry" but it only had to be coating with the gel and it was ready to use. No wet solutions were required. Eventually, photographers could purchase the glass plate already coated. The printing process would be the same as for the wet plate method. Because this was much easier and safer than the wet plate method, this tradesman was in Group B.

PRINTING AND PUBLISHING

Before the Second World War the Canadian Army did much of their own printing instead of sending material off to a civilian printer. Therefore, they required printing presses and qualified tradesmen to operate them. These were mostly RCE trades unless stated otherwise.

Lithographer

The Lithographer operates printing equipment. He must be able to produce a printed item from a copper, stone or zinc plate. This was a Group A trade. In 1939 it became obsolete and was replaced by the following three trades to separate the different aspects of the job. Group A.

Lithographer Draughtsman

This tradesman made drawings for lithographic printing. He prepared work on several different media including cloth, negative, zinc plates, stone and other material. He used different stencils to do lettering in different fonts. The Lithographer Draughtsman did not operate the printing equipment but he had to be familiar with the printing process. Group A.

Lithographer Machine Minder

This tradesman operated a rotary lithographic printing press. This press transferred data from stone or metal plates onto paper. The plates were prepared by the Lithographer Draughtsman. The Lithographer Machine Minder had to clean and maintain the press and make minor adjustments. Before printing, he had to prepare the ink and add dyes if printing was to be in colour. He was required to make a print run of 10,000 copies in five colours while maintaining the same colours. He could make minor alterations to the data on the plates. After printing, he could remove all data from the plates so that they could be reused. Group A.

Helioworker

The Helioworker mixed gum reversal and helio solutions used in the printing process. The main ingredient in the gum reversal solution is gum arabic which is a natural secretion of the acacia tree. This is mixed with phosphoric acid. It is used when printing photographs in the lithographic printing process. The zinc plate to be used for printing would have the gum reversal solution applied with a soft brush, then a negative is then layed over the solution. The solution hardens in direct relation to the amount of light received through the negative, causing different shades and thereby creating a picture on the plate.

Helio solutions were used in the printing of drawing or photographs. The picture is covered in gelatine and the plate is covered in a fine layer of asphalt powder. The two items are then pressed together. The unhardened gelatine is washed away, creating a relief effect of the picture. The plate is then washed with chloride acid in multiple stages. The different depths in the asphalt fill with ink, creating a picture that appears to have depth to it. It is a complicated process and therefore a Group A trade.

Lithographer Prover

The Lithographer Prover prepared the plate for printing. He would place the plate on a proof press and apply ink to it using a roller. He would add paper if required. He would print a sample copy of the material and check it for quality or any kind of errors. The proof press was a small printing press used to make sample copies before sending the plate to the Lithographer Machine Minder for the print run. Group A.

The Helioworker and the Lithographer Prover were later merged into a single trade.

Photowriter

This tradesman added text and symbols to negatives. He could erase unwanted details on a dry or wet plate negative. The Photowriter would be knowledgeable in the photography process as well as that of lithographic printing and chemistry. Group A.

Printer Machine Minder

The Printer Machine Minder was tasked with the maintenance of the printing equipment. He set up the machinery for printing and looked after the press during the print run. He would make any necessary repairs. This trade existed in the RCASC and RCE. Group A.

Printer Compositor

The Printer Compositor prepared metal plates that were used in the printing process. He would add metal letters and other characters to a metal plate that was used in the lithographic printing press. RCASC. Group B.

Sterotyper

The Sterotyper made duplicate copies of the composed type made by the Printer Compositor. He did this by pressing the plates into wood fibre mats to create a mold. He then filled the mold with molten metal. When hardened, he shaved and trimmed the plate. Spare copies of printing plates were needed in the event that a plate was to break during a print run. Group A.

RAILWAY

Until the 1950's the Canadian army had every type of tradesman that was needed to accomplish any task. If the army needed something, there was a soldier who could provide that service. This included printing presses, making false teeth, getting one's eyes checked and making spectacles. The army even had soldiers who could build railway tracks and operate a railway. Originally called the Canadian Overseas Railway Construction Corps in February 1915, they were later renamed the Canadian Railway Troops in 1917. The Railway Troops were not part of the Canadian Corps and operated independently with their headquarters located at the British Army's General Headquarters in France.

Blockman

The Blockman operated the track signals to control the movement of military railway trains. He worked from a signal tower at a railway yard or switching point. He would receive messages by telephone to inform him of approaching trains. He would then set the appropriate signal to direct the trains onto the correct tracks to avoid a collision. Group B.

Brakeman and Shunter

The Brakeman and Shunter was employed in a railway yard. He moved railway cars from place to place in the yard. He would couple or uncouple the cars as necessary and make brake connections from car to car. Moving the cars from one location to another is known as "shunting." The cars would be moved to make repairs or to assemble trains. Group B.

Carriage and Wagon Repairer

When I started to research into the many obsolete trades that are described in this book, I originally thought that this person must have made repairs to wooden wagons used by the army in the Boar War era before automobiles came into common use. I found that this was not the case. I discovered that the "carriage" that he repaired was the undercarriage of a railway car. The "wagon" is the top, wooden part of the car. Repairing the undercarriage of a railway car is no easy feat. First, the car had to be lifted off the ground with a crane. The Carriage and Wagon Repairer would remove the wheels and replace any broken or worn parts including the brakes. He would drill out and replace any broken studs. He could repair the automatic vacuum brake system. Finally, he would lubricate as necessary and then reassemble the carriage. The Carriage and Wagon repairer would also repair, if necessary, the coupling connections on either end of the car.

Repairing the wagon, or top part of the car, would be an easy job compared to repairing the carriage. This tradesman would check for defects and repair as necessary. In addition to the mechanical skills needed to repairing the undercarriage, he also had to be a skilled carpenter.

Surprisingly, considering the skills needed to do this job, The Carriage and Wagon Repairer was a Group B trade.

Checker Number Taker

The Checker Number Taker kept track of incoming and outgoing shipments by railroad. Before a train departed, he would make note of the contents of every car including the car number, the engine number, the name of the railroad owing the car and the date and time of arrival or departure. By comparing records, it could be determined if the train arrived at its destination with none of the contents missing. Group C.

Cleaner Locomotive

The Cleaner Locomotive was employed in a roundhouse. A roundhouse is a place where locomotives were repaired. When an engine arrived at the roundhouse for repairs, it would stop on a section of track that could be rotated, like a lazy susan, so that the engine could go into any of the several garages in the building. After being repaired the locomotive would drive out of the building and be rotated around so that it could proceed on the desired track without having to go in reverse.

While the locomotive was in the building for repairs, the Cleaner Locomotive would clean and oil all the moving parts. He would also fire the boiler and check the steam pressure. This was a Group C trade.

Photo of a railway roundhouse courtesy of Reinhard Wohlgemuth

Draughtsman Railway Construction

As the name implies, this person made drawings for the construction of railway tracks. During the First World War, small narrow gauge railways were constructed to move supplies to the front and to bring wounded troops to the rear. This was a Group A trade.

Fireman Locomotive

The Fireman Locomotive kept the locomotive running by keeping the boiler fired. Before leaving the railway yard, he would ensure that the coal car is fully loaded with coal and that the cistern was full of water. When the train is ready to leave, the Fireman Locomotive would fire the boiler and shovel coal into it to keep it fired during the trip. He would open a valve, when necessary, to inject water from the cistern into the boiler. The boiler turned the water into steam which was used to power the engine. He had to know the heat in the boiler by observing the colour of the fire, and know how much water to inject.

The Fireman Locomotive would also act as an assistant to the engineer by watching for block and shunt signals. He would also be familiar with the operation of the brakes. Group C.

Fitter Locomotive Diesel

This tradesman made repairs to diesel locomotives. He could do a complete overhaul of an engine including the inspection and repair of ignition, brakes, clutches, differentials, gear boxes, transmissions, fuel injection systems, pumps and valves. He had to fit components such as crankshafts and bearings, pistons and rings, connecting rods and camshafts to the correct clearance and alignment.

Fitter Locomotive Steam

This tradesman did the same job as the Fitter Locomotive Diesel, but on a steam engine instead of a diesel powered one. He had to repair some parts that were not applicable to diesel engines such as the water injector, safety valves and steam gauges.

Railway Engine Driver

This person was, in other words, a train driver, which came to be known at a later date as an "engineer." The Railway Engine Driver could operate steam, diesel or electric powered locomotives. He must know what to do, and to take charge of the situation, in the event of a derailment. Group A.

Platelayer

Using the diagrams made by the Draughtsman Railway Construction, the Platelayer would prepare the ground for the laying of tracks. After ensuring that the ground was level, the tracks would be layed and the distance between them would be checked. When it was sure that everything was correct, spikes would be driven to hold the rails in place. The Platelayer could bend rails slightly to create a curve. He would ensure that switches and crossings were properly constructed. If the tracks were on raised ground, which is often the case, the Platelayer would ensure that proper drainage is in place and the hill is of the correct grade. He was required to estimate the time, material and labour required for a job. The Platelayer would have a large crew of non-trade soldiers to do the manual labour required. Group B.

Surveyor Railway

This tradesman did the surveying required for the laying of a railway. This information would be used by the Draughtsman Railway Construction to draw the plans for the building of the tracks. Group A.

Traffic Operator Railway

The Traffic Operator Railway supervised the flow of traffic on a railroad. He would maintain records showing the location of all railway cars. He would know the capacity of all rail yards and sidings. He would prepare time tables for the departure and arrival of trains. Before being allowed to work at this trade, a potential candidate must be already qualified as a Blockman and also as a Brakeman and Shunter. Group A.

This photo shows one of the narrow gauge railways that the troops built to move supplies to the front and the wounded to the rear. They had complete miniature trains with engines, but as this photo shows, they also used individual cars pulled by horses. Photo courtesy of Fred Wade

The strength of the Canadian Railway Troops grew to 14 battalions by the end of the First World War. They had a total of 14,877 troops compared to the British railway troop strength of 7,340.

During the First World War they built 1,169 miles of standard gauge railway and 1,404 miles of two foot wide narrow gauge railway.

The narrow gauge railway connected the main railway system with the troops at the front line. Small steam or internal combustion engines brought the cars most of the way. On the final section of track the cars would be pulled by men or horses. They brought ammunition and other supplies to the front and took back the wounded.

The photo above shows one of the narrow gauge railways passing through the ruined town of Lievin. Some of the railway troops were billeted in the cellars of the buildings in the foreground.

During the First World War, 1,977 railway troops were killed, injured or captured. The Canadian Railway Troops were demobilized in 1919.

In the area just to the rear of the trenches, the light tramways were constructed and maintained by the Canadian Engineers, not the railway troops. The railway troops built narrow gauge railways between the main rail lines and the front. The worked as far forward as it was safe to do so during daylight hours. The last section was completed by the Engineers under cover of darkness.

*The photo at above shows tanks being loaded onto a train. The railway troops brought 460 tanks up to the front lines in one night for an attack on Cambrai. The pile of wood on top was used to fill in obstacles such as ditches. It could be released from inside the tank. (The tanks are British.)
Photo from Canadian Railway
and Marine World September 1919.*

*This photo shows ammunition being brought to the front lines.
National Archives Photo PA-1757*

SUPPLY

**Storeman Technical Signal Stores
Storeman Technical Signals and Wireless
Storeman Technical Engineer
Storeman Technical Motor Transport
Storeman Technical Weapons
Storeman Technical Clothing and General Stores
Storeman Technical Traffic
Storeman Technical Airborne Equipment
Storemen Technical Medical
Storeman Technical Dental**

All of the above RCOC trades were trained in basic caretaking of equipment. The only difference was the type of equipment that they looked after.

Storeholder RCOC

The Storeman RCOC worked in a QM stores or a small warehouse. He did all paperwork associated with the issue, receipt and shipping of stores. He would also take inventory and arrange stock in bins. The Storeman RCOC also packed stores for shipment. He must be familiar with ordnance catalogues and numbering systems. Group B.

Storeman Departmental

Some of the duties of this storeman and the Storeholder RCOC overlap. Both of these storemen had to deal with the issue, receipt and shipment of goods. The Storeholder RCOC had to put the stores away and occasionally perform an inventory. The Storeman Departmental did not unpack or look after the goods once they were unpacked. Instead, he went into more detail with the shipping process. He would deal with carriers and railway agents to arrange shipments and would deal with any damage claims that arose from the shipments. He needed a good knowledge of accounting, railway documentation, routing of shipments and the procedure for the shipment of ammunition. This was an RCOC Group C trade. This trade is a lower grade than the Storeholder RCOC because he did not have the responsibility of looking after the stores once they were unpacked. The Storeman RCOC would work at a unit QM, while the Storeman Departmental would probably look after shipments for an entire base.

Foreman Departmental

Although not in alphabetical order, I have listed the Foreman Departmental last as one should read the duties of the Storeholder RCOC and Storeman Departmental first. The Foreman Department must have been a Storeman before advancing to this trade. In addition to the duties of a storeman, he would account for the dollar value of the stores when doing inventory. The Storeman simply had to account for articles as to whether they were missing or not.

He also had to submit estimates of requirements for future use. The Foreman Departmental would instruct and supervise the storehouse personnel. He would have a through knowledge of the army regulations governing accounting, what to do about deficiencies and other supply procedures. Group B.

Assistant Foreman Department

As the name implies, this person was an assistant to the Foreman Departmental. It was a Group C RCOC trade. He could advance to Foreman Department and therefore to Group B and a pay raise.

VEHICLE MECHANICS

Body Builder Metal

The Body Builder was not in charge of building muscles on the troops. This tradesman built and repaired bodies of automobiles. The army often wanted a new configuration of the body of a truck. For example, a pickup truck could have a roof added to make it into an office vehicle. Other vehicles would be configured to be used as switchboard vehicles or dental vans. Metal cupboards might be needed inside the van to store parts, etc. Before 1942, most trades were in one pay group only. The class one Body Builder was a Group A trade, while the class two was in Group B. After 1942 most trades were spread over two or three pay groups. This was a very short-lived trade. It was new in 1941 and merged with the Panel Beater in 1942. It was an RCOC trade.

Coach Painter

The Coach Painter was a painter of wooden or metal automobile bodies. Before painting, he would prepare the surface by sanding or making minor repairs as necessary. He would be highly skilled at mixing colours. He could also give a good finish of varnish to wooden bodies. Keep in mind that from the early 1900's until about 1940 most automobiles had a lot of wooden parts unlike today's vehicles which are built mostly of metal and plastic. He had to know the amount of paint that would be required for a job before mixing the colours. The Coach Painter had to know how to paint a vehicle in camouflage pattern. He also had to be a first rate sign painter. This trade was RCOC and RCASC. Group B.

Coach Trimmer

The Coach Trimmer repaired cushions, canvas and leather parts of automobiles. They also made or repaired convertible tops for cars and tarps for the back of cargo trucks. They could also rebuild the springs in a seat if necessary. This trade was RCOC and RCASC. Group B.

Fitter MV

The Fitter MV (MV stands for motor vehicle) made replacement parts for vehicles of all types including tracked. He could build parts from scratch if necessary or grind parts to make them the correct tolerance. Today's mechanics simply order the parts they need from the supply system. This was a new trade in 1941. Class one and two of this trade were in Group B while the class three personnel were in Group C. He must have been previously qualified as a Motor Mechanic. The Fitter MV existed in several corps.

Motor Mechanic

The Motor Mechanic must be able to repair any part of a wheeled or tracked vehicle. To advance to class one, he must also be able to repair tires, and be qualified as a superior Fitter. The job today is known as a Vehicle Tech. This trade existed in several corps. The Motor Mechanic had to be previously qualified as a Driver Mechanic. Group B. The Motor Mechanic existed in several corps

Motor Assembler

The Motor Assembler was the Motor Mechanic's helper. Group C.

Panel Beater

The Panel Beater shaped metal panels for dashboards, lamps, and other objects. He also shaped panels on automobiles when they became damaged, such as bent fenders. This trade would later be renamed the Body Repairman. The Panel Beater belonged to RCOC and RCASC. Group B.

Upholsterer

The Upholsterer re-upholstered automobile seats. At the class one level the Upholsterer was Group A, while at the class two level, the trade was

Group B. This was a new trade in 1941. RCOC

Vulcanizer

The term "vulcanize" was used in the 1940's and earlier to refer to the repair of tubes for automobile tires. The trade was renamed several times. It would later be called the Mechanic Tire Repair, and still later the Tire Repairman. This trade existed in RCOC and RCASC. Group C.

Wheeler

The Wheeler repaired the wooden parts of wagons and automobiles and wooden wheels on wagons and artillery guns. From the early 1900's until the 1940's automobiles had many wooden parts, unlike today's vehicles which are made mostly of metal. One of his jobs was to repair the wooden spokes of an automobile wheel. This is how the Wheeler got his name. He also built automobile or wagon parts that were made from wood such as the windshield frame, or truck tailgates. He could also paint the finished product but he was not required to mix the colours. The Wheeler had to do some metal work, such as replacing the metal tyre on a wooden wheel. At the class one level, he had to build wooden automobile and wagon bodies and wheels from scratch. This was a Group B trade.

Note that there was also a trade called "Carpenter and Wheeler" who was an assistant to either the Carpenter or the Wheeler. Carpenters wore the same badge as the Wheeler. They can be found in the Fortress Section where you can also see a picture of the metal version of this badge.

The Wheeler's original job was the repair of wooden wagons such as those shown in the photo of Canadian troops in South Africa. (The Carriage Smith also made repairs to these wagons. See Farrier.) When Automobiles first came into use, they had many wooden parts. The wheels had wooden spokes and truck bodies were made of wood. Dashboards, windshield frames, steering wheels and many other parts were made of wood on early automobiles. The Wheeler gradually converted to the repair of wooden parts on automobiles.

Photo: Bennett collection

My thanks to Massey-Ferguson Ltd for the photograph of their painting of Bain Wagons

The wagons in the photo were made by the Bain Wagon Company. They were known as "Wagons GS MD Mk1" (Wagons General Service, Militia Department, Mark 1.) The Bain Company evolved into a tractor company called Massey-Harris and is today known as Massey-Ferguson Ltd.

WATER TRANSPORT

Canada took over responsibility for the Esquimalt and Halifax garrisons from the British on 18 January 1906. Responsibilities included resupply of the artillery batteries at George's Island and McNab's Island on the east coast. The government purchased two steamships from the British named the Lily and the Alfreda. These ships acted as ferry service for the artillery troops from other parts of Canada who went out to the island batteries for training during the summer months. They also towed targets for the Navy and coastal artillery. The RCASC operated the water transport section until 1948. [5 and 12]

Engineer Water Transport Steam

The Engineer Water Transport Steam operated and maintained the engine on a steamship. He stoped and started the engine and controlled the speed. He performed daily maintenance on the engine by lubricating, greasing, etc., and made minor repairs when required. He could repair the reduction gears, propeller shaft, bilge pumps, electrical system, starter engine and injectors.

The SS Alfreda
Courtesy of the Department of National Defence

Mechanist Coxswain

The Mechanist Coxswain could make repairs to the engine, and he was the captain of the ship and was in charge of the entire crew. He would pass his propulsion requirements to the Engineer Water Transport Steam who would make the necessary adjustments to the engine. The Machanist Coxswain steered the ship himself or delegated and directed the steering to another crew member. The Engineer Water Transport Steam did not concern himself with the steering; he only cared about the engine and the speed of the vessel. The Machanist Coxswain was a skilled mechanic and could, if necessary, rebuild the engine or make major repairs such as rebore cylinders, grind valves, replace or adjust values, pistons, tappets, gears, etc. He could also make repairs to the water pump, magnetos and injectors. The Engineer Water Transport Steam looked after the engine on a daily basis and performed minor maintenance but not major repairs. The Mechanist Coxswain had to have a Master of a Tugboat certificate. Group A.

Shipwright

The Shipwright was a sea-going carpenter. He made repairs to wooden ships. He could build wooden frames to hold ships when out of the water. The Shipwright could repair the keel, ribs, masts or bulkhead of a ship. He could bend lumber to use in curves of a ship's hull. He also had to caulk the seams to make the ship watertight. Group A.

Stevedore

The Stevedore was a labourer that loaded and unloaded cargo into or from the hold of a ship. This was a Group C trade.

Stoker Fireman

The Stoker Fireman fed coal to boilers in steam operated engines such as in steamships. Group C.

Waterman Boatman

Waterman and boatman are two different jobs. The Waterman Boatman trade included both of them. As a waterman, he would be in charge of small craft such as a punt, cutter, flat, dinghy, steamer, launch, power boat or rowboat including the crew. He would be responsible for safety precautions and plotting the course on a chart. When performing the duties of a boatman, the Waterman Boatman would be responsible for fastening a large craft to the dock. He would lay out the coils of rope in preparation and when docking, make all necessary knots to fasten the ship to the dock. The Waterman Boatman had to know the rules for the operation of steam, sail, and rowing craft, and the correct size of anchor for each. A Group C trade.

From the original two ships, the Water Transport built up a fleet of 14 vessels with a staff of 125 officers and men. They delivered food, ammunition, personnel, mail and movies to remote outposts along the coast and on islands. Some of their stops included Fort Sandwich, York's Redoubt, Sydney, Saint John, Shelburne and Saint John's.

The crews of the Water Transport were members of the RCASC. They wore civilian cloths for the first 12 years of service. In 1918 they adopted a blue uniform similar to that of the navy. During the Second World War the army ordered that since they were members of the army that they would wear battledress like all other soldiers. The lowest rank in Water Transport was a Sergeant.

WOODWORKING

Woodworker
Machinist Wood

The Woodworker was renamed the Machinist Wood in 1938. This tradesman set up and operated a variety of woodworking machines such as circular saws, jig saws, band saws, wood lathes and grinders. He made wooden parts for the assembly of doors, door and window frames and sashes and furniture. He would sometimes assemble these items, but mostly the parts would be used by the Carpenter in his building projects. The Machinist Wood also set up machines for others to use by selecting the proper blade and making trial cuts. He also operated other woodworking machines such as sanders, where he would select the appropriate sanding belt and install it in the machine. He would be familiar with the different types of wood and how to apply various finishes. This was a RCOC Group B trade.

Pattern Maker

The Pattern Maker made wooden patterns of pulleys, bearings, pistons, pinion wheels and other items. He had to do wood turning and machining, and be able to set up and operate any woodworking machine used in pattern making. He must have knowledge of allowances to be made for the contraction of various metals and alloys. He must be good at fractional and decimal arithmetic. At the class one level, he must be able to make paper patterns that other Pattern Makers can follow, taking into consideration the allowance for contraction and machining. He must also have a thorough knowledge of foundry work. At this level, he must be able to make wooden patterns for more complicated items such as carburetor bodies, small internal combustion water-cooled cylinders, etc. This trade existed in RCOC and RCE. Group A.

Wood Turner and Machinist

The Wood Turner and Machinist made items out of wood using a lathe. Group B.

UNKNOWN TRADES

Mechanist Instrument Maker

The duties of this 1930's tradesman are unknown to me.

Surveyor Ordnance

The duties of this tradesman are unknown to me. It was a Group A trade that existed in the 1930s. If you have any information about this trade please contact the author.

Operator B2 RC Signals

This was a Signals trade that existed in the 1930s for which I have been unable to find a job description. His duties are described in a publication called "General Instruction No. 2 for the RCCS." If anyone knows where to find this book please contact the author (see back of book).

General Information

Note that most of the trades did not have a badge. This does not mean that they were any less of a tradesman. The distinguishing mark of a tradesman was whether or not one received trades pay, not if one had a trade badge or not. The badge was just a nice thing to have. Members of the army who were not tradesmen, such as infantry, artillery, armoured and some others, were considered to be simply "soldiers." They did not receive trades pay.

Trade badges were to be worn on the upper right arm only. NCO's wore the badge above their chevrons; privates were to wear their trade badges mid way between the shoulder and elbow. During the Second World War they were moved to the lower left arm, where skill-at-arms badges were previously worn.

NON-TRADESMEN

The following soldiers were not considered to be tradesmen in the period before the Second World War. (There are no doubt others.)

- Most combat arms troops, such as infantryman, gunner AFV, gun layer, etc.
- Batman (servant)
- Batman Driver
- Bandsman
- Bandmaster
- Cyclist
- Driver IC (after June 1939, was a trade before that)
- Field Security (intelligence)
- Fire Fighter RCE
- Fireman Stationary Engineer (steam engines with boilers such as steam shovels)
- Mechanical Transport

- Medic
- Motorcyclist and despatch riders other than Signal Corps personnel
- Occupational Therapist Assistant
- Operator Key Punch (punches holes in tabulating cards)
- Personal Identification (fingerprinter)
- Provost (military police)
- Regimental Policeman
- Remedial Physical Training Instructor
- Runner
- Sanitary Dutyman (a helper to the Sanitary Assistant)
- Stretcher Bearer
- Signaller (see Communications section)
- Unit Projectionist
- Pioneer other than infantry
- Artillery Driver (horses and ammo trains)

Cyclist

The Cyclist was not a trade but many people assume that it was so I have decided to include some information on this job. The Cyclists were combat troops, not tradesmen. They were trained in a role similar to that of cavalry except with bicycles instead of horses. This might sound silly to us today, but on good terrain, a bicycle can travel farther and faster than a horse. Upon arrival at their destination, they would simply discard the bicycle and fight like infantry. In the trench warfare of the First World War this turned out to be impracticable. They ended up being used mostly as infantry in the trenches, but also worked as observers, labourers, runners and stretcher bearers. The Corps Cyclist Battalion consisted of 16 officers and 305 other ranks.

Mechanical Transport

Like the Cyclist, the Mechanical Transport was not a trade. He looked after vehicles in a military compound when not in use by the soldiers. He kept track of mileage and dates that the vehicle was taken out and of any needed repairs. I have seen Canadian uniforms wearing the MT badge (both with and without wings). As this was not an official trade, the badge was probably a British badge worn unofficially (perhaps with local permission).

SKILL AT ARMS

ADDITIONAL PHOTOGRAPHS
These photographs became available just prior to going to press.

DR First World War

This was the DR badge used during the First World War. Wings were added to the badge sometime after the war. Compare with the photo on page 27.

MG badge

The MG badge in metal with a wound stripe. Metal SAA badges and wound stipes were discontinued after the First World War.

All photographs from the Bennett collection.

This soldier has the LG badge in cloth and a wound stripe. He is not an instructor. Compare it with the photo on page 17. Wound stripes are discussed in Part Five.

LG badge

Part Two

T Badges

1942-1955

1942 to 1945

This part of the book is divided into two time periods. The first one deals with badges and trades as they existed from 1942 to 1945. The second time period will cover 1946 to 1955.

August 1942

The Canadian Women's Army Corp (CWAC) had been formed in August 1941 but were not part of the army. In March 1942, the CWAC became a corps of the army and began to wear the same rank and other badges as the men. Their role was to be employed in non-combat duties to free up the men for combat. They had 30 trades at first, later increasing to 55.

September 1942

In these modern times, many old trades were becoming obsolete and many new trades were being created. The vast majority of Canadian soldiers were unskilled in anything except basic rifle use. The army needed tank mechanics and other tradesmen. While the Canadian Army was in England, training for the invasion of Hitler's Europe, many soldiers were sent on courses at British Army schools. Upon successful completion of a course, all students - both British and Canadian - would be awarded the applicable trade badge for their new trade. Upon return to their unit, these soldiers were told to take down the badge, as it was not authorized for wear on the Canadian uniform. This created a lot of bad feelings amongst the troops. They felt that they had earned the badges and should be allowed to wear them. The commander of the First Canadian Army in England, LGen Crerar, agreed and told Ottawa that the badges were important to the soldiers, and that they should be allowed to keep them.

With almost 200 different trades in the army, it was decided that this was too many to create a separate trade badge for each. The decision was made to abolish all existing trade badges and create a new trade badge that would be common to all army personal, much in the same manner as had been done with the instructors badges in 1940. The result was the "T" for "tradesman" badges. [1]

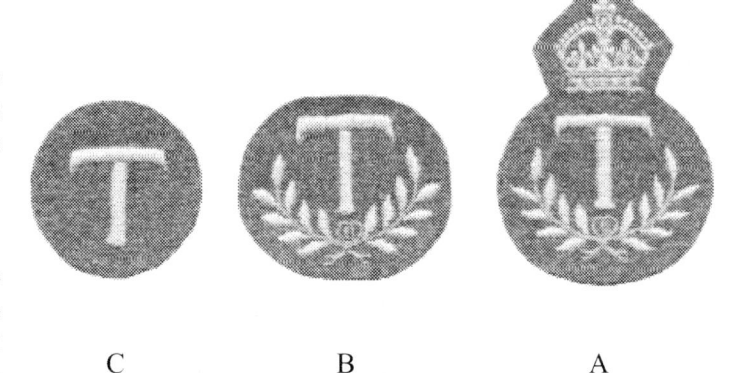

C   B   A

Group "C" trades wore a "T" for "Tradesman" without a wreath or crown. Group "B" trades wore a "T" with a wreath. Group "A" wore a badge with a letter "T" surrounded by a wreath and crown.

The groups were based on degree of difficulty. It was considered that trades in group "C" were fairly easy to learn, with group "B" being more difficult, and group "A" being the most difficult to master.

Before 1942 most trades were in one group only. A few of them were in two groups and only a couple were in all three groups. When these new badges came out, most trades were spread out over two or three groups. A newly qualified tradesman might begin in group "C". As he advanced in skill, he would be able to move to group "B" or "A". Some trades belonged to only one group and advancement to another group was not possible.

As you have seen in Part One of this book, this system of three trade groups had been in use since the 1920's. The only difference was that separate trade badges were done away with and now all trades have a common badge, including trades that previously had no badge at all.

Groups were tied to rank as follows: [2]

- Private to L/Cpl   T
- Cpl and L/Sgt   T with wreath
- Sgt and above   T with wreath and crown

The rules governing the wear of the "T" badges was as follows: [3]

- Not to be worn on shirts or greatcoats.
- Not to be worn by RCE sergeants and above

- who wore the grenade badge.
- Not to be worn by instructors and assistant instructors who wore the "CI" or "AI" badge. (This was originally allowed when the T badges first appeared but was disallowed in March 1943.)
- To be worn by privates on the upper right arm midway between the shoulder and the elbow.
- To be worn by NCOs on the right arm above the rank badge. This was changed by amendment 16 to the dress regulations in 1943 to be on the right forearm 6.5 inches from the bottom or above any service chevrons.
- To be worn by WOs on the right forearm below the rank badge. This was changed by amendment 16 to be above the rank badge.
- The badges were to be worn in Canada only except for personnel on the Canadian hospital ship.

Although it was not allowed by NDHQ, many soldiers continued to wear the British trade badges. This was often tolerated by the unit because everyone from Pte to General agreed with the practice. It is not uncommon to find Canadian uniforms in various museums today with British trade badges on them. Therefore, finding a badge sewn onto a Canadian uniform is not proof that it is a Canadian badge. The CWAC wore the mens khaki badges at this point. (They received their own colour badges later.)

November 1942

Trades pay as of November 1942: [4]

Daily pay for men $1.30
Daily pay for CWAC $0.90

Trades pay	Group C	25 cents
	Group B	50 cents
	Group A	75 cents

December 1942

Now it gets confusing. Orders in December 1942 brought back the class system where each trade group was divided into classes, now called grades. However, it was not like the system used before 1942 where each group was broken down into three classes. Group "A" was divided into three grades. Group "B" was divided into two grades, and group "C" remained with a single grade. Thus, there are now the following several different trade classifications. [5]

Group A, Grade I	"T" in wreath and crown
Group A, Grade II	"T" in wreath
Group A, Grade III	"T"
Group B, Grade I	"T" in wreath
Group B, Grade II	"T"
Group C, Grade I	'T'

This must have been very confusing. As you can see from the chart above, a tradesman who was a Group "A", Grade III, would wear the same badge as a tradesman in Group "B", Grade II, and all tradesmen in Group "C".

December 1942

Skill-at-arms badges were being phased out of use, the vast majority of them being abolished. By 1942, the only badges still authorized for wear were the following:

crossed flags	signallers and signalmen
crossed cannons	gunnery staff course an instructors RCA
crossed rifles	marksman
L	gun layer
MG	machine gunner
R	height takers and rangtakers and plotters of RCA & MG units

March 1943

The whole period of 1942 to 1944 seems to be a time of sorting out the proper wear of badges. NDHQ kept changing orders, and moving badges to different locations, and trying to decide which badges a soldier could wear and when he could wear them. In 1943 it was decided that a soldier could not wear both a tradesman badge and an instructor badge. Orders were sent out to all schools stating that instructors were to remove their trade badges. [6]

Strangely, in this time of standardization, the Royal Canadian Engineers managed to get authorized to wear their own distinctive badge: a flaming grenade. It was worn by Sergeants and Staff Sergeants only (not Lance Sergeants). Soldiers wearing the Engineer badge were not to wear the "T" badge. The badge was not new. It had been in use since the First World War. It was discontinued with the advent of the "T" badges in 1942 and authorized again in 1943.[6]

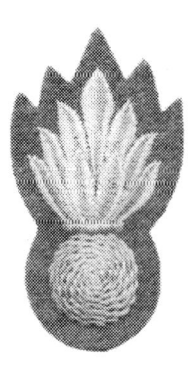

1944

Previously, WO's had worn their trade badge below their rank badge. Amendment 16 to War Dress Regulations in 1944 reversed this instruction. WOs were to wear the "T" immediately above their rank badge. This explains why you might see some old photographs showing the badge being worn above the rank badge and others showing the badge below the rank badge. For NCOs the location was changed from the upper right arm above the rank badge, to the lower right arm above the service chevrons. There was no change for the location of the badge to be worn by privates.[7]

Also In 1944, the grades within groups of tradesman badges were abolished, and they returned to the original 1942 system of three badges for three groups. The system of breaking down the groups into different grades with some grades wearing the same badge as a different grade in a different group must have been very confusing. It seems to me that this was not a well thought-out decision. My assumption seems to be confirmed by the fact that they did away with this and returned to the previous system.[8]

The Tank Badge

This badge is often stated as a First World War tank trade badge. It is not a trade badge at all. Although it depicts a First World War tank, the badge was issued in 1944. It was a formation badge and was worn on the right shoulder by all personnel of tank battalions, the Canadian Armoured Corps, training centres and tank regiments.[9]

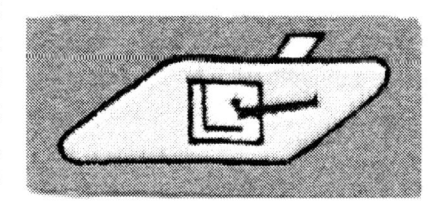

TRADES AS THEY EXISTED 1942 TO 1945
AMMUNITION

Ammunition Examiner
This trade now spread out over all three trade groups.

ARTIFICERS AND ARMOURERS

The Artificers and Armourers became members of the new corps of RCEME when it was formed in 1944. They were previously members of the RCOC Engineering Branch.

Armament Artificer (Fitter)
This trade became obsolete in 1942 or '43. The members of this trade were remustered to one of the new trades of Armament Artificer AA or Field.

Armament Artificer (Instruments)
This trade was split into three, approximately 1943, as follows:

Armament Artificer Instruments AA
Armament Artificer Instruments CD
Armament Artificer Instruments Field

These three trades worked on the optical and electrical instruments on artillery weapons. The only difference between the three was the role of the unit and the different weapons in use in each environment. The three roles were Anti-Aircraft, Coast Defence and Field Artillery. Some of the instruments they worked on included equilibrators, levels, elevating and transversing mechanisms and sights. They also worked on parts of the guns that did not really fall into the category of "instruments". They could inspect the breech block, measure the bore of the barrel for wear, inspect and repair brakes and other parts of a gun. An artificer was expected to make parts from scratch if they were unavailable. They also repaired non artillery items such as binoculars, predictors, plotters, range finders, etc. These artificers could also find electrical faults and repair cables. These were Group A trades and would hold the rank of S/Sgt or higher.

Armament Artificer (Wireless)
No change to this trade during this time period.

Artificer RCA

This trade was moved from Group B to Group A in 1941. In 1943 two new trades were created to repair artillery weapons as described below. These new trades operated at the Group A level only. The Artificer RCA was then spread over all three Group levels. At the Group C level, they made minor repairs to the guns under field or base conditions. New applicants for this trade had to be qualified as a Fitter Group C before applying. At the Group B and A levels, they made more complicated repairs. In fact, at the Group A level, there was very little difference between this trade and the Armament Artificer Field which is probably why this trade became obsolete in 1946.

Armament Artificer AA
Armament Artificer Field

Both of these trades repaired artillery weapons. One worked on Anti-Aircraft guns and the other on field artillery. They could disassemble and repair breech mechanisms, gears and hydraulic jacks. When not busy repairing guns, they were often tasked to repair a variety of items such as flame throwers, stoves, tools, machinery and various other pieces of equipment. These were Group A trades with the rank of S/Sgt or higher.

Engine Artificer

This trade now spread over groups C and B.

Armourer

This trade now spread over groups C and B.

Armourer IC RCOC Workshop

This trade became obsolete approximately 1943 and is now included with the Armourer.

Armament Artificer MV

This was a new trade approximately 1943. At first, vehicles were repaired by the Fitter, but as the job became too big for them to handle as a secondary task, this trade was initiated to do vehicle repairs. They were very highly skilled vehicle mechanics. MV stands for "motor vehicle". Although it does not specify, MV was understood to refer to wheeled vehicles only. (See the following trade for repair of tracked vehicles.) They could be employed in the field or in a base workshop. Like most artificer trades, these tradesmen were in Group A and held the rank of S/Sgt or higher. This tradesman must have previously been a superior Vehicle Mechanic MV.

Armament Artificer AFV

This was a new trade created at the same time as the Armament Artificer MV above. This tradesman made repairs to tracked vehicles. He must have previously been a superior Vehicle Mechanic AFV.

Armament Artificer Radar

This was a new trade approximately 1943. They performed complex repairs to radar equipment. This was a Group A trade and held the rank of S/Sgt or higher.

Armament Artificer (Electrical)

This was a new trade approximately 1943. The Armament Artificer (Electrical) was a highly skilled electrician. Prior to the mid 1930's there were only three types of artificers. They were the Armament Artificer (Fitter), Armament Artificer (Instruments) and the Artificer Artillery. With the use of vehicles, wireless radios and other new inventions, the workload for these artificers became too great and too varied. The Armament Artificer (Electrical) was one of several new trades created at this time to repair the new equipment. They repaired all types of electrical equipment in vehicles and buildings except radios. These were repaired by the Armament Ariticer (Wireless). Some of the equipment they repaired included lighting systems, ignition systems, generators, chargers, circuit breakers, etc. This tradesman would have previously been an Electrician Vehicle and Plant. This trade was Group A and held the rank of S/Sgt or higher.

ARMOURED

Fitter IC Tank

This was a new trade in 1941 and was obsolete by 1943. It was then included with the new trade of Vehicle Mechanic.

Gunner Operator

This was a new trade in 1943. It was not a new job. The job had been in existence for many years but what is new is that it was elevated to trade status. The Gunner Operator operated wireless radio equipment and fired the weapons on a tank including the cannon, machine gun and bomb thrower (a type of grenade launcher). He had to strip and clean the weapons when necessary. He would also maintain and charge the vehicle batteries. A new member of this trade must have previously been a Gunner AFV which was a non-trade job. A Gunner AFV did the same job except for the operation of the radio equipment and looking after the batteries. This was a Group C trade.

Operator CAC

The Operator Canadian Armoured Corps was a signaller who operated radio equipment in an armoured vehicle. He had less responsibility than the Gunner Operator (above) because he was not required to maintain the vehicle weapons. However, both of these trades were Group C.

The RCAC also had Driver Mechanics, Driver Operators, Motor Mechanics, Electrician MV, bandsmen, clerks, stewards, and storemen. These trades were common to most corps.

ARTILLERY

Master Gunner

No change to this trade during this time period. The Master Gunner continued to wear his unique badge as shown in Part One.

Fitter Gun

This trade now spread over Groups C and B. He would have to become an Armament Artificer in order to reach the Group A level and a higher rank. He would be a Sgt or lower rank.

Surveyor RCA

This trade now spread over all three trade groups. A new person in this trade would begin at the Group C level and if he acquired the necessary skills and leadership abilities, he could advance to Group B and later to Group A without changing trades. In this time period, groups were tied to rank so a soldier needed to be good at his trade and his soldierly skills and leadership in order to advance.

Battery Surveyor

This trade became obsolete in the early 1940s. It was included with the Group C level of Surveyor RCA.

Meteorological Observer

This tradesman was, in layman's terms, a weatherman. This was an artillery trade because the weather conditions had an affect on the firing of artillery weapons. It was a new trade in the early 1940's. See this trade in Part Three for more information. The Meteorological Observer worked at the Group B and A levels.

Operator Kine-Theodolite

This tradesman operated a photographic angle measuring instrument to improve the accuracy of anti-aircraft artillery. See this trade in Part Three for more information. This was a new trade in the early 1940s and trade was spread over all three trade groups.

Operator Radar

The Operator Radar operated radar equipment to find targets in an anti-aircraft unit. He would carry out maintenance on the equipment and the associated diesel engine. He could line up radar and follow the target smoothly and would pass his findings via radio to his headquarters. He would need to know radio procedure including the phonetic alphabet. This was a new trade approximately 1943. Group C.

Electrician Radar

This was a new trade created approximately 1944 to repair radar equipment. He would perform regular maintenance on the radar and its associated diesel electric generator. This trade was spread over all three trade groups.

CHEMICALS

Chemical Technician

This was a new trade created approximately 1943. This tradesman mixed and analysed chemical solutions. He would find the melting point of certain chemicals, carry out distillations, extractions, crystallizations and other laboratory procedures. He could find quantitative volumetric and gravimetric values, ions and radicals. He had to be aware of the danger of mixing certain chemicals for the production of war gases and explosives. This trade was spread over the three trade groups. Group A members of this trade supervised those working at the Group B and C levels of this dangerous job. An RCE trade.

Operator Chemical Plant

The Operator Chemical Plant took the next logical step after the work of the Chemical Tech above. The Chemical Tech mixed and analysed chemical solutions. The Operator Chemical Plant would then measure the solutions and put them into reaction vessels for use. He would control the temperature of the chemicals while in the reaction vessel to prevent overheating. He must be aware of the safety precautions in handling chemicals. These solutions were highly corrosive, inflammable and/or explosive. The Operator Chemical Plant would be knowledgeable in the packing and care and transportation of the chemicals while in or out of the reaction vessels. This RCE trade had members at all three group levels.

CLERKS

Clerk

No change to this trade during this time period.

Clerk Stenographer

This trade became obsolete in 1938 but was resurrected in the early 1940s only to be made obsolete for the second time in 1945.

Clerk Departmental

Obsolete 1945 and combined with Clerk above.

Clerk Superintending

No change to this trade during this time period except that it was no longer applicable to RCE after the creation of the Clerk Engineer Accountant.

Accountant Signals

This was a new trade approximately 1943 created to perform accounting of signals equipment. It was spread over all three trade groups.

Clerk Engineer Accountant

This was a new trade approximately 1943 created to perform accounting of engineer equipment. It was a Group A trade.

Court Reporter

No change to this trade during this time period.

Operator Punch Card Tabulating Machine

This RCOC tradesman set up and operated tabulating machines to automatically read and analyze punch cards. He would be assisted by the Operator Key Punch which was a non-trade soldier. See this trade in Part Three for more information. This trade was spread over Groups B and A. It was a new trade approximately 1943.

COMMUNICATIONS

Cable Splicer

No change to this trade during this time period.

Despatch Rider

No change to this trade during this time period.

Draughtsman RC Signals
Draughtsman Signals

This trade now spread over Groups C and B. The name was changed slightly from Draughtsman RC Signals to Draughtsman Signals.

Driver Operator

This trade previous existed in RC Sigs only. During the Second World War, it became available to soldiers of other corps. The trade now exists in CAC, RCA, RCE, CIC, RCEME and CDC as well as RC SIGS. It was still a Group C trade.

Electrician Signals

This trade now spread over all three trade groups.

Fitter Signals

This trade now spread over all three trade groups.

Foreman of Signals

No change to this trade during this time period.

Instrument Mechanic Signals

This trade now spread over all three trade groups.

Lineman Signals

This trade now spread over Groups C and B.

Lineman Mechanic

This trade now spread over all three trade groups.

Loftman

No change to this trade during this time period. Messenger pigeons were still in use during the Second World War. The author's father was a member of this trade.

Cipher Operator
Operator Cipher

This was a new trade approximately 1943. In 1945 the two parts of the name were reversed to Operator Cipher. Most Signals trade names began with the word "operator". It was created to operate the newly invented cipher machines for the encryption of messages. He had to encrypt messages at a minimum rate of 20 groups per minute. See Part Three for more details on this tradesman and a photo of a cipher machine. This was a Group C trade.

Operator Fixed Wireless Station

This was a new trade approximately 1943. They sent and received messages by morse code using a regular or semi-automatic key with a minimum of 18 w.p.m. Some of them worked on high speed circuits at speeds of over 300 w.p.m. using a Creed or Kleinchsmidt perforator. They did not get involved with any other type of communications. The Operator Wireless and Line also sent and received messages by morse code but he did not specialize in this type of communications; they also used voice radio, line, lamps and switchboard. The Operator Fixed Wireless Station worked in morse code only. This trade was spread over Groups C and B.

Operator Monitor Signals

This RC SIGS tradesman copied morse code in a foreign language. He could set up, pack and move his equipment and make minor repairs such as replacing tubes. He also operated direction finding equipment to find enemy radio stations. He could copy morse code manually or by typing it as it was received. Copying morse code in a foreign language is not much more difficult than copying it in English. Each letter of the alphabet is the same. There were only a few differences such as accent marks. Also the codes for procedure would be different (for the end of message, new message, end of sentence, over, out, etc). The Operator Monitor Signals would need to learn these procedural codes but would not need to learn a new language. He would understand the message only one letter at a time. The result was that the operator may not be able to read the message that he had copied down. This trade was spread over Groups B and A.

There were approximately 60 soldiers in this trade. It was formed in 1944. The new members of this trade had already been in the military. They came from the artillery, infantry, the armoured corps, the newly formed Electrical and Mechanical Engineers, RCASC, RCOC, and even some RCAF and RCN and some soldiers form the Signal Corps who were members of other Signals trades. The existence of this new trade was secret. The members were not allowed to tell anyone the details of their job or where they were going. The 60 members of this trade were divided into two troops of 30. Together with cooks, drivers and other trades, they formed a new unit called "Number One Canadian Special Wireless Group" with a total strength of 336 soldiers.

The unit was sent to northern Australia where their job was to intercept and record Japanese radio messages. As stated above, part of the training for this trade was to pack up and move the radio equipment. Vehicles were provided for this but it was soon found to be impracticable in the jungles of northern Australia. A permanent camp was set up near Darwin.

As the English alphabet has 26 letters and the Japanese has 72 symbols, the Japanese doubled up the letters after using up the first 26. A Japanese symbol could be represented in morse code by BA, BE, CO, or DU or many other combinations of letters. For example, the Japanese symbol "tse" was represented by BO. The letters OS represented the symbol "ku".

The Operator Monitor Signals used direction finding equipment to find a Japanese radio station. The Op Mon Sigs used two radios; one to monitor the sending station and one for the receiving station. He would copy down the message which would be unreadable to the Canadian operator. It would consist of a jumble of one and two letter groups. These groups would have been scrambled using a crypto machine before being sent. After recording the message and the reply, it would be sent to members of the Intelligence corps who were with the unit for deciphering. (The allies had been able to construct one of their cypher machines from plans that were stolen from the Germans.) The plain language message would then be translated by Japanese speaking members of the Intelligence corps. (The OC of the int section had been raised in Japan; the son of Canadian missionaries). The message would then be sent to allied headquarters in Melbourne.

After the war, the unit was sent to Chilliwack, BC where it was disbanded and the trade abolished. Before being released, the members of this trade were sworn to secrecy for a period of thirty years. Most of these tradesmen took their release after the war. Those wishing to stay in the army probably remustered to other Signals trades such as Operator Special or Operator Fixed Wireless Station. [10]

Operator Special Signals

The goal of this tradesman was to glean information from enemy radio messages in voice or morse code. He could set up and maintain a wireless telegraphy station. Using direction finding equipment, he would find and monitor enemy radio stations. He could copy morse code at a minimum of 15 w.p.m. as well as messages in cipher or in a foreign language. These operators had to be familiar with enemy radio procedures (see Operator Monitor Signals above.) This was a new trade approximately 1943 and was the beginnings of the trade today known as Communicator Research. You can read about this trade in Part Three. The Operator Special Signals worked at the Group C and B levels.

Operator Switchboad

This trade became obsolete in the 1930s and the duties were included with that of the Operator RC Signals (later named Operator Wireless and Line). The trade was revived approximately 1943 and worked at the Group C level.

Operator Wireless and Line

This trade now spread over Groups C and B.

Signaller Artillery
Signaller Infantry

As mentioned in Part One, the signaller was a skill and not a trade. The Signaller Artillery and the Signaller Infantry finally became trades approximately 1943. They were no longer required to send and receive messages with flags. The additional duty of switchboard operation was included with this new trade. There were Group C trades. Complete details of these trades can be found under "Signaller" in Part Three.

Operator Keyboard

This trade now spread over Groups C and B.

Electrician Wireless
Wireless Mechanic
Telecommunication Mechanic Coast Artillery
Telecommunication Mechanic Heavy-Anti-Aircraft
Telecommunication Mechanic Light Anti-Aircraft
Telecommunication Mechanic Field
Telecommunication Mechanic Lines of Communication

With the creation of RCEME in 1944, the RCOC trades of Electrician Wireless and Wireless Mechanic were replaced by the above five new trades.

The first three trades were basically the same except for the type of artillery weapons used by the unit. They repaired all radio equipment as well as machinery used by the gun crews such as motors, gear reducers, roller bearings and generators.

The duties of the Telecommunication Mechanic Field was slightly different. They repaired all unit radio equipment but not machinery. Instead they repaired other communication equipment such as telephones.

The Telecommunication Mechanic Lines of Communication repaired radios in units other than artillery. They also repaired generators, transformers, circuit breakers, teleprinters, switchboards, repeaters, etc. They could be assigned to a fixed wireless station to repair the high-powered transmitters and receivers used by the Operator Fixed Wireless Station. This tradesman must have previously been a Telecommunication Mechanic Field. They would then require additional training to repair teletype equipment, switchboards and fixed wireless station equipment.

All five of these trades worked at all three group levels. They were RCEME trades only and did not exist in RC SIGS.

COOKS

These trades became members of the RCASC in 1942. Previously they could be members of any corps.

Cook
This trade now spread over Groups C and B.

Baker
This trade now spread over all three trade groups.

Butcher
This trade now spread over Groups C and B.

Cook Hospital
This trade now spread over all three trade groups.

DENTAL

Dental Assistant
This trade now spread over Groups C and B.

Dental Tech
This trade now spread over all three trade groups.

Dental Instrument Repairer
Instrument Repairer Dental
This trade was renamed in the early 1940s from Dental Instrument Repairer to Instrument Repairer Dental. It was spread over Groups C and B.

DRIVERS

Driver Mechanic
Approximately 1943 this trade was split into three as follows:

Driver Mechanic MV
This tradesman drove and maintained all types of wheeled vehicles. This trade existed in most corps. In the Signal Corps, this trade replaced Driver MT RC Signals. Group C.

Driver Mechanic Carrier
This tradesman drove and maintained all types of tracked vehicle but not tanks.

Driver Mechanic Tank
This tradesman drove and maintained tanks as well as other tracked and wheeled vehicles. This trade existed only in armoured and artillery units. The artillery had a vehicle known as a M7 which was a 105mm gun on a sherman tank chassis. Group C.

Driver Transportation Plant
This trade now spread over all three trade groups.

For Engine Hand IC see Fortress section.

For Driver Operator see Communications section.

For Electrical and Mechanical trades see RCEME

EQUESTRIAN

Farrier
One might think that this trade would be obsolete by the 1940s but they would be incorrect. This trade now spread over Groups C and B.

FIELD ENGINEERS

Operator Special Engineering Equipment
This trade now spread over all three trade groups.

Fitter Special Engineering Equipment
The Operator Special Engineering Equipment drove many different types of engineering vehicles such as bulldozers, graders, steam shovels, cranes, etc. This trade was created to make repairs to those vehicles. It was spread over all three trade groups.

FORESTRY

Driver IC Tractor Forestry
Driver IC Tractor
Approximately 1943, the Driver IC Tractor Forestry was combined with the Driver IC Tractor which was previously a non-trade job. The two trades combined was then called Driver IC Tractor. This trade existed in Forestry and RCE. It was spread over Groups C and B.

Edgerman Forestry
Now spread over Groups C and B.

Engine Artificer Forestry
This trade became obsolete approximately 1943 and was replaced by the regular Engine Artifi-

cer instead of having a separate trade for the Forestry (see Artificers).

Fitter Tractor Forestry
This trade now spread over all three trade groups.

Foreman Departmental Forestry
This trade became obsolete in the early 1940s and the duties were included with the Foreman of Works Bush Forestry.

Foreman of Works Bush Forestry
The duties of this trade now include the duties of the Foreman Departmental Forestry which became obsolete. This trade was then spread over all three trade groups.

Foreman of Works Mill Forestry
This trade now spread over all three trade groups.

Log Canter Forestry
No change to this trade during this time period.

Motor Mechanic Forestry
This trade became obsolete approximately 1943 and was replaced by the regular Motor Mechanic instead of having a separate trade for the Forestry. (See Motor Mechanic in Parts One and Two.)

Sawdoctor
This trade now spread over all three trade groups.

Sawfiler Forestry
No change to this trade during this time period.

Sawyer Forestry
This trade now spread over all three trade groups.

FORTRESS COMPANY

Blacksmith
This trade now spread over Groups C and B. In 1944 this trade existed in RCASC, RCOC, RCEME, CIC AND RCE.

Blacksmith's Helper
Obsolete. The Blacksmith's Helper became the Blacksmith Group C. The Blacksmith trade was spread over Groups C and B. Formerly the Blacksmith was Group B only.

Boilermaker
This trade now spread over Groups C and B.

Bricklayer
This trade now spread over Groups C and B.

Carpenter and Joiner
Carpenter
In 1938, four different carpentry trades were combined to create the Carpenter and Joiner. One of those trades had been called "Carpenter" (see Fortress Company in Part One). Approximately 1944 the name of Carpenter and Joiner was shortened to simply Carpenter. This trade now spread over Groups C and B. The trade existed in most corps during this time period.

Concretor
This trade now spread over Groups C and B.

Diver
This trade now spread over all three trade groups.

Draughtsman Architectural
Draughtsman Engineering
Draughtsman Architectural and Engineering
The former trades of Draughtsman Architectural and Draughtsman Engineering were combined into a single trade. This new trade was spread over all three trade groups. It became known as Draughtsman A and E.

Draughtsman Topographical
This trade now spread over Groups C and B.

Electrician
This trade now spread over all three trade groups.

Engine Fitter IC and Pump
The Engine Fitter IC and Pump operated, maintained and repaired small engines such as generators, air compressors, pneumatic tools and pumps.

He could do a complete overhaul of the engine including grinding valves, adjusting magneto, replace pistons, etc. On pumps he could replace fuel and water pipes. He could bend, braze and solder pipes. This was a new trade approximately 1943 and was spread over Groups B and C.

Engine Fitter Steam Reciprocating

This tradesman operates and maintains reciprocating steam engines. He would repair steam and water and boiler pipes and joints. This was a new trade approximately 1943 and was spread over Groups C and B.

Engine Hand IC
Engine Hand

There was no change in this trade during this time period except that the letters IC were dropped form the name. The Engine Hand is listed in Part One of the book under "Drivers" because it was previously named Engine Driver IC.

Engineer Works Foreman

Obsolete 1943. This trade was included with the Foreman of Works.

Foreman of Works

This trade now spread over all three trade groups.

Instrument Mechanic RCE

Obsolete 1944. There was an Instrument Mechanic in the new corps of RCEME. The Instrument Mechanic RCE was deemed unnecessary.

Mason

This trade was now spread over Groups C and B.

Mechanic Refrigeration Plant

This was a new trade in 1943. His job was the installation and maintenance of all types of refrigeration equipment including condensers, compressors and motors. He would assemble or repair all necessary pipes and ducts. He would also test the available electrical circuit for the proper voltage. He also checked old refrigeration equipment for leaks using Freon detectors and refilled them after making repairs. He would ensure that the thermostat is working properly. The Mechanic Refrigeration Plant could also make repairs to electrical wiring and repair copper pipes. An applicant for this trade must be a Group A Electrician. The Mechanic Refrigeration Plant was a Group A trade.

Mechanist Electrical

No change to this trade during this time period except that the name of Mechanist Electrical RCE was shortened to simply Mechanist Electrical.

Mechanist Machinery

No change to this trade during this time period except that the name of Mechanist Machinery RCE was shortened to simply Mechanist Machinery.

Miner

This trade now spread over Groups C and B.

Minor Diamond Setter
Driller Diamond Setter

Approximately 1943 the Minor Diamond Setter was renamed Driller Diamond Setter. This trade was then spread over all three trade groups.

Minor Mechanic or Driller
Driller Diamond and Rotary

Approximately 1943 the Minor Mechanic or Driller was renamed the Driller Diamond and Rotary. This trade was in Groups C and B.

Operator Light and Power Plant

This tradesman worked in a power generating station to provide light and power to an army base. They operated and maintained and repaired turbine engines, generators, boilers, thermal and magnetic coil-tripping devices, overload and reverse current relays, air compressors, pumps, transformers and other equipment. There were three types of plants that they could be employed in: steam reciprocating, internal combustion or ignition compression. Different types of repairs would need to be done, depending in which of the three types of plants he was employed. In a steam reciprocating plant, he would be required to repair boilers, pumps, stokers, thermostatic controls and float switches. An internal combustion plant would require much the same type of repairs as an automobile engine such as valve grinding, piston fitting, decarbonizing, replacement of oil and air filters, etc. In a compression ignition plant, he would replace fuel pumps, injectors, oil, fuel and air filters. This trade was spread over all three group levels. The Group C Operator Light and Power Plant must have been an Electrician before working in this trade. This was a new trade approximately 1943.

Like all trades that were spread over all three group levels, the Group C worker was an apprentice or helper and did only minor repairs. The Group B tradesman was able to work mostly independently; asking for help only with complicated repairs. The Group A Operator Light and Power Plant would be in charge of the plant and would supervise the other workers. Their rank would increase with each jump to the next trade group.

Operator Steam Power Plant

Contrary to this tradesman's name, he did not necessarily operate a steam power plant. It would be more accurate to say that he operated a boiler to supply hot water or steam heating or power. The boiler could be portable; not necessarily in a steam power plant. He would stoke the fire by shovelling fuel (usually coal) into the boiler or adjust the flow of oil and air to the burners in a oil-fired boiler. He would make adjustments as necessary to maintain the required steam pressure, and keep the water at the required level. The Operator Steam Power Plant would occasionally shut down the boiler for maintenance. In this case, he would remove ashes, adjust all valves, lubricate moving parts and make repairs to pipes and fittings. This trade was spread over all three trade groups. This was a new trade approximately 1943.

Painter

Obsolete by 1943. This trade was merged with the Painter and Decorator below.

Painter and Decorator

This trade now spread over Groups C and B.

Pioneer RCE

No change to this trade during this time period.

Plumber and Pipe Fitter

This trade now spread over Groups C and B.

Quarryman

This trade now spread over Groups C and B.

Rigger

This trade now spread over Groups C and B.

Riveter

This trade now spread over Groups C and B. It also existed in RCEME.

Sawyer

This trade now spread over Groups C and B. It also existed in RCEME.

Sheet Metal Worker

The Sheet Metal Worker assembled, repaired and installed sheet metal. This was a new trade approximately 1942. He could manipulate the sheet metal into any desired shape. He could cut it with metal shears or bend it with a special machine. He punched holes along the edge so that the sheets could be joined with rivets. When assembling sections of sheet metal, he would join them by soldering, welding, rivetting, bolting or brazing. This trade was spread over Groups C and B. The Sheet Metal Worker also existed in RCASC, RCE and RCOC (later RCEME).

Steamfitter

This trade now spread over Groups C and B.

Stoker Stationary Engine

No change to this trade during this time period.

Surveyor Engineering

This trade now spread over all three trade groups.

Surveyor Topographical

This trade now spread over all three trade groups.

Wellborer

This trade now spread over Groups C and B.

GEOMATICS

The role of this group of trades changed dramatically during this time period. Previously, the duties of these trades were mainly surveying and map making. All of these trades became obsolete and new ones were created. Although still involved with map making, they are no longer involved with surveying. Instead, an emphasis was placed on art work. Surveying was done by the Surveyor Topographical who was part of the fortress section above.

Computer Trigonometrical

Obsolete early 1940s. The duties of this trade are now included with the Surveyor Topographical.

Surveyor Cadastral & Engineering

Obsolete early 1940s. The duties of this trade are now included with the Surveyor Topographical.

Surveyor Trigonometrical

Obsolete early 1940s. The duties of this trade are now included with the Surveyor Topographical.

Draughtsman Cartographic

This was a new trade in 1945. This tradesman made maps for reproduction. They would draw maps from scratch, reduce or enlarge existing maps, make corrections or revisions to existing maps, make corrections to maps based on aerial photographs and make corrections to maps on zinc printing plates. When a map is ready to be printed, the Draughtsman Cartographic would reproduce the map on a zinc printing plate. He would need a good knowledge of the lithographic printing process. This trade was spread over all three trade groups. (See Printing section for the Lithographer trade and information on printing.)

Draughtsman Graphic Arts

This was another of the new trades that were created in 1945. This tradesman made paintings, illustrations, sketches, posters and other art work for army publications. This trade was spread over all three trade groups.

Photogrammetrist

At the Group C level, the Photogrammetrist made drawings for engineering plans. They also did lettering using draughting instruments. The Group B and A levels of this trade had a different job. They created topographical maps from aerial photographs. The duties of this trade and the skill levels changed over the years. This was a new trade in 1945. More information can be found in Part Three.

INFANTRY

Pioneer

This trade become obsolete after WWI but was revived in 1950.

INTELLIGENCE

Wireless Intelligence Linguist

The Linguist was a new trade approximately 1943. His job was the translation of foreign language radio transmissions into English or from English into another language. At the Group C level, each Linguist needed to be good, but not 100 percent fluent, in one language used by the enemy forces during the Second World War. At the Group B level, the Linguist needed to be fluent in one language of the enemy and be able to conduct interrogations of prisoners as well as performing the duties of the Group C Linguist. He had to possess a good knowledge of enemy organization, especially their signal service. He had to be familiar with enemy wireless and telegraph procedure and terminology. Members of this trade could be of any corps. Group C and B only.

Members of the Canadian Intelligence Corps were not tradesman during this time period.

MATERIALS

Equipment Repairer

No change to this trade during this time period.

Textile Refitter

This trade now spread over Groups C and B. This trade also existed in RCEME after their split from RCOC.

Saddler

Surprisingly, this trade was still in existence after the Second World War. It was spread over Groups C and B. It existed in RCOC, RCASC and RCEME.

Saddle Tree Maker

This trade now spread over Groups C and B. It was RCOC only.

Shoemaker

This trade now spread over Groups C and B. This was an RCOC trade but there were also shoemakers in the Medical corps (see Shoemaker Orthopaedic).

Tailor

This trade now spread over Groups C and B.

Workshop Supervisor

No change to this trade during this time period.

MEDICAL

Chiropodist

This was a new trade approximately 1943. A Chiropodist, in layman's terms, is a foot doctor. He diagnoses and treats ailments affecting the feet. He would remove corns and bunions. In order to be a member of this trade, the soldier must be a graduate of a school of chiropody and be licenced by a province of Canada to practice in this field. This was a Group A trade.

Instrument Mechanic Surgical

This trade now spread over all three trade groups.

Laboratory Assistant

This trade now spread over all three trade groups.

Laboratory Technician

This was a new trade in 1943. The Lab Tech performed the same duties as the Laboratory Assistant but he worked on more complicated projects. A potential applicant for this trade needed a university degree whereas the Laboratory Assistant did not. Both of these trades were spread over all three group levels.

Masseur

This trade now spread over all three trade groups.

Nursing Orderly

The medic finally became a trade approximately 1942 with the name of Nursing Orderly. The medic had been in existence since the First World War but was not previously a trade. His job was the care of the sick and wounded. He would also remove wounded soldiers from a battlefield although there were also non-trade soldiers called stretcher bearers who would carry out this duty. The Nursing Orderly worked in a hospital or in the field. In a hospital ward, he would have the additional duties of ward cleanliness, patient admission and discharge procedures. He would care for patients in many ways including bathing, feeding, taking temperatures, taking pulse and administering enemas and catheters. He could apply simple dressings and sterilize equipment The Nursing Orderly worked at the Group C and B levels. There were also Nursing Sisters who performed similar work but were more skilled and were of officer rank. Nursing Sisters worked in hospitals and did assist wounded soldiers on a battlefield.

Shoemaker Orthopaedic

This trade was new in 1943. The Shoemaker Orthopaedic made special shoes to correct deformities of the foot. He would fit shoes or boots with arch supports or he could take an impression of the patient's foot and custom build necessary supports. Before working at this trade, a soldier would have to be a regular Shoemaker Group B. This was a Group A RCAMC trade. (The regular shoemaker can be found in the Materials section.) In order to be a Shoemaker Orthopaedic, the soldier would have to remuster from RCOC to RCAMC.

Operating Room Assistant

This trade now spread over all three trade groups.

Optician

An Optician makes eye glasses. He would cut and polish the eye pieces and insert them into a frame and adjust them for fit to an individual head. They did not test vision; this was the job of the Optometrist. To be employed in this trade, the soldier must be licenced by a province of Canada as an Optician. This was a new Group B trade approximately 1943.

Optometrist

An Optometrist tests eyes for vision and writes a prescription for the creation of eye glasses. He would prescribe corrective lenses for nearsightedness, far-sightedness or astigmatisms. The Optometrist could also check for colour blindness and prescribe eye exercises to correct muscular faults in the eyes. He could also inspect eyes for damage and recommend surgery if necessary. To be employed in this trade, the soldier must be licenced by a province of Canada to practice Optometry. This was a new Group A trade.

Pharmacist and Dispenser
No change to this trade during this time period.

Radiographer
This trade now spread over all three trade groups.

X-Ray Maintenance Tech
Mechanic X-Ray
This trade was renamed to Mechanic X-Ray in 1942. Still a Group A trade.

Sanitary Assistant
This trade now spread over Groups C and B.

Sanitary Inspector
The Sanitary Assistant had been a trade since the 1930s. That trade was now spread over Groups C and B. The Sanitary Inspector was a new trade for work at the Group A level. He would inspect, instruct and advise on all matters pertaining to hygiene. He tested water and milk for contamination, inspected food for signs of spoilage and advised on sewage disposal. The Sanitary Inspector would have been a Sanitary Assistant Group B before being promoted into this position. This was a new trade approximately 1943

Wardmaster
This trade now spread over Groups C and B.

Workshop Foreman Field Hygiene
This supervisor would be in charge of a group soldiers whose duties were the construction of sanitary appliances such as outhouses. These small buildings could be constructed of wood, tin, sheet metal, brick or concrete. They also constructed appliances for the kitchen such as fly traps and grease traps. Their skills were also put to use making small items for the kitchen such as funnels, cans and metal boxes. The crew also looked after water and sewage disposal. They could, if requested, build incinerators of brick or concrete for the burning of contaminated material

Most of the soldiers in this crew were non-tradesmen except for Bricklayers and the Workshop Foreman Field Hygiene. This trade was created at the start of the Second World War and became obsolete in 1946. He must have previously been a Bricklayer, Carpenter or Tinsmith in order to be accepted into this trade. He must also be able to read blueprints and have a good knowledge of arithmetic and the Army Manual of Hygiene and Sanitation. (See Bricklayer in the Fortress section of Part One.)

This trade existed in Groups C and B.

MILIARY POLICE

The Canadian Provost Corps was created in 1940 but the members of this corps were not considered to be tradesmen during this time period. See Military Police in Part One and in the 1946 to 1955 time period of this part of the book.

MUSICIANS

Bandsman
The Bandsman, formerly an appointment only, was made a Group C trade in 1943. Members of the band continued to wear their unique badges as described in Part One.

Bandmaster
The Bandmaster, formerly an appointment only, was included with the Bandsman trade when it was created. He continued to wear his unique badge that was a combination of trade and rank badge.

Drummer, Fifer, Cymbal Player
Bugler
Trumpeter
All of the above musicians were included with the Bandsman trade. They were not separate trades, however, they continued to wear their unique badges.

PARACHUTE TRADES

Parachute Packer
The First Canadian Parachute Battalion was

formed in July 1942. At first, parachute training was conducted in England and U.S.A. In 1943 the Canadian Parachute Training Centre opened in Shilo, Manitoba. This trade was created at that time to pack the parachutes. A used parachute would be spread out on a long table to removed all tangles and check for damage. The parachute would then be properly folded and packed. The harness would also be inspected for damage and a static line attached. The static line is attached to a cable inside the aircraft and pulls open the parachute when the soldier jumps out. The Parachute Packer must be qualified as a parachutist. This was a Group C trade. (Part Four is devoted to parachute badges and information about Canadian parachute forces.)

Parachute Rigger

This trade is slightly different from the Parachute Packer described above. Both of these trades packed parachutes for soldiers to use in parachuting. The Parachute Rigger had additional duties above those of the Parachute Packer. This tradesman could also make repairs to parachutes. The Parachute Packer checked parachutes for damage but did not make repairs. The Parachute Rigger also packed large parachutes for cargo drops. This tradesman worked at the Group C and B levels. At the Group C level he would pack parachutes and was no different than the Parachute Packer. At the Group B level, he performed the additional duties described here. The Parachute Packer was Group C only; therefore, he might wish to become a Parachute Rigger in order to advance to Group B.

There was also a trade called Rigger in the RCE (see Fortress section). This trade had nothing to do with parachute packing.

PHOTOGRAPHY

Photographer Wet Plate
Photographer Dry Plate
Photographer

The Photographer Wet Plate and the Photographer Dry Plate were combined into a single trade called simply "Photographer". This new trade was spread over all three trade groups. It was an RCE trade.

Photographer Cinematograph

This was a new trade approximately 1943. His duties were the production of documentary movies. The trade was spread over all three trade groups. He could be a member of any corps.

POSTAL

Postal Sorter

This trade was created approximately 1942 to conduct post office duties for the troops during the Second World War. The Postal Sorter performed all the jobs that one would be familiar with at a civilian post office. They sold money orders and postage stamps as well as sorting the mail and determining the cost of postage. They distributed incoming mail to the units on the base. When a soldier was posted (transferred) to another base, the Postal Sorter would keep a record of his new address and ensure that his mail is forwarded. In addition to all the duties of a civilian post office, the Postal Sorter needed to know the method of handling confidential and secret material. This trade worked at the Group C and B levels.

Postal Supervisor

The Postal Supervisor was the Group A level for the Postal Sorter. He would be in charge of a military post office including any vehicles belonging to the Canadian Postal Corps. He would instruct and supervise the Postal Sorter.

PRINTING AND PUBLISHING

Lithographer

Obsolete by 1943. This trade was combined with the Lithographer Machine Minder.

Lithographer Draughtsman
Draughtsman Lithographer

Approximately 1943, the Lithographer Draughtsman was renamed the Draughtsman Lithographer. This trade was spread over all three trade groups.

Lithographer Machine Minder

This trade now spread over all three trade groups.

Helioworker
Lithographer Prover
Helioworker and Litho Prover

The Helioworker and the Lithographer Prover were combined into a single trade called Helioworker and Litho Prover. It was spread over all three trade groups.

Photowriter
This trade now spread over all three trade groups.

Printer Machine Minder
This trade now spread over all three trade groups.

Printer Compositor
This trade now spread over Groups C and B.

Sterotyper
Obsolete early 1940s.

RAILWAY

Blockman
This trade now spread over Groups C and B.

Brakeman and Shunter
This trade now spread over Groups C and B.

Carriage and Wagon Repairer
This trade now spread over Groups C and B.

Checker Number Taker
No change to this trade during this time period.

Cleaner Locomotive
No change to this trade during this time period.

Fireman Locomotive
No change to this trade during this time period.

Fitter Locomotive Diesel
This trade now spread over all three trade groups.

Fitter Locomotive Steam
This trade now spread over all three trade groups.

Railway Engine Driver
Engine Driver Railway
The Railway Engine Driver was renamed Engine Driver Railway in the early 1940s. This trade was spread over all three trade groups.

Platelayer
This trade now spread over Groups C and B.

Traffic Operator Railway
This trade now spread over all three trade groups.

The following two trades became obsolete by 1943 because the army was no longer in the business of building their own railroads.

Draughtsman Railway Construction
Obsolete. Members of this trade were included with the new trade of Draughtsman Architectural and Engineering. (See Fortress section.)

Surveyor Railway
Obsolete. Members of this trade were remustered to Surveyor Engineering. (See Fortress section.)

RCEME

These trades were formally listed under the section heading of "Electrical and Mechanical". They were mostly RCOC trades. The Corps of Royal Canadian Electrical and Mechanical Engineers was formed in 1944 and most of these trades became members of this new corps.

Coppersmith
This trade now spread over Groups C and B. It became obsolete in 1945.

Draughtsman Mechanical
This trade now spread over all three trade groups.

Electrician Fitter
Electrician RCEME
When the new corps of RCEME was formed in 1944, it was decided that they needed their own electrician trade. The Electrician Fitter was renamed Electrician RCEME.

Fitter
This trade now spread over all three trade groups.

Grinder Precision
This trade now spread over Groups C and B.

Instrument Mechanic
This trade now spread over all three trade groups.

Instrument Mechanic Field
Instrument Mechanic Field Survey
Instrument Mechanic Heavy Anti-Aircraft
Instrument Mechanic Light Anti-Aircraft
These were four new trades created in 1943 to repair optical, electrical, and mechanical instruments on artillery weapons. Their duties were slightly different from each other depending on their environment and the type of weapons used there. If you read the Artificer section, you will find that there were already Artificer trades making this type of repairs. The difference was their level of skill. The Artificers were experts and worked at the Group A level. These tradesmen made less difficult repairs and worked at th both the Group B and A levels. They could fit new lenses, prisms, mirrors and bubbles to optical sights. In addition to repairing artillery instruments, they repaired binoculars, compasses, predictors, range finders, plotters and other items found in an artillery unit. Before becoming a member of this trade, applicants must have been an Instrument Mechanic of any group level.

Instrument Mechanic Typewriter and Cipher
This was a new trade approximately 1943. They repaired all types of office machines including typewriters, cipher machines and duplicators. This new trade did not replace the trade of Typewriter Mechanic (below) although both trades made repairs to typewriters.

The Typewriter Mechanic worded only at the Group C and B levels and did not repair cipher equipment or duplicating machines. The Instrument Mechanic Typewriter and Cipher made more complicated typewriter repairs including complete disassembly and rebuilding. They used lathes and grinders to make repairs to damaged parts. On cipher machines, they could make repairs to both the electrical and mechanical portions for the machine as well as the rotors that create the codes. (See the Communication section in Part Three for a photograph and information on the operation of a cipher machine.)

This tradesman worked at the Group B and A levels. Before becoming a member of this trade, applicants must have been an Instrument Mechanic of any group level.

Machinist Metal
This trade now spread over Groups C and B.

Mechanist
No change to this trade during this time period.

Millwright
This trade now spread over all three trade groups.

Moulder
The Moulder now spread over Groups C and B.

Senior Projectionist
This was a new trade approximately 1943. It might seem strange, at first, for a RCEME tradesman to be a projectionist. The Senior Projectionist set up and showed 16mm movies and slide projectors. He also trained unit projectionists (The unit projectionist was a non-trade soldier.) The justification for this being a RCEME trade is that he also made repairs to the projector when required. Showing a movie was not a simple matter with this equipment and it was not unusual that something went wrong with the projector or the film in the middle of a movie. By combining the projectionist with the repairer meant that it was not necessary to call for a repair person when help was needed. Time would be of the essence to finish the movie within the time allocated so that the soldiers could move on to their next class or job. He could also clean and splice film and select the appropriate lens for current conditions. The film would sometimes break during a showing. The Senior Projectionist also repaired amplifiers, convertors, transformers and other related equipment. This trade was spread over Groups C and B. It also existed in the RCASC.

Tinsmith
This trade now spread over Groups C and B.

It existed in RCE and RCASC as well as RCEME.

Tinsmith and Whitesmith

This trade was obsolete by 1943 and included with the Tinsmith above.

Toolmaker

This trade now spread over all three trade groups.

Turner

This trade now spread over Groups C and B. It existed in RCE and RCASC as well as RCEME.

Typewriter Mechanic

This trade now spread over Groups C and B. It existed in RCASC as well as RCEME.

Watchmaker

This trade now spread over Groups C and B.

Welder Acetylene

This trade now spread over Groups C and B.

Welder Electric
Welder Gas and Electric

Approximately 1943 the Welder Electric was renamed Welder Gas and Electric. This trade now spread over Groups C and B.

This is not a complete list of the new RCEME trades. Others can be found in various sections such as Artificers, Vehicle Mechanics and other sections appropriate for their job. A new group of Telecommunications trades can be found in the Communications section. This section lists RCEME trades that did not fit into any other category. During this time period there were no weapons techs other than Artificers and Armourers. The next part of the book will include a section on the new weapons tech trades.

SUPPLY

Storeholder RCOC
Storeholder

The name of this trade was shortened to simply Storeholder. It was now spread over trade Groups C and B.

Storeholder MV

This storeman controlled spare parts for motor vehicles. The regular storeholder above looked after uniforms and other equipment required by the soldiers. To be a member of this trade, a soldier must have previously been a Storeman Technical and Departmental and be a qualified driver IC. (Driver IC was a non trade soldier.) This trade was spread over Groups C and B and existed in RCASC, RCOC and RCEME. It was a new trade in 1943.

Storeman Technical and Departmental

All of the various types of Storeman Technical listed in Part One were combined with the Storeman Departmental approximately 1943 to create the Storeman Technical and Departmental.

Foreman Departmental

This trade now spread over Groups C and B.

Assistant Foreman Departmental

This trade was obsolete by 1943 and included with Foreman Departmental at the Group C level.

VEHICLE MECHANICS

These trades are now part of the new corps of RCEME. (Some of them were still members of other corps in 1943 but were gradually changed to RCEME.)

Body Builder Metal
Panel Beater
Panel Beater (Body Repair Man)

The Body Builder Metal and the Panel Beater were combined into a single trade called Panel Beater (Body Repair Man). It was spread over Groups C and B. This trade existed in RCASC as well as RCEME.

Coach Painter

There was no change to this trade during this time period. It existed in RCASC as well as RCEME.

Coach Trimmer
Upholsterer
Coach Trimmer and Upholsterer

The Coach Trimmer and the Upholsterer were merged together into a single trade approximately 1943. This new trade was spread over Groups C and B.

Electrician MV

This was a new trade around the end of 1942. Their job was to repair electrical problems on motor vehicles. They had to be previously qualified as a Driver Mechanic. It became obsolete in 1945 and was included with the trade of Electrician Vehicle and Plant. This trade existed in CAC and RCASC.

Electrician Vehicle and Plant

This was a new trade in 1945. This tradesman repaired electrical components of vehicles and machinery. The Electrician Vehicle and Plant worked on circuitry in lighting equipment, ignition systems, generators, motors, chargers, electric welders, etc. He repaired circuitry and circuit breakers in workshops but not in houses or office buildings, that was the job of the regular electrician which was an RCE trade (see Fortress section). This trade was spread over all three trade groups.

Electroplater

This was a new trade approximately 1943. The Electroplater covered metal objects with a coating of chrome, tin, nickel, gold or other metal to make the objects shiny and rustproof. This was done by submerging the object in a vat of pre-mixed chemicals. After coating the object in the solution, it would be hung up on a hook and an electrical current would be applied. The electricity made the solution adhere to the object. This trade was spread over Groups C and B.

Fitter MV

The Fitter MV must have been previously qualified as a Driver Mechanic. It became obsolete in 1945. Its members remustered to one of the new trades of Vehicle Mechanic AFV or Vehicle Mechanic MV. This was a RCASC trade.

Fitter AFV

This was a new trade in the early 1940s. They made repairs to tracked vehicles. It became obsolete in 1945 and was included with the new trade of Vehicle Mechanic AFV.

Motorcycle Mechanic

This was a new RCOC trade created in 1942 for the repair of motorcycles. It was a very short lived trade and became obsolete in 1945 when it was included in the new trade of Vehicle Mechanic MV.

Motor Mechanic

The Motor Mechanic had to be previously qualified as a Driver Mechanic. This trade became obsolete in 1945. Its members remustered to one of the new trades of Vehicle Mechanic AFV or Vehicle Mechanic MV. It was a CAC and RCASC trade.

Motor Assembler

This trade became obsolete in 1943.

Vehicle Mechanic MV

This was a new trade that came into being in 1945 after the formation of RCEME. Most of the trades that worked on vehicle repair were made obsolete and included with this new trade. They made all types of repairs to wheeled vehicles. These tradesman also made recoveries to vehicles that were broken down in the field or were stuck in mud or ditches. This trade operated at all three trade levels. It existed in the new corps of RCEME as well as several other corps. The soldiers who remustered to this new trade did not change corps except for those in RCOC who became RCEME. Soldiers in RCASC, RC Sigs and others changed trades but not corps.

Vehicle Mechanic AFV

This was a new trade in 1945. It was similar to the Vehicle Mechanic MV above except that they worked on tracked vehicles instead of wheeled vehicles. (AFV stands for armoured fighting vehicle.) This trade worked at all three trade groups. Like the Vehicle Mechanic MV, personnel remustering to this new trade did not change corps except for those in RCOC who became RCEME.

Push Cycle Repairer

The Push Cycle Repairer was, in other terms, a bicycle repairman. This was a new trade in 1942. The army had used bicycles since before the First World War. He made repairs to army bicycles including wheel alignment, painting, replacing spokes, adjusting brakes, adjusting handle bars and seats and anything else that could go wrong with a bicycle. This was a Group C trade.

Vulcanizer
Mechanic Tire Maintenance

The Vulcanizer was renamed Mechanic Tire Maintenance. The trade was spread over all three trade groups.

Wheeler

This trade now spread over Groups C and B.

WATER TRANSPORT

Engineer Water Transport Steam
Engineer Water Transport Diesel
Engineer Water Transport Gasoline

The Engineer Water Transport Steam was replaced by two trades for ships with diesel or gasoline engines. These trades are spread over the three trade groups.

Foreman Fore and Aft

This was a new trade in 1943. His job was the supervision of Side-Runners, Winchmen, Hatch Tenders and a gang of civilian longshoreman. These people were involved with the loading of supplies on a ship. The Foreman Fore and Aft would ensure that the loading and unloading of cargo was properly carried out. He was also responsible to check the hoisting equipment for defects and proper operation. He was responsible for the safety of the gang including proper lighting, first-aid facilities, the provision of drinking water, ensuring the gangway and other passages are clear and other safety precautions. He must have full knowledge of the duties of the Side-Runner, Winchman and Hatch Tender. There were several new trades in Water Transport in 1943. The jobs were not new. People had been doing these jobs for many years. What is new is that the job was elevated to trade status. This was a Group C trade.

Hatch Tender

This is one of several new Water Transport trades created in 1943. The job was not new. The Hatch Tender had been in existence for many years as a non-trade job. It was now elevated to trade status. The Hatch Tender was in charge of loading the cargo into a ship's hold. He would direct the Winchman in the operation of the crane using hand signals. He would ensure that the cargo is properly stowed. The Hatch Tender would check the rigging, nets, hooks, ropes and other gear used in loading the cargo to ensure that it is in good condition. He would check the knots and slings before the cargo is lifted. He would supervise the Stevedores, longshoreman or other labourers. Although the Hatch Tender was in charge of loading the cargo, he came under the supervision of the Foreman Fore and Aft who supervised this trade as well as several others. This was a Group C trade.

Skipper Water Transport 1st Class

This was a new trade approximately 1943. The Skipper Water Transport 1st Class would be in complete charge of a steam, gasoline or diesel-powered ship and its crew. He would plot the course and keep ship's log. Previously the Mechanist Coxswain had doubled as the captain of the ship. The Skipper Water Transport 1st Class must possess a Tug Boat Master's Certificate. This was a Group A trade.

Mate Water Transport 1st Class

This was a new trade approximately 1943. The mate was a member of the crew and not a labourer. He was the assistant to the captain. It was a Group A trade.

Mechanist Coxswain

No change to this trade during this time period except that with the creation of the Skipper Water Transport 1st Class, the Mechanist Coxswain no longer doubled as the captain of the ship and could concentrate on engine repairs.

Shipwright

This trade is now spread over the three trade groups.

Side-Runner

The Side-Runner supervised the cargo in the hold of a ship. He would ensure that cargo is unloaded and stored properly. He would consider the properly handling of explosives, inflammables, or corrosive material. The Side-Runner must be familiar with the hand signals of the Hatch Tender and the Winchman. He could fill in for the Hatch Tender if required. This was another of several new Water Transport trades created approximately 1943. These jobs were not new, but were newly elevated to trade status. The Side-Runner was a Group C trade.

Stevedore

This trade became obsolete approximately 1943. Former members of this trade could remuster to Hatch Tender, Side-Runner or Winchman. These tradesmen were replaced with civilian longshoremen.

Stoker Fireman

Obsolete approximately 1943.

Winchman

The Winchman operated steam-powered or electric winches. The winch was used to load or unload cargo into the haul of a ship. He would watch the Hatch Tender and obey his hand signals. The Winchman was also responsible to keep the winch lubricated and make minor repairs. Now Group C, the Winchman was formerly a non-trade job. It was elevated to trade status in the early 1940s.

Waterman Boatman

No change to this trade during this time period.

WOODWORKING

Machinist Wood

This trade now spread over Groups C and B.

Pattern Maker

This trade now spread over all three trade groups.

Wood Turner and Machinist

Obsolete approximately 1943.

Trivia

In August 1944 the self propelled artillery of the 3rd division, known as priests, were exchanged for 25 pounder towed artillery pieces. Some of the priests were converted to APC's by removing the gun, mantlet, seats and ammo carriers and adding armour plate on the front. Many of the drivers of this new unit, called the 1st Canadian Armoured Carrier Regiment, were former gunners of the 3rd division. The same soldiers who had driven the vehicles when they were self propelled artillery. [11]

UNKNOWN TRADES

Nursing Orderly Mental
Technical Supervisor Radio

The duties of the above tradesmen are unknown to me. They existed in the 1942-44 time period. If you have any information about these trades please contact the author.

1946 to 1955

1946

In 1946 the size of the "T" badges was reduced by approximately 50% and each trade was to be divided into four groups, instead of three. The previous badges, referred to as Groups C, B and A were replaced by these smaller badges called Groups 1, 2, 3 and 4. [12]

This was the beginning of the four group system of levels of expertise that is still in use today. Lateral progression was allowed. This means that moving from one group to a higher group was not tied to rank as was the case before 1946. Thus, a private could advance from group one to group two to group three and still remain a private. It was acknowledged that some soldiers were good at their trade, but made poor leaders. This system enables the soldier to advance in skill and trades pay without having to advance in rank. This system was abolished upon unification in 1968 and we returned to the system of skill being tied to rank progression.

The names were changed from "C, B, A"
(named lowest to highest) to "1, 2, 3, 4"

Previous

Group C	T
Group B	T with wreath
Group A	T with wreath and crown

New

Group 1	T
Group 2	T with wreath
Group 3	T with crown
Group 4	T with wreath and crown

Trades C, B and A became 1, 2 and 3 at first. Tradesmen then had to take a test if they wanted to advance to a higher group level.

September 1946

The Canadian Women's Army Corp was disbanded.

1951

The Canadian Women's Army Corp was reactivated as a militia corps. They did not really exist as a corps but were spread out to work in all the reserve force units across Canada. Some with wartime experience were called up for full time duties.

December 1951

In 1951 there was much discussion at army headquarters as to whether or not the combat soldiers should receive trades pay. All of the trades mentioned so far in this book received extra pay for their skills.

On the one side of the argument, the average infantryman was not as skilled or educated as the soldiers who could repair radios or vehicles, or make dentures or maps, or drive a tank, etc.

On the other hand, the combat troops had the hardest, dirtiest and most dangerous jobs in the army. Surely they should get something extra for their labours.

The Vice Chief of the Defence Staff did not agree to the term "tradesman" being applied to combat soldiers. After much debate a compromise solution was reached. It was decided to call the combat troops "specialities". This would mean that they would receive extra pay in four levels the same as the four levels for tradesmen. They would not get to be called "tradesmen" and they would not get to wear the "T" badge.

The money that the specialties received would be called "group pay" instead of "trades pay". The amount of money would be the same as trades pay. Therefore a Group 1 specialty would receive the same amount of money as a Group 1 tradesman which was up to $6.00 per month in 1951. I can imagine what the average infantryman thought of this: "who cares what you call it; just give me the six bucks!"

This was to take effect 1 December 1951.

In the list that follows, specialties are indicated with the letter "S" after the name.

1952

The CWAC received the "T" badges in their own distinctive colours, drab on beach brown. (In April 1964 the CWAC was disbanded once again when women were fully integrated into the individual army corps in non-combat jobs.)

1954

In 1954 the definitions of "tradesman" and "specialty" were as follows:

tradesman   A trained soldier who has qualified for employment in army duties, generally in the administrative or technical fields, which require particular skills and knowledge.

specialist   A trained soldier with particular skills in RCAC, RCA or RCIC.

Some trades such as Despatch Rider that existed before 1951, were changed to specialties at that time. In accordance with the new definition of a specialty in 1954, all specialties that were not members of RCAC, RCA or RCIC reverted back to tradesman status.

Even some specialties within those three corps, such as Master Gunner, were changed back to tradesman status, leaving only the hard fighting troops to be known as specialties.

Many changes were made to the driver trades in 1954. Driver Mechanic Tracked became a tank driver in RCAC only. Driver Mechanic Wheeled became a driver in RCAC only, to correspond with their Driver Mechanic Tracked. Drivers in all other corps were renamed Driver Mechanical Transport. The Driver Operator existed only in RCA, RCE and RCEME. In all other corps they were renamed. This was a change back to the situation before the Driver Operator trade existed, when each corps had their own name for this trade. See the driver chart at the end of Part Two.

Gender Reference

Many times in this book, you will find that a tradesman is referred to as "he". This is not meant to be sexist or politically incorrect. It is meant to reflect the reality of the times. There were no women tradesmen in the army corps except in the CWAC. Therefore to refer to a clerk in an army corps as "he" would be correct as there were no women in these trades until 1964. The only exception were the Nursing Sisters in the Medical Corps. (See Women in the Canadian Army page 218.)

TRADES AND SPECIALTIES AS THEY EXISTED 1946 TO 1955

During this time period you will notice some trades that were reduced to "nil strength". This means that the trade was not obsolete, but there were no people doing the job. These trades existed on paper only and had no soldiers currently enlisted.

AMMUNITION

Ammunition Examiner
Groups
1-3, 1-4 in 1947, 2-4 in 1953

The group level was changed in 1947 to add the Group 4 level. In 1953, it was changed again. This time to delete the Group 1 level. This meant that the trade was no longer available for direct entry. Civilians wishing to join this trade, must first join the army in some other trade and then remuster to Ammunition Examiner after completing Group 1.

ARTIFICERS AND ARMOURERS

Most of the Artificers were no longer with us by 1946. What happened to them? With the formation of RCEME in 1944, the technical trades were moved from RCOC to RCEME.

The many types of fitters were combined into two trades called Fitter Signals in the Signal Corps and simply Fitter in all other corps. These trades can now be found in the communications, RCEME, weapons, or vehicle sections. Two new fitters were created to work on locomotives and can be found in the Railway section.

Armament Artificer Radar	see Telecommunication Mechanic in Communications.
Armament Artificer Wireless	see Telecommunication Mechanic in Communications.
Engine Artificer	see Mechanic Stationary Engine in Construction Engineers.
Armament Artificer Electrical	see RCEME.
Armament Artificer Instruments CD	see Weapons Techs.
Armament Artificer Instruments AA	see Weapons Techs.
Armament Artificer Instruments Field	see Weapons Techs.
Armament Artificer AA	see Weapons Techs.
Armament Artificer Field	see Weapons Techs.
Armourer	see Weapons Techs.
Armament Artificer MV	see Vehicle Mechanics.
Armament Artificer Vehicle	see Vehicle Mechanics.

ARMOURED

Fitter 1-3

The Fitter trade could be found in several different corps. It became obsolete in the Armoured Corps in 1950.

Gunner Operator (S) 1
Gunner Signaller (S) 1-2

This Group C trade is now a Group 1 trade under the new system. It was changed to a specialty in 1951. The name was changed to Gunner Signaller in 1954. At this time a Group 2 level was added.

Operator CAC 1
Operator RCAC 1

The Operator CAC was renamed Operator RCAC in 1947 due to the title "Royal" being added to the corps name. The trade then became obsolete in 1949 and was replaced with the Driver Operator.

Driver Operator (S) 1
Signaller RCAC (S) 1-2

The Driver Operator was not a new trade. It had existed since 1939 in the Signal Corps. This was an attempt to give all signallers in all corps the same name. This trade was changed to a specialty in 1951.

In 1954 the name was changed in RCAC to Signaller RCAC and the group level was changed to add Group 2. The name Driver Operator continued to be used as a trade in RCA, RCE and RCEME

In 1954 there was a major reorganization of RCAC specialties. The Driver Operator was renamed Signaller RCAC, and several new specialties were created (listed below).

Leading Assault Trooper (S)   1

This was a new specialty in 1953; it was reduced to nil strength in 1954. It was deemed to be required in wartime only. See Part Three for a job description.

Gunner-Driver Mechanic Tracked (S)   2
Gunner-Driver Mechanic Wheeled (S)   2

These were a new specialties in 1954. The Gunner-Driver Mechanic tracked was a combination of gunner and tank driver. The Gunner-Driver Mechanic Wheeled was a combination of gunner and wheeled vehicle driver. There was no specialty for someone who was a gunner only.

Signaller-Driver Mechanic Tracked (S)   2
Signaller-Driver Mechanic Wheeled (S)   2

These were a new specialties in 1954. The Signaller-Driver Mechanic tracked was a combination of signaller and tank driver. The Signaller-Driver Mechanic Wheeled was a combination of signaller and wheeled vehicle driver.

Specialist RCAC (S)   3

This was a new specialty in 1954. See Part Three for a job description.

Before 1954, the Driver Mechanic Tracked existed in several corps. In that year the specialty was changed (but not the name) to be a tank driver in RCAC only. In this part of the book this trade is listed under Drivers but it will be moved to the armoured section in Part Three.

ARTILLERY

Master Gunner (S)   3, changed to 4 in 1947

The class one and class two Master Gunners were previously in Group A, while the class three Master Gunner was in Group B. Under the new system, all Master Gunners were placed in Group 3. This was later changed to Group 4. The Master Gunner trade was changed to a specialty in 1951, and changed back to a trade again in 1954.

Electrician Radar

This trade became obsolete in 1946. The job was then included with the trade of Telecommunication Mechanic. See the Communication section for details.

Fitter Gun
Fitter   1-3

The Fitter Gun was replaced by the Fitter which was a trade that was common to several corps. The Fitter became obsolete in the Artillery in 1950.

Surveyor RCA   1-4

See Part Three for detailed information about this trade.

Surveyor RCA Flash Spotting   2-3
Surveyor RCA Radar   1-3
Surveyor RCA Sound Ranging   2-3
Technical Assistant Survey   2

These were new trades created in 1955. They were in addition to the previous trade of Surveyor RCA which remained in use. Flash spotting and sound ranging had been in use since the First World War but were not considered to be trades or specialties until 1955. See Part Three for details. All of these new trades except Surveyor RCA Radar had to be previously qualified as a Surveyor RCA Group 1.

Meteorological Observer   3

The Meteorological Observer formerly worked at Group B and A levels. It is now a Group 3 trade.

Operator Kine-Theodolite (S)   1-3

This trade was changed to a specialty in 1951 and changed back to a trade again in 1954. See Part Three for detailed information about this trade.

Operator Fire Control AA (S)   1
Operator Fire Control Coast Artillery (S)   1

The Operator Fire Control's job was to find the range and plot targets. These were new trades in 1950 and were changed to specialties in 1951.

Operator Fire Direction Coast   1

In 1954 the Operator Fire Control AA became obsolete. The Operator Fire Control Coast Artillery was renamed Operator Fire Direction Coast and was changed back to being a trade.

Operator Fire Direction HD   1
In 1955 the word coast was changed to Harbour Defence.

Operator Radar
This trade was downgraded to non-trade status in 1946.

Operator Radar AA   1-2
In 1954 the Operator Radar was elevated to trade status once again with the new name of Operator Radar Anti-Aircraft.

Operator Radar Coast   1
This was a new trade in 1954. There were now separate trades for the field and coastal artillery.

Operator Radar Harbour Defence   1
In 1955 the word coast was changed to Harbour Defence.

Operator Predictor   1
This was a new trade in 1954. See Part Three for more information.

Operator Searchlight   1
This was a new artillery trade in 1954.

Signaller Artillery   1
Driver Operator (S)   1
In 1949, the Signaller Artillery was replaced by the Driver Operator who was both a driver and a signaller. The Driver Operator trade was common to several corps. The idea was to give all signallers the same name regardless of corps affiliation.

This trade was changed to a specialty in 1951. The new trade of Driver RCA, which was created in 1954, was not a signaller and did not replace this trade.

Technical Assistant RCA AA (S)   1-3
Technical Assistant RCA Coast (S)   1-2
Technical Assistant RCA Field and Medium(S) 1-2
These were new trades in 1948 and were changed to be specialties in 1951.

Technical Assistant AA   3
Technical Assistant Coast   2-3
Technical Assistant Field and Medium   1-2
In 1954 the letters RCA were dropped from the name and the group levels were changed. These specialties were also changed to trades at this time.

Technical Assistant AA   3
Technical Assistant Harbour Defence   2-3
Technical Assistant Field   1-3
In 1955 the names of these trades were changed slightly. The Technical Assistant Coast was renamed to Technical Assistant Harbour Defence. The Technical Assistant Field and Medium was renamed to Technical Assistant Field. See Part Three for details.

Gun Number RCA (S) 1, changed to 1-2 in 1954
This was a new speciality in 1951. The Group 2 level was added in 1954. See Part Three for a detailed job description.

Clerk Operations (S)   1
This soldier worked in coastal artillery units. It was a new specialty in 1951, and changed to a trade in 1954. See Part Three for a job description.

In 1954 the specialties of Driver RCA and Driver RCA Tracked were created. See Driver section for details.

CHEMICALS

Chemical Tech   1-3
Operator Chemical Plant   1-3
These trades were reduced to nil strength in 1949. They were deemed to be required in wartime only. Both trades were abolished in the early 1950s. They were RCE trades.

CLERKS

Clerk
Clerk Superintending
Clerk Administrative   1-3
The Clerk and the Clerk Superintending were combined in 1946 to create the Clerk Administrative. This clerk could be a member of any corps.

Accountant Signals
Clerk Engineer Accountant
Clerk Accounting   1-3
The Accountant Signals and the Clerk Engineer Accountant were combined in 1946 to create the Clerk Accounting. This new clerk could be a member of any corps. Soldiers employed as Accountant Signals or Clerk Engineer Accountant would probably

have had no change in their job except for the name change.

In 1949, this policy was reversed. The Clerk Accounting was dissolved and replaced by the following corps specific trades:

Clerk Accounting RC SIGS	2-3
Clerk Accounting RCASC	1-3
Clerk Accounting RCAMC	2-3
Clerk Accounting RCAPC	2-3
Clerk Accounting RCOC	1-3
Engineer Accountant	2-4

The above trades that did not exist in Group 1 would have been a Clerk Administrative at that level. The Engineer Accountant could also have been a Storeman Clerk or a Clerk Typist at the Group 1 level. The Engineer Accountant worked on papers for the following tasks:
- Authorization for construction projects
- Procurement
- Admin for civilian employees
- Financial accounting
- Engineer stores accounting

In 1950, the Clerk Accounting RCAPC was replaced by the following two trades:

Clerk Accounting Institutes 1-3
Clerk Accounting Pay 1-3

The Clerk Accounting Pay worked in the pay office and looked after the soldier's pay records. The Clerk Accounting Institutes did the accounting for the messes (kitchens and clubs).

The Clerk Accounting RC SIGS became obsolete in 1953.

Clerk RCASC 1-3

The Clerk Accounting RCASC was renamed Clerk RCASC in 1954. There was a clerk by this name once before in the 1930s. (See Part One.)

Clerk Stenographer 3, changed to 2-3 in 1953.

The Clerk Administrative was the regular office clerk who replaced the previous trade of "Clerk". The Clerk Admin was not required to learn shorthand as was the case for the Clerk. Therefore the Clerk Stenographer was brought back again. This trade had been made obsolete in 1938, brought back in the early 1940s, made obsolete for the second time in 1945, and brought back for the third time in 1948. This time the Clerk Stenographer could be a member of any trade. Previously it had been a Signal Corps trade. In 1953 the group levels were changed to include Group 2.

Operator Punch Card Tabulating Machine 1-3
Operator Punched Card Machines 1-3

This trade could be found in RCASC and RCOC. In 1954 the name was changed to Operator Punched Card Machine. See Part Three for details.

Court Reporter 4

The Court Reporter drew its recruits from the ranks of the Group 3 Clerk Admin. This was a RCASC trade.

Clerk Typist 1

This was a new trade created in 1953. He was not really much of a clerk and was not required to be skilled at office work such as filing. He was simply a typist. If something had to be typed up, this soldier could do that but not much more. Which explains why the trade existed at the Group 1 level only.

The Clerk Typist could be a member of any corps and the trade was not reflected in unit establishments like other trades. This meant that there was no limit to the number of Clerk Typists that a unit could have. All other trades had establishment limits for the number of soldiers of each trade that a unit was entitled to have. Soldiers in excess of establishment entitlement would not receive trades pay.

The Clerk Typist existed in 1953 only and was obsolete by the end of the year. Perhaps this trade existed on a trail basis only and things just did not work out. No reason was given for its demise.

Steward 1-2

The Steward was made a trade in 1954. This was previously a non-trade job. He could be a member of any corps. See Part Three for a job description.

For Storeman Clerk see Supply Section.

COMMUNICATIONS

Cable Splicer 3

Despatch Rider (S) 1

In 1946, the DR was downgraded to non-trade status. It was revived in 1950 as a Group 1 trade under the new system. Before being a DR, this soldier had to be qualified driver wheeled. In 1951 this trade was changed to a specialty; in 1954 it was changed back to a trade.

Draughtsman Signals 1-2

Signaller Artillery
Signaller Infantry
Driver Operator (S) 1

The Driver Operator trade originally existed in RC Sigs only. By 1949 it existed in six different corps.

The Signaller Artillery and the Signaller Infantry were upgraded to trade status in 1943. In 1949, these trades were dissolved and replaced by the Driver Operator.

The Operator RCAC was also replaced by the Driver Operator in the Armoured Corps. The Driver Operator was also created in RCE and RCEME. It was still in use in RC Sigs as well. The object was to make all signallers in all corps members of the same trade.

In 1951 the Driver Operator was changed from a trade to a specialty.

In 1953 this specialty was eliminated in RC SIGS.

In 1954 the Driver Operator was changed back to being a trade. Also in 1954, the trade was renamed in the armoured corps and infantry, leaving it existing only in RCA, RCE, and RCEME.

Driver Electrician 2-3

The Driver Electrician was a new trade in 1953. His job was to operate and maintain generators and power distribution equipment and look after battery charging for the radio vehicles. Before being accepted into this trade at the Group 2 level, he would be a Driver Mechanic Wheeled Group 1.

Fitter Signals

The Fitter Signals became part of the new Vehicle Mechanic trade in 1945. This does not mean that these personnel changed corps. They would have changed trades to Vehicle Mechanic but would still be a member of the Royal Canadian Corps of Signals. The Vehicle Mechanic trade existed in several corps. See the Vehicle Tech section for a list of corps.

Fitter 1-3

The gap left by the absence of the Fitter Signals was filled by the Fitter which was a trade that was common to several corps. Some of the former Fitter Signals probably remustered to this trade. However, the Fitter became obsolete in the Signal Corp in 1950 and the personnel probably became Vehicle Mechanics.

Foreman of Signals 4

The Foreman of Signals had to have previously been a Radio or Line Mechanic Group 3.

Lineman Signals 1-2
Lineman Field 1-2
Lineman Permanent Line 1-2

The Lineman Field and the Lineman Permanent Line had been combined into a single trade in the 1930s. In 1949, it was once again split into two trades.

Loftman 1

Obsolete 1947.

Operator Cipher 1-2

Before becoming an Operator Cipher Group 1, this soldier had to be already qualified as an Operator Keyboard, Clerk Administrative or Clerk Stenographer Group 1.

Operator Fixed Wireless Station 1-3

Operator Monitor Signals

This trade became obsolete in 1946 and its members were merged with the Operator Special. (This refers to the small percentage of soldiers who remained in the army after the war. The vast majority of troops of all corps took their release as soon as possible after returning to Canada.)

Operator Special Signals
Operator Special 1-3

In 1946 the word "Signals" was dropped from this trade. In 1953 this trade was reduced to nil strength. It still existed on paper but there were no members.

Operator Switchboard 1

The Operator Switchboard operated both base and field switchboards and had to be familiar with office duties and battery charging.

Operator Wireless and Line
1-2, changed to 1-3 in 1953

This trade was known as the "OWL". The Group level was changed in 1953 to include Group 3.

Operator Keyboard
Teletype Operator
Operator Teletype
Operator Keyboard 1-2

This trade went through several name changes during this period. Originally called the Operator Keyboard, the name was changed to Teletype Operator after the war. In 1947 it was changed to Operator Teletype. In 1950 it was renamed once again, this time back to the original name of Operator Keyboard. His job was to operate teletype equipment.

RCEME COMMUNICATION EQUIPMENT REPAIR TRADES

Telecommunication Mechanic Coast Artillery
Telecommunication Mechanic Heavy Anti-Aircraft
Telecommunication Mechanic Light Anti-Aircraft
Telecommunication Mechanic Field
Telecommunication Mechanic Lines of Communication
Electrician Radar
Armament Artificer Radar
Armament Artificer Wireless
Instrument Mechanic Signals
Electrician Signals

In 1946 all of the above trades were combined into a single trade.

Telecommunication Mechanic
1-4, changed to 1-3 in 1947

This new trade originally operated at all four group levels in 1940, but in 1947 the Group 4 was deleted and replaced with two new artificer trades.

Telecommunication Artificer Wireless 4
Telecommunication Artificer Radar 4

These two new trades replaced the Group 4 Telecommunication Mechanic in 1947. These were RCEME trades. Signals did not have a radio repair trade working at the Group 4 level in this time period.

Radio Mechanic 1-3
Radar Mechanic 1-3

In 1947, the new trade of Telecommunication Mechanic was replaced by two new trades. One of them was the Radio Mechanic which existed in both RCEME and RCSIGS. The old trade was RCEME only.

The other new trade was the Radar Mechanic which existed in both RCEME and RCA.

In 1950, the above trades become obsolete in RCEME and RCA leaving only the Radio Mechanic as a Signals trade.

Telecommunication Mechanic Field 1-3
Telecommunication Mechanic Radar 1-3
Telecommunication Mechanic
Line of Communication 1-3

The above new trades were created to replace the Radio Mechanic and the Radar Mechanic in RCEME. Note that they went back to using the name Telecommunication Mechanic. The Telecommunication Mechanic Line of Communication replaced the Lineman Mechanic in RCEME but not in Signals. No trade was created to replace the Radar Mechanic in RCA.

Radio Tech 1-3
Radar Tech 1-3

In 1955 the Telecommunication Mechanic Field was renamed Radio Technician. The Telecommunication Mechanic Radar was renamed the Radar Technician. The Telecommunication Mechanic Line of Communication would be renamed in 1956. (This part of the book only covers activity up to 1955.)

Radio Artificer 4
Radar Artificer 4

In 1955 the Telecommunication Artificer Wireless was renamed the Radio Artificer. The Telecommunication Artificer Radar was renamed the Radar Artificer.

RC SIGS COMMUNICATION EQUIPMENT REPAIR TRADES

Radio Mechanic 1-3
This trade, when it was created in 1947, existed in both RCEME and RC SIGS. In 1950 it was renamed in RCEME.

Lineman Mechanic
Line Mechanic 1-3
After the creation of RCEME in 1944 this trade existed in both RCEME and RC SIGS. The name was shortened to Line Mechanic in 1947. This trade was the forerunner of the Terminal Equipment Tech. In RCEME the name was changed to Telecommunication Mechanic Line of Communication in 1950.

Telegraph Mechanic 1-3
This was a new trade in RC SIGS in 1950. They made repairs to teletype, cipher and telegraph equipment, leaving the Line Mechanic to repair switchboards, telephones, and repeaters.

In summary, RCEME took over the duties of radio and radar equipment repairs from RCOC in 1944. At this time RC SIGS also created their own radio repair trade. Both RCEME and RC SIGS did radio repairs at the Group 1-3 level but only RCEME had artificers who worked at the Group 4 level. In 1950, the names were changed in RCEME to make them separate trades from those in the Signal Corps. There is a chart at the end of this part of the book that will enable you to follow the many changes mentioned here.

CONSTRUCTION ENGINEERS

The Construction Engineer Section was formerly known as the Fortress Company. These were RCE trades and all pers had to undergo basic corps training before proceeding on their individual trades training.

Blacksmith 1-2 originally, later 1-3
The Blacksmith became obsolete in 1947 and their duties were taken over by the Welder. In 1953 the Welder was made obsolete in RCE (but still continued in RCEME). When the Welder was made obsolete, the Blacksmith was brought back. The Blacksmith was originally employed at the Group 1-2 levels under the new system. When the trade was reinstated in 1953, it was given employment at Group 1-3.

Boilermaker 1-2
This trade was reduced to nil strength in 1949. It was deemed to be required in wartime only. It became obsolete in 1953.

Bricklayer 1-2
The Bricklayer included the duties of Mason after 1946 when the Mason trade became obsolete.

Carpenter 1-2, changed to 1-3 in 1953
The group level for this trade was increased to included Group 3 in 1953.

Concretor 1-2

Diver 1-4
This trade was reduced to nil strength in 1949 and became obsolete in 1953.

Draughtsman A & E 1-3 originally, later 1-4
This trade was started at the Group 1-3 levels under the new system, but was changed to be Group 1-4 in 1947.

Draughtsman Topographical 1-2

Driller Diamond Setter
Driller Diamond and Rotary
Driller 1-3
In 1946 the Driller Diamond Setter and the Driller Diamond and Rotary were combined into a single trade. This trade was reduced to nil strength in 1950. It was deemed to be required in wartime only. It became obsolete in 1953.

Electrician 1-3

Engine Fitter IC and Pump
Engine Hand
Mechanic Stationary Engine 1-2
These two trades, along with the Engine Artificer, were combined to create the new trade of Mechanic Stationary Engine in 1946. This trade was reduced to nil strength in 1950 and made obsolete in 1952. Most trades that were reduced to nil strength eventually became obsolete; very few were reactivated.

Fitter 1-3
Fitter RCE 1-3

The Fitter existed in RCOC, RCA and RCE. It also existed in other corps under different names such as Fitter Signals and Fitter Gun. In the mid 1940s all of these different fitter trades were combined into a single trade called simply Fitter. In 1950 it became obsolete in all corps except RCEME and RCE. In the Engineers the trade was renamed Fitter RCE making it a separate trade from the RCEME Fitter.

In 1947 the Mechanic Special Engineering Equipment became obsolete and the Fitter took over the job of repairing this equipment from 1947 to 1950. In 1950 a new trade called Mechanic RCE was created for this role. The Mechanic RCE and the Fitter RCE both worked on the repair of special engineering equipment. See Field Engineers for details.

Foreman of Works
4 only, changed to 3-4 in 1947

The group level for this trade was changed in 1947 to include the Group 3 level. It was previously Group 4 only. Candidates for this trade had to be a Group 2 in any construction trade.

Mason

This trade became obsolete in 1946 and the duties were included with the Bricklayer trade.

Mechanic Refrigeration Plant
Equipment Mechanic 1-3

The Mechanic Refrigeration Plant was renamed Equipment Mechanic in 1946. This new trade made repairs to kitchen equipment and utensils in addition to refrigeration equipment. It was reduced to nil strength in 1950 and was obsolete by 1953.

Mechanist Electrical 4

Members of this trade would have previously been an Electrician Group 3

Mechanist Machinery 4

Prospective members of this trade could be a Group 3 of any mechanical trade.

Miner 2

Operator Light and Power Plant 2-4
This trade became obsolete in 1952.

The trades that were employed in the light and power plant (Operator Light and Power Plant) and the heating plant (Stationary Engineer) and the refrigeration plant (Equipment Mechanic) all eventually became obsolete and were replaced with civilian workers. This was the beginning of a trend that was to accelerate in the Canadian Forces over the years with more and more tradesmen being replaced with civilians, especially after 1995. Before 1950, whatever the job, there was a tradesman in uniform to do it.

Painter and Decorator
Painter 1-2

The trade of Painter that existed in the 1930's and earlier was made obsolete in the early 1940s and combined with the trade of Painter and Decorator which had been two separate trades until that time. In 1946 The Painter and Decorator was combined with the trade of Coach Painter to create a new trade called "Painter". The Coach Painter trade had existed in RCASC and RCEME.

For Pioneer see Field Engineers

Plumber and Pipe Fitter
Plumber 1-3

The name of Plumber and Pipe Fitter was shortened to Plumber in 1946.

Quarryman 1-2, changed to 2 only in 1947

The trade of Quarryman was originally set up under the new system to work at the Group 1-2 levels. This was changed in 1947 to be Group 2 only. It was reduced to nil strength in 1950. The trade of Miner continued to be in use after 1950.

Rigger 1-2

This trade was reduced to nil strength in 1950 and was obsolete by 1953.

Riveter
Structural Steel Worker 1-2

The Riveter was renamed the Structural Steel Worker in 1947. It was then reduced to nil strength in 1950 but was reactivated in 1953.

Engine Fitter Steam Reciprocating
Operator Steam Power Plant
Steamfitter
Stoker Stationary Engine
Stationary Engineer 1-3

The Engine Fitter Steam Reciprocating, the Operator Steam Power Plant, the Steamfitter and the Stoker Stationary Engine were all combined in 1946 to create the new trade of Stationary Engineer. This tradesman worked in the base heating plant. The Stationary Engineer trade became obsolete approximately 1952.

Sawyer 1-3

The trades of Sawfiler Forestry, Sawyer Forestry and Saw Doctor were all made obsolete in 1946 and their duties included with this trade. The Sawyer was reduced to nil strength in 1949.

Sheet Metal Worker 1-2, changed to 1-3 in 1953

This trade existed in RCE, RCASC and RCEME. In 1949 it became obsolete in RCASC and RCEME. The RCEME personnel were transferred to RCE. Instructions for this trade did not state what happened to the RCASC personnel. They probably changed to other trades within RCASC. In 1953 the group level was changed to add a Group 3 level.

Surveyor Engineering 1-4
Surveyor Topographical 1-4

Welder 1-3

This trade became obsolete in RCE in 1953 but continued in RCEME. The duties were assumed by the Blacksmith which was revived from nil strength status. (See Blacksmith above and Welder in the RCEME section).

Wellborer

This trade was reduced to nil strength in 1949. It became obsolete in 1952 or '53.

A few of the Construction Engineer trades listed here were RCE but were not really construction trades; they were machinists. These trades were the Fitter RCE, the Mechanic RCE and the Machinist Machinery. When the new trade badges were issued in 1956, these trades wore a different badge than the construction trades. Therefore, in the next part of the book these trades will be moved to the Materials section.

COOKS

Cook 1-4

The Cook Hospital became obsolete and was included with this trade.

Master Cook 4

The Cook trade was originally set up to be Group 1-4 under the new system. In 1947 it was reduced to Group 1-3 and the trade of Master Cook was created to work at the Group 4 level. This was a very short-lived trade. By 1949 it was obsolete and the Cook trade was changed back to work at the Group 1-4 levels. The trade of Master Cook would be initiated once again in the 1960s.

Baker 2-3

Butcher 1-3
Meat Cutter 1-3
Butcher 1-3

The Butcher trade became obsolete in 1947 and was replaced with the Meat Cutter trade. The Meat Cutter was more like the modern grocery store butcher. He cut up meat but did not kill animals. The previous trade of Butcher was required to be knowledgeable in the slaughter of animals. The Meat Cutter operated only at the Group 1-2 levels. The Group 3 Meat Cutter was to be activated in wartime only. In 1949 the Meat Cutter was renamed Butcher. This new Butcher trade had the duties of the Meat Cutter and not the duties of the previous Butcher which was required to kill animals and prepare the meat for consumption. The new Butcher trade, like the Meat Cutter, existed on paper at the Group 1-3 levels but actually only operated at Group 1-2. No members of this trade existed at the Group 3 level during peacetime. The Group 3 level was activated with the outbreak of the Korean War and remained in use after the war until the trade was made obsolete about 1960.

Cook Hospital

This trade became obsolete in 1946 and all personnel were remustered to the Cook trade. It was replaced by a course that any Group 3 Cook could attend.

DENTAL

Dental Assistant 1-2

Dental Tech 1-3, changed to 1-4 in 1954
The Group 4 level was added to this trade in 1954.

Instrument Repairer Dental 1-3
Dental Equipment Repairer 1-3
The Instrument Repairer Dental was renamed in 1950 to Dental Equipment Repairer. It had been called the Dental Instrument Repairer in the 1930s.

DRIVERS

Driver Mechanic MV
Driver Mechanic Carrier
Driver Mechanic Tank
Driver Mechanic 1
Driver Mechanic Tracked (S) 1, changed to 1-2 in 1954
Driver Mechanic Wheeled (S) 1

Approximately 1943, the trade of Driver Mechanic had been split into three trades as named above (MV, Carrier and Tank). In 1946, this decision was reversed and these trades were once again combined into a single trade called Driver Mechanic. This new Driver Mechanic included the Driver IC Tank personnel who were previously non tradesmen. The Driver IC Tank was a driver only and did not do repairs or maintenance which is why they did not receive trades pay. These personnel now had to become Driver Mechanics and Driver IC Tank became obsolete.

In 1947 this new trade of Driver Mechanic was split into two. These new trades were called Driver Mechanic Tracked and Driver Mechanic Wheeled for the drivers of tracked and wheeled vehicles. The Driver Mechanic Tracked existed in RCE, RCEME, RCAC and RCA. The Driver Mechanic Wheeled existed in most corps. In RCEME, the Driver Mechanic Wheeled and the Driver Mechanic Tracked could progress to Tire Repairman Group 2 or Vehicle Tech Group 2. After 1950, he could no longer progress to Vehicle Tech, only to Tire Repairman. In other corps he could progress to a Group 2 trade applicable to that corps.

Both the Driver Mechanic Wheeled and the Driver Mechanic Tracked were changed from trades to specialties in 1951.

In 1954 the Driver Mechanic Tracked was changed (but not the name) to be a tank driver in RCAC only. Members of this specialty who were RCA were remustered to Driver RCA Tracked. In RCE and RCEME a specialty for drivers of tracked vehicles was deleted.

At the same time, the Driver Mechanic Wheeled was limited to RCAC personnel only. Members of this specialty who were RCA were remustered to Driver RCA. Those drivers who were infantry were remusterd to the new specialty of Infantry Driver. All former members of the Driver Mechanic Wheeled who were neither RCAC, RCA or RCIC were remusted to the new trade of Driver Mechanical Transport.

Driver RCA Tracked (S) 1
This specialty was created in 1954 for RCA tracked drivers who were formally members of the Driver Mechanic Tracked specialty. The Driver Mechanic Tracked became a tank driver in RCAC only.

Driver RCA (S) 1
This specialty was created in 1954 for wheeled vehicle drivers who were formally RCA members of the Driver Mechanic Wheeled specialty. The Driver Mechanic Wheeled became an RCAC specialty only.

Infantry Driver (S) 1-2
This specialty was created in 1954 for wheeled vehicle drivers who were formally infantry members of the Driver Mechanic Wheeled specialty.

Driver Mechanical Transport 1
This trade was created in 1954 for wheeled vehicle drivers who were formally members of the Driver Mechanic Wheeled specialty and were not RCA, RCAC or RCIC.

Note that the RCASC driver was not a separate trade at this time. They were included with the Driver Mechanic Wheeled and later Driver Mechanical Transport. See Drivers in Part Three for more information on this.

Driver Transportation Plant

In 1946 this trade was made obsolete and the personnel were transferred to the trade of Operator Special Engineering Equipment. See Field Engineers.

"Driver Wheeled" was not a trade. This was a course. Many non-trade soldiers and tradesmen alike took the driver wheeled course to learn how to drive. This did not change their status as a soldier or a tradesman. Several trades, such as Driver Mechanic Wheeled, Driver Mechanic Tracked and Despatch Rider had to take this course as a prerequisite before taking their trades training. Many non-trade soldiers, such as the Artillery Gun Number also took this course. It was never the name of a trade.

For Driver Operator see Communications

EQUESTRIAN

Farrier

Obsolete. The army decided in 1948 that the Farrier was no longer required.

FIELD ENGINEERS

Operator Special Engineering Equipment
2-3 originally, 1-3 1947

This trade now included the personnel and duties of the Driver Transportation Plant which became obsolete in 1946. This trade was originally set up to be Group 2-3 under the new system but was changed in 1947 to be Group 1-3.

Fitter Special Engineering Equipment
Mechanic Special Engineering Equipment 2-3

The Fitter Special Engineering Equipment was combined with the Fitter Tractor Forestry in 1946 to create the new trade of Mechanic Special Engineering Equipment. This trade was very short-lived however, and became obsolete in 1947. The job of repairing this equipment fell to the Fitter.

The Fitter trade had existed for some time in RCOC, RCE and other corps under different names such as Fitter Signals and Fitter Gun. In the mid 1940s all of these different fitter trades were combined into a single trade called simply Fitter. This new trade existed in RCA, RCE, RCAC, RC SIGS, RCASC and RCEME. See Fitter in Construction Engineers for more information.

Mechanic RCE 2-3

This trade was created in 1950 to make repairs to special engineering equipment. Before becoming a member of this trade, he must be qualified as a Group 1 of any RCE trade. The Fitter RCE and the Mechanic RCE worked together. The Fitter could create parts in a metal workshop when necessary.

Pioneer RCE
Pioneer (S) 1
Pioneer RCE (S) 1

Around the time of the Second World War (during the war I think but I was unable to put a year on this), the role of the Pioneer RCE changed. The name was changed from Pioneer RCE to simply Pioneer. The Pioneer RCE was a tradesman's helper (an apprentice) to any RCE trade. The new role for the new Pioneer was to assist the infantry with engineer tasks. This trade was changed to a specialty in 1951 which indicates that it was a field profession. However, the infantry started their own pioneer trade in 1950.

When the infantry pioneer (see Pioneer RCIC) was created in 1950, the name of this trade was changed back to Pioneer RCE once again to differentiate between the two. The duties were not changed. This Pioneer worked at the Group 1 level only. To get to Group 2 he would remuster to Field Engineer. As the infantry had their own pioneer trade, this trade was not really required and was made obsolete in 1954. A Group 1 level was added to the Field Engineer trade to replace the Pioneer RCE.

Field Engineer (S) 2-4, changed to 1-4 in 1954

This was a new specialty in 1951. They worked at the Group 2-4 levels only. Field Engineers would be any RCE trade at the Group 1 level. When the Pioneer RCE became obsolete in 1954, a Group 1 level was added to this trade. Also in 1954, the Field Engineer was changed to a trade.

Driver Operator (S) 1

This trade was new in RCE in 1949. It had existed before that in RC SIGS. In 1951 it was changed to be a specialty. In 1954 it was changed back to being a trade.

FIRE SERVICE

Fire Fighter 1-2, changed to 1-3 in 1953

This was a new trade in 1946. He had existed previously as a non-trade soldier. The Fire Fighter was a RCE trade. A Group 3 level was added in 1953.

FORESTRY

Driver IC Tractor

This trade became obsolete in 1946 and the personnel transferred to the trade of Operator Special Engineering Equipment. See Field Engineers.

Edgerman Forestry 1-2
Edgerman

The Edgerman Forestry was shortened to simply Edgerman in 1946. The trade was reduced to nil strength in 1949.

Fitter Tractor Forestry

This trade became obsolete in 1946 and the personnel transferred to the trade of Mechanic Special Engineering Equipment. See Field Engineers.

Foreman of Works Bush Forestry 4

This trade was reduced to nil strength in 1949.

Foreman of Works Mill Forestry 4

This trade was reduced to nil strength in 1949.

Log Canter Forestry 1

The name of Log Canter Forestry was shortened to Log Canter in 1946. The trade was reduced to nil strength in 1949.

Sawdoctor
Sawfiler Forestry
Sawyer Forestry

These three trade became obsolete in 1946. See Sawyer in the Construction Engineer section.

All of the Forestry Corps trades were either obsolete or reduced to nil strength by 1949. The trades that were at nil strength were not obsolete; they were simply not required and no personnel were recruited or trained for these trades. It was thought that they would be needed again some day but most nil strength trades were never reactivated and were eventually removed from the list of army trades.

The Forestry Corps trades that were at nil strength were all obsolete by 1953. The Sawyer (not to be confused with the Sawyer Forestry) still existed in RCE but at nil strength since 1949. (See Construction Engineers).

FORTRESS COMPANY

The Fortress Company was renamed the Construction Engineer Company.

GEOMATICS

Draughtsman Cartographic
Cartographer 1-4

A Cartographer is a map maker. This trade was created by merging the Draughtsman Cartographic with the Draughtsman Lithographer and the Photowriter in 1947. (The Draughtsman Lithographer and the Photowriter were previously listed in the Printing section. The Draughtsman Cartographic was a very short-lived trade. It was created in 1945.)

Draughtsman Graphic Arts
1-3, changed to 1-4 in 1947

This trade was originally set up to work at Group 1-3 levels under the new system. The Group 4 level was added in 1947.

Photogrammetrist 1-3, changed to 2-4 in 1947

This trade was originally set up to work at the Group 1-3 levels but this was changed to be Group 2-4 in 1947.

GLIDERS

Glider Pilot (S) 2-4, changed to 3-4 in 1953

The Glider Pilot was a new specialty in 1953. He could be a member of any corps. Later in 1953 the Group 2 level was eliminated, making this a Group 3-4 trade. Glider pilots had been used by the army since the Second World War. They finally became a specialty in 1953 and they become obsolete in 1954 as being no longer required.

INFANTRY

Signaller Infantry
Driver Operator (S) 1
Infantry Signaller (S) 1-2

The Signaller Infantry was renamed Driver Operator in 1949. The Driver Operator was a trade that was common to several corps. The idea was to give all signallers the same name, regardless of corps affiliation. Details can be found in the Communication section. This trade became a specialty in 1951.

In 1954, this process was reversed and the name was changed to Infantry Signaller to match the other infantry specialties. This specialty was Group 1-2.

Pioneer RCIC (S) 1

This was a new trade in 1950. Their main job was the building and dismantling of obstacles such as ditches, tank traps and defensive positions. They also did minor bridging and demolitions. These tasks were done on a larger scale by the Field Engineer. The Pioneer RCIC performed these jobs at the infantry battalion level.

There had been pioneers in the infantry during the First World War and there were also whole units of soldiers called "Pioneer Battalions". These battalions were not part of the infantry nor the Field Engineers and were not considered to be tradesmen, which is why they are not listed in this book. They were more like carpenters and labourers than Field Engineers. The Field Engineer was not a tradesman either until after the Second World War. The infantry pioneers and the pioneer battalions were disbanded after the war. The infantry pioneers became infantrymen and the personnel from the pioneer battalions were recruited as Field Engineers.

After the infantry pioneer trade was abolished in the 1920s, each infantry battalion had bricklayers and carpenters to carry out the jobs formerly done by the pioneer. These trades are described in the Fortress and Construction Engineer sections. These carpenters and bricklayers were infantry corps and not RCE. Neither the infantry pioneer nor the pioneer battalions existed during the Second World War.

In 1950, this new trade of Pioneer RCIC was created to replace bricklayers and carpenters in the infantry.

Be careful not to confuse this trade with the Pioneer RCE which was a different trade altogether. The Pioneer RCE was not employed at pioneer duties as described above. See Part One for his job description. Pioneer duties in the RCE were carried out by the Field Engineer. (The role of the Pioneer RCE was changed during the Second World War to be similar to that of the infantry pioneer. See Field Engineers in this part of the book.)

The Pioneer RCIC could also be employed outside of an infantry unit, such as in defence of a Signal Regiment.

This trade was changed to a specialty in 1951.

Infantry Pioneer (S) 1, changed to 1-3 in 1954

In 1953 the Pioneer RCIC was renamed Infantry Pioneer to match the other infantry specialties which all had the word "infantry" in their name. This specialty operated at the Group 1 level only. In 1954 this was changed to be Group 1-3.

Infantry Anti-tank Gunner (S)
1, changed to 1-3 in 1954

This was a new specialty in 1951. Originally Group 1 only, this was changed to be Group 1-3 in 1954.

Infantry Mortarman (S) 1, changed to 1-3 in 1954

This was a new specialty in 1951. Originally Group 1 only, this was changed to be Group 1-3 in 1954.

Infantry Sniper (S) 1

This was a new specialty in 1951.

Infantry Stretcher Bearer (S) 1

This was a new specialty in 1951. There were stretcher bearers in all corps but they were non-tradesman. Only in the infantry were they made into a specialty. In 1954, this specialty was changed to a trade. It was the only trade in the infantry. All other infantrymen were either specialties or non-tradesmen.

Leading Infantryman 1, changed to 1-3 in 1954

This was a new specialty in 1951. Originally Group 1 only, this was changed to be Group 1-3 in 1954.

Medium Machine Gunner (S) 1
Infantry Machine Gunner (S) 1-3

The Medium Machine Gunner was a new specialty in 1951. In 1954 the name was changed to Infantry Machine Gunner and the group level was increased to be Group 1-3.

Infantry Driver (S) 1-2

In the infantry, the name of the Driver Mechanic Wheeled was changed to Infantry Driver to match the other infantry specialties witch all had the word "infantry" in their name. This specialty was Group 1-2 while the Driver Mechanic Wheeled worked only at the Group 1 level.

INSTRUCTORS

If you have read Part One of the book, you may remember reading about the Assistant Instructor. There was a badge for instructors with the letters "AI" on it. An Assistant Instructor was not a trade. A soldier could be an instructor and also a member of a trade such as Operator Signals. Or perhaps he was not a member of any trade, such as an artilleryman or infantryman.

In 1946 being an instructor was made a trade so that instructors could receive trades pay. A soldier who was previously employed as an instructor, would now be able to remuster (change trades) from his current trade to one of the new instructor trades. For trades such as the Operator Signals, they were already receiving trades pay, so this meant little difference to them. For instructors in the combat arms such as infantry or artillery, it meant that they would start collecting trades pay which gave them a substantial raise in pay. This was before the combat arms started collecting group pay in December 1951.

Instructor 1-4

This trade was formed in 1946 to give instructors trades pay. In 1947 it became obsolete and was replaced by all of the following instructor trades.

Instructor RCAC (S) 1-3, later 3 only.

This was a new trade in 1947; it was changed to a specialty in 1951. In 1952 the group level was changed to be Group 3 only. This specialty was changed back to a trade in 1954; it was eliminated in 1955. The Instructor RCAC taught driving and maintenance on both wheeled and tracked vehicles, tank gunnery and regimental communications. He had to be previously qualified as a Driver Mechanic Tracked Group 1, a Driver Mechanic Wheeled Group1, and either a Gunner Operator Group1 or a Driver Operator Group 1. (The Gunner Op was renamed the Gunner Sig in 1954.)

Instructor RCE (S) 1-4

This was a new trade in 1947; it was changed to a specialty in 1951. Obsolete 1953.

Instructor RC SIGS (S) 1-2

This was a new trade in 1947; it was changed to a specialty in 1951. This specialty was changed back to a trade in 1954.

Instructor RCASC (S)
1-3, changed to 2 only in 1953

This was a new trade in 1947. It was changed to a specialty in 1951 and the group level was changed to be Group 2 only in 1953. This specialty was changed back to a trade in 1954.

Instructor RCOC (S) 1-2, upgraded to 1-3 in 1949.

This was a new trade in 1947; it was changed to a specialty in 1951. The group level was changed to Group 1-3 in 1949. This specialty was changed back to a trade in 1954. They taught RCOC organization, stores, administration and staff duties. They had to be previously qualified as either a Storeman RCOC Group 1 or a Clerk Accounting RCOC Group 1.

Instructor RCAMC (S) 1-2

This was a new trade in 1947; it was changed to a specialty in 1951. This specialty was changed back to a trade in 1954.

Instructor Arctic Training (S)
1-2, changed to 2 only in 1953

This was a new trade in 1947. It was changed to a specialty in 1951 and the group level was changed to be Group 2 only. These instructors could be a member of any corps but were probably mostly infantry.

This specialty was changed back to a trade in 1954.

T Badges 1946-1955

Instructor Parachute Training (S)
1-2, changed to 2-3 in 1953
This was a new trade in 1947; it was changed to a specialty in 1951. The group level was changed to be Group 2-3 in 1953. These instructors could be a member of any corps but were mostly infantry. They were employed at Rivers, Manitoba. See Part Four for more information.
This specialty was changed back to a trade in 1954.

Instructor Airportability (S)
1-2, changed to 2 only in 1953
This was a new trade in 1947; it was changed to a specialty in 1951. This instructor could be a member of any corps. They were employed at Rivers, Manitoba. See Part Four for more information on this trade.
This specialty was changed back to a trade in 1954.

Instructor Air Supply (S)
1-2, changed to 2-3 in 1953
This was a new trade in 1947; it was changed to a specialty in 1951. This trade existed in RCE, RCASC, RCAMC, RCOC and RCEME. The group level was changed to Group 2-3 in 1953.
This specialty was changed back to a trade in 1954.

Instructor Infantry Anti-Tank (S)
1-2, changed to 2 only in 1951
This was a new trade in 1947; it was changed to a specialty in 1951. The group level was changed to be Group 2 only.
This specialty was changed back to a trade in 1954; it became obsolete in 1955.

Instructor Infantry Mortar (S)
1-2, changed to 2 only in 1951
This was a new trade in 1947; it was changed to a specialty in 1951. The group level was changed to be Group 2 only.
This specialty was changed back to a trade in 1954; it became obsolete in 1955.

Instructor Infantry Medium Machine Gun (S)
1-2, changed to 2 only in 1951
This was a new trade in 1947; it was changed to a specialty in 1951. The group level was changed to be Group 2 only.
This specialty was changed back to a trade in 1954; it became obsolete in 1955.

Instructor Infantry Carrier and Flame (S) 1-2
This was a new trade in 1947; it was changed to a specialty in 1951. It was obsolete by 1953.

Instructor Infantry Pioneer (S)
1-2, changed to 2 only in 1951
This was a new trade in 1947; it was changed to a specialty in 1951. The group level was changed to be Group 2 only. This specialty was changed back to a trade in 1954; it became obsolete in 1955. They had to be previously qualified as an Infantry Pioneer Group 1.

Instructor Physical Training (S)
1-2, changed to 2 only in 1953
Assistant Instructor Physical Training 2-3
This was a new trade in 1947. It was changed to a specialty in 1951 and the group level was changed to be Group 2 only. This instructor could be a member or any corps.
In 1954 the name was changed to Assistant Instructor Physical Training (AIPT) and the group level was changed to be Group 2-3. The AIPT was a trade; not a specialty. All instructors would eventually be renamed "Assistant Instructors".

Instructor Infantry Battalion (S) 3
This was a new trade in 1947; it was changed to a specialty in 1951. It was obsolete by 1953.

Instructor Medium Machine Gun Battalion (S) 3
This was a new trade in 1947; it was changed to a specialty in 1951. It was obsolete by 1953.

Instructor Anti-Aircraft Guns (S) 1-3
This was a new trade in 1947; it was changed to a specialty in 1951. This instructor was deleted in 1953 and included with the Instructor Anti-Aircraft. RCA.

Instructor Anti-Aircraft Radar (S) 1-3
This was a new trade in 1947; it was changed to a specialty in 1951. This instructor was deleted in 1953 and included with the Instructor Anti-Aircraft. RCA.

Instructor Anti-Aircraft (S)
4, changed to 2-4 in 1953

This was a new trade in 1947; it was changed to a specialty in 1951. This was a senior artillery instructor in several artillery subjects. The group level was changed to be Group 2-4 in 1953 because the Instructor Anti-Aircraft Guns and the Instructor Anti-Aircraft Radar were merged in with this specialty.

This specialty was changed back to a trade in 1954.

Instructor Field Artillery (S)
1-4, changed to 2-4 in 1953

This was a new trade in 1947; it was changed to a specialty in 1951. The Group 1 level was eliminated in 1953. RCA.

This specialty was changed back to a trade in 1954.

Instructor Coast Artillery Radar (S) 1-3

This was a new trade in 1947; it was changed to a specialty in 1951. This instructor was deleted in 1953 and included with the Instructor Coast Artillery. RCA.

Instructor Coast Artillery Guns (S) 1-3

This was a new trade in 1947; it was changed to a specialty in 1951. This instructor was deleted in 1953 and included with the Instructor Coast Artillery. RCA.

Instructor Coast Artillery (S)
4, changed to 2-4 in 1953
Instructor Harbour Defence

This was a new trade in 1947; it was changed to a specialty in 1951. This was a senior artillery instructor in coast artillery subjects. The group level was changed to be Group 2-4 in 1953 because the Instructor Coast Artillery Radar and the Instructor Coast Artillery Guns were merged in with this speialty.

This specialty was changed back to a trade in 1954.

In 1955 the name of this trade was changed to Instructor Harbour Defence.

Instructor RCEME (S)
1-3, changed to 2-3 in 1953

This was a new trade in 1949; it was changed to a specialty in 1951. The Group 1 level was eliminated in 1953. This specialty was changed back to a trade in 1954. They had to be previously qualified as a Group 1 in any RCEME trade.

Instructor Rifle Company (S) 1-2

This was a new trade in 1949; it was changed to a specialty in 1951. It was obsolete by 1953.

Instructor C Pro C (S) 2-3

This was a new specialty in 1953. It was changed to be a trade in 1954. They had to be previously qualified as a Service Policeman Group 1.

Instructor Driver Mechanic Tracked (S) 2

This was a new specialty in 1953. Members were RCAC, RCA and RCE. Later the same year, this instructor was eliminated in RCE. It was changed to be a trade in 1954.

Instructor Driver Mechanic Wheeled (S) 2

This was a new specialty in 1953. It existed in RCAC, RCA, RCE, RC SIGS, RCIC, C Pro C, RCASC and RCOC. It was changed to be a trade in 1954. They had to be previously qualified as a Driver Mechanic Group 1.

Instructor Regimental Communications (S) 2

This was a new specialty in 1953. It existed in RCAC, RCA, RCE, RC SIGS, RCIC and RCEME. Later the same year, this instructor was eliminated in RC SIGS; it was not required in that corps as most of its members were already trained in communications. It was changed to a trade in 1954. Due to the subject matter, this instructor had to be previously qualified as a Driver Operator Group 1.

Instructor Tank Gunnery (S) 2

This was a new specialty in 1953. It was changed to a trade in 1954; it was eliminated in 1955. It was an RCAC trade.

Senior Instructor Infantry 3

This was a new trade in 1954; however, it was eliminated by January 1955.

Senior Instructor RCASC 3

This was a new trade in 1954.

Note that most of the instructor trades were only Group 1 or 2. This would later be raised to a mini-

mum of Group 3. Keep in mind that rank was not tried to group level after 1946. It was possible that the instructor could be a Group 2 Sergeant.

All of the infantry instructor trades and the Instructor Tank Gunnery were eliminated by 1955. This was because the Leading Infantryman specialty was upgraded to Group 1-3 and the Group 3 level of this trade was expected to do the instructing. In the Armoured Corps, the new trade of Specialist RCAC had instructing as part of his job description.

INTELLIGENCE

Intelligence Specialist (S) 1-3

This was a new trade in 1946. The Intelligence Specialist was responsible for doing paperwork for an intelligence investigation. To qualify for this trade, a soldier had to first be qualified as a Clerk Administrative Group 1. This was a C Int C trade.

This trade was changed to a specialty in 1951.

Investigator Intelligence 1-2
Intelligence Investigator (S) 1-2

This was a new trade in 1946. Their job was to gather information to advise the commanding officer of enemy status or activity. This was a C Int C trade. In 1948 the Investigator Intelligence was renamed the Intelligence Investigator.

This trade was changed to a specialty in 1951.

Intelligence Investigator 1-3

In 1953, the two trades of Intelligence Specialist and Intelligence Investigator were combined into one trade. Intelligence Specialist was chosen for the name of this combined trade. In 1954 this specialty was changed back into a trade and was renamed Intelligence Investigator. Yes, you read correctly, this is not a typing error. The two combined trades were named Intelligence Specialist in 1953 and renamed Intelligence Investigator in 1954. The new trade of Intelligence Investigator was Group 1-3. The old trade by the same name was Group 1-2.

Wireless Intelligence Linguist
Linguist (S) 1-2
Intelligence Linguist (S) 1-3

The Wireless Intelligence Linguist translated foreign language radio transmissions into English.

In 1945 the Wireless Int Linguist became obsolete and was replaced by the Linguist. The job of this new trade was to translate written documents into English. The Linguist was trained by C Int C personnel but he could be a member of any corps. He had to know at least one foreign language. He was basically a translator and did not gather intelligence. This trade was changed to a specialty in 1951

At the Group 2 level, they were required to conduct interrogations in the enemy's language. They were required to have a general knowledge of organization of enemy forces, especially intelligence, police and signal units. They were also required to learn the political, geographical and historical background of enemy countries.

Most members of this trade worked from written documents only but some continued to translate information from foreign language military and civilian radio stations. These personnel were required to learn enemy radio procedure.

In 1953 the name of this specialty was changed from Linguist to Intelligence Linguist. The group level was changed to include Group 3. In spite of the name, members of this specialty could be of any corps, however, they were trained by C Int C personnel. In 1954, the Intelligence Linguist was changed back to being a trade instead of a specialty.

Plotter Air Photo (S) 1-3

This was a new specialty in 1953. There task was to gather intelligence form aerial photographs and to plot details onto aerial photographs. This was a C Int C specialty. The Plotter Air Photo was changed from a specialty to a trade in 1954.

LAUNDRY

Laundry Operator 1-2
Laundry and Bath Operator 1-2

This was a new trade in 1950. The Laundry Operator was employed in the operation of the RCOC mobile laundry and bath unit (MLBU). Once again, I want to remind the reader that you must differentiate between a trade and job. The MLBU was not new. It had been in operation during the Second

World War. What is new is that the Laundry Operator was elevated to tradesman status. Prior to 1950, he was considered to be just an ordinary soldier doing his job and not a tradesman. As a tradesman, he would start to receive trades pay. Non-tradesmen did not receive trades pay.

In 1953 the trade was renamed Laundry and Bath Operator because they operated shower facilities for the soldiers. The old name indicated that they did laundry only, which would not be correct. See this trade in Part Three for more information.

MATERIALS

Equipment Repairer
Textile Refitter
Leather and Canvas Worker 1-2
Leather and Textile Worker 1-2

The Equipment Repairer and the Textile Refitter were combined into a single trade in 1946 with the name of Leather and Canvas Worker. The Coach Trimmer and Upholsterer (see Vehicle Mechanics) were also included in this trade. In 1953 the trade was renamed Leather and Textile Worker.

Saddler
Saddle Tree Maker

The Saddler and the Saddle Tree Maker become obsolete in 1946.

Shoemaker 1-2, changed to 2-3 in 1953

The trade of Shoemaker Orthopaedic became obsolete in 1946 and his duties were added to that of the regular Shoemaker. A job description for the Shoemaker Orthopaedic can be found in the medical section.

Because of the extra duties that were added to this trade when the Shoemaker Orthopaedic became obsolete, the group level was changed from Group 1-2 to Group 2-3. (Although the Shoemaker Orthopaedic became obsolete in 1946, the Group 3 level was not added to this trade until 1953.) The Shoemaker Orthopaedic was a medical corps trade. Shoe repair at the Group 1 level would now be done by the new trade of Shoe Repairer.

Shoe Repairer 1

In 1953, when the Shoemaker trade was changed from Group 1-2 to Group 2-3, this trade was created to work at the Group 1 level. The Shoemaker performed more complicated jobs at the Group 2 level and orthopaedic work at the Group 3 level. This tradesman made simple repairs and was therefore only a Group 1 trade. The Shoe Repairer could be of any corps; the Shoemaker was an RCOC trade.

Tailor 1-2, changed to 1-3 in 1953

The group level for the Tailor was upgraded to Group 1-3 in 1953.

Workshop Supervisor

This trade became obsolete in 1946.

MEDICAL

Chiropodist 3
Obsolete 1947.

Instrument Mech Surgical 1-3

Laboratory Assistant 1-3

Laboratory Tech 4
Technical Assistant Medical 4

The Laboratory Tech was renamed Technical Assistant Medical in 1947. The trade was then reduced to nil strength in 1949.

Masseur
Physiotherapy Aide 1-3, changed to 2-3 in 1947
Physio-Occupational Therapy Aide 2-3

The Masseur was replaced by the Physiotherapy Aide in 1946. The duties changed from rubbing sore muscles to exercising injured muscles and joints. The Group 1 level was deleted in 1947. In 1953, the trade was renamed to Physio-Occupational Therapy Aide.

Nursing Orderly
Nursing Assistant 1
Medical Assistant 1-2

The Nursing Orderly was renamed the Nursing Assistant in 1946. In 1947 the trade was renamed again to Medical Assistant. A Group 2 level was added.

Senior Medical Assistant 3

This was a new trade in 1947, created to do medical work at the Group 3 level.

Master Medical Assistant 4

This was a new trade in 1947, created to do medical work at the Group 4 level. This was a very short-lived trade. It was reduced to nil strength in 1949 and became obsolete in 1950.

Operating Room Assistant 2, changed to 3 in 1947

The Operating Room Assistant was originally set up to work at the Group 2 level under the new system in 1946. This was changed to Group 3 in 1947. The Operating Room Assistant would have previously been a Medical Assistant Group 1.

Optician 2, changed to 3 in 1947
Optometrist 3, changed to 4 in 1947

The Optician and the Optometrist were both reduced to nil strength in 1949. They were deemed to be required in wartime only. In peacetime the job would be done by civilians. Soldiers are entitled to free eyeglasses as part of the medical coverage provided by the army. Civilian Opticians and Optometrists would make regular visits to the army bases to see soldiers who had an eye appointment They would test their eyes and make eyeglasses as required.

Pharmacist and Dispenser
Pharmacist 4

The name of the Pharmacist and Dispenser was shortened to Pharmacist in 1946.

Radiographer 1-4, changed to 1-3 in 1947
Master Radiographer 4

In 1946 the Mechanic X-Ray became obsolete and its personnel included with the Radiographer trade. The Radiographer was originally set up to work at the Group 1-4 levels but in 1947 the Group 4 was deleted and the new trade of Master Radiographer Group 4 was created to take its place.

Mechanic X-Ray

This trade became obsolete in 1946 and the personnel remustered to Radiographer.

Sanitary Assistant
Sanitary Inspector
Hygiene Assistant 1-3

In 1946, the Sanitary Assistant and the Sanitary Inspector were combined into a single trade called the Hygiene Assistant. Also included in this new trade is the Sanitary Dutyman which was previously a non-trade soldier. The Sanitary Dutyman was a helper to the Sanitary Assistant.

Shoemaker Orthopaedic

The Shoemaker Orthopaedic trade became obsolete in 1946. The task of making orthopaedic shoes and inserts was added to the duties of the regular Shoemaker. It was decided that this job did not have to be done by a medical corps tradesman. The Shoemaker is listed in the Materials section.

Wardmaster 2

This trade became obsolete approximately 1948. The duties were included with that of the Medical Assistant.

Workshop Foreman Field Hygiene
Obsolete 1946.

MILITARY POLICE

Service Policeman (S) 1-2

Like several other trades listed in the book for the first time, the job of military police was not new. The Canadian Military Police Corp was created in 1914 for the First World War but was disbanded in 1920. After 1920 soldiers were provided by each unit to police their own troops. Soldiers chosen for police duty were called "Regimental Police". They wore an armband with the letters "RP" on it. Personnel on police duties remained infantrymen (or whatever their trade was). Being chosen for RP duties did not change their trade to service policeman.

The Canadian Provost Corps was created in 1940 but the Service Policeman was not made a trade until 1946. Before 1946 it was just a job, not a trade. In 1953, this trade was changed to a specialty. In 1954 it changed back to a trade once again.

"Special Investigator" was a course; not a trade. Students had to be a Service Policeman Group 2 in order to attend. It qualified the Service Policeman to investigate crimes involving military personnel. It did not change their trade.

Fingerprint Classifier 1-2
Fingerprint Tech 1-3, changed to 3 only in 1953.
Fingerprint Classifier 2-3

The Fingerprint Classifier was a new trade in 1946. In 1947 the name was changed to Fingerprint

Tech and the group level was upgraded from Group 1-2 to Group 1-3.

This was originally a RCASC trade and not C Pro C. In 1953 the group level was changed from Group 1-3 to Group 3 only. The corp affiliation was changed from RCASC to C Pro C. After 1953, new recruits for this trade must be a Group 2 Service Policeman. This was the only way a Service Policeman could advance to Group 3 at that time.

In 1954 the name was changed back to the original name of Fingerprint Classifier. At this time the group level was changed to Group 2-3.

MUSICIANS

Bandsman 1-2, changed to 1-3 in 1947

The Bandsman was originally set up under the new system as Group 1-2. This was upgraded to Group 1-3 in 1947.

Bandmaster 3, changed to 4 in 1947

The Bandsman trade was created approximately 1943 or '44. Before that it was a non-trade appointment. The Bandsman and the Bandmaster were originally both members of the Bandsman trade. The Bandmaster was an appointment, not a separate trade at that time. The Bandmaster would make more money because of his higher rank but would receive the same amount of trades pay as other band members.

When the new group system was initiated in 1946, the Bandmaster was made a separate trade from the Bandsman. The Bandsman was originally set up at Group 1-2 and the Bandmaster was Group 3, giving the Bandmaster more trades pay than the Bandsman. In 1947 the Bandsman was upgraded to Group 1-3 and the Bandmaster upgraded to Group 4.

More maple leaves were added to the Bandmaster Badge. Previously there were three leaves on each side. This was increased to five. I don't have an exact date for this but it happened approximately 1946; the same year that the Bandmaster became a separate trade.

As band badges were a combination of rank and trade badge, they were not classified as trade badges. Therefore, the band members continued to wear their unique badges during this period when almost all other trades wore the "T" badges.

The Drummer, Fifer, Cymbal Player, Bugler and Trumpeter were not separate trades and are included within the Bandsman trade.

PARACHUTE TRADES

Parachute Packer
Parachute Rigger
Parachute and Safety Equipment Worker 1-3
Safety Equipment Tech 1-3
Parachute Packer 1
Parachute Rigger 2-3, changed to 1-3 in 1953

In 1946, the Parachute Packer and the Parachute Rigger were combined into a single trade called the Parachute and Safety Equipment Worker. This was a RCASC trade.

In 1949, the trade was renamed from Parachute and Safety Equipment Worker to Safety Equipment Tech. Also, at this time, the corps affiliation was changed from RCASC to RCOC.

In 1950, the trade was split into two called the Parachute Packer and the Parachute Rigger bringing things back to the way they were in 1943. There were a couple of differences between these new trades and the old ones of the same name. The old trades were RCASC; these new ones were RCOC. Also, they worked at different group levels that did not overlap as previously. See these trades in the 1942 to 1945 time period for their job descriptions.

The Parachute Rigger had to have previously serviced as a Parachute Packer and had to pass a jump course before that.

In 1953, the Parachute Packer trade was abolished and the duties incorporated into the Parachute Rigger trade. The Parachute Rigger was changed to work at Group 1-3 instead of 2-3.

Despatcher Air Supply (S) 1

This was a new RCASC specialty in 1953. In 1954 it was changed to a trade. See Part Three for a job description.

PHOTOGRAPHY

Photographer 1-4
Photographer Cinematograph 1-3

Photographer Cinematograph was renamed Photographer Cinematographic in 1954.

For Photographer Cartographic see the Printing section.

POSTAL

Postal Sorter
Postal Supervisor
Postal Clerk 1-2, changed to 1-3 about 1951

In 1946, the Postal Sorter and the Postal Supervisor were combined into a single trade called the Postal Clerk. In 1949 the Poster Clerk was reduced to nil strength. It was thought that it would be required in wartime only.

With the outbreak of the Korean War in 1951 the trade was reactivated and upgraded to include Group 3. It was previously Group 1-2. The Postal Clerk was not reduced to nil strength again after the Korean War and is still in use today.

PRINTING AND PUBLISHING

Draughtsman Lithographer
Photowriter

The Draughtsman Lithographer and the Photowriter were combined with the Draughtsman Cartographic to create the Cartographer in 1946. See Geomatics section.

Lithographer Machine Minder
Lithographer 1-4

The name of the Lithographer Machine Minder was shorted to Lithographer in 1946.

Helioworker and Litho Prover
Photographer Cartographic 1-4

In 1946 the Heliowoker and Litho Prover was replaced with the Photographer Cartographic. Their duties were not the same. The Helioworker and Litho Prover mixed ink and applied images to printing plates. (The Helioworker and the Litho Prover were once separate trades. See Part One for a detailed job description). The Photographer Cartographic applied images of maps to printing plates. This was an RCE trade. In the next part of the book this trade will be moved to the Geomatics section.

Printer Machine Minder 1-2

This trade was reduced to nil strength in 1953. The Lithographer probably had to look after the printing machinery himself after the absence of the Printer Machine Minder.

Printer Compositor 1-2

This trade was reduced to nil strength in 1949.

By 1950 the Lithographer and the Printer Machine Minder were the only two trades left in the printing section. The Lithographer was the person in charge of the printing process while the Printer Machine Minder looked after the equipment. After 1953, the Lithographer would be the only trade left in this section.

RAILWAY

Blockman 1-2
Brakeman and Shunter 1-2
Carriage and Wagon Repairer 2
Checker Number Taker 1
Cleaner Locomotive 1
Engine Driver Railway 2-3
Fireman Locomotive 1
Fitter Locomotive Diesel 1-3
Fitter Locomotive Steam 1-3
Platelayer 1-2
Traffic Operator Railway 1-3

In 1949 all of the railway trades were reduced to nil strength and by 1953 they were all obsolete.

RCEME

Draughtsman Mechanical
Draughtsman Electrical and Mechanical
1-3, changed to 1-4 in 1953

The Draughtsman Mechanical was renamed the Draughtsman Electrical and Mechanical approximately 1948. The group level of this trade was upgraded in 1953 to include Group 4.

Electrician RCEME
Electrician Control Equipment 1-3
Electrical Mechanic 1-3

In 1945 the Electrician RCEME was renamed Electrician Control Equipment. In 1949, the trade was renamed again to Electrical Mechanic. This change was made to match the Electrical Artificer (formerly the Armament Artificer Electrical).

Armament Artificer Electrical
Electrical Artificer 4

The Armament Artificer Electrical was renamed the Electrical Artificer in 1949. He would previously have been an Electrical Mechanic Group 3.

Fitter 1-3

The Fitter trade had existed in several corps. By 1950 it was obsolete in all corps except RCE and RCEME. In RCE the trade was renamed Fitter RCE. It also become obsolete in RCEME in 1953 leaving only the Fitter RCE. In RCEME the Fitter was replaced with the Gun Mechanic which can be found in the Weapons Tech section.

Grinder Precision 1-2
Obsolete 1947.

The Instrument Mechanic has been moved to the weapons section.

Instrument Mechanic Field
Instrument Mechanic Field Survey
Instrument Mechanic Heavy Anti-Aircraft
Instrument Mechanic Light Anti-Aircraft
Instrument Mechanic Typewriter and Cipher
Watchmaker

All of the above trades were new in 1943 except for the Watchmaker. In 1946 all of these trades became obsolete and their duties included with that of the Instrument Mechanic (now in the weapons section).

Watchmaker 1-3

In 1946, the Watchmaker trade became obsolete and was included with the Instrument Mechanic trade. In 1947, the Instrument Mechanic was split into two trades for the repair of electrical and optical instruments and the Watchmaker was made a separate trade once again. (The Instrument Mechanic is now in the weapons section.)

Machinist Metal 1-3
Machinist Fitter 1-3

The Machinist Metal was renamed the Machinist Fitter in 1953.

Mechanist

This trade became obsolete in 1945 and was included with the new trade of Vehicle Mechanic. See the Vehicle Tech section.

Millwright 1-3

The Millwright was reduced to nil strength in 1949. It was deemed to be required in wartime only. It became obsolete approximately 1952.

Moulder 1-2

The Moulder was reduced to nil strength in 1949. It was deemed to be required in wartime only.

Senior Projectionist 1-2
Projector Mechanic 1-2

The Senior Projectionist was renamed the Projector Mechanic in 1953.

Sheet Metal Worker 1-2

In 1949, this trade became obsolete in RCEME and the personnel were transferred to RCE.

Tinsmith
Obsolete 1946.

Toolmaker 1-3

Turner 1-2
Obsolete 1947.

Typewriter Mechanic

1-2, changed to 1-3 in 1948. 1-2 in 1953
The Typewriter Mechanic was set up in 1946 to work at the Group 1-2 levels. This was upgraded in 1948 to be Group 1-3. In 1953 it was changed back to Group 1-2 once again. Complicated repairs at the Group 3 level would be done by the Telecommunication Mechanic Line of Communication. (See Communication section.)

Welder Acetylene
Welder Gas and Electric
Welder Acetylene or Electric 1-2
Welder 1-3

In 1946 the two types of welders were combined into a single trade. Then, In 1947 the name of the Welder Acetylene or Electric was shortened to simply Welder and the Group level was changed to be Group 1-3. In 1953, the Welder become obsolete in RCE but continued to be used in RCEME.

Driver Operator (S) 1

This was a new trade in 1949. It was common to several corps including RCEME. In some corps it replaced other trades such as Signaller Artillery. There was no previous signaller in RCEME. In 1953, the Driver Operator was changed from a trade to a specialty.

Other RCEME trades can be found in the Communications, Vehicle Mechanics and Weapons Tech sections.

SUPPLY

Storeholder
Storeholder MV
Storeman Technical and Departmental
Foreman Departmental 1-3

In 1946, the four different storeman trades were replaced by nine different trades as follows:

Storeman Signals and Wireless 1-2
Storeman Engineer 1-2
Storeman Motor Transport 1-2
Storeman Weapons 1-2
Storeman Clothing and General Stores 1-2
Storeman Traffic 1-2
Storeman Airborne Equipment 1-2
Storeman Medical 1-2
Storeman Dental 1-2

The Group level of these nine trades was reduced to Group1-2.

Storeman Medical 1-3
Storeman RCOC 1-3
Storeman Supplies RCASC 1-2

In 1949, the nine different storeman trades created in 1947 were reduced to three trades. The only one that was unchanged was the Storeman Medical. All of the others had their duties combined into two trades. The Storeman RCOC worked in the base QM and RCOC warehouses. The Storeman RCASC looked after RCASC supplies. The Storeman Medical was a member of the Medical corps and was responsible for medical supplies.

Storeman Clerk 1-3

This was a new trade in 1949. The Storeman Clerk was more of an accountant than a storeman. He could be a member of any corps. This trade will be listed in the clerk section in Part Three with a detailed job description.

VEHICLE MECHANICS

Panel Beater (Body Repair Man)
Panel Beater 1-3
Body Repairman 1-3

The name of Panel Beater (Body Repair Man) was shortened to Panel Beater in 1946. In 1947 the name was changed to Body Repairman.

Coach Painter

Obsolete 1946. See Painter in Construction Engineer section.

Coach Trimmer and Upholsterer

Obsolete 1946. This trade was included with the new trade of Leather and Textile Worker. (See Materials section.)

Electrician Vehicle and Plant 2-3

Obsolete 1947.

Electroplater

Obsolete 1946.

Vehicle Mechanic MV
Vehicle Mechanic AFV
Vehicle Mechanic 2-3

In 1945, these two trades, along with the Fitter Signals and the Mechanist, were combined to create the new trade of Vehicle Mechanic. This trade was no longer split to work on tracked or wheeled vehicles.

Vehicle Mechanic Tracked
2-3, changed to 1-3 in 1950
Vehicle Mechanic Wheeled
2-3, changed to 1-3 in 1950

In 1947 this decision was reversed and the trade was split into two once again for the repair of tracked and wheeled vehicles. The Vehicle Mechanic Wheeled existed in RCAC, RCA, RCE, RCASC RC SIGS and RCEME. The Vehicle Mechanic Tracked existed in the same corps with the exception of RCASC and RC SIGS.

The Vehicle Mechanic Tracked Group 2 had to be previously qualified as a driver tracked or driver wheeled. (These were courses, not trades.) To advance to Group 3, he had to be previously qualified as a Group 2 or a Vehicle Mechanic Wheeled Group 3 or a Recovery Mechanic Group 2.

In 1950 the group level was changed to be Group 1-3. Previously, the Driver Mechanic Tracked or the Driver Mechanic Wheeled could progress to Vehicle Mechanic. After the Group 1 level was created in these trades, the Driver Mechanic was no longer eligible to become a Vehicle Mechanic.

In 1954 the Vehicle Mechanic tracked was eliminated in all corps except RCEME. The Vehicle Mechanic Wheeled was eliminated in all corps except RCEME and RCASC. The RCASC mechanics worked in the Transport Companies where a large number of trucks were required to bring the daily supplies to the army in the field. See Transport Operator in Part Three for more information.

Armament Artificer MV
Armament Artificer AFV
Armament Artificer Vehicle 4
Vehicle Artificer 4

In 1946, the Armament Artificer MV and the Armament Artificer AFV were combined into a single trade with the name of Armament Artificer Vehicle. In 1947 the name was changed to Vehicle Artificer. In order to be a Vehicle Artificer, a soldier needed the following qualifications:

- Vehicle Mechanic Tracked Group 3 + Vehicle Mechanic Wheeled Group 1 or
- Vehicle Mechanic Wheeled Group 3 or
- Recovery Mechanic Group 3 + Vehicle Mechanic Tracked Group 3

Push Cycle Repairer
Obsolete 1946.

Mechanic Tire Maintenance 1-3
Tire Repairman 2-3, changed to 1-3 in 1953

In 1947, the Mechanic Tire Maintenance was renamed Tire Repairman and the group level was changed to Group 2-3. In 1953 the group level was changed back to Group 1-3.

Wheeler 1-2
Obsolete 1947.

Recovery Mechanic 2-3

This was a new trade in 1950. His task was the recovery of broken down or stuck vehicles. He had to be previously qualified as a Vehicle Mechanic Tracked or Wheeled Group 1. The Recovery Mechanic became obsolete in 1955 and the duties included with the trades of Vehicle Mechanic Tracked and Vehicle Mechanic Wheeled.

WATER TRANSPORT

Engineer Water Transport Diesel
Engineer Water Transport Gasoline
Engineer Water Transport 2-4

The two types of Engineer Water Transport were combined into a single trade in 1946. The trade was reduced to nil strength in 1949.

Foreman Fore and Aft 1

This trade was reduced to nil strength in 1949.

Mate Water Transport 1st Class
Mate 3
Waterman Boatman
Seaman 1-3

The name of Mate Water Transport 1st Class was shortened to simply Mate in 1946. Later that year it was combined with the Waterman Boatman and renamed to Seaman. The group level was changed to Group 1-3. This trade was reduced to nil strength in 1950.

Hatch Tender 1

This trade was reduced to nil strength in 1949.

Mechanist Coxswain
Obsolete 1946.

Shipwright 1-3

This trade was reduced to nil strength in 1949.

Side-Runner

This trade was downgraded to non-tradesman status in 1946.

Skipper Water Transport 1st Class
Skipper 4
Master Seaman 4

The name of Skipper Water Transport 1st Class was shortened to simply Skipper in 1946. However, it was renamed to Master Seaman later that year. This trade was reduced to nil strength in 1949.

Winchman

This trade was downgraded to non-tradesman status in 1949.

The last trip for the Water Transport was to McNab Island in March 1948. The Water Transport was shut down and all the trades were reduced to nil strength by 1949 except for the Seaman. The Seaman probably had some duties to do in the closing process. This trade met the same fate as the others in 1950. All Water Transport Trades were obsolete by November 1953.

WEAPONS TECH

All of these Weapons Tech trades were RCEME

Armament Artificer AA 4
Armament Artificer Field 4

Armament Artificer CD 4

This trade was created in 1948 for the repair of Coast Defence Artillery.

Armament Artificer Instruments CD 4
Armament Artificer Instruments AA 4
Armament Artificer Instruments Field 4
Instrument Artificer CD 4
Instrument Artificer AA 4
Instrument Artificer Field 4

In 1947 the Armament Artificers Instruments were renamed Instrument Artificers.

Instrument Artificer HD

In 1955 the Instrument Artificer Coast Defence was renamed Instrument Artificer Harbour Defence.

Instrument Mechanic 1-3
Instrument Mechanic Electrical 1-3
Instrument Mechanic Optical 1-3

In 1947 the Instrument Mechanic was split into two trades for the repair of electrical and optical components of weapons.

Armourer 2-3, changed to 1-3 in 1953

The group level for this trade was changed in 1953 to be Group 1-3.

Small Arms Artificer 4

This trade was created in 1948 for the repair of small arms such as rifles and machine guns. Before getting into this trade, a soldier must have been an Armourer Group 3.

Gun Mechanic 1-3

The Gun Mechanic was a new trade in 1953. It was created to replace the Fitter which became obsolete in RCEME that year.

Fire Control System Tech AA 1-3
Fire Control System Artificer AA 4

These were new trades in 1955. They made repairs to various weapon systems.

WOODWORKING

Machinist Wood 2

This trade was reduced to nil strength in 1950.

Pattern Maker 1-3

Driver Trades 1930 to 1955

There were many changes to the many different driver trades during this time period. This flow chart will make it easier to follow them. The Driver Operator was a combination of driver and signaller. Note that the RCASC driver was not a separate trade at this time. They were included with Driver Mechanic Wheeled, later called Driver Mechanical Transport.

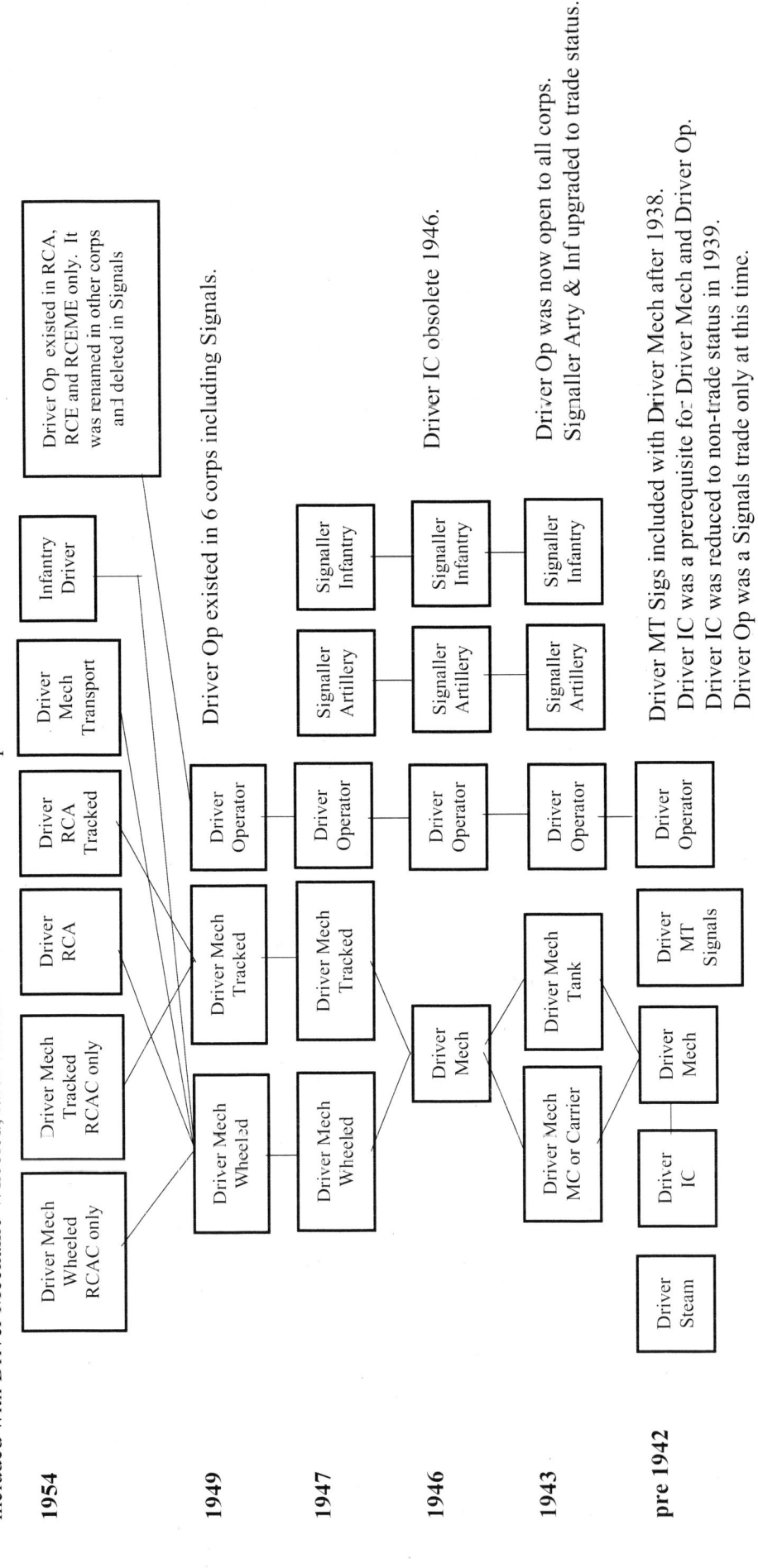

1954

| Driver Mech Wheeled RCAC only | Driver Mech Tracked RCAC only | Driver RCA | Driver RCA Tracked | Driver Mech Transport | Infantry Driver |

Driver Op existed in RCA, RCE and RCEME only. It was renamed in other corps and deleted in Signals.

1949

| Driver Mech Wheeled | Driver Mech Tracked | Driver Operator |

Driver Op existed in 6 corps including Signals.

1947

| Driver Mech Wheeled | Driver Mech Tracked | Driver Operator | Signaller Artillery | Signaller Infantry |

Driver IC obsolete 1946.

1946

| Driver Mech | Driver Operator | Signaller Artillery | Signaller Infantry |

1943

| Driver Mech MC or Carrier | Driver Mech Tank | Driver Operator | Signaller Artillery | Signaller Infantry |

Driver Op was now open to all corps. Signaller Arty & Inf upgraded to trade status.

pre 1942

| Driver Steam | Driver IC | Driver Mech | Driver MT Signals |

Driver MT Sigs included with Driver Mech after 1938. Driver IC was a prerequisite for Driver Mech and Driver Op. Driver IC was reduced to non-trade status in 1939. Driver Op was a Signals trade only at this time.

Communication Equipment Repair Trades 1947 to 1955

Another confusing area is the communication equipment repair trades. This task was shared by RCEME and RC Sigs. Sometimes the jobs overlapped and sometimes they were shifted from one corps to the other. Here is a flow chart that will help to clarify the situation.

Abbreviations: Tel = Telecommunications   Mech = Mechanic   Tech = Technician   The number is the Group level

1955

| Radar Tech 1-3 RCEME | Radio Tech 1-3 RCEME | Radar Artificer 4 RCEME | Radio Artificer 4 RCEME | Tel Mech Line of Comms 1-3 RCEME | | Radio Mech 1-3 RC Sigs | Line Mech 1-3 RC Sigs | Telegraph Mech 1-3 RC Sigs |

The 1955 changes were changes in name only.

1950

| Tel Mech Radar 1-3 RCEME | Tel Mech Field 1-3 RCEME | Tel Artificer Radar 4 RCEME | Tel Artificer Wireless 4 RCEME | Tel Mech Line of Comms 1-3 RCEME | | Radio Mech 1-3 RC Sigs | Line Mech 1-3 RC Sigs | Telegraph Mech 1-3 RC Sigs |

Radar and Group 4 radio repairs were done by RCEME only. The Telegraph Mech made repairs to teletype, cipher and telegraph equipment

1948

| Radar Mech 1-3 RCEME | Radio Mech 1-3 RCEME | Tel Artificer Radar 4 RCEME | Tel Artificer Wireless 4 RCEME | Line Mech 1-3 RCEME | | Radio Mech 1-3 RC Sigs | Line Mech 1-3 RC Sigs |

The RCEME Telecommunications trades were each split into two, one for Radio and one for Radar. Radio repairs were now being done by both RCEME and RC Sigs.

1947

| Tel Mech 1-3 RCEME | Tel Artificer 4 RCEME | | Line Mech 1-3 RCEME / Line Mech 1-3 RC Sigs |

RCEME trades   RC Sigs trades

The Line Mechanic found faults and made repairs to line terminal equipment. This job was done by both RC Sigs and RCEME. Before 1950, all other communication equipment repairs were done by RCEME. Before RCEME was formed in 1944 all equipment repairs were done by RCOC engineering branch.

This chart is continued in the communications section of part three.

The "T" Badges

Large khaki.
Group C, B and A

Large Red.
Group C, B and A

Small Khaki.
Group 1, 2, 3 and 4

Small Red.
Group 1, 2, 3 and 4

Small Brown (CWAC).
Group 1, 2, 3 and 4

Small Blue
Group 1, 2, 3 and 4

St. Edwards (queen's) Crown.

I have seen this badge only in red but according to the ordnance catalogue it was produced in both Group 3 and 4 in brown, khaki and red (but not blue). The St. Edward's crown was used only from 1952 to 1956. Most soldiers probably continued to wear the badge with the old Tudor crown during this period.

Part Three

**Trade Badges
1956 to Date**

TRADE BADGES 1956 TO DATE

In 1956, the army finally got their wish to have trade badges for every profession. Well, almost. Trades that had a lot in common were grouped together. For example, bakers, butchers and cooks all wore the same badge.

All members of the army were divided into one of three status blocks: tradesmen, specialties or assistant instructors. The definition of each block was as follows:

Tradesmen: are trained soldiers who have qualified for employment in Army duties, generally in the administrative or technical fields, which require particular skills and knowledge.

Specialties: are trained soldiers who have qualified for employment in duties in RCAC, RCA, or RCIC, generally related to the fighting roles of these corps, which require particular skills and knowledge. (The specialties began to wear trade badges at this time).

Assistant Instructors: are Warrant Officers or NCO's who are specially qualified to carry out instructional duties.

Starting in 1966, tradesmen and specialties were combined and everyone in the armed forces was deemed to have a trade. The trade of instructor became obsolete in 1968. Most trades were open to women except field units.

Each block of trades was divided into four levels of expertise called "Groups". This had been in effect since 1946 with the four "T" badges.

LEVELS

Each trade has four badges representing four levels of expertise. The badges are of the same basic design as the "T" badges, but with a different cental picture for each group of related trades in place of the letter "T".

In October 1966 there was a complete overhaul of the pay structure. The four levels of expertise remained in effect, but each trade was placed into one of seven "pay fields". The first pay field was for recruits before doing basic training, and the second pay field was for recruits after completing basic training. Pay fields three to seven were for trades pay. Pay field four would receive a higher rate of trades pay than someone in pay field three. For example, a Postal Clerk was placed in pay field three, while a Cook was placed in pay field four. A Cook of equivalent rank and training would receive more trades pay than a Postal Clerk. Each trade was placed into one of the seven pay fields based on their working conditions, knowledge required, hazards, consequences of error and other conditions. Some examples of pay field five trades would be Medical Assistant, Radio Operator, Lineman and Infantryman. Pay fields six and seven were mostly technicians.

Specialties were done away with at this time and all members of the army were considered to be tradesmen. Many trades were eliminated. Some 350 trades (in the army, navy and air force combined) were reduced to less than 100.

The four levels of expertise remained in effect within each pay field. Advancement in the new pay fields was once again tied to rank. Lateral progression had been allowed from 1946 to 1966. (See 1946 for information on lateral progression.)

Pay Level   Pay fields 3 to 7

8. WO1
7. WO2
6B S/Sgt
6A Sgt
5. Cpl
4. Pte Group 2 or 3
3. Pte Group 1
2. Pte trained
1. Pte recruit

> For example, a Private qualified Group 1, would get paid for this level of rank and training, plus extra trades pay. The amount of trades pay to be determined by the pay field in which his trade was placed. The pay level was a combination of rank and group.

The term "pay level" was changed over the years. In the 1970's it was called "Trade Qualification Level" (TQ). In the 1990's it was shortened to "Qualification Level" (QL).

This book will use the term "1-4" to mean the four levels of expertise represented by the four badges, and does not refer to the 1956, 1966 or 1990's terminology. This will enable me to use just one system to describe all the badges in the book without having to use different names for different years. For example, the 2nd level badge could be a group 2, or a TQ4, or a QL4. It simply means that this is the 2nd badge in the series of four, without regard to the name, year or colour of the badge.

ORDER LISTING

The trades are listed in alphabetical order by grouping of similar trades. This way, all the trades of one branch of the army are found together. For example, all the armoured trades are together in one grouping. Putting the names in a strict alphabetical order was not possible because many of the trades have changed their names over the years. A "gunner" was later renamed "crewman", and the badge was redesigned. Both of these trades can be found under "A" for "armoured". Some trades were renamed, but the badge was not redesigned. Other trades have been merged together or split apart. If you have difficulty finding a certain trade, the index at the back of the book should enable you to find it.

COLOURS

The badges were produced on several different background colours to match several different uniforms as follows:

Khaki	Battledress and TW 1956 to 1968
Red	Guards and Rifle Regiments (except RWR)
GreenRWR	Royal Winnipeg Rifles
none	CF 1968 to 1985
Black	DEU 1985 to present
Green	Garrison Dress 1985-1998
Blue	Optional Dress Blue uniform (private purchase)

By looking at the list of colours above, you can see that there are two main sets of badges. The first big issue in 1956, which was discontinued in 1968, and the second issue of the current badges which began in 1985.

These three dates, 1956, 1966, 1968 and 1985, are referred to often throughout the remainder of the book. Sometimes the year 1968 is replaced by the words "upon unification" or "as a result of unification". The year 1966 was a very important year. It was in 1966 that the pay and trade structure was completely changed and many trades eliminated. Some trade badges began or ended in other years, but the vast majority first appeared or disappeared in 1956, 1966, 1968 or 1985.

The unification law was passed in 1968 but the old uniforms continued in use as late as 1971. Changes due to unification were still occurring in the late 1970's. See the page on unification for details. Many of the old hat badges remained in use up to the mid 70's.

When trades badges made their re-appearance in 1985, there was one trade per badge. There was no longer a group of trades wearing the same badge as in 1956.

Reminder: If you are not familiar with military acronyms, there is a list at the back of the book.

SKILL AT ARMS

The new trade badges, in four different levels, show the skill or expertise of the wearer as well as the trade. So, although skill-at-arms badges are no longer in use, the modern trade badges, with the skill level incorporated into the badge, are in essence, both trade and skill badges combined.

MISSING BADGES

It is not possible to collect all four levels of badges for all trades. Some of them were never made. For example, Driver Mechanic Tracked existed only in levels one and two.

There were some trades for which no badge was ever produced even though the trade did exist at that level. For example, the Gun Layer trade was originally Group 1 to 2 only. It was later increased to Group 3 but no badge for that level was ever produced.

Some trades are designated "non-direct entry trades". This means that you cannot join one of these trades as a civilian. One must first join the military in another trade, and after meeting the necessary qualifications, apply for remuster to the desired trade. That is the reason that some trade badges do not exist at the first or second level.

Some trades exist only in the Khaki version as these trades were eliminated before the uniforms were changed in 1968. No trade badges were produced for the CF uniform (1968-1985). The battledress and CF uniforms were both in use during the transition period 1968 to 1971. Some new trades exist in Black and Green for the new uniforms but do not exist in khaki.

GENDER

The CWAC was abolished and female members were fully integrated into the army corps in 1964. Most trades were open to women by 1966 except field units. Today, women can join any army trade. (See Women in the Army page 218.)

UNIFICATION 1968

This book would not be a complete record of badges of the Canadian Army of the 20th century without a few words on the subject of unification. With the CF Reorganization Act of 1 February 1968, the Canadian Army, the Royal Canadian Air Force, and the Royal Canadian Navy were amalgamated into one single force. The old Army, Navy, and Air Force uniforms were replaced by a single uniform. This CF uniform was made to appear as unmilitary as possible. Unit identification was replaced by the single word "Canada". There were no shoulder epaulets. Unification was highly unpopular and many senior ranks resigned because of it, especially in the Navy. As you may have noticed in the "colours" section, the CF uniform had no trade badges.

In the mid 1980's, after a change of government, separate force uniforms made a reappearance, complete with epaulets. Trade badges came back into use, and unit shoulder identification was back in style. By the 1990's most of the traditions relating to uniforms had returned. Units whose uniforms did not conform to the rest of the army, (guards, rifle regiments, and highland regiments) had been permanently removed from the regular force order of battle.

Also as part of the unification process, the names of the army corps were replaced with "branches". For example, "The Royal Canadian Corps of Signals" became the "Communications and Electronics Branch". Although Sigs personal today technically belong to the Communications and Electronics Branch, the word "Signals" has reappeared on their shoulder titles. Even the words "Army", "Air Force", and "Navy" are being used again although these formations do not technically exist. Since 1968, they have been called the land, air, and sea elements of the Canadian Forces.

When the Corps became branches, some trades were moved around from one corps to a different branch, not necessarily the new branch that replaced their old corps. Some corps were amalgamated into a single branch. The Canadian Provost Corps and the Canadian Intelligence Corps were joined into the new Security and Intelligence Branch. They have since been changed back to two separate "branches".

Also as a result of unification, some trades disappeared altogether, others became common to all three elements, and some moved from land to air element (or some other combination of the three elements). Photo and Meteorological Techs became air element only.

The only method of unit identification that a member of the forces had, was his hat badge and collar badges. If the hat was removed, which was normally done while indoors, it became difficult to tell if a member was an infantryman or an air force cook, or any other trade of any element. One could tell by the collar badges, but they are small and not familiar to many people.

Lateral progression was no longer allowed. Progress in one's trade meant that they must also advance in rank. It was no longer possible to be a group three private. Now, someone who is good at their trade but not good enough to get promoted would not be allowed to remain in the forces. Previously, as long as a soldier did his job well, he could remain in the army, but without promotion if he did not have leadership abilities. This was implemented in 1966. The unification process actually began several years before the unification act of 1968.

In summary, technically Canada still does not have an army, navy, or air force. We have one single force. My thoughts on the subject, and those of many of my peers, can be summed up by the following observations. At the time of unification, many countries sent observers to get first hand information about this unique event. To this date, no other country has decided to follow our example. However, most of the traditions (as far as uniforms and badges and terminology are concerned) have returned. Unification had many good points. There was no reason to have three different kinds of leave passes for a member to go on holidays. Also, there was no reason to have three different recruiting centres. Elimination of triplication of paperwork, and the joining of recruiting centres and some trades was a good idea. The elimination of our traditions was not.

BADGES NOT ISSUED IN 1956

When the majority of trade badges were issued in 1956, some trades were still without a badge. Trades that did not have a badge were authorized to continue wearing the "T" badges until a badge was issued for their trade.

Trades that did not have a badge in 1956:

Airplane Tech	Badge was authorized at a later date, sometime after 1960.
Gunner	Badge was authorized at a later date, in use by Sep 1958.
Fire Fighter	The Fire Fighter, because they did not have a badge of their own, decided to wear the Field Engineer trade badge. Field Engineer and Fire Fighter were both Engineer trades. This was contrary to the orders that trades without a badge were supposed to continue wearing the "T" badge. The Fire Fighters never did get a badge of their own as the trade was abolished before a badge was made. [1]
Transport Op	The RCASC Transport Op was considered to be no different than the other drivers until it became a separate trade in 1957. The badge was first issued in 1960.
Disciplinarian	This badge was first issued sometime after 1960.
Parachute Instructor	Badge was authorized at a later date, in use by Sep 1958.
Public Relations	This badge was first issued sometime after 1960.
Air Supply	Badge was authorized at a later date, in use by Sep 1958.
Fire Safety	This badge was first issued in 1961, after the decision to make the Fire Fighter obsolete in 1960.

TRADE PROGRESSION AND NAMES

Trade progression in the 1950's and 1960's was not what it appears to be by someone looking at the trade badges today. Although most badges were produced in four levels, it does not necessarily mean that personnel in any given trade could progress from group one through to group four. Some trades were limited to certain group levels. In order to go higher, they had to change trades, usually to a closely related trade but not always. The Clerk Administrative is a good example. The clerk badge exists in all four group levels, so one would assume that a clerk could begin at group one and proceed up to group four. This is not the case. The Clerk Administrative could advance only as far as group three. The group four badge was worn by the Court Reporter. See the clerk progression chart for details. This is just one example. The same situation existed in several other trades.

Some trades changed their name at different levels. The cook badge exists in all four levels, but the cook trade, in the 1950's, existed in only group one to three. The group four badge was for a trade called "Master Cook". This is actually a trade change in name only, and is in reality a group four cook. This same situation applied to the Vehicle Tech and other trades.

COURSES

After basic training, the new recruit would then proceed to one of the many military schools to learn his trade. Upon completion of the course, he would become a group one, and would then be posted to his new unit.

Group two was usually done by "on-the-job-training" at the unit. Groups three and four meant a trip back to the corps school for another course. (This varied for some trades.)

JOB vs TRADE

Before unification, it was common for soldiers to be misemployed. This meant that a soldier could work for years at some job that was not his trade. For example, the Royal 22nd Regiment had a tailor. This soldier may have worked for many years as a tailor but he was not a tailor by trade. He was an infantryman. Tailors were members of the Royal

Canadian Ordnance Corps. Another example is the butcher. This trade was abolished about 1959 but soldiers were still employed in this job after this date. Their trade was cook, not butcher. Many people confuse jobs with trades. So keep in mind that if you hear about a soldier who was employed in a certain job, it does not necessarily mean that this was his trade.

An example of how the trades are listed is show below with explanatory notes.

INFANTRY (note 1)

Flash - just before going to press I learned that the trade numbers for all trades had recently been changed. Both old and new trade numbers are shown.

(Note 2)

Infantry Mortarman (note 3)
Khaki (note 4)   2-4 (note 5)

Fires Motars. The 1985 version of the badge remains unchanged from the original 1956 design. **(Note 6)**

1. This is the trade grouping. All similar trades will be grouped together. For example all infantry trades will be grouped together and all medical trades will be grouped together. The trades will be in alphabetical order by this grouping, not by the individual trade names.

2. There will be at least one photo of the trade badge for this trade. If there are no others, then the badge has not changed in appearance or this trade no longer exists. The text below each badge will tell you if the trade is obsolete. (There are a couple of trades for which no badge was ever made. This will be indicated.)

3. This is the name of the trade. Some trades have been renamed over the years. If this is the case you will see another line below this one with the new name and trade number. The new name may, or may not, be accompanied by a redesigned badge. The name will also include the trade number for trades after unification.

4. This is the background colour of the badge.

5. This tells you in how many levels the badge was produced. In this case the badge was not made in level one. The term "1-4" will be used for all badges, referring to the four levels of expertise. For the newer badges, this may mean QL3-6.

6. This is the job description. There will be a brief explanation of the trade and any other pertinent information. It will also tell you the corps or branch of the army to which this trade belongs. It will tell you if the trade no longer exists.

AIRCRAFT TECH   Khaki   2-4

Airplane Tech Group 2-3
Helicopter Tech Group 2-3
   The above two trades were merged together in 1963 to form the Aircraft Tech.
Aircraft Tech Group 1-3
Aircraft Artificer   Group 4 only, renamed in 1963
Master Aircraft Tech Group 4 only

This badge was not among the original trade badges issued in 1956. These were new trades in 1960. They made repairs to L19 Cessna and Nomad aeroplanes and Voyager helicopters. They performed mechanical work (excluding instruments and electrical systems), not body work. This badge is often listed as a airframe tech which is not correct. Instrumentation and electrical repairs were performed by Aircraft Instrument-Electrical Techs. The L19 was a light observation aircraft used by artillery units and armoured recce squadrons to find the enemy. These tradesmen had to be able to service, inspect, test and repair aeroplanes and helicopters. They had to lubricate the aircraft and make repairs to mechanical parts, fuel, ignition, cooling systems and external power supplies for startup.

These trades began at the Group 2 level. Potential recruits had to be a Vehicle Mechanic Wheeled or a Vehicle Mechanic Tracked. The Airplane Tech and Helicopter Tech trades merged at the Group 4 level to become the Aircraft Artificer. In 1963 the Aircraft Artificer was renamed the Master Aircraft Tech.

In 1963 The Airplane Tech and the Helicopter Tech were combined at the Group 1-3 levels to become the Aircraft Tech. After the merger, a Group 1 level was added but no badge was ever made that I was able to find. They were RCEME trades. These trades no longer exist as all aircraft repairs are now done by air element personnel. This change was made in 1966.

Aircraft Instrument-Electrical Tech   Group 1-3
Master Aircraft Instrument-Electrical Tech
Group 4 only

In 1964 two trades were added to work on the instruments and electrical systems in aircraft. Obsolete in the army in 1966.

Courtesy Dept of National Defence DGPA

AMMUNITION

Ammunition Examiner 423   Khaki   2-4
Ammunition Tech 921 (00169-01) Black   1-4
                                    Green   1-4

The Ammunition Examiner is responsible for inspection, disposal, storage, testing, repair and safe transportation of ammunition and explosives. He checks ammunition for serviceability by looking for cracks, splits, dents, corrosion and leaks. He must also make repairs to ammunition cases if necessary. If ammunition is found to be obsolete, unsafe or unserviceable he must be able to destroy it with explosives. Storage areas must be checked to ensure that they are safe and maintained at the proper temperature. The Ammunition Examiner also has to make reports on his findings and supervise work crews in the storage area. He must know the proper maintenance and storage methods for chemical weapons. He must have a good knowledge of chemistry.

The Ammunition Examiner, in 1956, began at the Group 2 level. New personnel for this trade would come from the Group 1 Clerk Accounting RCOC or Storeman RCOC trades. In 1960 the trade was renamed Ammunition Tech. Originally a RCOC trade, upon unification it became a EME trade. In 1974, the trade was moved to the Logistics Branch.

After unification it was possible to enter directly into this trade, but about 1990 it returned to a non-direct entry trade. In other words, there is no direct entry for civilians into this trade. To become an Ammunition Tech, one must join the military in some other trade, then remuster to Ammo Tech at the QL5 level. The first two badges (QL3 and QL4) are no longer used in the regular force, but are still used in the reserve force where direct entry into this trade is still possible. The new badge is similar but not exactly identical to the old battledress badge shown. The circle around the letter "A" is now in the shape of a maple leaf.

ARMOURED

Gunner-Signaller   Khaki   1-2 
This soldier operated radio equipment in a tank, in addition to being able to fire the tank's gun. In 1957 the Group 1 was eliminated. This trade became obsolete 1963 when its duties were included with the new crewman trade. [2]

                                    Khaki   1 and 2 only
Gunner-Driver Mechanic Tracked
Group 2 only, obsolete 1963.
Gunner-Driver Mechanic Wheeled
Group 2 only, obsolete 1963.
Gunner RCAC   Group 1-2   obsolete 1963

Not one of the original 1956 badges, it was first issued in 1957 or '58. It was worn by three different specialties. The Gunner fired the tank's main gun. The other specialties were a combination of two jobs, one being the Gunner, the other being a driver. The Gunner RCAC, without the driver combination, was a new specialty in 1956. This was the reason for the delay in the creation of this badge. Prior to 1956, there was no such thing as a tank gunner without the signaller or driver combination.

Crewman RCAC   Group 1-2

In Nov 1963 there was a complete reorganization of the RCAC trades and specialties. All of the former specialties were replaced with a new specialty named Crewman RCAC. A crewman was a combination of the following four specialties:
Driver Mechanic Tracked
Gunner RCAC
Signaller RCAC
Gunner-Signaller

There was now only one specialty to operate all aspects of the tank. One person would drive, one operate the radio, and one to fire the gun, but they were all of the same specialty and were interchangeable. The only other specialty in the tank would be the Crew Commander, the soldier in charge. (See Specialist RCAC.) The tank in use at this time was the centurion.

Driver Mechanic Tracked   Khaki 1 and 2 only

The job of this soldier was to drive and maintain tanks. This was a RCAC specialty. The definition of Driver Mechanic Tracked changed over the years. Before 1954 a Driver Mechanic Tracked was a tracked driver in any corps (Group 1 only). In 1954 a Driver Mechanic Tracked was changed to mean a tank driver in RCAC only (Group 1-2). Other corps that had tracked vehicles had to rename their people such as the Driver Tracked RCA in the artillery. Drivers of tracked vehicles other than tanks wore the regular drivers trade badge (see Drivers).

At the Group 2 level he had to teach and assess student drivers.

The name "driver mechanic" is misleading. This person had to do a lot of vehicle maintenance on the tanks, especially repairing tracks, but he was not as skilled as a mechanic (see "Vehicle Mechanic Tracked" under Vehicle Techs). The job of this person was to drive the tank and do maintenance but not to fire the gun. This specialty became obsolete in Nov 1963 when the jobs of driver, signaller, and gunner were all combined into one specialty called Crewman RCAC.

Khaki 1 and 2 only
Signaller RCAC   Group 1-2
Signaller-Driver Mechanic Tracked
Group 2 only
Signaller-Driver Mechanic Wheeled
Group 2 only

These three specialties were signallers and drivers of tracked and wheeled vehicles, but not tanks. The badge is not shown because it was the same badge as worn by Signallers in other Corps (See Communications for photo and explanation. A photo can also be found on the Armoured Corps trade progression chart.) The badge existed in Groups 1 to 3, but in the Armoured Corps it was used in Groups 1 and 2 only. The Signaller RCAC was better trained in communications skills than the Gunner-Signaller but was not trained in firing the tank weapons.

These trades became obsolete in Nov 1963 when the Gunner-Signaller trade became part of the new Crewman trade. After that a signaller and a gunner were interchangeable and these trades were no longer required. The Signaller RCAC and the Signaller-Driver Mechanic Tracked were remustered to crewman. The Signaller-Driver Mechanic Wheeled became part of the new Crewman Recce trade described in this section.

Driver Mechanic Wheeled   Khaki 1 only

In the Armoured Corps, the drivers of wheeled vehicles were called Driver Mechanic Wheeled to correspond with their Driver Mechanic Tracked specialty. The Driver Mechanic Wheeled was formerly a driver in any corps but in 1954 it was changed to mean a driver in RCAC only. After this, the badge was used at the Group 1 level only. It had previously been used at both the Group 1 and Group 2 levels when it was used by other corps. The trade was renamed Driver Mechanical Transport in all other corps. The badge not shown because it was the same badge as worn by drivers in other Corps. (See Drivers for photo and explanation. A photo can also be found on the Armoured Corps trade progression chart.) Although this person was well trained in vehicle maintenance, he was not a mechanic. (See Vehicle Techs.) Obsolete Nov 1963 when this job was included with the new Crewman Reconnaissance RCAC trade.

Trade Badges 1956 to Date

Specialist RCAC   Khaki   3 only
Crew Commander RCAC (1963-1966)

This soldier was a commander of a tank and crew. They could also serve as second in command of a troop of tanks and their crews. They assisted the troop commander in the control, co-ordination, fire and movement of the troop. They handled the routine administration details for the troops, such as resupply of fuel, ammo and repairs. They could assume the duties of the troop commander if necessary. Also, they were the instructors for the troop in the subjects of driving, maintenance of both wheeled and tracked vehicles, gunnery, and communications procedures and equipment. The word "they" in this case means one tank commander per tank in a troop of four tanks. The duties mentioned above would be shared by these four soldiers. To be a specialist, he had to be skilled in the trades of gunner, driver mechanic tracked and signaller. In 1963 he was renamed Crew Commander RCAC.

This trade became obsolete in 1966 and was replaced with a Group 3 level of the Crewman RCAC trade.

Crewman Reconnaissance RCAC   Black 1-4
                                  Green 1-4

This specialty was formed in Nov 1963 by the amalgamation of the following three specialties:
Driver Mech Wheeled
Signaller-Driver Mech Wheeled
Gunner-Driver Mech Wheeled

In the same way that all the tracked trades were combined into one trade called Crewman RCAC, all of the wheeled trades were combined into the Crewman Reconnaissance RCAC trade.

This soldier worked in the Reconnaissance Squadron (RECCE) of an Armoured Regiment. His job was to drive and service wheeled recce vehicles, operate communication equipment, fire heavy machine guns and use demolitions. He could progress to Crew Commander.

The job of the RECCE Squadron was to go ahead of the tanks and look for enemy. They would try to observe the enemy without engaging them. They would then advise the tanks on their best course of action.

This trade was short-lived. It was created in 1963 and become obsolete in 1966. However, the badges were created in 1985. Perhaps they were made in error or perhaps there was thought of bringing this trade back into service. The former is the more likely of the two scenarios. These badges were never worn by any member of the CF. The numbers and colours above show which badges were produced. In spite of this, the specialty existed only at the Group 1 and Group 2 levels. No badge was ever produced for the battledress uniform. The Crewman Recce was absorbed into the Crewman trade in 1966.

The Recce Squadron still exists in an armoured unit today but there is no special trade that is employed there. Members of the Recce Squadron are of the same Crewman 011 trade that are employed in the tanks. Instead of the Ferret Scout Car which is pictured on the trade badge, they now use the Coyote light armoured vehicle which is equipped with thermal imagining surveillance equipment. See Crewman 011 at the end of this section.

Assistant Instructor RCAC   Khaki   4 only
Master Crewman RCAC (1963-1966)

The Assistant Instructor RCAC was an instructor at RCAC schools. The trade called Instructor RCAC became obsolete in 1955. That was a Group 3 trade. It was replaced in 1956 with the Assistant Instructor RCAC which was a Group 4 trade. (See Instructors or trade progression chart for photo of badge.)

In 1963 the Assistant Instructor was replaced by the Master Crewman. His job was to assist with the administration and training of a tank or recce squadron. Also, he had to prepare and conduct courses for RCAC personel, as the instructor had done before him. There was no badge for this trade.

In 1966, this trade became obsolete and was replaced with a Group 4 level of the Crewman RCAC trade.

In November 1963, eleven RCAC trades were narrowed down to just four as follows:

Before Nov 1963	After Nov 1963
Driver Mech Tracked	Crewman RCAC
Gunner RCAC	"
Gunner Driver Mech Tracked	"
Signaller RCAC	"

SKILL AT ARMS

Gunner Signaller   Crewman RCAC
Signaller Driver Mech Tracked   "
Driver Mech Wheeled   Crewman Recce RCAC
Gunner Driver Mech Wheeled   "
Signaller Driver Mech Wheeled   "
Specialist RCAC   Crew Commander RCAC
Assistant Instructor RCAC   Master Crewman RCAC

In October 1966, these four trades were then combined into a single trade called Crewman RCAC. In 1968 the name was shortened to simply Crewman.

Leading Assault Trooper   Group 1 only

The job of the Leading Assault Trooper was similar to that of an infantryman except that the he was employed in an armoured unit. This specialty existed from 1953 to approximately 1964, however it was really only utilized in 1953. In 1954 the trade was reduced to nil strength. What trade badge they wore is unknown. Perhaps the trade never really existed except on paper as it was created in 1953 and had no members by 1954. They performed infantry and pioneer duties in an armoured unit. See Support Trooper under the duties of the present day Crewman.

Crewman 011 (00005-01)   Black 1-4
                                                  Green 1-4

In 1966 all of the above specialties were combined into one trade. The duties of driver, gunner, signaller, recce and crew commander have not changed. It is just that all of these jobs are now done by the members of a single trade. In fact a couple of new jobs have been added. Some positions, such as the driver, would be filled with junior tradesmen while others, such as the crew commander, would be filled by senior NCO's with many years of experience and who are at the fourth level of expertise. (Group 4 is now known as QL6.) The current jobs in an armoured unit are:

Gunner   The gunner is required to maintain the gunnery equipment and assist the other members of the crew in their duties. He could be a gunner in a Leopard tank or a Coyote light armoured vehicle which is equipped with a 25 mm gun. In the reserve forces, the gunner could also be employed in a Cougar which has a 76mm gun. This vehicle was formerly used in the regular force as a tank simulator for training. It is no longer used in the regular force.

Driver   The driver is required to drive and maintain the vehicle and assist the other members of the crew in their duties. He could be required to drive any of the unit vehicles including the Leopard tank, Coyote reconnaissance vehicle, Cougar light armoured vehicle, or any of the unit light wheeled vehicles.

Recce Crewman   This soldier is a member of the Recce Squadron (see Crewman Reconnaissance previously described), now equipped with the Coyote light armoured vehicle.

Recce Surveillance Operator   This soldier is required to maintain and operate the surveillance equipment on the Coyote reconnaissance vehicle. This vehicle is equipped with several high technology surveillance systems as follows:

1. Night Observation Device Long Range (NODLR). This is a thermal imaging device that enables the operator to see things in the dark up to 3,000 metres away. This device is currently being replaced by the Forward Looking Infa Red (FLIR) which has approximately double the range of the NODLR.
2. A video camera for creating daytime videos with a range of up to 9,995 metres.
3. A laser range finder that can tell the operator the distance of the object he is viewing.
4. Standard radar which can detect objects up to 24 kilometres away.

These observation devices can be mounted on a mast that extends above the vehicle or they can be mounted on two small tripods that sit on the ground away form the vehicle. The mast, being higher, is more efficient. On the other hand, the tripods are less noticeable if the crew does not want to be observed. They are also required to assist other members of the crew in their duties.

Trade Badges 1956 to Date

*Above:
Centurion tank
(photo LDSH Archives)*

*Left:
Coyote recce vehicle
(photo DND)*

Support Trooper — The Support Trooper was formerly known as the Assault Trooper (see Leading Assault Trooper in this section). They are still known as Assault Trooper to the members of an armoured regiment. Their combined infantry and pioneer training give them the ability to deal with obstacles or provide defence for the recce squadron. The assault troop is now equipped with the modern Bison armoured vehicle which replaced the M113 tracked armoured personnel carrier. The crew are equipped with C6 machine guns, grenade launchers, 60mm motars, M72, Carl Gustav and Eryx anti-tank weapons. They also have minefield clearing equipment and Claymore command detonated mines. For observation they have the NODLER and night vision goggles. The Eryx has a thermal image device. For pioneer duties they are equipped with chainsaws, auger and other pioneer tools. Their main functions are as follows:

1. Clear obstacles for the advance of the recce squadron.
2. Provide defence for the surveillance crews. The crew is vulnerable when the mast is deployed. If they had to provide their own defence, one or two other surveillance crews would be required, taking them away from other surveillance duties.
3. They could act as a recce crew to do route reconnaissance

Patrol Commander — This soldier would be in charge of a recce patrol using the Coyote light armoured vehicle. They have to be skilled in battle procedure, gunnery and enemy vehicle recognition. They also had to be prepared to take charge of a dismounted recce patrol. As stated earlier, these duties are all performed by members of the same trade. Jobs like this one would be filled by the more senior members.

Crew Commander — This is the soldier in charge of a tank and its crew. He also has to provide supervision and instruction for the crew and other members of the tank troop. See the job description for the old pre-unification Crew Commander above. There are four tanks in a troop. The Troop Commander, who is an officer, would also be the crew commander of the number one tank. The crew commander of the second tank would be a senior NCO. He would also be the second in command of the troop and would take over if anything happened to the troop officer. The other two crew commanders would be less experienced and lower in rank.

The single trade of Crewman could, over a period of many years, be employed at all of the above jobs.

An Armoured Regiment

An armoured regiment, when fully up to strength would consist of four tank squadrons and one recce squadron. Since the 1950's, the only armoured unit to have four squadrons was the one stationed in Germany. The others in Canada had only three squadrons. Today, an armoured unit consists of only two squadrons of tanks plus a recce squadron.

Each squadron consists of 14 tanks. There are four tanks to a troop, with three troops to a squadron, which makes a total of 12 plus two for the squadron headquarters.

It seems likely that in the near future the Canadian army will be an army without tanks. The Leopard tanks were purchased in the early 1970's and are approaching the limit of their useful lifespan. They will probably be replaced with a wheeled armoured vehicle.

The recce squadron has three troops. Each troop has seven light armoured vehicles (LAV's) used for surveillance duties, plus two LAV's for the squadron headquarters.

The assault troop has 47 personnel mounted in five Bison armoured vehicles.

The support trooper has not been used since 2002.

OTHER TRADES

The armoured corps also had the following trades before unification which were common to all corps:

Bandsman	Group 1-3
Clerk Administrative	Group 1-3
Steward	Group 1-2
Storeman Clerk	Group 1-3

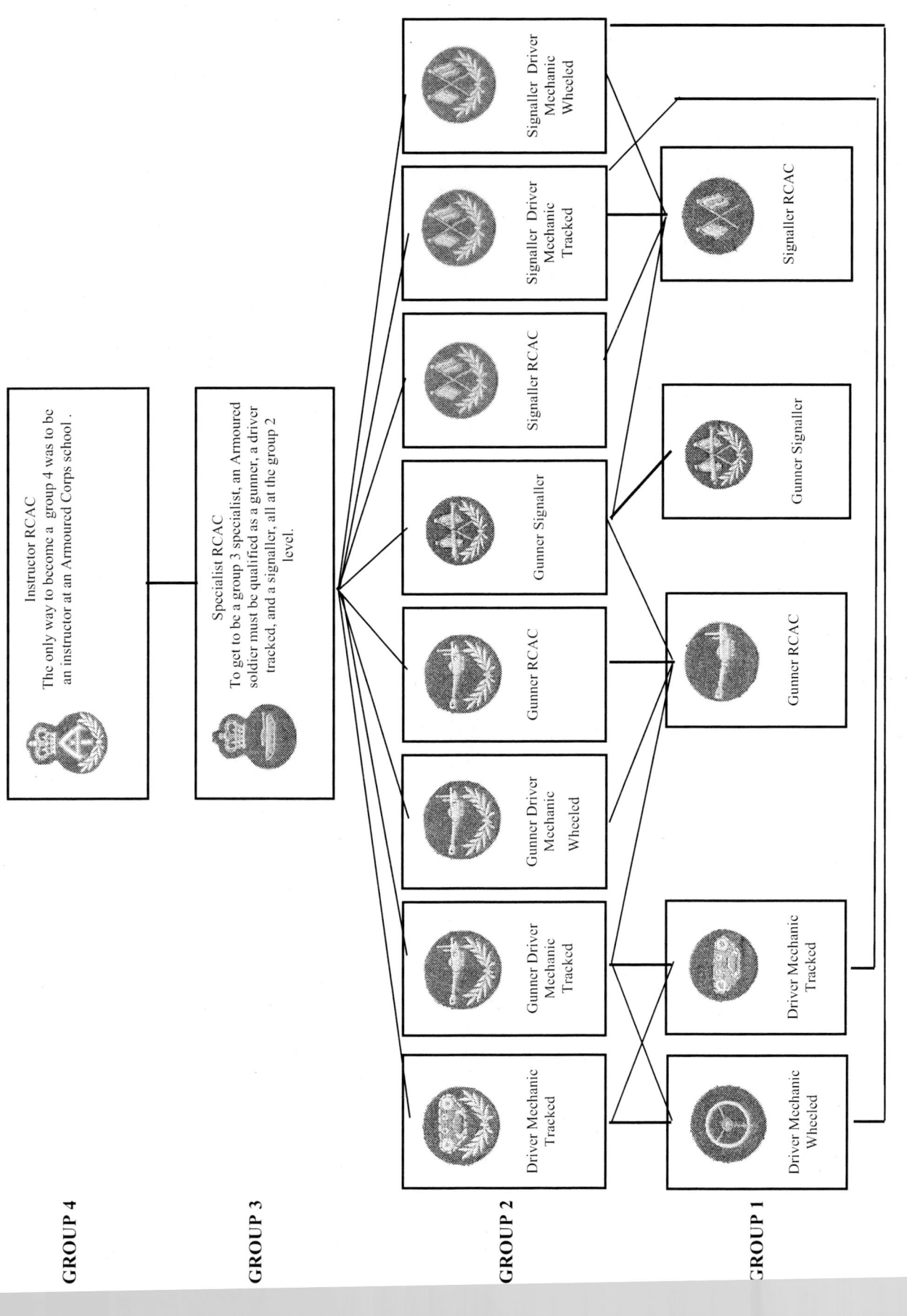

ROYAL CANADIAN ARMOURED CORPS TRADE PROGRESSION 1956-1963

GROUP 4

Instructor RCAC
The only way to become a group 4 was to be an instructor at an Armoured Corps school.

GROUP 3

Specialist RCAC
To get to be a group 3 specialist, an Armoured soldier must be qualified as a gunner, a driver tracked, and a signaller, all at the group 2 level.

GROUP 2

- Driver Mechanic Tracked
- Gunner Driver Mechanic Tracked
- Gunner Driver Mechanic Wheeled
- Gunner RCAC
- Gunner Signaller
- Signaller RCAC
- Signaller Driver Mechanic Tracked
- Signaller Driver Mechanic Wheeled

GROUP 1

- Driver Mechanic Wheeled
- Driver Mechanic Tracked
- Gunner RCAC
- Gunner Signaller
- Signaller RCAC

The RCAC also had the following trades which were common to all corps:
Bandsman 1-3, Clerk Admin 1-3, Steward 1-2, Storeman Clerk 1-3

ROYAL CANADIAN ARMOURED CORPS TRADE PROGRESSION 1963-1968

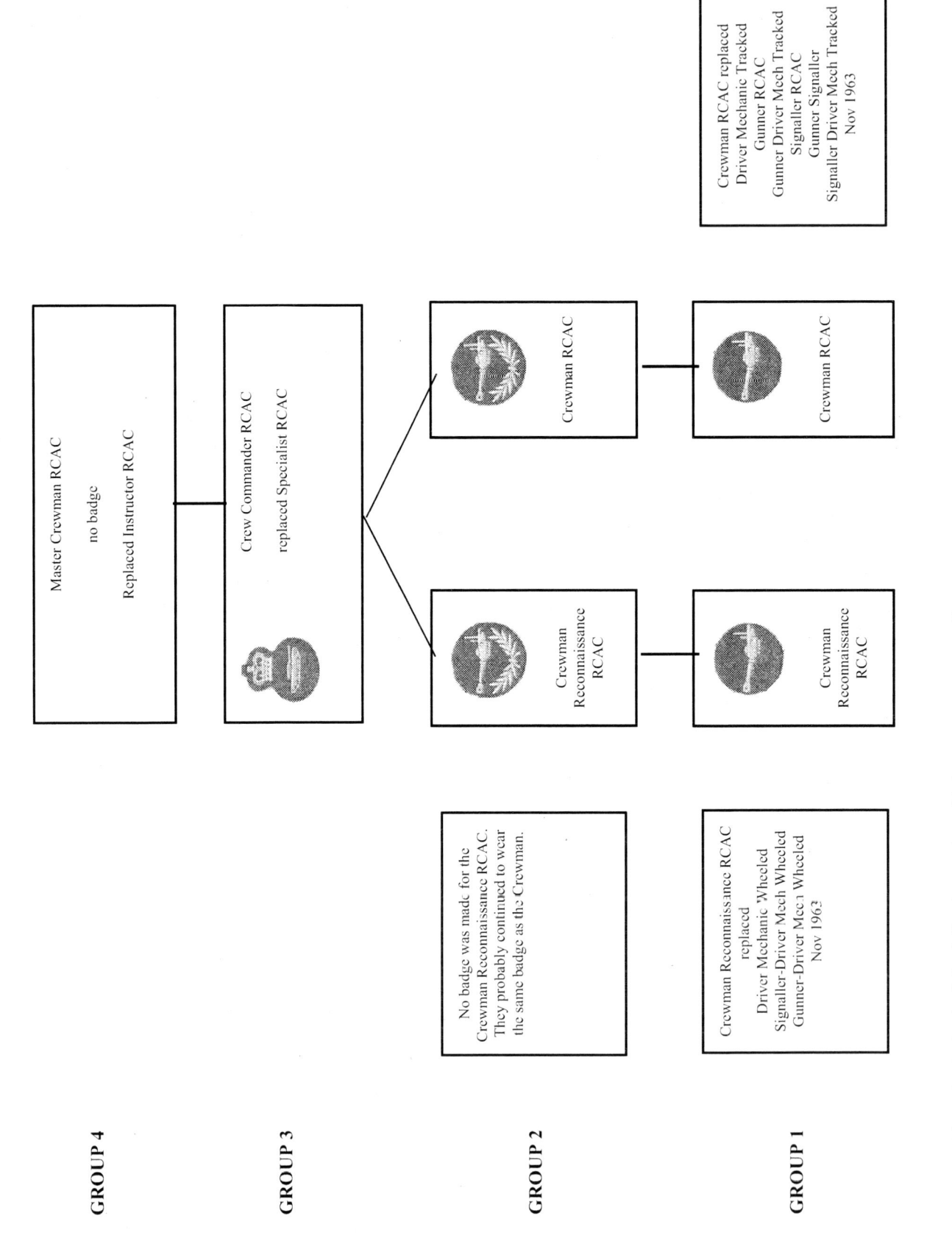

GROUP 4

Master Crewman RCAC
no badge
Replaced Instructor RCAC

GROUP 3

Crew Commander RCAC
replaced Specialist RCAC

GROUP 2

Crewman RCAC

Crewman Reconnaissance RCAC

No badge was made for the Crewman Reconnaissance RCAC. They probably continued to wear the same badge as the Crewman.

GROUP 1

Crewman RCAC

Crewman RCAC replaced
Driver Mechanic Tracked
Gunner RCAC
Gunner Driver Mech Tracked
Signaller RCAC
Gunner Signaller
Signaller Driver Mech Tracked
Nov 1963

Crewman Reconnaissance RCAC

Crewman Reconnaissance RCAC replaced
Driver Mechanic Wheeled
Signaller-Driver Mech Wheeled
Gunner-Driver Mech Wheeled
Nov 1963

The RCAC also had the following trades which were common to all corps:
Bandsman 1-3,   Clerk Admin 1-3,   Steward 1-2,   Storeman Clerk 1-3

ARTILLERY

Gun Number RCA Khaki 1-2

Prior to the Second World War, there were skill-at-arms badges for "Layers" and "Gunners". (See Part One.) The Layer operated the sighting device and laid the gun on target. The remainder of the detachment (det) were called Gunners and they performed the duties of ammunition handlers, fuse setters, loaders and gun movers. All of these skills were combined into one new specialty named "Gun Number". Each job for the seven man detachment had a number. Each "number" of the det had specific duties to bring the gun into action.

The positions of a gun detachment had been numbered for decades, but it did not become the name of a specialty, with group pay, until 1953. The letter "L" for "Layer" appears on the badge for all members of the det.

The exact duties for each member of the det varied slightly depending on which gun was in use over the years. The complete description of each job would take up many pages. A gun det consisted of six or seven members depending on the gun. Most guns used during the First and Second World Wars had a six man det, while the newer 105mm had a seven man det. Very briefly, here are the basic duties of the gun det.

The Number 1 was the Detachment Commander who would be a Sergeant. The Sergeant would be only a Group 2 as that is as far as the trade went before 1958 when the Group 3 was created, but he had the experience and rank to supervise the remainder of the det. He would respond to fire orders from the command post and control the firing of the gun and expenditure of ammunition. He would be responsible for the safe operation of the gun and would check that no live round remained in the gun after firing is complete. He would assist the other members of the det with setting up the trail legs, and would look through the bore to ensure that the field of fire is not obstructed by the crest of a hill or other obstacle. The number one position had to be skilled in the duties of all members of the det.

The Number 2 is responsible to ensure that the brake in engaged. He opens and closes the breech and sets the range on the range indicator. If the gun needs to be moved to change target, he will man the right wheel.

The Number 3 is the layer. He puts the gun on target and fires the gun. If the gun needs to be moved, he will attend to the left wheel.

On the 105mm, both number 2 and 3 are layers and number 2 would fire the gun. Number 2 would be responsible for elevation and number 3 for the bearing.

After firing, the next round of ammunition must be readily available. It is the job of the Number 4 to be standing by with the next round. When the Number 2 opens the breech, Number 4 inserts the round, and Number 2 closes the breach while Number 4 is off to fetch another round.

Number 5 looks after the supply of ammunition. When in action at least six rounds should be readily available for use. The Number 5 would place these rounds on a canvas on the ground to prevent dirt or mud from adhering to them and getting into the breech. He is responsible to set the fuses so that the round is ready to fire. He gives the next round to be fired to the Number 4. He is responsible for any unused shells to be made safe.

Number 6 works together with Number 5. He helps set the fuzes. In the days of horse drawn artillery, Numbers 5 and 6 were responsible to "unhook" and "hook in" the team of horses. Number 4 would also assist with this job.

Depending on the gun, there may be a seventh member of the det. Older guns such as the 18 pounder and the 25 pounder had a six man det. If there is a Number 7 he is responsible for any ammunition and other equipment that remain on the vehicle. He would also set up and man the machine gun if one was issued to the gun det.

The last number, whether it be number 6 or number 7, would also be the second in command of the det.

The above job descriptions will vary slightly depending on the gun in use. The 25 pounder was in use from about 1942-1957. In 1957 the army acquired the 105 and the 155. The 105 become obsolete in some units in 1968 but remained in use with other units as late as 1993. The 155 was replaced in 1968 with the M109 self propelled howitzer. [3]

25 pounder
Courtesy RCA Museum

To advance to Group 2, a Gun Number must also be qualified as a driver wheeled or tracked. It was important to be able to drive large vehicles as the guns in this era were towed, not self propelled. The specialty existed in Group 1 and 2 only. After Group 2, the Gun Number could become a Assistant Instructor. (See Artillery trade progression chart.)

An Artillery Regiment is divided into sub-units called "batteries". In the 1960's there were four batteries per regiment and eight guns per battery. Today there are only three batteries per regiment with only six guns each.

Everyone thinks of artillery as being used in the field against enemy troops. The Royal Canadian Artillery also had anti-aircraft guns for air defence and coastal guns to be used against ships. These three roles were all manned by members of the same specialty.

Normally, an artillery battery would be fired at a target that is beyond the sight of the gun det. This is called indirect fire. In the case of coastal artillery, the guns would fire at a ship that is within sight. This is called direct fire. Direct fire could also be used in the field in self defence if a battery is attacked by enemy tanks or other fighting vehicles.

Gun Number RCA Field
Group 1-2, Group 1-3 after 1963.
Gun Number RCA Anti-Aircraft
Group 1-2 (1958-1963 only)
Gun Number RCA Harbour Defence
Group 1 only (obsolete 1960)

In 1958 the Gun Number RCA specialty was split into three, with anti-aircraft artillery and harbour defence becoming separate specialties. The Gun Number RCA Anti-Aircraft Group 1 had to be skilled in the duties of a member of the det of a 90mm anti-aircraft gun or a 40mm anti-aircraft gun. To advance to Group 2, he also had to be a qualified driver. There was no Group 2 for the Gun Number RCA Harbour Defence specialty. They could become a Technical Assistant Group 2 and eventually an Assistant Instructor Group 3. The anti-aircraft artillery and harbour defence personnel continued to wear the same trade badge as the field artillery units. Harbour defence artillery became obsolete approximately 1960.

Six inch coastal artillery gun at Merry Hill Vancouver
Courtesy RCA Museum

Honest John 762mm rocket, 1961-1969

In July 1963, a Gun Number RCA Field Group 3 was created in place of the Assistant Instructor. The Gun Number RCA Group 3 was highly skilled in several complicated procedures including the duties of numbers two to ten on the 155mm howitzer and numbers two to eleven on the 762mm rocket (The 762mm "Honest John" rocket had been brought into service in 1961.) He was also skilled at sighting of guns and rockets, electrical systems on the 762mm rocket, setting fuzes and arming warheads on the 762mm rocket, construction of gun pits, serviceability of ammunition, first aid for white phosphorus burns, estimating ranges, be able to act as section commander, electrical theory, instruct other members of the det and much more. (See Artillery trade progression charts.)

No badge for the Group 3 Gun Number was ever made. Some of them would be of Warrant Officer rank and therefore did not wear trade badges. For others it was simply not an important matter. The important thing was to qualify for the group pay. Wearing the badge was nice, but not the reason for wanting advancement.

The Assistant Instructor in Field Artillery Group 3 and the Assistant Instructor in Anti-Aircraft Artillery Group 3 both became a Gun Number Field Group 3. Also in 1963, the Gun Number RCA Anti-Aircraft was incorporated back into the Gun Number RCA Field trade. The Gun Number Group 1 was then limited to employment on the 105mm howitzer. Only after progressing to Group 2 could he be employed on the 155mm gun.

Above: M109 self propelled 155mm howitzer (model A1, range 14 km) photo by author

Top Right: (model A3/4, range 18 km) Courtesy RCA Museum

Black 1-4
Green 1-4

Artilleryman 021
Artilleryman Field 021 (00008-01)

In 1968 the Artillery received the M109 self propelled 155mm howitzer. The Gun Number was renamed Artilleryman in 1966. Their duties today are to drive, maintain, and fire artillery systems, but not rockets which were no longer in use after 1969. In 1986 Anti-Aircraft Defence became a separate trade once again. Because of this, the Artilleryman was renamed Artilleryman Field. The instructor trade is obsolete (the assistant instructor in gunnery still exists but this is in addition to the four levels of expertise and not in lieu of one of them). The Artilleryman trade now exists in four levels instead of three. The trade goes from QL3 to QL6 (same as Group 1-4) since 1966, but the badge was not created until 1985.

Driver Operator
Group 1 only, renamed May 1958
Signaller RCA
Group 1-3

The Driver Operator, in addition to driving, sent messages using artillery voice procedure at the sub-unit level. When firing their guns, the artillery uses voice procedure (the format for sending messages) that is different from other units. Communications at the regimental level and higher was done by RC SIGS.

This trade originally had different names in different corps. It was called Signaller Artillery, Signaller Infantry and Operator RCAC in the armoured corps. In 1949 it was decided to give all these tradesman the same name as their jobs were identical, that is to drive and operate a radio. They were all renamed Driver Operator. The Signaller Artillery and the Driver Operator trades did not progress past Group 1. To get to Group 2 a signaller would have to become a Gun Number.

In 1958 the process was reversed. Each corps thought that it was be a good idea to give their own tradesman a unique name. In the artillery, the trade was renamed Signaller RCA. (In RCE and RCEME the name was changed to Driver Radio Operator).

The Driver Operator, and later the Signaller RCA wore the crossed flags signaller badge that was common to signallers of all corps (see communications section for details or artillery trade progression chart for a photo).

The Signaller RCA, in 1958, was authorized at the Group 1-3 levels instead of Group 1 only for its predecessor trades. The trade became obsolete in 1966.

Be careful not to confuse the Driver Operator with the Driver RCA described next. The Driver RCA was a driver only and was not qualified to operate radio equipment. The Driver Operator wore the crossed flags badge, while the Driver RCA and Driver RCA Tracked wore the steering wheel badge. The Gunner-Signaller badge is often referred to as an artillery signaller badge, which is incorrect. (See Gunner-Signaller in the armoured section.)

Driver RCA
Group 1 only in 1954,
increased to Group 1-2 in 1957.

This was a new trade in 1954 to replace the Driver Mechanic Wheeled. After 1954 Driver Mechanic Wheeled was a name for armoured corps drivers only. The trade name of Driver RCA was unique to the Artillery, but the job and badge was the same as that for drivers in other corps (see drivers). Their duties were to drive and service unit wheeled vehicles. In order to advance to Group 2, he must also be qualified as a gun number, and could be used as a Gun Number when required. Obsolete 1966.

The M548 is used to carry ammunition to the guns. Being tracked it can go wherever the M109 can go. Photo by author.

Driver RCA Tracked
Group 1 only in 1954,
increased to Group 1-2 in 1957.

This was a new trade in 1954 to replace the Driver Mechanic Tracked. The Driver Mechanic Tracked, after 1954, was an RCAC trade only and meant a "tank driver". The trade name was unique to the Artillery, but no badge is shown because the badge is the same as that for wheeled drivers. (see drivers). Their duties were to drive and service unit tracked vehicles. In order to advance to group 2, he must also be familiar with the duties of a gun number and could be used as a gun number when required. Obsolete 1966.

The above three trades became obsolete in 1966 and were combined with the duties of the Artilleryman.

Khaki 1-3
There were four trades who wore this badge:
Technical Assistant
Anti-Aircraft
Group 3 only
Technical Assistant Harbour Defence Group 2-3
Technical Assistant Field
Group 1-3
Technical Assistant Survey
Group 2 only

These trades performed roughly the same duties, but for different branches of the artillery. In 1960 the Harbour Defence trades became obsolete and in 1963 all other Technical Assistants were merged into one trade called Technical Assistant RCA.

Technical Assistant RCA   Group 1-3

His duties were
- Set up and use a director for orientation of the guns.
- Set up charts, tables and graphs to plot and determine firing data.
- Plot bearings using a map and compass.
- Read meteorological reports and determine the effect of weather on firing.
- Determine projectile fuse settings.
- Observe the shot and calculate corrections.

They were employed in a troop, battery, regimental command post or a forward observation post. Using the director he would set up the initial orientation of the guns. This would later be checked, and corrected if necessary, by the surveyor who used more accurate instruments. (See surveyor in this section.)

They could progress to either Assistant Instructor Group 4 or Master Gunner Group 4. (In 1963 the Assistant Instructor Group 4 was renamed Chief Gunnery Assistant Group 4.)

The badge depicts a plane table on a tripod. This was a 2.5 square foot board divided into 1000 metre squares. The Technical Assistant did his plotting on the plane table.

Artillery Technician

The Technical Assistant RCA was renamed in 1966 to Artillery Technician. It became obsolete shortly after unification. The duties were included with that of Artilleryman.

Artillery Operators   Khaki 1 and 2 only

The artillery operators badge was worn by six trades.

Operator Radar Anti-Aircraft
Group 1-2
Clerk Operations
Group 1 only
Operator Predictor
Group 1 only

The above three trades were employed at Anti-Aircraft units.

Operator Radar Harbour Defence
Group 1 only
Operator Fire Direction Harbour Defence Group 1

Operator Searchlight   Group 1 only

The second group of three trades were employed at harbour defence units.

The Artillery Gun Number could be employed in Field Artillery, Anti-Aircraft Artillery or Coastal Artillery (Harbour Defence). It was all the same specialty but not the same people. A Gun Number might be trained in only one of these three roles. Occasionally a Gun Number would be transferred from a field unit to an anti-aircraft or harbour defence unit but this was not the norm. At Harbour Defence and Anti-Aircraft units, the Gun Number would man the guns but people wearing this badge ran the facility. They would man the searchlights, do the necessary paperwork, operate radar equipment, and decide which targets to shoot at and which ones not to shoot at as the gunners might be untrained at ship and aircraft identification. The six inch coastal artillery gun was used for direct fire. This means that the gunner would shoot directly at the target in view. Artillery is normally fired over long distances at a target that is not visible from the weapon site. This is called indirect fire. Harbour Defence was abandoned in the 1950's and by 1960, all of the above trades were obsolete except the Operator Radar Anti-Aircraft who lasted until 1963 when the anti-aircraft trades were merged back in with the field artillery trades. The Operator Radar Anti-Aircraft is not the trade that operated counter-battery radar. (For counter-battery radar see Artillery Survey trades. For more info on the Operator Radar Anti-Aircraft see Artilleryman Air Defence.)

The badge shows a plotting table with grids and crossed lightning bolts.

Artilleryman Air Defence 022 (00009-01)
Black   1-4
Green   1-4

Originally, the Gun Numbers of Field Artillery, Anti-Aircraft Artillery and Coastal Artillery units were all members of the same trade. By 1960 coastal artillery was obsolete. All of the artillery operator trades were also obsolete except for the Operator Radar Anti-Aircraft. Radar operators had been required at both coastal artillery batteries and any location where anti-aircraft artillery was employed. When the harbour defence units closed down, the radar operators were no longer required at those locations but were still needed wherever anti-aircraft artillery was stationed.

Anti-Aircraft Artillery became a separate specialty in 1958 but was merged back in with the Field Artillery specialty in 1963, only to emerge again as a separate trade in January 1986. The name of the trade was changed from Gun Number Anti-Aircraft to Artilleryman Air Defence. Their duties are to operate and maintain air defence missiles and gun systems. In this age of advanced technology, missiles are replacing guns as the best weapon for air defence. Since about 2000 the weapons in use for air defence are ADATS (air defence and anti tank system) which is a self propelled vehicle mounted weapon with a supply of eight missiles, the Javelin which is a shoulder fired missile, and the 35mm gun.

The Operator Radar Anti-Aircraft trade no longer exists. The job is now included with the Artilleryman Air Defence trade. The anti-aircraft radar system that is now in use is called the Skyguard. An Air Defence unit will operate two 35mm guns per Skyguard.

Reminder: Combat troops before unification were referred to as "specialties". After unification they were called trades.

These photos show air defence weapons currently in use by the Canadian Armed Forces. Above is the ADATS, a self propelled weapon that carries eight missiles.
To the right is the Javelin. It can be shoulder fired with a single missile or with three missiles mounted on a post as shown.
Below is the Skyguard anti-aircraft radar system with two 35mm guns attached. Photos courtesy of 18 Air Defence Regiment.

40mm Bofors anti-aircraft (used about 1942-1985) Courtesy RCA Museum

Surveyor RCA   Khaki   1-4

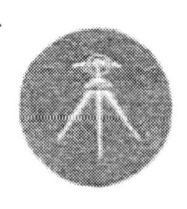

The main objective of artillery survey is to reduce the amount of ranging. Ranging means to fire the guns, observe where the shell lands and then adjusting for inaccuracy. The more accurate the survey, the less the amount of ranging that is required. Other types of surveying can be used to find enemy artillery.

The surveyor determines the map coordinates and the height above sea level for the gun position. Using a precision bearing on which the guns are pointed result in more accurate firing data. This is achieved by the accurate measurement of angles and distances and height on a specified point on a line. This is called orientation.

Group 1 in this trade was a prerequisite for Flash Spotting and Sound Ranging. There was no Group 1 in those two trades. They did survey by fixation which is the defining of a position by observation or sound, rather than the orientation methods described above. The Surveyor RCA Group 1 could also simply proceed to Surveyor RCA Group 2. The Surveyor Radar and the Operator Kine Theodolite were separate trades that progressed from Group 1 to Group 3. All Surveyor trades were combined at the Group 4 level. Obsolete 1966.

Chief Locating Assistant   Group 4 only

Approximately 1960 the Surveyor Group 4 was renamed the Chief Locating Assistant. His job was to organize and control survey parties. He also instructed in practical survey subjects including sound ranging, radar, basic electronics and counter bombardment. The prerequisites were to first be a Group 3 in any artillery survey trade. This trade was renamed in 1966. See Chief Locator below in this section.

Surveyor RCA Flash Spotting

Khaki 2 and 3 only

The purpose of flash spotting is to locate hostile batteries or mortars by cross observation of the gun flashes. For this to work properly, several observation posts must be set up over a wide area and connected by telephone or radio to a central station. After several sightings from different observation posts, using cross triangulation, the location of the target can be determined. Obsolete approximately 1958.

Surveyor RCA Radar   Khaki 1-3

Members of this trade operated M33C radar equipment to determine the position of enemy artillery and mortars. This is known as "counter-battery radar". Reduced to Groups 2-3 in Mar 1962. Obsolete 1966.

Surveyor RCA Sound Ranging

Khaki 2 and 3 only

The purpose of sound ranging is to locate hostile batteries or mortars by the report of their guns. For this to work properly, several recording posts, usually six, must be set up over a wide area and connected by wire to a central station. Each microphone must be accurately surveyed so that the exact location is known. When an enemy gun fires, the sound would arrive at each microphone at a slightly different time. Using a sound ranging recorder the operator could find the time intervals between the firing of the guns and the arrival of the sound at each microphone. (Sound spreads at 337.6 metres per second.) After collecting enough data, using triangulation, the surveyor could determine where the sound of an artillery round came from and produce the location and even calibre of the enemy guns. This information could be used to bring counter battery fire down upon the enemy position. The trade became obsolete in 1966 and the equipment was eventually replaced by radar.

Operator Kine-Theodolite   Khaki 1-3

The kine-theodolite is a photographic angle measuring device. It records the angle of shell bursts in the air. This information is then used to improve the firing of artillery at aircraft. After setting up the theodolite on a tripod, the operator would connect the cables, ensure that the instrument is level, and load the film. After photographing the air burst, and developing the film, the theodolite would give the angle in relation to the target. The operator must be able to develop his own film.

He then had to compute any necessary corrections using mathematical instruments and computations. He had to find the bearing and angle using logarithms and trigonometry. The Operator Kine-Theodolite also had to be a qualified driver, and have a sound knowledge of electricity, optics and photography. The word "kine" refers to the "kine-film" which was the type of film used in this instrument. The Surveyor RCA also used a theodolite but not in the same manner as this tradesman. Surveyors used a simpler model of theodolite only to measure vertical and horizontal angles in conjunction with field artillery. This tradesman worked with anti-aircraft artillery and used a type of theodolite that used film as its recording media. They wore the survey badge. This piece of equipment and the trade become obsolete in the early 1960's.

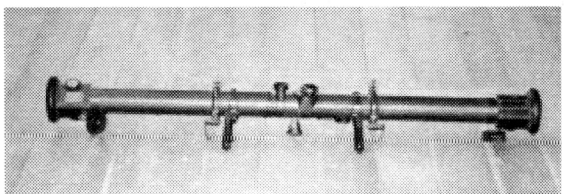

Equipment used by Artillery Survey
At the top of the page is a theodolite used by surveyor RCA and Operator Kine Theodolite. The Surveyor used it to survey positions. The Operator Kine Theodolite used a different model of this instrument that used film to measure the angle of shells in the air. (photo courtesy of the CF).

Above is a rangefinder. The operator would look into the two eyepieces in the centre and would see out through two different viewers located near the end of the instrument. Where these two different views crossed, a distance would be indicated in the viewfinder. (photograph by the author with the rangefinder provided by Allan Kerr)

Changes in 1966

There was a complete reorganization of army trades in 1966. About 350 trades in the army, navy, and air force were reduced to less than 100. This included several artillery trades. As mentioned earlier in this section, the driver and signaller trades were made obsolete and were included with the duties of the Artilleryman. The Technical Assistant was renamed Artillery Technician. This was a short-lived trade and after unification, it was also included with the duties of the Artilleryman.

Artillery Surveyor
Artillery Locator

All of the above survey trades, with the exception of those that were already obsolete, were combined in 1966 into two trades called Artillery Surveyor and Artillery Locator. The Artillery Surveyor replaced the Surveyor RCA while the Artillery Locator replaced the other artillery survey trades. Like the Artillery Technician these were very short-lived trades, lasting only from 1966 until 1968 when they too were made obsolete and the duties were included with that of the Artilleryman.

Chief Artilleryman
Chief Locator

There were a couple of exceptions to the trend of combining trades together. The Group 4 level of the Artilleryman and Artillery Surveyor became separate trades known as Chief Artilleryman and Chief Locator. The Chief Locator was not new and is described above under its old name of Chief Locating Assistant. Once again, these changes made in 1966 lasted only until unification in 1968 when they were also made obsolete and they became the Group 4 level of the Artilleryman trade.

Artillery Survey Today

All of the artillery survey trades have been obsolete since 1968. However the job still needs to be done. The modern day Artilleryman must learn the duties of the former trades of Gun Number, Driver RCA, Tech Assistant and Surveyor RCA.

Surveying is now done using the Gun Laying and Position System (GLPS pronounced glips). The GLPS is a tripod mounted positioning and orienting device that includes a gyroscope, an electronic theodolite and a rangefinder. All of the old surveyor jobs rolled into one piece of equipment, eliminating the need for more than one survey crew. For data transfer, the GLPS interfaces digitally with the command and control computers. It can provide orientation to an accuracy of 0.2 mils in a little over five minutes.

The theodolite does the same job as the theodolite of the 1950's but does not require a separate tradesman to operate it. The built in rangefinder can measure distances up to two kilometres.

The GLPS is not limited to any particular weapons system but can be used with howitzers, radar or meteorological stations.

Trade Badges 1956 to Date

Khaki 1-4

Meteorological Observer
Group 3 only
Meteorological Assistant
renamed 1957 Group 1-3, after 1961 Group 2-3
Chief Meteorological Assistant
Group 4 only
Meteorological Tech 121
Group 1-4 after 1966

This person's job was weather prediction using electronic weather observation and recording equipment. They collected data using weather balloons, barometers, barographs, thermometers, slide rules and other instruments. They had to have a knowledge of physics including air pressure, gas laws, resolution of forces, heat and the effects of meteorological conditions on the flight of an artillery round. They also required a good knowledge of logarithms and trigonometry. This was an artillery trade because weather has an effect on the firing of artillery shells. They had to have a complete understanding of meteorological conditions on the flight of an projectile.

In 1957 the Meteorological Observer was renamed the Meteorological Assistant. The group level was changed to be Group 1-3 instead of Group 3 only. However, in 1961 the Group 1 level was deleted. Also in 1961, the Chief Meteorological Assistant was added to work at the Group 4 level. See Part Two for name changes of this trade before 1957.

In 1966 the Met Assistant and the Chief Met Assistant were combined into a single trade called Meteorological Tech that worked at all four group levels.

The trade no longer exists in the army. Since unification, it is an air element trade. However, the requirement for weather prediction in the artillery still exists. Therefore a few air force Meteorological Techs, as they are now called, are posted to each artillery regiment. So if you ever see an artillery regiment on parade you will easily be able to spot the Meteorological Techs. They will be the guys in the blue uniforms. If this seems strange that we would abolish the trade in the army and then send air force tradesman to do their job in a combat unit, you must keep in mind that an artillery unit is a part of the Canadian Forces and we do not really have an army or an air force. (Read the article on "unification" if you are not familiar with this concept.)

The Locating Battery

In the 1950's and 1960's, the soldiers in the surveyor and meteorological trades were members of the locating battery. An artillery regiment was made up of four gun batteries and one locating battery. Today an artillery unit consists of three batteries only. The locating battery has been abolished. The Artilleryman trade now includes the jobs of the former surveyor trades.

Instructors

Instructors in all corps were renamed Assistant Instructors in 1955. There were three Assistant Instructors in the artillery, one for each branch:

Assistant Instructor Field Artillery
Assistant Instructor Anti-Aircraft Artillery
Assistant Instructor Harbour Defence

These trades existed only at the Group 3 and 4 levels. Their job was to instruct in all aspects of technical and administrative handling of artillery for their particular branch. The Group 3 instructor taught up to troop level. The Group 4 taught up to regimental level with the principals of tactics and locating added. These instructor trades were employed at the artillery school.

There was a badge for Assistant Instructors with the letters "AI" on it. (See instructors in this part of the book.) The badge was supposed to be for all corps but apparently it was not used in the artillery. There had been a badge for artillery instructors in the 1940's which consisted of cross gun barrels with a crown above (See artillery in part one.) This badge could no longer be used because the crown for Queen Elizabeth was different than that of the previous king. The Ordnance catalogue of 1958 shows that the old badge was still in the supply system and had not yet been replaced with a newer version.

The course instructions for the assistant instructor's course in 1955 states that the students had to learn, among many other things, the methods of instruction and the duties of the Assistant Instructor in Gunnery. The Assistant Instructor Field Artillery was a trade while the Assistant Instructor in Gunnery (AIG) was a position and not a trade. The exact difference in their duties remains unclear. The only differences that I could find was that the Assistant Instructor Field Artillery was a full time job/trade at a military school. The Assistant Instructor in Gunnery was a part time job/appointment in a field unit. The AIG might also be employed as a battery sergeant-major, or some other job depending on rank. (If you have more information on the differences between these two artillery instructors please contact the author.)

Before 1958, most Artillery trades only went as far as Group 2. The only way for a Gun Number to advance to Group 3 was to become an instructor. In July 1963 the Group 3 instructor was replaced by the Gun Number Field Group 3, leaving only the Group 4 instructor.

Chief Gunnery Assistant equal to group 4

Harbour Defence became obsolete in the late 1950's. Approximately 1960 the Assistant Instructor Field trade was renamed Chief Gunnery Assistant. They taught gun drill, gun position recce, gun placement, command post procedures and information about ammunition and other related equipment.

The Chief Gunnery Assistant was equal to a Group 4. Prerequisites were to be a Group 3 Gun Number or a Group 3 Technical Assistant. Although the name does not describe his position, his job was mainly that of instructor.

Assistant Instructor in Gunnery

Some time after 1958 the cross guns badge came back for the Assistant Instructor in Gunnery, but without the crown. It was one of only four badges authorized for wear by Warrant Officers. Another was the Master Gunner badge and the other two were RCAC badges. If worn by a Sergeant or a Staff-Sergeant, the badge would be worn on top of his rank badge on both sleeves. Mostly this badge was worn

by Warrant Officers who wore it on the right sleeve only, below the rank badge.

In 1966 all Assistant Instructors in all corps were replaced with a single trade, regardless of corps affiliation. At this time the Chief Gunnery Assistant trade became obsolete. It had existed only from approximately 1960 to 1966. The Assistant Instructor in Gunnery remained but as stated above, this was a part time appointment and not a trade, even though there was a unique badge for it. A few other jobs, drummer for example, had a unique badge but were appointments, not trades. See Instructors for more information.

Assistant Instructor of Gunnery Field

After unification, the Instructor as a trade became obsolete. However, the position of Assistant Instructor in Gunnery remains to this day. It is a position in addition to the four levels of trade badges and does not take the place of one of them as before.

The badge is still in use today, slightly modified for the new Canadian Forces uniform. The current dress regulations describe it as Assistant Instructor of Gunnery (not "in Gunnery").

Assistant Instructor of Gunnery Air Defence

This soldier instructs in anti-aircraft artillery techniques. The badge was created when Air Defence became a separate trade in 1986.

Current dress regulations show only three badges authorized for wear by Warrant Officers. All three of them are artillery badges. They are the two instructor's badges and the Master Gunner badge. (Note that the Master Gunner badge can now be worn by soldiers other than artillery. See Army Technical Warrant Officer at the end of this part of the book.) These badges are called "Army Master Occupational Badges".

Artillery Schools

Since 1871 each battery of artillery had operated their own school. The Royal Canadian School of Artillery was formed at Shilo, Manitoba in 1946. The Anti-Aircraft branch had their own school in

Picton, Ontario. This was closed in 1960 when the army decided to cease training in anti-aircraft artillery. In 1968 as a result of unification, the school in Shilo was renamed the Canadian Forces School of Artillery. In 1970 it was moved to Gagetown, New Brunswick as part of the Combat Arms School. In 1975 anti-aircraft training was resumed (at the field artillery school) because of the need for the air defence unit in Lahr, Germany. In 1979 the Combat Arms school was replaced with separate schools for artillery, armoured and infantry. The artillery portion was called the Field Artillery School. A separate air defence school was opened in Chatham, New Brunswick in 1985. In 1996 the Air Defence School moved to Gagetown and the two artillery schools were merged and named the Royal Canadian Artillery School.

Master Gunner   Khaki   equal to group 4
                         Black
                         Green

The trade of Master Gunner is an ancient one. When cannons were first brought into use with the military in the 1300's they were muzzle loaded. Gun powder had to be inserted, then tamped down to the correct density. Getting the correct amount of powder and tamping it down correctly required a highly skilled individual. If the gun powder was packed too tight or too loose, it would not fire properly or not at all. Or worse, the cannon could explode. Firing the cannon in its early days was almost as dangerous for the gunners as for the enemy. The individual who did this job became known as the Master Gunner.

Today the Master Gunner is an artillery expert in ballistics, ammunition design, weapon design, repair and calibration.

This badge took the place of the Group 4 badge. There was no Group 4 badge for the gunners prior to 1985 other than instructors and the Master Gunner. (Artillery Surveyors had a Group 4 badge.) This was one of only four trade badges authorized for wear by WO's. (Currently there are only three badges authorized for wear by WO's. The fourth was an armoured corps badge, now obsolete.)

Obtaining accuracy with artillery is a complicated matter. Many factors must be considered. The Master Gunner would be consulted on many of these factors, such as:
- Variations in muzzle velocity. Muzzle velocity is the speed of the round as it leaves the gun. This can change over time due to wear on the barrel.
- The Master Gunner must be able to calibrate the guns. This is done by comparing the firing of a gun with that of a previously set standard.
- Determine the jump, which is the vertical movement of the barrel when the gun is fired.
- Ballistic Co-efficient. A complicated procedure that would need a whole book to explain. (There is such a book.) Basically it is the measure of the shell's carrying power in flight. Shells will lose velocity at different rates depending on their power.
- The effects of temperature of the charge. The higher the temperature, the higher the muzzle velocity.
- The weight and nature of the shell. The greater the weight, the less the muzzle velocity, but more carrying power.
- Terrain must be considered when firing uphill or downhill.
- Meteorological conditions. The higher the temperature the farther the shell will travel. The effect of wind must also be considered.

The Master Gunner would be employed with a field artillery unit, or at a research centre or a staff position or at the artillery school.

The badge was, and still is, worn on the lower right sleeve below the rank badge. A Master Gunner had to be at least a WO2 which is called a Master Warrant Officer today. The gun faces to the right so that when worn on the sleeve it points to the wearer's front. There have been several slightly different varieties of this badge over the years. Two of them are shown here. The top picture is the newest type and is still in use today except for colour changes for the new uniform. It has been produced with black and green backgrounds for the DEU and Garrison dress uniforms. The lower picture is an older version, and there may be other varieties.

The course for the Master Gunner was replaced in 2003 by the Army Technical Warrant Officer course. You can find information about it at the end of this part of the book.

Before unification, Artillery Sergeants and Staff Sergeants wore the gun badge above their rank badge. This does not mean that they were Master Gunners. A Sergeant could not be a Master Gunner. It only designated the wearer as being a senior NCO in the Artillery. This was common in several corps. Engineer and Signal Sergeants also wore a corps symbol above their rank badges. A second type of gun badge was produced for this purpose with the gun pointing to the left. This was so that a badge could be worn on each sleeve and both of them would be pointing to the front. If both badges faced to the right, when worn on both sleeves, one of them would be pointing to the rear. The Master Gunner wore only the one facing to the right. These badges were also produced in metal for Sergeants and Staff Sergeants to wear on the tropical worsted (TW) uniform. See Part Five of the book for more information on corps badges worn by senior NCO's.

OTHER TRADES

The artillery also had the following trades before unification which were common to all corps:

Bandsman Group 1-3
Clerk Administrative Group 1-3
Instructor Parachute Training Group 2-3 (Most parachute instructors were infantry, but the artillery had at least one)
Steward Group 1-2
Storeman Clerk Group 1-3

ROYAL CANADIAN ARTILLERY 1953 TO 1963
(Anti-Aircraft and Harbour Defence were separate specialties from 1958 to 1963. (HD obsolete 1960))

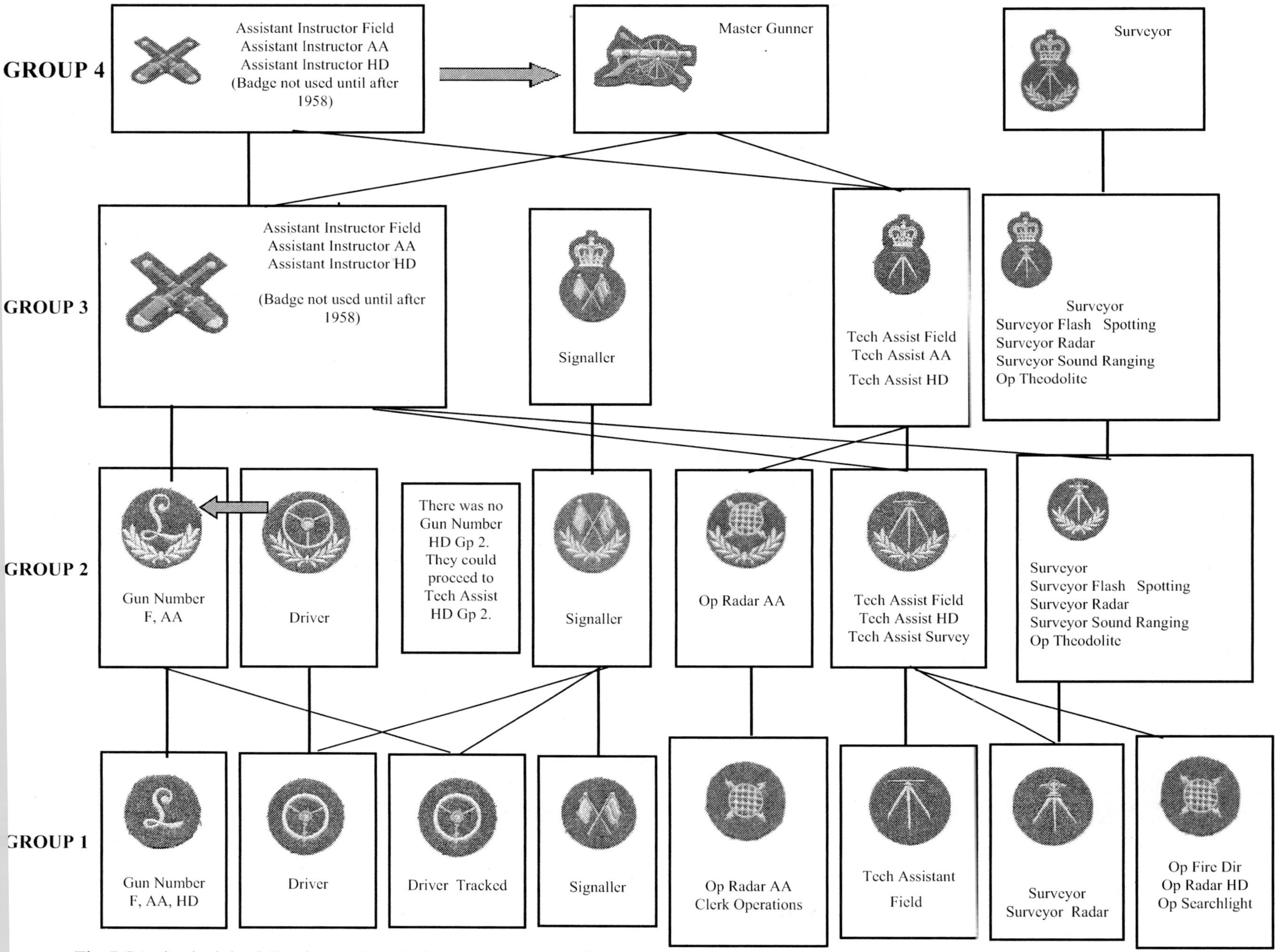

GROUP 4

- Assistant Instructor Field / Assistant Instructor AA / Assistant Instructor HD (Badge not used until after 1958)
- Master Gunner
- Surveyor

GROUP 3

- Assistant Instructor Field / Assistant Instructor AA / Assistant Instructor HD (Badge not used until after 1958)
- Signaller
- Tech Assist Field / Tech Assist AA / Tech Assist HD
- Surveyor / Surveyor Flash Spotting / Surveyor Radar / Surveyor Sound Ranging / Op Theodolite

GROUP 2

- Gun Number F, AA
- Driver
- Signaller
- Op Radar AA
- Tech Assist Field / Tech Assist HD / Tech Assist Survey
- Surveyor / Surveyor Flash Spotting / Surveyor Radar / Surveyor Sound Ranging / Op Theodolite
- There was no Gun Number HD Gp 2. They could proceed to Tech Assist HD Gp 2.

GROUP 1

- Gun Number F, AA, HD
- Driver
- Driver Tracked
- Signaller
- Op Radar AA / Clerk Operations
- Tech Assistant Field
- Surveyor / Surveyor Radar
- Op Fire Dir / Op Radar HD / Op Searchlight

The RCA also had the following trades which were common to all corps except the Meteorological Observer which was RCA only:
Bandsman 1-3,　Clerk Admin 1-3,　Instructor Para 2 only,　Meteorological Observer 1-4,　Steward 1-2,　Storeman Clerk 1-3

ROYAL CANADIAN ARTILLERY 1963 TO 1968 - Gun Number Anti-Aircraft merged back in with Gun Number Field
- Assistant Instructor Gp 3 replaced with Gun Number Gp 3
- Assistant Instructor Gp 4 replaced with Chief Gunnery Assistant
- Surveyor Gp 4 replaced by Chief Locating Assistant

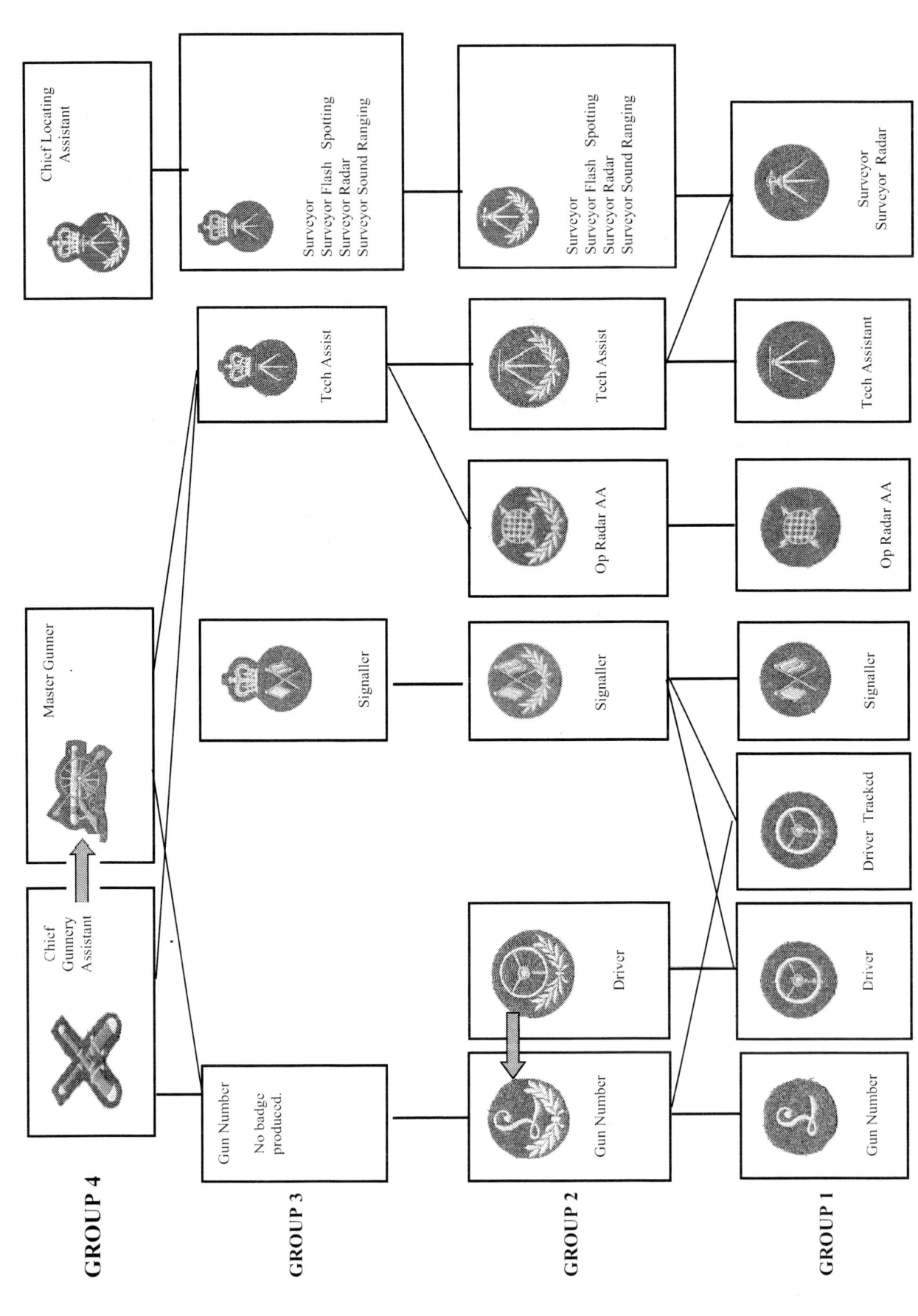

GROUP 4
- Chief Gunnery Assistant → Master Gunner
- Chief Locating Assistant

GROUP 3
- Gun Number (No badge produced.)
- Signaller
- Tech Assist
- Surveyor / Surveyor Flash Spotting / Surveyor Radar / Surveyor Sound Ranging

GROUP 2
- Driver
- Gun Number
- Signaller
- Op Radar AA
- Tech Assist
- Surveyor / Surveyor Flash Spotting / Surveyor Radar / Surveyor Sound Ranging

GROUP 1
- Gun Number
- Driver
- Driver Tracked
- Signaller
- Op Radar AA
- Tech Assistant
- Surveyor / Surveyor Radar

The RCA also had the following trades which were common to all corps except the Meteorological Observer which was RCA only:
Bandsman 1-3,   Clerk Admin 1-3,   Instructor Para 2 only,   Meteorological Observer 1-4,   Steward 1-2,   Storeman Clerk 1-3

ARTILLERY BRANCH 1985 TO 2004

Master Gunner

Instructor in Gunnery Air Defence

Instructor in Gunnery.

Note:
Anti-Aircraft, now called Air Defence, split from the Field Artillery trade for the second time in 1986.

There were no trade badges from 1968 to 1985.

LEVEL 4

LEVEL 3

LEVEL 2

LEVEL 1

CLERKS

ADMINISTRATIVE CLERKS

                Khaki   1-4
                Red   1-3

Clerk Administrative Group 1-3

The duties of the Clerk Admin were to draft and type correspondence and forms, keep records and other clerical work. They made copies of paper work using mimeograph, or hectograph machines. (See Draughtsman Signals for a description of how these machines work.) There was no "administration branch" of the army in 1956, so administrative clerks wore this trade badge together with the hat badge of the corps that they belonged to, except Sig Clerks who wore the Signals trade badge. There had been a "Corps of Military Staff Clerks" formed in 1912, but it was disbanded in 1946.

This badge existed in Groups 1-4, but this is misleading. The Clerk Admin could only advance as far as Group 3. The fourth level badge was worn by other trades (discussed in this section). Watch out for other instances of this throughout the book. Just because a badge exists in four levels does not mean that one trade wore it at all four of those levels.

In the Engineers the Clerk Admin could advance to Group 4 by remustering to Engineer Accountant after Group 1, or he could advance to Clerk Admin Group 3 but no further. (see clerks chart).

All Clerk Admin personnel were trained at the RCASC school regardless of corps affiliation.

Clerk Stenographer   Group 2-3
Stenographer   renamed 1966

The Clerk Stenographer trade became obsolete in 1945 but the army quickly had a change of mind and the trade was reinstituted in 1948. His duties were similar to the Clerk Admin except that he also had to be able to work in shorthand. The Clerk Steno had to take dictation at 80 words per minute. This trade existed at the Group 2-3 levels only. The Group 2 Clerk Steno was recruited from the Group 1 Clerk Admin. The trade existed in RCASC, RCAMC, RC SIGS, and RCOC. The name of this trade was shortened in 1966 to simply Stenographer. It became obsolete in 1968.

Court Reporter   Group 4 only

The Group 4 badge was worn by the Court Reporter. The trade existed at the Group 4 level only and drew its personnel from the ranks of the Group 3 Clerk Stenographer RCASC. This trade was RCASC only. The Court Reporter had to record the statements of witnesses and other court proceedings. They had to have a good knowledge of court procedure and be able to take notes stenographically at 140 words per minute. The Court Reporter became obsolete upon unification but was reactivated in 1999. You can read about the modern day Court Reporter further on in this section.

Operator Punched Card Machines
                Group 1-3 renamed
Punch Card Equipment Operator Group 1-3
Chief Punch Card Equipment Operator
                Group 4 only

A Punched card is a thin cardboard card about the size of a U.S. dollar bill. Holes punched in the card at certain places had certain values. An IBM 026 Keypunch Machine was used to punch the holes. An IBM 602 Calculation Punch Machine was used to multiply, add, divide and subtract the values of the holes and arrive at an answer. The answer would then be punched into the card by this same machine. A small amount of alphabetic information could be punched in as well as numbers. Other IBM machines were used for duplication and sorting of the cards, and there was one for printing text on the cards. The cards could find information such as the total cost of trades pay for a certain group level of a certain trade, or the value of all the uniforms in the stores, etc. A single typing error would ruin a card and it would have to be re-done. There was no way to correct an error if a hole was punched in the wrong place. In 1960 the name of the Operator Punched Card Machines was changed to Punch Card Equipment Operator. This tradesman could be a member of RCASC or RCOC. Remington Rand equipment was used at RCOC installations, while IBM equipment was used by RCASC.

In 1960, RCAPC personnel became eligible to join this trade. After Jan 1964 RCASC personnel were no longer permitted to be members of this trade.

A Group 4 level was added in 1960, and was named Chief Punch Card Equipment Operator. This was an RCOC trade. RCASC personnel could not advance to Group 4 because the Chief Punch Card

Equipment Op worked at RCOC installations where they used Remington Rand equipment and the RCASC personnel were trained only on the IBM equipment. The Chief Punch Card Equipment Op had to be able to produce punched cards for the operation of the UNIVAC computer. The UNIVAC was the first commercial computer and was first used in 1951 at the US Bureau of Census. That computer is now in the Smithsonian museum. It replaced tabulating machines to read the punch cards much faster. It was produced by Remington Rand and used by RCOC but not RCASC. A Clerk Accounting RCOC Group 3 could also be a potential Chief Punch Card Equipment Op. Both RCASC and RCOC Punch Card Equipment Operators had the option to switch to Computer Programmer Group 4 RCAPC. (See Computer Programmer under Financial Clerks.)

Administrative Clerk 831   Black 1-4
                                  Green 1-4

In 1966 all clerical work was combined into one trade The Clerk Administrative was renamed Administrative Clerk. The new badge is a slightly modified version of the old Public Relations badge. (See Public Relations.) An Administration Branch trade. Now obsolete. See RMS Clerk.

FINANCIAL CLERKS   Khaki 1-4

This badge was worn by several trades who were involved with financial services as follows:

Clerk Accounting RCAMC
Group 1-3
This tradesman did accounting for medical supplies. Obsolete 1964.

Clerk Accounting Pay   Group 1-3
Pay Clerk   Group 1-3

The Clerk Accounting Pay was renamed the Pay Clerk in 1958. A member of the RCAPC, they worked in pay offices. He could advance to Computer Programmer Group 4.

Clerk Accounting Institutes
                Group 1-3   renamed

Institute Bookkeeper Group 1-3

The Clerk Accounting Institutes was renamed Institute Bookkeeper in 1956. Members of the RCAPC, they did the accounting for the messes (dining halls and clubs). The Clerk Accounting Pay and the Clerk Accounting Institutes were formerly members of the same trade called Clerk Accounting RCAPC. It split into these two trades in 1949.

Clerk Accounting RCOC   Group 1-3

Members of this trade had to maintain accounts and control stock in QM stores and ordnance depots.

Clerk RCASC   Group 1-3

This trade used to be called the Clerk Accounting RCASC but in this corps the word "accounting" was dropped from the trade name. They kept detailed accounting records at supply depots, movement sections and POL sections.

Engineer Accountant   Group 2-4

There was no Group 1 in this trade. Members were recruited from the Group 1 Clerk Admin (RCE only). The Storeman Clerk (RCE only) could also become an Engineer Accountant. The Clerk Admin and the Storeman Clerk (RCE only) Group 2 could advance to Engineer Accountant Group 3. After unification this trade was called the CE Procedures Tech (see CE section for job description).

Storeman Clerk   Group 1-3

In spite of the name, this person was an accountant, not a storeman. This trade was concerned with the value of items such as spare parts in workshops, etc. In the Engineers, the Storeman Clerk had the option to switch to Engineer Accountant. This trade became obsolete in 1963. The personnel had to remuster to Clerk Accounting RCASC or RCOC or Engineer Accountant or Dental Storeman. The Storeman Clerk could be of any corps. (See "Supply" for storeman trades.)

Steward   Group 1-2

This person worked in the messes. He had to account for the cash and inventory (liquor) behind the bars. He also had many other duties. The Steward could be a member of any corps. See Steward further in this section for more information.

SKILL AT ARMS

Computer Programmer   Group 4 only

Yes, they had computers in the 1950's. The IBM 650 came into use with governments and universities in 1954. The Canadian army began using it in 1960. The IBM 650 computer was a room-sized machine that would be considered primitive by today's standards. The computer in my home that this book was written on is thousands of times more powerful than the 650. The room had to be kept cool and a crew of several people were needed to maintain the equipment.

The IBM 650. Photo courtesy of IBM

This was definitely not a desktop computer! Everything you see in the photo above are all parts of one computer. On the left are four Magnetic Tape Units for the storage of data. In the centre, with the chair in front, is the console where the operator controls the machine. The large parts at the centre rear are the central unit which is the brains of the machine and is today known as the Central Processing Unit (CPU) and can fit in the palm of your hand, the power supply and the storage unit. The CPU was almost 2 metres long and two metres tall by one metre wide and weighed a ton or so. The power supply was a similar size. The storage unit was for temporary storage of data until permanently stored on the magnetic tape reels. This unit could store up to 20,000 digits, or about 2,000 words. On the right is the read and punch unit where information was fed into the machine or collected from the machine by means of data recorded on punched cards. (See Punched Card Equipment Operator under administrative clerks.) The computer could read 200 cards per minute and punch out 100 cards per minute.

The IBM 650 was rented, not purchased, from IBM for $3,200 dollars (U.S.) per month. This was much more than the price of a new car in the 1950's. The machine was not operated by the Computer Programmer. The Punch Card Equipment Operator did that (RCAPC personel only as the RCOC used the UNIVAC computer made by Remington Rand). The Computer Programmer wrote the code (software), in machine language, that gave the computer its instructions. He was a member of the RCAPC. They were recruited from the Clerk Accounting Pay trade Group 3 or the Punch Card Equipment Operator Group 3 (RCAPC only).

The badge existed in Groups 1-4, but most clerk trades could only advance to the Group 3 level. Only the Engineer Accountant and the Computer Programmer wore the badge at the Group 4 level.

Data Processor

In 1966, all of the computer related trades mentioned above were combined into a single trade called Data Processor. This trade existed only from 1966 to 1968. After unification, it became obsolete and all computer duties became a speciality course for the Administrative Clerk until the personal computer came into use in the 1980s. I have not been able to find any information on this short lived trade as to their group levels or badge.

          Black   1-4
          Green 1-4

Finance Clerk
Accounting and Finance Clerk
Finance Clerk 841

In 1966, the many accounting trades were narrowed down to just one. In 1968 the Finance Clerk was renamed to Accounting and Finance Clerk, a member of the Logistics Branch. It was later renamed back to Finance Clerk. The badge was issued in 1985. Pay Clerks (Clerk Accounting RCAPC) were originally part of RCOC until they branched off to form the RCAPC in 1907. Ironically, in 1974, they became members of the Logistics Branch which is the successor to RCOC.

          Black   1-4

Resource Management
Support Clerk 836 (00298-01)

In Jan 1998, the Administrative Clerk, the Financial Clerk and the Construction Engineer Procedures Tech (CEP Tech) were combined to create the RMS Clerk.

As there were seven trades in the Logistics Branch and Admin Branch consisted only of the Admin Clerk, it was decided that this new combined trade would be a Logistics trade. The Administration Branch was dissolved.

The work done by the former CEP Tech is now done by RMS Techs and civilians in base construction units. (See CEP Tech in the CE section.)

Court Reporter 833 (00322-01)   No badge

Upon unification, the Court Reporter ceased to exist as a separate trade. It became a specialty of the Admin Clerk. After the Admin Clerk and the Finance Clerk were merged into a single trade in 1998, it was decided that the Court Reporter should become a separate trade once again. This happened in Sep. 1999.

They record audio and typed transcriptions of the proceedings of courts martial. They also provide legal clerk assistance and legal research and keep track of exhibits. Their recordings become an unbiased official account of the court proceedings. They must have excellent language comprehension with above average spelling and grammar.

The working rank of the Court Reporter is Warrant Officer, therefore there is no direct entry into this trade. Like the Court Reporter of old who drew their members from the Group 3 Clerk Stenographer, today the new members of this trade come from the RMS trade. A potential Court Reporter must be a WO or Sergeant with a minimum of two years in rank. While undergoing training, the new member would continue to wear the RMS trade badge. Upon successful completion of the training, the Sgt would be promoted to WO and would no longer wear a trade badge. Therefore trade badges for this trade are not required. With only 8 persons in this trade, it is the smallest in the army. The Court Reporter is a member of the Legal Branch, which had formally consisted only of lawyers which are of officer rank. (See RMS Clerk.)

Steward 862   Badges ?

Prior to unification the Steward wore the Clerk Accounting badge. The duties of the Steward were:
- Hygiene and sanitation of food handling
- Formal and informal dining room service
- Bar tending
- Accounting for bar stock
- Short order cooking
- Basic merchandising
- Fire safety
- Security of the building
- Etiquette and protocol
- Maintenance of equipment and facilities

In short, the Steward operated the messes. The mess is the soldiers' social club where they gather for informal drinks after work or a formal dinner or a social event such as a dance. This was a new trade in 1954. Before that the job was done by any soldier who happened to get picked for the task.

Before unification, this trade could advance only as far as Group 2. There was no possibility to advance further without remustering to another trade. Stewards were used in most corps. After unification, they became members of the Administration branch and could advance from TQ3 to TQ6 (equal to Groups 1-4 or QL3-6). The trade was later transferred to the Logistics Branch.

The Clerk Accounting Institutes did the accounting in the messes for items other than bar stock, such as furniture, dishes, etc.

In 1999 the Steward was abolished in the army and the job taken over by civilians. The trade still exists in the Navy. The Clerk Accounting Institutes' job is also now done by civilians.

I have not been able to find an example of this badge. Perhaps it did not get past the design stage and was never produced.

The Administration Branch

Originally, the Administration Branch consisted of the following trades:

Administrative Clerk
Cook
Draughtsman
Physical Training Instructor
Postal Clerk
Steward
CE Procedures Tech

Over the years, most of these trades were removed from the Administration Branch until, by 1978, only the Admin Clerk and the Postal Clerk, remained. Here is where the others went:

CE Procedures
Tech   moved to the Engineering Branch
Draughtsman   moved to the Engineering Branch
PTI   formed its own Branch.
Steward   moved to the Logistics Branch
Cook   moved to the Logistics Branch

In 1986 the Postal Clerks formed their own branch, leaving only the Administration Clerk in the Admin Branch.

In 1998 the Administration Clerk and the Financial Clerk were combined to create the RMS Clerk. This new trade was part of the Logistics Branch. The Administration Branch was dissolved.

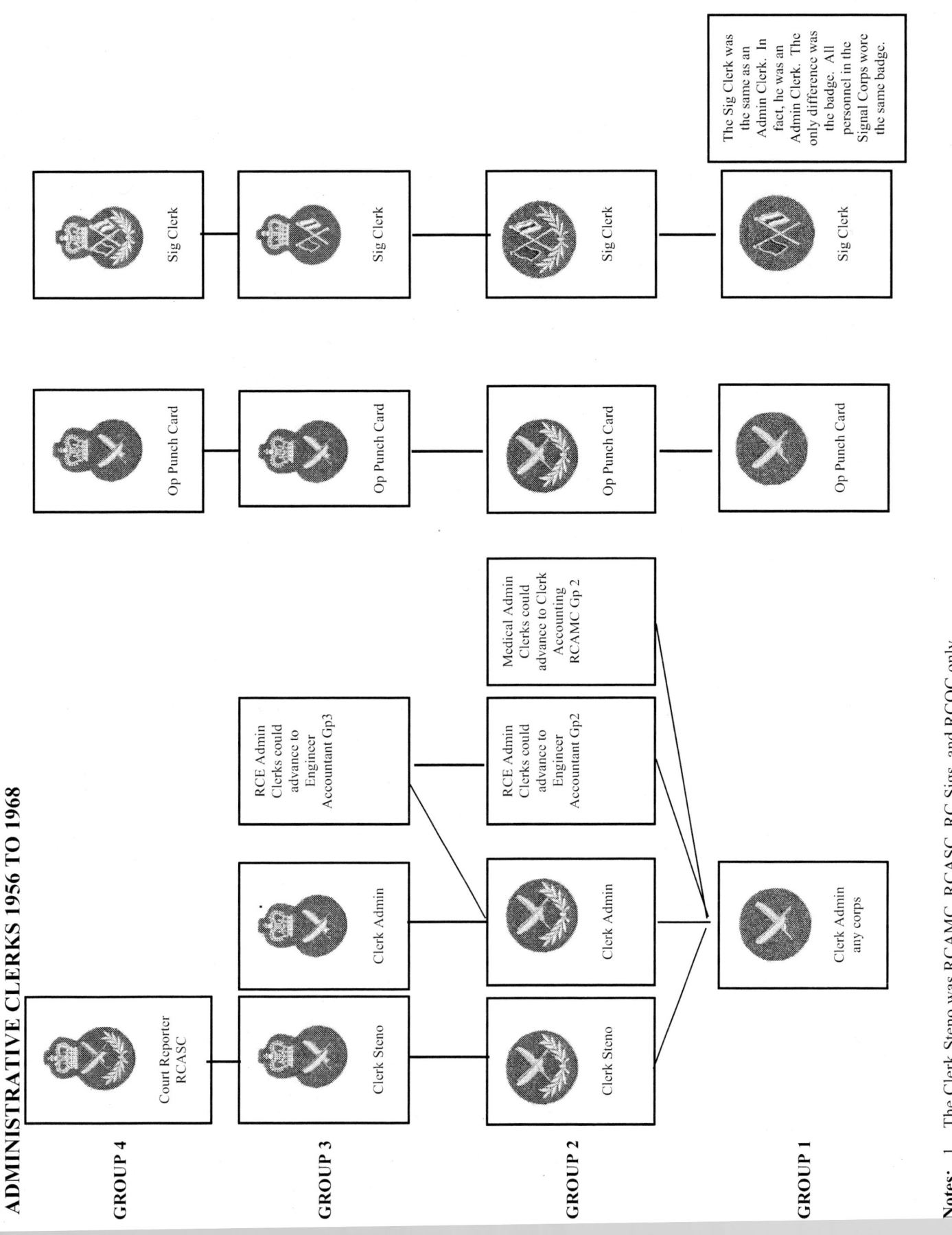

ADMINISTRATIVE CLERKS 1956 TO 1968

GROUP 4

- Court Reporter RCASC

GROUP 3

- Clerk Steno
- Clerk Admin
- RCE Admin Clerks could advance to Engineer Accountant Gp3
- Sig Clerk
- Op Punch Card

GROUP 2

- Clerk Steno
- Clerk Admin
- RCE Admin Clerks could advance to Engineer Accountant Gp2
- Medical Admin Clerks could advance to Clerk Accounting RCAMC Gp 2
- Sig Clerk
- Op Punch Card

GROUP 1

- Clerk Admin any corps
- Sig Clerk
- Op Punch Card

The Sig Clerk was the same as an Admin Clerk. In fact, he was an Admin Clerk. The only difference was the badge. All personnel in the Signal Corps wore the same badge.

Notes:
1. The Clerk Steno was RCAMC, RCASC, RC Sigs, and RCOC only.
2. Op Punch Card was RCASC or RCOC. After 1963 this was changed to RCOC and RCAPC.

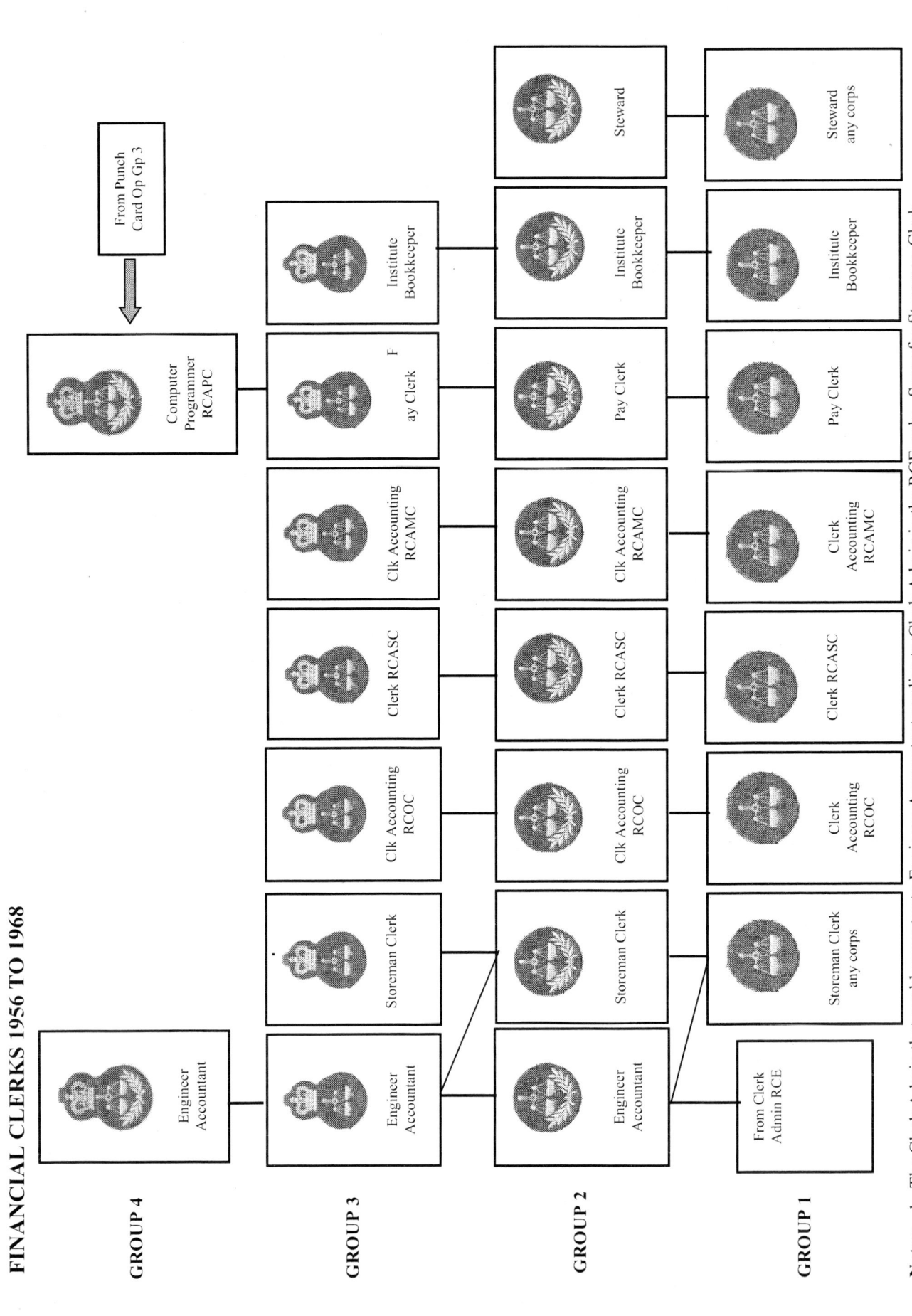

FINANCIAL CLERKS 1956 TO 1968

GROUP 4: Engineer Accountant

GROUP 3: Engineer Accountant | Storeman Clerk | Clk Accounting RCOC | Clerk RCASC | Clk Accounting RCAMC | Pay Clerk | Institute Bookkeeper | Computer Programmer RCAPC (From Punch Card Op Gp 3)

GROUP 2: Engineer Accountant | Storeman Clerk | Clk Accounting RCOC | Clerk RCASC | Clk Accounting RCAMC | Pay Clerk | Institute Bookkeeper | Steward

GROUP 1: Storeman Clerk any corps (From Clerk Admin RCE) | Clerk Accounting RCOC | Clerk RCASC | Clerk Accounting RCAMC | Pay Clerk | Institute Bookkeeper | Steward any corps

Notes:
1. The Clerk Admin that could remuster to Engineer Accountant applies to Clerk Admin in the RCE only. Same for Storeman Clerk.
2. The Storeman Clerk was obsolete after 1963.
3. The Clerk Accounting RCOC Gp 1 could advance to Ammo Tech Gp 2.
4. The word "accounting" was dropped from the Clerk Accounting RCASC to become Clerk RCASC.

COMMUNICATIONS

Signals   Khaki   1-4
                    Black   1-4
                    Green   1-4

The Royal Canadian Corps of Signals was responsible to install, maintain and repair communications equipment and provide communications by a variety of means including radio and line. The corps was renamed the Communications and Electronics Branch (it was originally called Communications and Electronics Engineering but the word "Engineering" was later dropped) as a result of unification, but the badge has remained unchanged. The same badge is worn by all army Signals trades. Note that this is the only coloured trade badge and one of the very oldest with the design remaining unchanged since 1908 and is still in use today.

1950's
LINE TRADES

Cable Splicer Group 3 only
The Cable Splicer made repairs to large multiple conductor cables. He must have been a Lineman Group 2 to advance to this trade.

Lineman Field Group 1-2
The Lineman Field laid telephone lines in tactical field locations. They used mechanical cable layers, line trucks and also laid cable by hand. They had to be able to make field repairs to damaged or broken line.

Lineman Permanent Line Group 1-2
The Lineman Permanent Line laid telephone lines in buildings. They also laid permanent overhead and underground line. They had to dig holes and erect telephone poles. They climbed poles to attach cross arms, insulators, lightening arresters and of course line.

Lineman 052 (00015-01) Group 1-3
This trade is a combination of two previous types of Lineman and the Cable Splicer. They were combined in March 1957. They could progress to Line Construction Foreman.

Line Construction Foreman Group 4 only
The LCF was a supervisor for the lineman trade. This was a new trade in 1957. Previously the Lineman went only as far as Group 2, then he could become a Cable Splicer Group 3. The new Lineman could now advance as far as Group 3 and then he could become a Line Construction Foreman. The Foreman had to survey routes, estimate manpower, equipment and material and supervise the line troop when constructing permanent lines.

The photo above shows Cable Splicers repairing an underwater cable in Halifax harbour. Both photos on this page courtesy of the Communications and Electronics Museum.

OPERATOR TRADES

Op Wireless and Line   Group 1-3 renamed
Radio & Telegraph Operator   Group 1-3

This tradesman operated radio equipment and sent messages by radio & morse code. In addition to radio duties, the OWL had to perform clerical duties in a message centre, build field antennas and setup and operate a field switchboard.

The Op Wireless and Line was renamed Radio & Telegraph Op in 1957 because "wireless" was then called "radio". Also "telegraph" was a more appropriate name for someone who sends messages by morse code than "line". The word "line" was used in the job description of the Lineman. There were minor differences between the old and new radio operator trades. The R&TG Op had to learn morse code at a slightly reduced speed. There was less training on line duties, and the fixed base switchboards were not taught. Training was given only on the portable field (SB22 model) switchboards.

SKILL AT ARMS

Chief Radio & Telegraph Operator   Group 4

This is the fourth level of expertise for the Radio & Telegraph Op trade. His job was to supervise and direct the operation of signal message centres and telegraph rely centres as well as field and fixed radio stations. This was a new trade approximately 1960. Before the creation of this trade, the R&TG Op could not progress past Group 3 except as an instructor.

Operator Keyboard   Group 1-2   renamed
Teletype Op   Group 1-2

This trade is known in modern times as the Teletype Operator. In fact, it was called the Teletype Operator once before. The name of this trade went through several name changes as follows:

- Operator Keyboard
- Changed to Teletype Operator in 1945
- Changed to Operator Teletype in 1947
- Changed back to Operator Keyboard in 1950
- Changed once again to Teletype Operator in 1957

His job was to send and receive messages by telecommunications (using teletypewriters) and operate tape rely equipment. He also had to do clerical duties in a Signals Message Centre and encrypt and decrypt messages using off-line cipher equipment. At the Group 1 level he would be employed in field duties only. At the Group 2 level, he could be employed in either static or field positions. Over the years this evolved so that the Tel Op was employed at mostly static positions while the Radio Op did the job in the field. The Op Keyboard had no progress past Group 2. The Tel Op however, could become a Group 3 Cryptographer and eventually a Group 4 Chief Cryptographer. He also had the opportunity to become a Cipher Op. See the Signals trade progression charts for 1956 and 1957.

Op Cipher   Group 1-2   renamed
Cipher Op   Group 2-3

This tradesman was responsible for encoding and decoding messages using off-line cipher equipment (this means that the message was encoded before being sent, not simultaneously as is done today with modern equipment). They also did encoding and decoding of messages without the use of cipher machines. Before 1957 the trade existed in Group 1 and 2 only and had no relationship to any other trade. Candidates for this trade had to be already qualified as an Operator Keyboard Group 1, or a Sig Clerk Group 1 or a Stenographer Group 1. This meant that a soldier who was already qualified as a Group 1 in one of these trades, had to take another course to become an Operator Cipher Group 1. In 1957 the Operator Cipher was renamed the Cipher Operator and the Group 1 level was eliminated. The prerequisites were also changed. To become a Cipher Op, he first had to be a Tel Op at the Group 1 level. See the Signals trade progression charts. When this trade became obsolete in 1963, the job was merged with that of the Teletype Operator who was then renamed the Teletype and Cipher Op. (See Teletype and Cipher Op later in this section for a picture of a crypto machine.)

Cryptographer   Group 3 only

A new trade in 1957. At the Group 2 level he would have been a Tel Op or a Cipher Op. Like the Cipher Op, this tradesman worked with codes. This trade was simply a more advanced level of the Cipher Op trade. He could go on to become a Chief Cryptographer Group 4. In 1963 this trade was merged with the Tel Op trade.

Chief Cryptographer   Group 4 only

This was the top level of expertise for the Cryptographer. In 1963, when the cipher, crypto and teletype trades were combined, this trade was renamed Chief Teletype and Cipher Op.

Operator Switchboard   Group 1 only

This person operated all types of permanent base switchboards and small field switchboards with up to 80 lines. They had to be able to answer 100 calls in 30 minutes. They were also required to take messages for receivers if there was no answer. These messages were called "phonograms". The answering machine had not been invented yet. When this trade became obsolete in 1961, the base switchboards were taken over by civilians, while the task of operating the field switchboards was added to the Radio and Telegraph Op trade.

Operator Fixed Wireless Station Group 1-3

This tradesman specialized in sending and receiving messages by morse code. The Operator Wireless and Line also used morse code, but only as a back up method for voice transmissions. Morse code can be heard when atmospheric conditions are bad and voice messages cannot be understood. Another advantage is that morse code signals (called "continuous wave") can be heard over longer distances than voice. They worked in static locations and not in field tactical situations like the Op Wireless and Line, hence the name Op Fixed Wireless Station. Beginners had to be able to send and receive at 18 words per minute. Experienced operators could work at much higher speeds. They would write incoming by hand and then type them. Many operators could skip this step and type the message as the code was heard. The Operator Fixed Wireless Station and the Operator Wireless and Line both became obsolete in 1957. The new trade of Radio and Telegraph Operator took over both of these jobs.

Operator Special Group 1-3

This trade was a well kept secret. It was one of the predecessors of the Comm Research trade. They were involved with the interception of enemy radio communications. They had to send and receive messages in voice or morse code or in a foreign language. They also had to operate direction finding equipment. Using this equipment, the operator could find the bearing of the transmitting station. These operators had to learn foreign voice procedures. (Voice procedure is the format for sending and receiving voice radio transmissions. It gives all operators a standard method so that each operator is not creating their own procedure.) The trade was reduced to nil strength in 1953 but it still existed on paper. In the early 1960's it was reactivated and was still in use in the mid 60's. See Communicator Research in this section. This trade became obsolete approximately 1965.

Draughtsman Signals Group 1-2

The main job of this tradesman was to draught diagrams to scale for the installation of permanent telephone lines, circuitry, cable diagrams for radio installations and power supply diagrams. They had to produce proposal drawings from oral or written instructions. After approval, they had to make copies of their work using mimeograph, or hectograph equipment. These were primitive copying machines by today's standards. They didn't have the luxury of photocopiers in those days. The mimeograph works by pressing ink onto paper through openings cut into a stencil. Liquid ink is added to the machine. Then the stencil is wrapped tautly around a metal cylinder. As the operator turns a crank on the side of the machine, the cylinder picks up ink and presses it through the stencil onto the paper. It can be a very messy job. I had the privilege of using one of these machines in my younger days. We called it a "Gestetner" which was the brand name of the manufacturer. If one is not careful, ink is liable to end up all over the place, including the desk, floor, finished product and the operator. The Hectograph works by making an impression into a gelatin slab, then after applying ink, using it to produce copies. I have never seen one of these machines but it sounds as if it is just as messy or perhaps worse.

The Draughtsman Signals also had to be quite skilled in map reading. He had to understand the use of map bearings and military map symbols. He had to orient the map and measure distances. This was required in order to draw line diagrams to the proper scale. Obsolete 1961.

Royal Canadian Corps of Signals
1903-2003

EQUIPMENT REPAIR TRADES

Radio Mechanic Group 1-3 renamed
Radio Equipment Tech Group 1-3

The Radio Mechanic was renamed the Radio Equipment Tech in 1958. The Radio Mechanic was the first line radio repair trade. They also repaired PA and intercom systems. Before 1950 all radio repairs were done by RCEME. After 1950, both Sigs and RCEME did radio repairs at the Group 1-3 level.

The equivalent trade in RCEME was called the Radio Tech. RC SIGS Radio Mechanics repaired their own radios while RCEME Radio Techs did repairs for the remainder of the army. If he was unable to repair the radio, it would be sent to the Radio Artificer RCEME who did repairs at the Group 4 (second line) level. In 1958, RC SIGS began doing radio repairs at the Group 4 level also. The Radio Equipment Tech could then progress to Master Radio Equipment Tech Group 4 or Foreman of Signals Group 4

Master Radio Equipment Tech   Group 4 only

This was a new trade in 1958 because at this time the RC SIGS began to do their own radio repairs at the Group 4 level. Previously Sigs did repairs only at the Group 1-3 level and RCEME did all Group 4 level repairs. The Master Radio Equipment Tech was also required to supervise the Group 1-3 levels of the trade.

Line Mechanic   Group 1-3   renamed
Terminal Equipment Tech   Group 1-3

The Line Mechanic was renamed the Terminal Equipment Tech in 1958 to more accurately reflect his duties. They installed and repaired line junction boxes, repeaters, switchboards, power supplies, and other telephone, telegraph and switchboard equipment. Before 1950 all teletype repairs were done by RCEME. After 1950, both Signals and RCEME did these repairs at the Group 1-3 level. The equivalent trade in RCEME was called the Communication Systems Tech. Note that in RCEME the Comms Systems Tech did the job of both the Telegraph Mechanic (later Teletype and Cipher Tech) and the Line Mechanic (later Terminal Equipment Tech) in Signals. RC SIGS TE Techs repaired their own equipment while RCEME Techs did repairs for the remainder of the army. If he was unable to repair the equipment, it would be sent to the Comms System Artificer RCEME who did repairs at the Group 4 (second line) level. In 1958, RC SIGS began doing radio repairs at the Group 4 level also. The Terminal Equipment Tech could then progress to Master Terminal Equipment Tech Group 4 or Foreman of Signals Group 4

Master Terminal Equipment Tech Group 4 only

This was a new trade in 1958 because at this time the RC SIGS began to do their own repairs at the Group 4 level. Previously Signals did repairs only at the Group 1-3 level and RCEME did all Group 4 level repairs. The Master Terminal Equipment Tech was also required to supervise the Group 1-3 levels of the trade.

TE Techs doing maintenance in the line junction room for a large switchboard

Courtesy of Communications & Electronics Museum

Telegraph Mechanic   Group 1-3   renamed
Teletype and Cipher Equipment Tech   Group 1-3

The Telegraph Mechanic was renamed the Teletype and Cipher Equipment Tech in 1958 to more accurately reflect his duties. They were the first line repair trade for telegraph and teletype equipment and off-line cipher machines and tape recorders. Before 1950 all teletype repairs were done by RCEME. After 1950, both Signals and RCEME did these repairs at the Group 1-3 level. The equivalent trade in RCEME was called the Communication Systems Tech. RC SIGS T&C Techs repaired their own equipment while RCEME Techs did repairs for the remainder of the army. If the T&C Tech was unable to repair the equipment, it would be sent to the Comms System Artificer RCEME who did repairs at the Group 4 (second line) level. In 1958, RC SIGS began doing radio repairs at the Group 4 level also. The Teletype and Cipher Equipment Tech could then progress to Master Teletype and Cipher Equipment Tech Group 4 or Foreman of Signals Group 4

Master Teletype and Cipher Equipment Tech
Group 4

This was a new trade in 1958 because at this time the RC SIGS began to do their own repairs at the Group 4 level. Previously Signals did repairs only at the Group 1-3 level and RCEME did all Group 4 level repairs. The Master T&C Tech was also required to supervise the Group 1-3 levels.

Foreman of Signals   Group 4 only

The Foreman of Signals was a supervisor for all equipment repair trades. Potential Foreman of Signals had to be a Group 3 technical trade. He had to prepare plans and supervise installation, testing, adjusting and repairs of all types. He also had to instruct in the technical trades. After 1958, when RC SIGS started doing their own Group 4 level repairs, the prerequisite to become a Foreman of Signals was changed to being a Group 4 in one of the above mentioned technical repair trades. (The job of the Foreman of Signals was different before 1948 when RC SIGS began doing radio repairs. You can read the previous job description in Part One of the book. You can also read more about the Foreman of Signals later in this section.)

DRIVER TRADES

Despatch Rider   Group 1 only.
Changed to Group 2 only in 1958.
More commonly know as DR, The Despatch Rider delivered messages by jeep and motorcycle. They also did convoy escort, vehicle maintenance, and when not busy, assisted the lineman with line laying. (See Despatch Rider in Parts One and Two for more information on this trade). Before 1958 the trade existed at the Group 1 level only with no chance of progression. In 1958 the trade was changed to Group 2 only. He would have been a Driver Mechanical Transport at the Group 1 level. There was no progression for the DR past Group 2. The trade became obsolete in 1964.

Photos show the DR Motorcycle Display Team at Vimy Barracks about 1952 with their new Triumph motorcycles. Courtesy of Joe Arsenault.

The RC SIGS motorcycle display team existed from 1952 to 1956. It was brought back in 1967 for Canada's centennial year but was disbanded again at the end of the year.

Driver Mechanical Transport   Group 1-2
This driver had to be able to operate all unit wheeled vehicles. He could advance to Group 2 in his own trade or become a DR or a Signals Electrician. This trade became obsolete in 1964 in RC SIGS but continued to exist in other corps.

Driver Electrician   Group 2-3 (1953-1957)
Signals Electrician Group 2-3 (1957 and after)
Formerly the Driver Electrician, this trade was renamed Signals Electrician in 1957. He was tasked with charging and maintaining the many large batteries that were used in radio vehicles. He also maintained small generators and field lighting equipment. He would have been a Driver Mechanical Transport at the Group 1 level before he could advance to this trade at the Group 2 level. (See more information about this trade under "Driver Signals" and "Radio Operator" later in this section.) Obsolete October 1966.

RCEME COMMUNICATION EQUIPMENT REPAIR TRADES

The RCEME communications trades wore the electrician badge (see picture on the chart at the end of this section). In 1956 the following RCEME trades were involved with the repair of communication equipment:

Radio Tech	Group 1-3
Radio Artificer	Group 4
Radar Tech	Group 1-3
Radar Artificer	Group 4
Telecommunication Mechanic Line of Communication	Group 1-3

The type of repairs done by the radio and radar technicians is obvious by their names. The Telecommunication Mechanic Line of Communication repaired all other types of communication equipment including switchboards, terminals, teletype, cipher and telegraph equipment. In the Signal Corps there were two different trades doing this work. The Terminal Equipment Tech for switchboards, terminals and power supplies, and the Teletype and Cipher Tech for the other equipment.

Communication System Tech.   Group 1-3
Communication System Artificer   Group 4
Later in 1956 the Telecommunication Mechanic Line of Communication was renamed to Communication System Tech. Also a Group 4 level

for this trade was created called the Communication System Artificer. This trade became obsolete in 1963. (You can read more information about these trades later in this section.)

1960's

Teletype Op. obsolete 1963
Cipher Op. obsolete 1963
Cryptographer obsolete 1963
Chief Cryptographer obsolete 1963

All of the above four trades were combined into the new trade of Teletype and Cipher Operator.

Teletype and Cipher Op. Group 1-3 new in 1963

In 1963 the trades of Teletype Op, Cipher Op and Cryptographer were combined to create this new trade. The T & C Op did both jobs of teletype operation and encoding/decoding messages.

Chief Teletype and Cipher Op.
Group 4 only. New in 1963.
This trade replaced the Chief Cryptographer in 1963. He supervised and directed operations of a signal centre a crypto centre or a tape relay centre.

Teletype Op. Group 1-4

In 1966 the name of the Teletype and Cipher Op was shortened to Teletype Operator. The Chief Teletype and Cipher Op became obsolete and was replaced by a Group 4 Tel Op.

The machine in the photo is a KL7 off-line crypto machine used in the army from the 1950's until the 1970's. The cylindrical portion held eight rotors of letters and figures. When the operator pressed a key on the keyboard, the KL7 would change the letter to a different one, making the resulting message unreadable. If the same letter was typed again, a different letter would result because the rotors turned after every character. The message was produced on a narrow tape with letters in five letter groups. The message could then be sent by radio. The receiving operator, by using the same arrangement of

Photo courtesy of John Alexander.

the rotors, could decipher the message by typing the five letter groups into the machine. The KL7 would then produce a tape in plain language. The KL7 was used by Teletype and Cipher Operators and also Radio and Telegraph Operators.

Communication System Tech
Communication System Artificer

In 1963, the Communication System Tech Group 1-3 and the Communication System Artificer Group 4, which were RCEME trades, became obsolete and all repairs of terminal equipment, switchboards and power supplies were taken over by the RC Signals Terminal Equipment Tech Group 1-3 and the Master Terminal Equipment Tech Group 4. All repairs of teletype and cipher equipment were taken over by the Teletype and Cipher Tech and the Master Teletype and Cipher Tech. Previously, both RC SIGS and RCEME had made these types of repairs. RCEME still did repairs on radio and radar equipment.

Driver Signals Group 1-3

In 1964 the DR, the Signals Electrician, and the Driver Mechanical Transport (in RC SIGS only) were combined, and the personnel absorbed into the new trade of Driver Signals. Their duties were a combination of the three old driver trades in RC SIGS. Namely, delivery of messages by jeep and motorcycle, battery maintenance, operating field lighting equipment and vehicle maintenance. At the Group 3 level, they also instructed soldiers of other trades on driving and vehicle maintenance. This very short lived trade became obsolete in 1969. Personnel were remustered to other trades in Communications Branch and also to other branches of the land forces.

Radio Operator 211   Group 1-4

With morse code being used less and less, the R & TG Op was renamed to simply "Radio Op" in 1966. Today morse code is no longer taught on the basic radio operator's course.

The photo shows the author, as a Radio and Telegraph Operator, on radio duty in the back of a 1950's radio van. The name of this trade changed several times over the years. It was called Operator Radio RC SIGS in the 1930's. After the war the name was changed to Operator Wireless and Line. In 1957 it was changed to Radio and Telegraph Operator. Then in 1966 it was changed again to Radio Operator. Finally in the year 2000 the trade was merged with the Teletype Operator and the name changed to Signal Operator. The radio in the photo is a C42 set.

Note the several large batteries under the table (they are black and one has the number 44 on it). Although the Radio Operator was trained in battery maintenance, he did so only while the batteries were in his vehicle. When they were removed from the vehicle they were maintained by the Driver Electrician (later renamed the Signals Electrician, and in 1964 renamed again to Driver Signals. See information about these trades above in this section).

CHIEFS, MASTERS AND FOREMEN

Before 1966 RC SIGS trades could advance only as far as Group 3. Qualified tradesmen could then advance to the Group 4 level as a Chief, Master, or Foreman. In 1966 these trades were abolished and replaced with a Group 4 level going by the same name as the first three levels of the trade. This applied to the following trades:

- Line Construction Foreman replaced with Lineman Group 4.
- Chief Radio and Telegraph Op replaced with Radio Op Group 4.
- Master Radio Equipment Tech replaced with Radio Tech Group 4
- Master Terminal Equipment Tech replaced with Terminal Eqpt Tech Group 4
- Chief Teletype and Cipher Op replaced with Teletype Op Group 4
- Master Teletype and Cipher Equipment Tech replaced with Teletype and Cipher Equipment Tech Group 4

SUPERVISORY TRADES

Foreman of Signals
Communications Op 214
Communications Tech 224

The supervisory trade for the technicians was called the Foreman of Signals. This trade has been mentioned several times in this book. It dates back to before the Second World War. He was the supervisor for all the technical trades from the Radio Mechanic and the Line Mechanic which were new in RC SIGS in 1948, to the six different communication repair trades that existed in the 1960's.

The earliest record that I have found showing the existence of a Foreman of Signals is dated 1937. The trade is probably older. See Part One of the book for a job description of the Foreman of Signals before 1948.

In 1966 the Foreman of Signals was renamed Communications Tech. An equivalent trade for the operators was created called the Communications Op. All technicians would become a Comm Tech at the Warrant Officer level, and all operators would become a Comm Op at the Warrant Officer level. There would be no more technicians or operators ranked WO or higher except for these two trades. There was no equivalent trade for the linemen.

The Foreman of Signals and the Comm Tech were not exactly the same. There was only one Foreman of Signals per unit and he was usually a Chief Warrant Officer, whereas after unification all technicians would became a Comm Tech upon reaching the rank of Warrant Officer.

These trades are now obsolete. The role of supervising and planning is still being done by senior members of the technical and operator trades, but without the necessity of changing trades. These are now positions, not trades. You can find more information about this further on in this section under the heading of "1996".

The Royal Canadian Corps of Signals war memorial was completed in 1963. It is located at Vimy Barracks in Kingston. The plaque on the front reads "To those in the Royal Canadian Corps of Signals who gave their lives for their country."

Photo by author

OTHER TRADES

The Royal Canadian Corps of Signals also had the following trades before unification which were common to all corps:

Assistant Instructor RC SIGS Group 3-4
To become a Sigs instructor, one first had to be a Operator Wireless and Line Group 2 and also be qualified as a Radio Mechanic Group 1 or a Lineman Group 1. In addition to teaching radio and line and office procedures, he was expected to teach regimental and ceremonial drill and corps history. Most army corps had soldiers who were instructors by trade. In today's army being an instructor is only a temporary job, not a trade. This trade became obsolete in 1964.

Clerk Stenographer Group 2-3
The Clerk Stenographer took messages by shorthand, later to be typed out in long form. The Stenographer first had to be a Clerk Admin at the Group 1 level Obsolete about 1968.

Steward Group 1-2
This person looked after the messes on Sigs bases. See clerks for a full job description

Storeman Clerk Group 1-3
This tradesman did accounting for the stores. See clerks for a full job description.

Bandsman Group 1-3
Like several other corps, RC Signals had their own corps bandsman until unification. See musicians for information about the RC SIGS band.

Assistant Instructor Air Supply Group 2-3
This trade was used in RC Signals until 1959 to teach the methods of delivering communications equipment and supplies (batteries, etc) by air.

Sig Clerk (Clerk Administrative)
The Sig Clerk was actually a Clerk Administrative. The only difference was the trade badge. All personnel in the Signal Corps wore the crossed flags trade badge, regardless of their trade. Clerk Administrative personnel in all other corps wore the clerk trade badge.

COMMUNICATIONS BRANCH EQUIPMENT REPAIR TRADES

In 1966 the RCEME and Sigs communications equipment trades were merged. After 1968 the new trades were part of the Communications and Electronics Branch. The radio repair trade adopted the old RCEME name of Radio Tech instead of the Signals name of Radio Equipment Tech. The Terminal Equipment Tech trade remained unchanged because this trade had been obsolete in RCEME since 1963. There had been no former equivalent to the Radar Tech in RC SIGS. They did repairs to anti-aircraft and counter battery radar equipment.

RC SIGS trades	**RCEME trades**
Radio Equipment Tech	Radio Tech
Master Radio Eqpt Tech	Radio Artificer
Terminal Eqpt Tech	Comm System Tech
Master TE Tech	Comm System Artificer
Tel & Cipher Eqpt Tech	Comm System Tech
Master T & CE Tech	Comm System Artificer
n/a	Radar Tech
n/a	Radar Artificer

Communication Branch trades
Radio Tech 221 (level 1-4)
Terminal Eqpt Tech 222 (level 1-4)
Tel & Cipher Tech 223 (level 1-4)
Radar Tech 231 (level 1-4)

RC SIGS BECOMES THE COMMUNICATIONS AND ELECTRONICS BRANCH

In 1976 the former RC SIGS personnel changed hat badges to the new Communications and Electronics Branch of the Canadian Armed Forces. (Originally called the Communications and Electronics Engineering Branch but the word "Engineering" was later dropped). This change officially took place in February of 1968 but the new hat badge was not approved until April 1972 and was not produced and issued until 1976.

1996

In January 1996 there was a complete revision of the technical trades in the Communications Branch. The supervisory trades of Comm Op and Comm Tech were abolished, and were not replaced. The job of supervising and planning still exists, but is now done by senior members of the operator and technical trades. Operators and technicians no longer change trades at the Warrant Officer level. All of the above mentioned technician trades were abolished and the following three new trades were initiated to replace them.

Strategic and Information Systems Tech 225

This technician was required to preform preventive and corrective maintenance on a variety of equipment including teletype, personal computers, secure voice and crypto machines. They also had to install and maintain cables. A complicated wiring installation might be required for computer networks, telephones and equipment using fibre optic cables. He or she also had to create and maintain accurate diagrams of the cable installation. The trade was very short lived and it became obsolete in June 2000. Their job was added to the remaining two communication technical trades.

Aerospace Telecommunications and Information System Tech 226

The job of this technician is to repair and maintain communications equipment used by the air element of the Canadian Forces. The Communications branch of the CF is responsible to provide communications repairs to the air and land elements. The navy has their own technicians who are not part of the Communications branch and have different names.

Land Communications and Information Systems Tech 227 (00110-01)

The Land Communications and Information Systems Tech is the land element equivalent of the above trade. They repair a large variety of communications equipment including radios, radio relay equipment, teletype equipment, radiation equipment, crypto equipment, portable satellite receivers, switchboards and telephones. Such a diversified assortment of equipment to repair by one trade required a more knowledgeable technician than the four different technicians who previously repaired this equipment. Some junior Sergeants were required to repeat their 6A course to qualify for this new trade. [4] (The new 6A course was not an exact repeat of the old one but now taught subject material required for this new trade. The 6A course is normally taken by Master Corporals to qualify for a promotion to Sergeant.) After the demise of the Strategic Communication System Tech, the task of repairing computers, teletype and cipher equipment was also added to this trade.

2000

Signal Operator 215 (00329-01)

The trades of Tel Op and the Rad Op were finally combined. This was a long overdue move and had been talked about for many years. The new trade was named Signal Operator.

Communicator Research 291 (00120-01)   Black   1-4
                                            Green   1-4

The job of Comm Research personnel is to intercept, analyse, and report data from foreign communication systems in voice and morse code. This trade evolved from others over the years. It first began as a RC SIGS trade called Operator Special during the Second World War (see Op Special in Part Two of this book, and in this section). That trade was reduced to nil strength in 1953, but reactivated in the early 1960's. A similar trade called Communications Special was started in the Navy in 1948. The name was changed to Communications Supplementary in the 1950's and then changed again to Radioman Special in 1960.

As a result of the trade regrouping in October 1966, the following trades were combined to create the Communication Research trade.

Navy   Radioman Special
Army   some Radio and Telegraph Operators RC SIGS
Army   Radio Intelligence Collator (an Intelligence Corps trade)
Air Force   some Communications Operators

The name was changed in 1968 from Communication Research to Communicator Research. There were no trade badges during the period 1968 to 1985. This badge was first introduced in 1985. They are still part of the Communications Branch but are the only trade with a separate trade badge.

The badge consists of the Signals flags with a flying "S" in front. The "S" on the badge stands for "special" with comes from the Radioman Special (Navy) and Operator Special (RC SIGS).

Driver Operator   Khaki 1-3
                                    Red   1-3

renamed Driver Radio Operator
                        Group 1-2 in 1958.

This badge was worn by non-Signal Corps communicators. It is the same as the Signals badge but without the colour. They were also commonly referred to as "Signallers". Their main duty was communications, so I have listed it in this section. There were other soldiers whose main job was to drive (see Driver section). At the Group 2 level, they also had the task of doing vehicle maintenance. For the Driver Operator to advance to Group 2 he also had to be qualified as a Driver Mechanical Transport. In RCEME the Driver Op could progress to Assistant Instructor RCEME Group 3.

The history of this trade is a bit confusing so I will repeat some of it here and lay it out in point form. (See Driver Operator in all previous parts of this book.)

- Prior to 1949, this trade had different names in different corps as follows:
- It was called Operator RCAC in the armoured corps.
- It was called Signaller RCA in the artillery.
- It was called Infantry Signaller in the infantry.
- It was called Driver Operator in all other corps.
- In 1949 the name was standardized to Driver Operator in all corps. The trade existed in RCAC, RCA, RCE, RC SIGS, RCIC and RCEME.
- In 1953 the trade was eliminated in RC SIGS. As the Signal Corps had extensively trained radio operators, there was no need for the Driver Operator.
- In 1954, the practice of using a common name in all corps began to be reversed. In RCAC the name was changed to Signaller RCAC. In the infantry it was changed to Infantry Signaller. The Driver Operator existed only in RCA, RCE and RCEME.
- In 1958 the artillery also changed the name of their Driver Operator to a name that was unique to their trade. They called it Signaller RCA leaving the Driver Operator only in RCE and RCEME. In these two corps the name was changed to Driver Radio Operator.
- In 1963 the Group 1 level was eliminated from the Driver Radio Operator trade.
- In 1963, the Infantry Signaller trade was abolished. (See infantry section for details.)
- Also in 1963 the Driver Rad Op trade was abolished in RCEME leaving this trade existed in RCE only.
- In 1964 the Signaller RCAC was abolished. (See armoured section for details.)

The last two trades in this group (Signaller RCA and Driver Radio Op in RCE) were abolished in 1966. Today most soldiers are trained to use radios as part of their own trade of infantry, artillery, etc.

See the Drivers section for information about drivers who were not also signallers.

Master Sig   Black and Green

This badge was intended to be worn by the Chief Comm Ops of each Brigade and the Master Comm Op at Army HQ. The Chief Comm Op makes communications plans and manages and allocates frequencies. The plan was never implemented and the badge was never worn. (Before unification a khaki version of this badge was worn by Sig Sgts above their rank badge. See Part Five.)

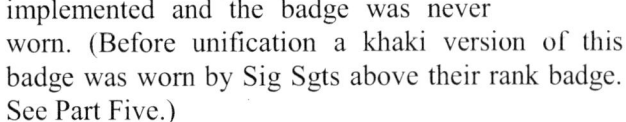

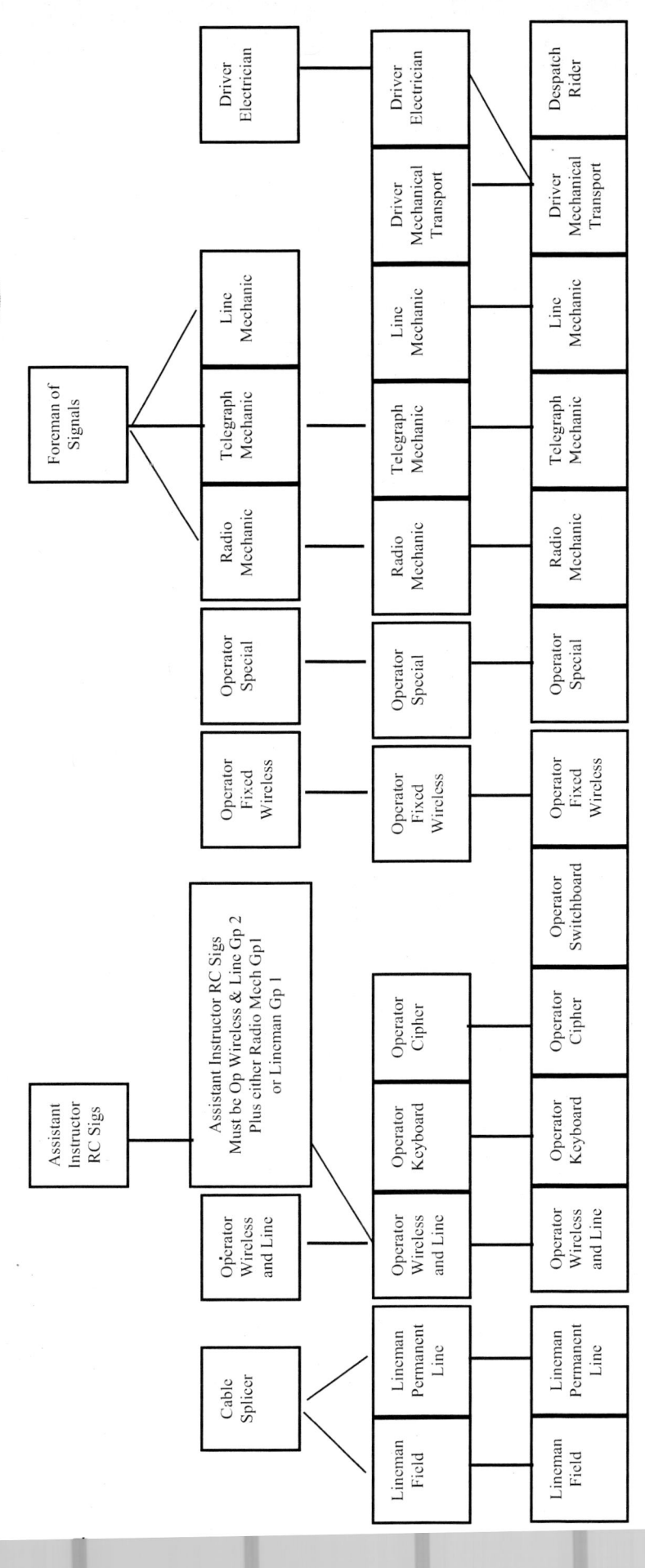

CANADIAN CORPS OF SIGNALS - 1956 - all Signals trades wear the trade same badge.

```
                                    Foreman of Signals
                    ┌──────────────┬──────┴──────┬──────────────┐
                    │              │             │              │
              Operator Fixed  Operator    Radio Mechanic  Telegraph   Line Mechanic   Driver Electrician
               Wireless       Special                     Mechanic
                                                                                            │
              Operator Fixed  Operator    Radio Mechanic  Telegraph   Line Mechanic   Driver Electrician   Driver Mechanical Transport
               Wireless       Special                     Mechanic
                                                                                                                  │
              Operator Fixed  Operator    Radio Mechanic  Telegraph   Line Mechanic                        Driver Mechanical Transport   Despatch Rider
               Wireless       Special                     Mechanic
```

```
      Assistant Instructor RC Sigs
                │
      Assistant Instructor RC Sigs
      Must be Op Wireless & Line Gp 2
      Plus either Radio Mech Gp1
      or Lineman Gp 1
   ┌────────────┬──────────┬──────────┬──────────┐
   │            │          │          │          │
 Cable      Lineman    Operator  Operator   Operator   Operator
 Splicer    Permanent  Wireless  Keyboard   Cipher     Switchboard
            Line       and Line

            Lineman    Operator  Operator   Operator
            Permanent  Wireless  Keyboard   Cipher
            Line       and Line

 Lineman
 Field

 Lineman
 Field
```

The RCCS also had the following trades: Bandsman Group 1-3, Sig Clerk 1-3, Clerk Stenographer 2-3, Draughtsman Signals 1-2, Steward 1-2, Storeman Clerk 1-3. Communications equipment repairs were also done by RCEME at the Group 1-3 level. RC Sigs did their own repairs while RCEME did repairs for all other corps. RCEME repairs for RC Sigs at the Group 4 level, and all radar repairs.

RCEME communication repair trades:

| Radar Tech Gp 1-3 | Radar Artificer Gp 4 | Radio Tech Gp 1-3 | Radio Artificer Gp 4 | Comm System Tech Gp 1-3 | Comm System Artificer Gp 4 |

ROYAL CANADIAN CORPS OF SIGNALS - 1957 - all Signals trades wear the trade same badge.

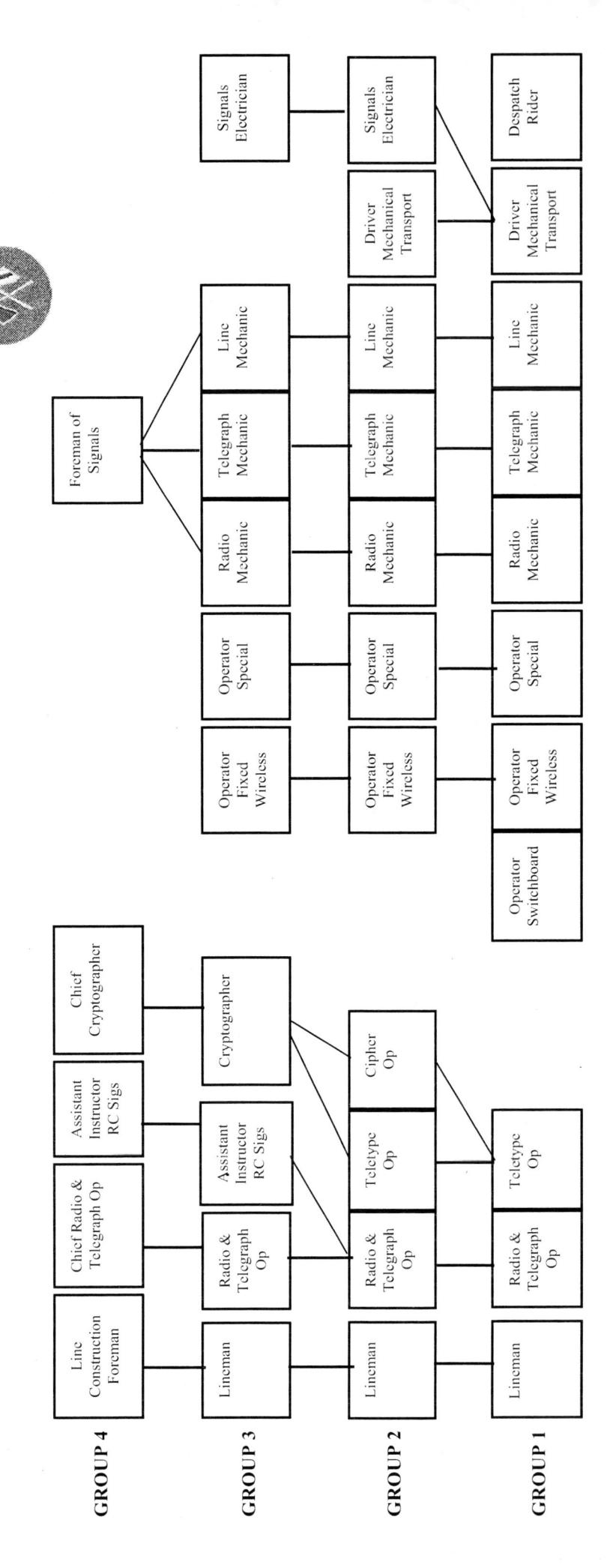

GROUP 4: Line Construction Foreman | Chief Radio & Telegraph Op | Assistant Instructor RC Sigs | Chief Cryptographer | Foreman of Signals | Signals Electrician

GROUP 3: Lineman | Radio & Telegraph Op | Assistant Instructor RC Sigs | Cryptographer | Operator Fixed Wireless | Operator Special | Radio Mechanic | Telegraph Mechanic | Line Mechanic | Driver Mechanical Transport | Signals Electrician

GROUP 2: Lineman | Radio & Telegraph Op | Teletype Op | Cipher Op | Operator Fixed Wireless | Operator Special | Radio Mechanic | Telegraph Mechanic | Line Mechanic | Driver Mechanical Transport

GROUP 1: Lineman | Radio & Telegraph Op | Teletype Op | Operator Switchboard | Operator Fixed Wireless | Operator Special | Radio Mechanic | Telegraph Mechanic | Line Mechanic | Driver Mechanical Transport | Despatch Rider

Notes:
1. The RCCS also had the following trades: Bandsman Group 1-3, Sig Clerk 1-3, Clerk Stenographer 2-3, Draughtsman Signals 1-2, Steward 1-2, Storeman Clerk 1-3.
2. Communications equipment repairs were also done by RCEME at the Group 1-3 level. RC Sigs did their own repairs while RCEME did repairs for all other corps. RCEME did repairs for RC Sigs at the Group 4 level, and all radar repairs.

RCEME communication repair trades:

Radar Tech Gp 1-3 | Radar Artificer Gp 4 | Radio Tech Gp 1-3 | Radio Artificer Gp 4 | Comm System Tech Gp 1-3 | Comm System Artificer Gp 4

CANADIAN CORPS OF SIGNALS - 1958-1963 all Signals trades wear the trade same badge.

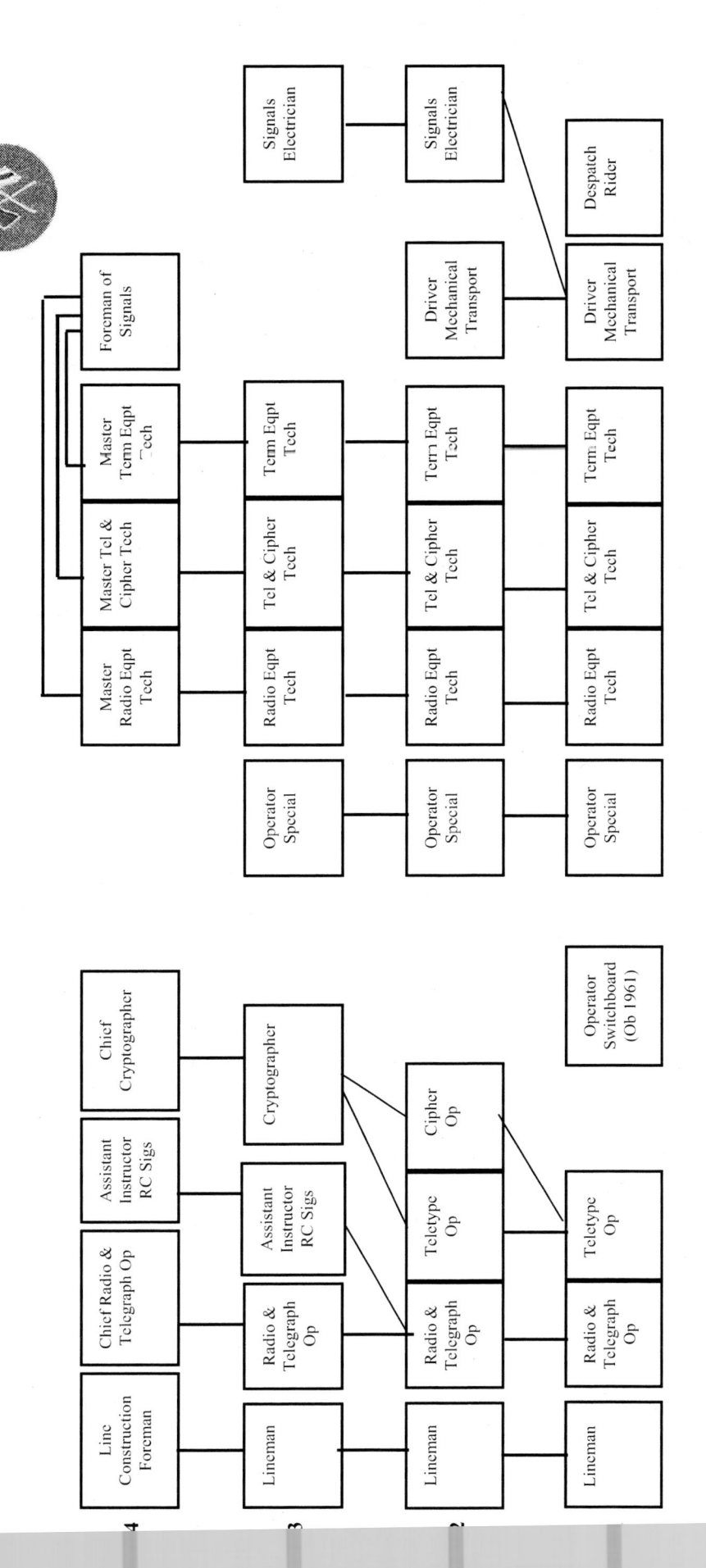

Level 4:
- Line Construction Foreman
- Chief Radio & Telegraph Op
- Assistant Instructor RC Sigs
- Chief Cryptographer
- Master Radio Eqpt Tech
- Master Tel & Cipher Tech
- Master Term Eqpt Tech
- Foreman of Signals

Level 3:
- Lineman
- Radio & Telegraph Op
- Assistant Instructor RC Sigs
- Cryptographer
- Radio Eqpt Tech
- Tel & Cipher Tech
- Term Eqpt Tech
- Signals Electrician
- Driver Mechanical Transport

Level 2:
- Lineman
- Radio & Telegraph Op
- Teletype Op
- Cipher Op
- Operator Special
- Radio Eqpt Tech
- Tel & Cipher Tech
- Term Eqpt Tech
- Signals Electrician
- Driver Mechanical Transport
- Despatch Rider

Level 1:
- Lineman
- Radio & Telegraph Op
- Teletype Op
- Operator Switchboard (Ob 1961)
- Operator Special
- Radio Eqpt Tech
- Tel & Cipher Tech
- Term Eqpt Tech

The RCCS also had the following trades: Bandsman Group 1-3, Sig Clerk 1-3, Clerk Stenographer 2-3, Steward 1-2, Clerk 1-3, Assistant Instructor Air Supply 2-3, Storeman Clerk 1-3, Assistant Instructor Air Supply 2-3. RC Sigs did their own repairs at all levels, while RCEME did repairs for all other corps. RCEME did all radar repairs.

RCEME communication repair trades:

- Radar Tech Gp 1-3
- Radar Artificer Gp 4
- Radio Tech Gp 1-3
- Radio Artificer Gp 4
- Comm System Tech Gp 1-3
- Comm System Artificer Gp 4

ROYAL CANADIAN CORPS OF SIGNALS - 1964-1973 - all Signals trades wear the trade same badge.

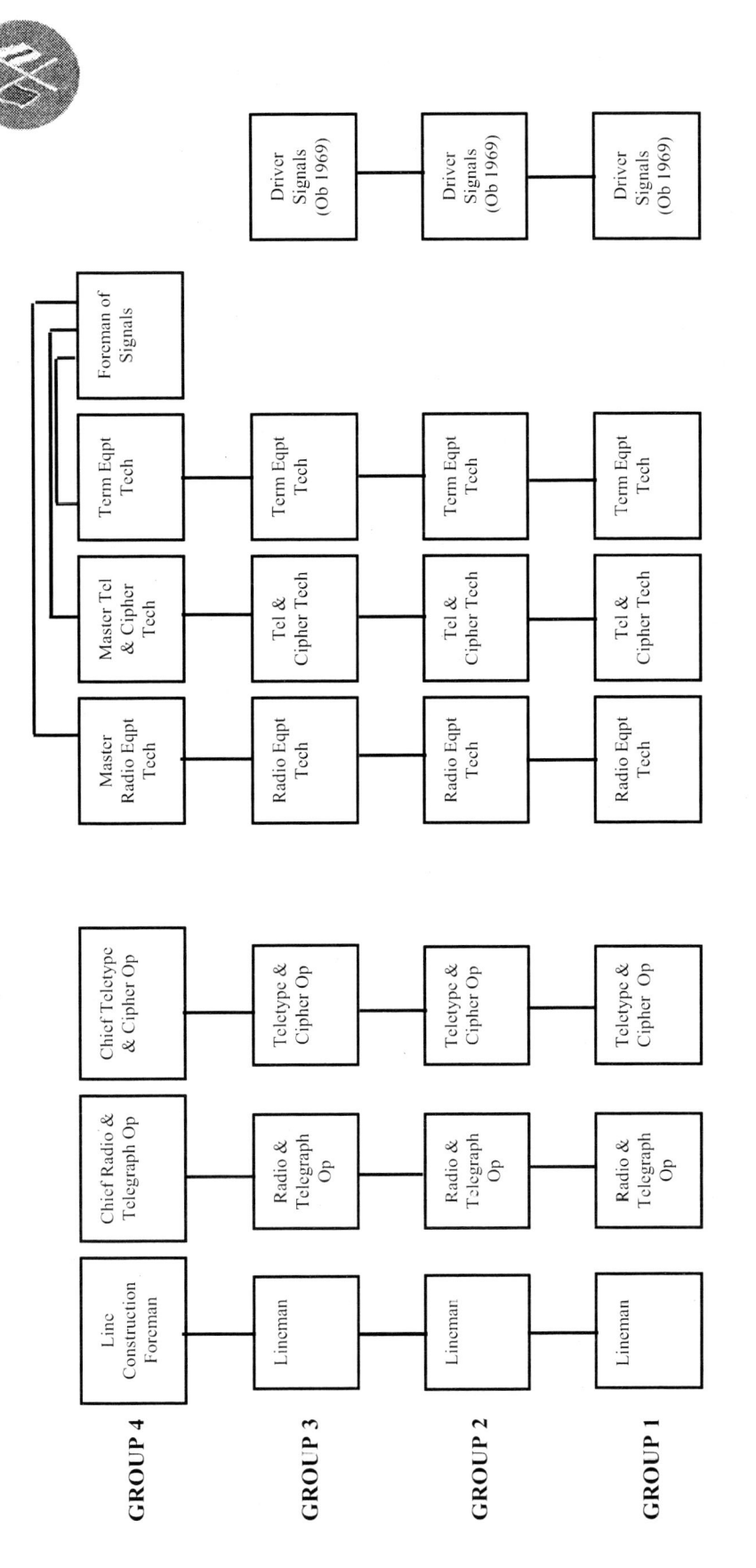

GROUP 4	Line Construction Foreman	Chief Radio & Telegraph Op	Chief Teletype & Cipher Op	Master Radio Eqpt Tech	Master Tel & Cipher Tech	Term Eqpt Tech	Foreman of Signals
GROUP 3	Lineman	Radio & Telegraph Op	Teletype & Cipher Op	Radio Eqpt Tech	Tel & Cipher Tech	Term Eqpt Tech	
GROUP 2	Lineman	Radio & Telegraph Op	Teletype & Cipher Op	Radio Eqpt Tech	Tel & Cipher Tech	Term Eqpt Tech	
GROUP 1	Lineman	Radio & Telegraph Op	Teletype & Cipher Op	Radio Eqpt Tech	Tel & Cipher Tech	Term Eqpt Tech	

Driver Signals (Ob 1969) — Driver Signals (Ob 1969) — Driver Signals (Ob 1969)

Notes:
1. The RCCS also had the following trades: Bandsman Group 1-3, Sig Clerk 1-3, Clerk Stenographer 2-3, Steward 1-2, Storeman Clerk 1-3.
2. The following trades RCCS trades are not shown on the chart: Operator Special (obsolete about 1965) & Communicator Research (new 1968)
3. RC Sigs did their own repairs while RCEME did repairs for all other corps. RCEME did all radar repairs.

RCEME communication repair trades:

| Radar Tech Gp 1-3 | Radar Artificer Gp 4 | Radio Tech Gp 1-3 | Radio Artificer Gp 4 |

Comm System Tech and Artificer became obsolete in 1964. These repairs were then done only by the RC Sigs Terminal Equipment Tech and the Teletype and Cipher Tech.

Communication Equipment Repair Trades 1955 to 2000

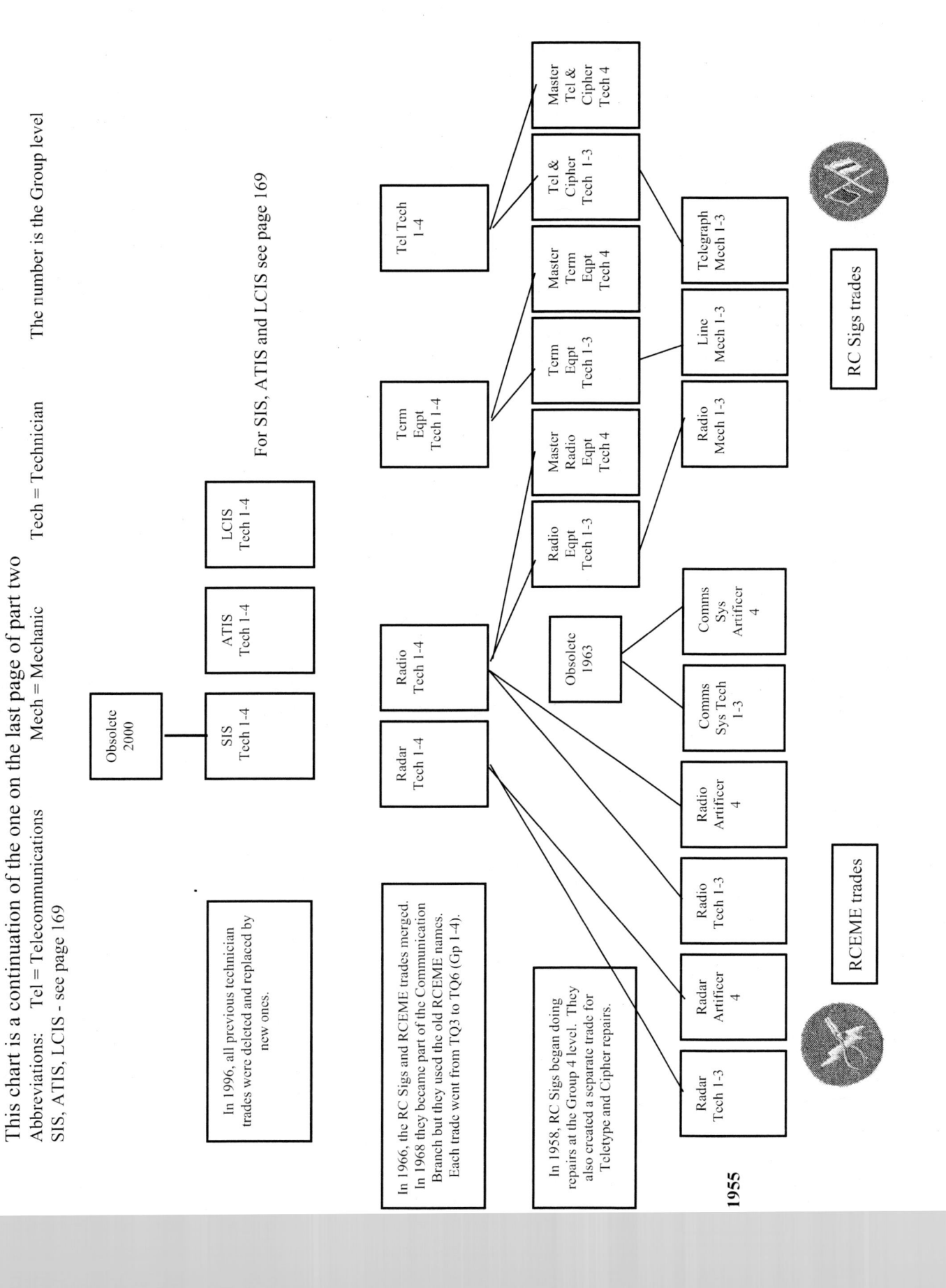

This chart is a continuation of the one on the last page of part two

Abbreviations: Tel = Telecommunications   Tech = Technician   The number is the Group level
Mech = Mechanic
SIS, ATIS, LCIS - see page 169   For SIS, ATIS and LCIS see page 169

Obsolete 2000 — SIS Tech 1-4 — ATIS Tech 1-4 — LCIS Tech 1-4

In 1996, all previous technician trades were deleted and replaced by new ones.

In 1966, the RC Sigs and RCEME trades merged. In 1968 they became part of the Communication Branch but they used the old RCEME names. Each trade went from TQ3 to TQ6 (Gp 1-4).

In 1958, RC Sigs began doing repairs at the Group 4 level. They also created a separate trade for Teletype and Cipher repairs.

Radar Tech 1-4 — Radio Tech 1-4 — Term Eqpt Tech 1-4 — Tel Tech 1-4

Radio Eqpt Tech 1-3 / Master Radio Eqpt Tech 4

Term Eqpt Tech 1-3 / Master Term Eqpt Tech 4

Tel & Cipher Tech 1-3 / Master Tel & Cipher Tech 4

Obsolete 1963: Comms Sys Artificer 4, Comms Sys Tech 1-3, Radio Artificer 4, Radio Tech 1-3, Radar Artificer 4, Radar Tech 1-3

Radio Mech 1-3 — Line Mech 1-3 — Telegraph Mech 1-3

1955

RCEME trades   RC Sigs trades

CONSTRUCTION ENGINEERS

Works Company Khaki 1-4

The Works Company, in 1956, included the following trades:

Blacksmith	Group 1-3
Bricklayer	Group 1-2
Carpenter	Group 1-3
Concretor	Group 1-2
Miner	Group 2 only
Painter	Group 1-2
Plumber	Group 1-3
Quarryman	Group 2 only
Sawyer	Group 1-2
Sheet Metal Worker	Group 1-3
Structural Steel Worker	Group 1-2
Foreman of Works	Group 3-4

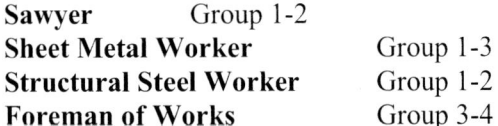

The Works Company, as this group of trades was known, carried out repairs to buildings, and the construction of new buildings. The badge is a "battlemented tower". The supervisor for these trades was called a "Foreman of Works" who wore the same badge. The tradesmen wore the badge at the Group 1 and 2 levels, and for three of the trades, Carpenter, Plumber, and Sheet Metal Worker, Group 3. The Foreman of Works wore the badge at the Group 3 and 4 levels. After Group 2, most of these trades had the opportunity to progress to a Foreman of Works Group 3, and later Group 4. If the Carpenter, Plumber or Sheet Metal Worker went to Group 3 in their own trade, instead of becoming a Foreman of Works, then they could never advance to Group 4. The Blacksmith was not allowed to become a Foreman of Works. They could advance as far as Group 3. See the CE trade progression chart.

The job of the Foreman of Works was to supervise and inspect construction, alteration and maintenance of buildings. He also had to estimate the cost of materials and labour.

The following trades were also part of the Works Company:

Draughtsman Architectural and Engineering
Surveyor Engineering
Surveyor Topographical
Electrician

There were two notable differences between these trades and the others in the Works Company. With the exception of the Electrician, they had the option, when ready to advance to Group 3, of becoming a Foreman of Works like the other trades in the Works Company, or proceeding to Group 3 in their own trade. The difference was that if they choose to go to Group 3 in their own trade, they had the prospect of later advancing to Group 4 in their own trade without becoming a Foreman of Works. The other Works Company trades could reach Group 4 only as a Foreman of Works, otherwise they could not advance past Group 3. (See the CE trade progression chart.)

The second difference between these trades and the others is that they did not wear the Works Company badge although they were members of the Company. These trades each had their own distinctive trade badges. These trades will be discussed individually beside the picture of their badge.

All RCE trades, when ready to become a Group 2, had the opportunity to change to a Field Engineer Group 2. That is because all Engineers had to undergo training as a Group 1 Field Engineer before taking their individual trades training. (See Field Engineers.)

The above list shows the Works Company trades that existed in 1956. The makeup of the Works Company was continually changing. Some changes took place in the next few years as follows:

- The Quarryman had been reduced to nil strength since 1950 and existed on paper only. The trade became obsolete approximately 1960.
- The Sawyer was not the same trade as the Sawyer Forestry. The Sawyer Forestry became obsolete in 1946 and the personnel were remustered to the Sawyer trade in the Works Company. This trade was reduced to nil strength in 1949 and became obsolete about 1960. (See Forestry trades in Part One and Two.)
- Here is the strange story of the Blacksmith and the Welder. The Blacksmith was deemed obsolete in 1947. In 1953 it was decided that the Welder would be a RCEME trade only and was not allowed in RCE. Therefore the Welder was removed from the RCE and the Blacksmith was revived to take over his job. They simply had a welder who was called a Blacksmith. In 1958, the Welder was revived in

- RCE once again and the Blacksmith made obsolete once again.
- The Mason was a new trade in 1958 which was created by combining the Bricklayer and the Concretor into one trade. The trade of Mason had existed before but had been obsolete since 1946. The Mason mixes, places, and finishes concrete, plaster and stucco. They also build and repair brick structures.
- The Minor became obsolete approximately 1960.
- The Structural Steel Worker became obsolete approximately 1960.
- The Surveyor Engineering became obsolete approximately 1960.
- The Draughtsman Topographical became obsolete in 1959. See the Geomatics section.

By 1963, there were only five trades that could become a Foreman of Works.

Carpenter   Group 1-3
Sheet Metal Worker   Group 1-3. (Obsolete 1966)
Mason   Group 1-3
Painter   Group 1-2
Plumber   Group 1-3

The Painter painted both interior and exterior of buildings and painted signs. The Sheet Metal Worker did installation and repair of sheet metal used in building construction and heating and ventilation systems. All of these trades except the Painter had the option of going to Group 3 in their own trade instead of being a Foreman of Works. (See the second CE trade progression chart.)

The following trades were no longer eligible to become a Foreman of Works:

Welder   Group 1-2 (obsolete 1966)
Minor   Group 2 only (obsolete approx 1960)
Draughtsman A & E   (had own badge)
Surveyor Engineering   (survey badge)
Surveyor Topographical   (survey badge)
Electrician   (had own badge)

All Engineers still had the opportunity to become a Field Engineer at the Group 2 level, but only after taking a course. The course was no longer a prerequisite for all Engineers.

Some information about the jobs of individual Works Company trades is given in this section. For more job descriptions see the earlier parts of this book.

The name of the company itself has undergone several changes. It was originally called a "Fortress Company", hence the battlemented tower badge. After the Second World War it was changed to a "Works Company". In the 1960's it was changed again to a "CE Section", and is currently called the "Engineer Services Company".

See CE Superintendent for the current use of the works badge.

Structures Tech 612   Black   1-4
                                Green   1-4

By 1985 the Works Company was called a Construction Engineer Section and each trade had its own distinctive badge. In 1966 three of the old works trades: Painter, Carpenter, and Mason were combined into one trade called a Structures Tech. They construct, repair and maintain buildings. The Sheet Metal Worker became obsolete in 1966.

The Structures Tech is now obsolete as this combined trade was merged with yet more trades to create the Construction Tech. (See Construction Tech in this section.)

Plumber
Plumber Gas Fitter 613   Black   1-4
                                Green   1-4

The last remaining trade that wore the original works company badge was the Plumber who was renamed Plumber Gas Fitter in 1966. They received their own badge in 1985.

renamed Plumbing & Heating Tech 646 (00304-01)

About 2000 the Plumber Gas Fitter was renamed again to Plumbing and Heating Tech. They Install and maintain plumbing and heating and gas systems. It includes the former trade of Stationary Engineer 623 (an air element trade) who operated the base heating plant. (You may recall from the previous part of this book that there was an army Stationary Engineer at one time. This trade became obsolete in the army about 1950.)

There were other trades in the Works

Company that I have not yet discussed. These trades were the Draughtsman, Electrician, and Surveyor. They had their own separate trades badge, and did not wear the Works Company badge. These trades are discussed separately, the Draughtsman and Electrician in this section, and the Surveyor in the Geomatics section.

Draughtsman A & E   Khaki   1-4
renamed Draughtsman 1966

In 1956 there were four draughting trades that wore this badge. The only one that we will discuss here is the one that was a member of the Works Company, namely the Draughtsman Architectural and Engineering Group 1-4.

The other three are discussed in other sections as follows:
Draughtsman Graphic Arts
see Geomatics section
Draughtsman Topographical
see Geomatics Section
Draughtsman Electrical and Mechanical
see RCEME section

The Draughtsman Architectural and Engineering could become a Foreman of Works when ready for Group 3, or he could remain a draughtsman right through to the Group 4 level. They prepared architectural and engineering sketches, working drawings, site plans and specifications for construction projects.

By 1963 he could still advance to Group 4 in his own trade but could no longer become a Foreman of Works. The name was shortened in 1966 to simply Draughtsman. See CE trade progression charts.

Construction Engineering Tech 611   Black   1-4
Green   1-4

This was a new trade in 1966. They originally wore the same badge as the Draughtsman. The CE Tech specialised in surveying and structural design.

After unification, the trade of Draughtsman (described above) became obsolete and was combined with this trade. This new Construction Engineering Tech would begin his or her career as a draughtsman. As they progressed through the next three levels of their trade, they would be required to learn surveying, elementary structural design and elementary field engineering skills.

There were no trades badges during the period of the CF uniform 1968 to 1985. When the second generation of trade badges were issued in 1985 the badge for the CE Tech was the same as the badge worn by the Draughtsman A & E.

Construction Tech 648 (00306-01)   Black   1-4
Green   1-4

About 2000 the CE Tech was combined with the Structures Tech to create the Construction Tech. The trade badge for the Construction Tech is the old Structures Tech badge. (See Chart).

Electrician 614   Khaki   1-4
Mechanist Electrical   Black   1-4
Green   1-4

There were eleven trades who wore this badge, but only two of them were members of the RCE. Six of them were RCEME trades involved with the repair of communications equipment (see Communications). Three of them were RCEME electricians (see RCEME).

Although only two of the eleven trades were RCE, the picture of the badge is placed here because all of the RCEME trades are now obsolete. (Each badge is shown only once in the text portion of this book.)

The two RCE trades who wore this badge were Electrician, Group 1-3 and the Machanist Electrical Group 4 only

The Electrician and the Mechanist Electrical were actually made up of the same people. He was called an Electrician from Group 1 through to 3, then he became a Mechanist Electrical at the Group 4 level. The Electrician had to be able to install, test and repair electrical fixtures and wiring in buildings. The Mechanist Electrical planned, inspected and tested electrical installations and supervised personnel in power plants, buildings and lighting systems. He was eventually renamed Electrician Group 4.

Electrical Distribution Tech 642 (00302-01)

About 2001 the Electrician was renamed the Electrical Distribution Tech. Their job was to install, repair and maintain electrical distribution systems. They also install lighting systems and fire and security alarms. The badge remains the same.

Trade Badges 1956 to Date

The tradesmen of the Works Company were members of the Corps of Royal Canadian Engineers

Surveyor Engineering   Group   1-4
Surveyor Topographical   Group   1-4

There were two surveyor trades that were part of the Works Company in 1956. They did not wear the Works Company badge, but neither did they have their own distinctive badge. They shared a survey badge with the Artillery Surveyor (see Artillery), the Cartographer, the Lithographer, and the Photogrammetrist. See Geomatics for information about these trades and see the Artillery section for a picture of the badge.

The Surveyor Engineering did surveying of building, road and airfield sites. The Surveyor Topographical did surveys of large tracts of land for map making. Both of these trades could become a Foreman of Works at the Group 3 level. The Surveyor Topographical also had the option to switch to Photogrammetrist at the Group 2 level. The Photogrammetrist did not exist at the Group 1 level, so all of their personnel were former Surveyor Topographical tradesmen. See Geomatics section for information about the Photogrammetrist. By 1963 the option for these two surveyor trades to become a Foreman of Works or a Photogrammetrist had been removed. They now simply proceeded from Group 1 through to Group 4 in their own trade. Approximately 1960 the Surveyor Engineering trade became obsolete. The job is now done by civilian contractors.

Topographical Surveyor 141   Black   1-4
                                                   Green   1-4

In 1966 the name of this trade was changed from Surveyor Topographical to Topographical Surveyor. Members could no longer become a Foreman of Works after 1962. After 1966 this became a non-direct entry trade. Prospective members came from other engineering trades.

New badges (of the same design) were made in 1985 for the new uniforms. In 1998 the trade was merged with the Map Reproduction Tech to become the Geomatics Tech and is no longer part of the CE section. See Geomatics section for details.

Refrigeration and Mechanical   Black   1-4
Tech 641 (00301-01)

This tradesperson operates and maintains refrigeration, heating, ventilation, and air conditioning systems. It was not part of the Works Company in the 1950's. It is a new trade in the CE section. It was an air element trade (Refrigeration Tech 621) until 2003.

CE Procedures Tech 631   Black   1-4
                                   Green   1-4

This trade was formerly called the Engineer Accountant and wore the accounting trade badge in the 1950's. They did all CE related paperwork including production schedules, works control and reception, contract administration, civilian pay, hiring, relations and human resources, and budgets and finance. The trade is obsolete as of 1998. Former CEP Techs were remustered to RMS Clerk. (See Clerks for information about the Engineer Accountant and the RMS Clerk.)

This job is now done by a combination of RMS clerks and civilians.

SUPERVISORY TRADES

Construction & Maintenance Tech 615   No badge
Mechanical Systems Tech 625

In 1966 the Foreman of Works was replaced by two trades. The Construction and Maintenance Tech was the supervisor for the "61" series of trades that have been discussed in this section. They were the trades from what remains of the old Works Company that were involved with construction and repair of buildings. The Mechanical Systems Tech was the supervisor for the "62" series of trades. These were engineering trades which were all air element. They included the following:

- 621 Refrigeration and Mechanical Tech

- 622 Electrical Generating Systems Tech
- 623 Stationary Engineer
- 624 Water, Sanitation, Petrol, Oil, and Lubrication Tech

CE Superintendent 649 (00307-01) No badge

Approximately 2000, the two supervisory trades of Construction & Maintenance Tech and Mechanical Systems Tech were combined into one trade called the CE Superintendent.

The "61" series and the "62" series of trades were combined and are now known as the "64" series of trades. All the CE trades were renumbered. The current status of the CE trades is as follows:

- 641 The Refrigeration and Mechanical Tech became an army trade as well as an air force trade. (now 00301-01)
- 642 Electrical Distribution Tech (now 00302-01)
- 643 Electrical Generating Systems Tech (an air force trade)
- 646 Plumbing and Heating Tech (now 00304-01)
- 647 The Water, Sanitation, Petrol, Oil, and Lubrication Tech was renamed the Water Fuel and Environmental Tech (an air force trade.)
- 648 Construction Tech (now 00306-01)
- 623 The Stationary Engineer is the now obsolete. The job is now included with the trade of Plumbing and Heating Tech.

Reminder: all trade numbers were changed in 2005.

The CE Superintendent could be army or air force and could be in charge of any of the above CE trades. Normally an army CE Superintendent would be posted to an army base to supervise the construction trades, while an air force CE Superintendent would supervise the mechanical trades on an air base. They are however, both members of the same trade.

CE Superintendent badge   Black 1-4
                                      Green 1-4

As stated above there is no badge for the CE supervisory trades. The CE Superintendent is of Warrant Officer rank or above and therefore does not wear a trade badge. However a badge was made for him when the new set of trades badges were produced in 1985. The design is the same as the old Foreman of Works badge, the battlemented tower. The badge was produced in all four levels even though the CE Superintendent would be at least a TQ5 (third level of expertise). The badge was produced in error and was never worn at any level.

The Corps of Royal Canadian Engineers is now known as the Military Engineering Branch, 1903-2003.

OTHER TRADES

The Corps of Royal Canadian Engineers also had the following trades before unification which were common to all corps:

Clerk Administrative   Group 1-3

In the Engineers, members of the Clerk Administrative trade had the option to become an Engineer Accountant at the Group 2 level or they could become a Clerk Administrative Group 2. If they decided to stay with the Clerk Administrative trade, they had another chance to become an Engineer Accountant when they were ready to advance to Group 3. This was their last opportunity to do so. If they chose to advance to Clerk Admin Group 3, then they could advance no higher. The Engineer Accountant trade went from Group 2 to 4.

Storeman Clerk   Group 1-3

The Storeman Clerk, in the RCE, had the same opportunities as the Clerk Admin to change to the Engineer Accountant trade at the Group 2 or Group 3 levels.

Bandsman   Group 1-3
Steward   Group 1-2
Assistant Instructor Air Supply   Group 2-3
Driver Mechanical Transport   Group 1-2

Driver Operator   Group 1 only

The Corps of Royal Canadian Engineers had the greatest variety of trades under a single hat badge. They can be found throughout this book, listed under their various occupation groups. You have already seen a large group of them in the Construction Engineer section. Others can be found as follows:

Trade Badges 1956 to Date

Engineer Accountant - see Clerks
Field Engineer - see Field Engineer
Fire Service - see Fire Service
Fitter RCE - see Materials Tech
Operator Special Engineer Equipment - see Field Engineer and Materials Tech
Machinist Machinery - see Materials Tech
Photographer - see Photographer
Mechanic RCE - see Materials Tech
Welder - see Vehicle Tech

The Royal Canadian Engineers were heavily involved in map production. At one time or another they had the following trades working in this field:
Cartographer
Draughtsman Graphic Arts
Draughtsman Topographical
Lithogrpher
Training Aids Artist
Photogrammetrist
Geomatics Tech
Map Reproduction Tech

You can find information about these trades under its current heading of Geomatics.

COOKS

Catering   Khaki   1-4

This badge was worn by four trades:

Baker	Group 2-3
Butcher	Group 1-3
Cook	Group 1-4 (1942-1962)
	Group 1-3 1961-1966
Master Cook	Group 4 only (new 1960)

Together, these trades were known as the "catering" group of trades. The badge depicts a ladle, cleaver, and rolling pin. The Cook trade began approximately 1938. Before that, a cook was any soldier who was picked for the job. They had no special training to be a cook. Usually the individuals chosen were selected because of their inabilities in their own profession. One can imagine the quality of the meals. After 1938, Cook was a trade but training was done mostly by on-the-job-training. After August 1942, all cooks were members of the RCASC and were sent on a course to learn the trade. In addition to food preparation, the course included the fundamentals of nutrition, hygiene and sanitation, use and care of kitchen equipment and food storage. Candidates for the course had to be medically examined and certified to be free of infectious diseases. At the Group 3 level, the Cook also had to learn menu planning.

The Baker had to begin as a Cook. All Cooks had the option of becoming a Baker at the Group 2 level. There was no Group 1 Baker.

In 1960 the Group 4 Cook was replaced with a new trade called a Master Cook. The Master Cook was responsible for organizing and supervising feeding arrangements and cooking. They also had to supervise the kitchen and staff, and be able to organize and preside over the preparations for a formal mess dinner. (The mess is the place where soldiers eat.)

The Butcher trade was unrelated to the Cook trade except for the fact that they wore the same trade badge. The Baker and Butcher trades were absorbed into the Cook trade in 1964.

In 1966 the Master Cook was replaced by a Group 4 Cook once again. There was no difference between the Group 4 Cook and the Master Cook. It was simply a name change. In the 1960's quite a few trades identified their group four level by a name other than that used by the first three levels. The name usually began with Master or Chief. (For example the Master Terminal Equipment Tech was eventually renamed Terminal Equipment Tech Group 4.)

Cook 861 (00164-01)   Black   1-4
                         Green   1-4

The badge was redesigned in 1985. They prepare meals, from box lunches to formal banquets. They must be able to cook in a modern kitchen or from the back of a truck or a trailer in the woods. Since unification, this had been a Logistics trade.

DENTAL

Khaki   1-3

Dental Assistant Group 1-2
Dental Technician Clinical Group 3-4 (1956-1963) Group 3 only 1963-1968.
Technical Dental Therapist Group 4 only (new 1963)

The Dental Assistant assists or performs dental duties including installing rubber dams, making appointments, reception and other

ROYAL CANADIAN ENGINEERS WORKS COMPANY 1956

Chart does not show trades that were not eligible to become a Foreman of Works, such as Electrician, Blacksmith, & Sawyer.

All trades wore the Works Company badge unless otherwise indicated

Surveyor Topo Could go to Photogrammetrist

All RCE trades had the option to switch to Field Engineer when ready to advance to group two.

The Miner & Quarryman did not exist at the Gp 1 level. They were recruited as already trained civilians. The Quarryman had been at nil strength since 1950.

group 4
- Foreman of Works

group 3
- Foreman of Works
- Surveyor
- Surveyor
- Draughtsman

group 2
- Bricklayer | Concretor | Painter | Miner | Quarryman | Structural Steel Worker | Carpenter | Plumber | Sheet Metal Worker
- Surveyor Topographical | Surveyor Engineering | Draughtsman
- Surveyor Topographical | Surveyor Engineering | Draughtsman A & E

group 1
- Bricklayer | Concretor | Painter | Structural Steel Worker | Carpenter | Plumber | Sheet Metal Worker
- Surveyor Topographical | Surveyor Engineering | Draughtsman A & E

ROYAL CANADIAN ENGINEERS CE SECTION 1963

All trades wore the Works Company badge.

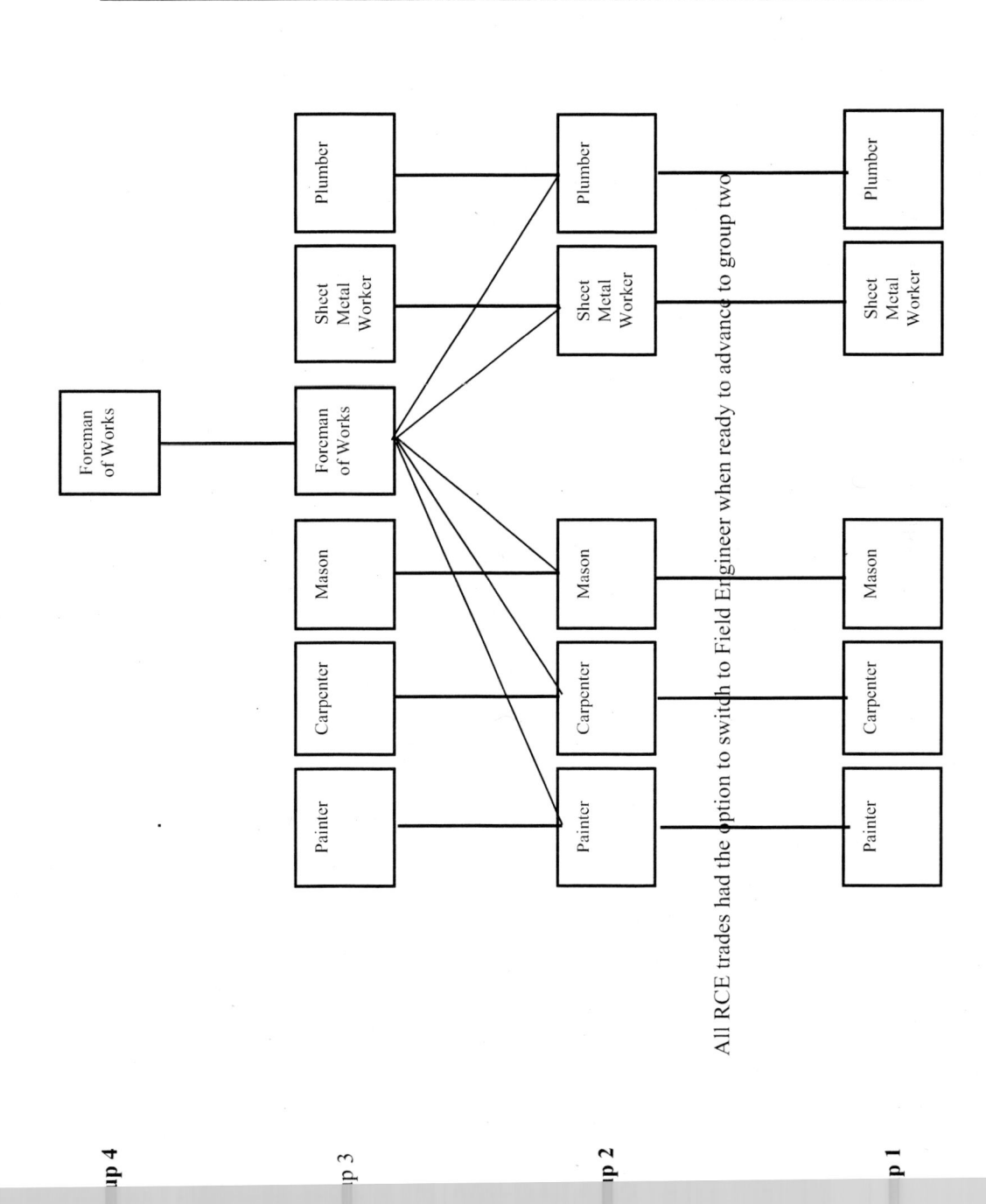

Chart does not show trades that were not eligible to become a Foreman of Works:

Electrician - Gp 1-3
Mechinist Electrical - Gp 4 only
Draughtsman A & E - Gp 1-4
Surveyor Topographical - Gp 1-4
Welder - Gp 1-3, new 1958

Now Obsolete

Blacksmith
Sawyer
Miner
Quarryman
Structural Steel Worker
Surveyor Engineering

All RCE trades were still eligible to switch to Field Engineer after group one, but they had to pass the Field Engineer course as it was no longer a prerequisite for all RCE trades.

Bricklayer and Concretor now included with new trade of Mason.

Group 4: Foreman of Works

Group 3: Foreman of Works — Painter, Carpenter, Mason, Sheet Metal Worker, Plumber

Group 2: Painter, Carpenter, Mason, Sheet Metal Worker, Plumber

All RCE trades had the option to switch to Field Engineer when ready to advance to group two

Group 1: Painter, Carpenter, Mason, Sheet Metal Worker, Plumber

ENGINEER SERVICES COMPANY TO 2004

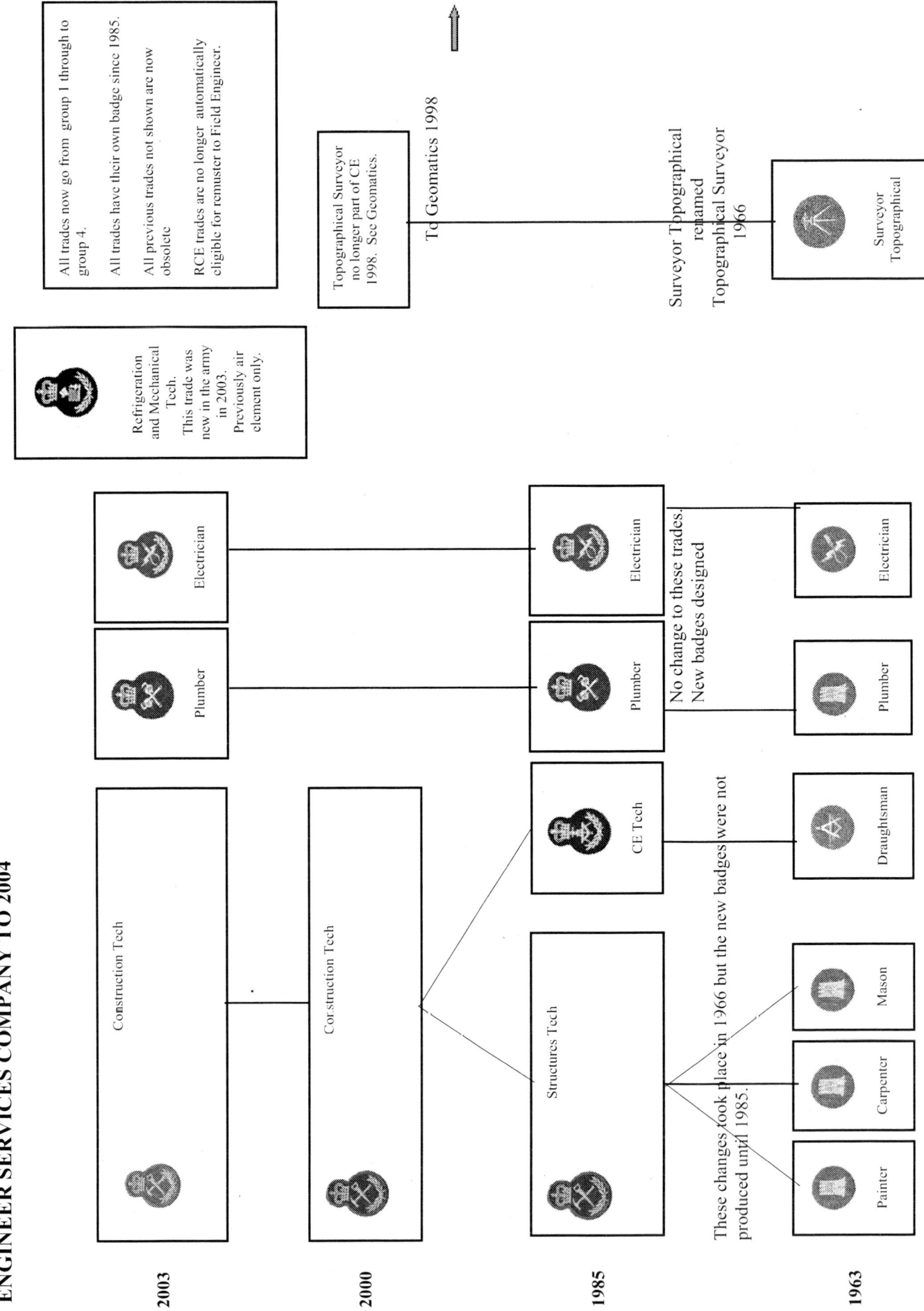

All trades now go from group 1 through to group 4.
All trades have their own badge since 1985.
All previous trades not shown are now obsolete.
RCE trades are no longer automatically eligible for remuster to Field Engineer.

Refrigeration and Mechanical Tech. This trade was new in the army in 2003. Previously air element only.

Topographical Surveyor no longer part of CE 1998. See Geomatics.

To Geomatics 1998

Surveyor Topographical renamed Topographical Surveyor 1966

1966 — Surveyor Topographical

2003 — Construction Tech

2000 — Construction Tech

1985 — Structures Tech | CE Tech | Plumber | Electrician

2003 — Plumber | Electrician

No change to these trades. New badges designed

1963 — Painter | Carpenter | Mason | Draughtsman | Plumber | Electrician

These changes took place in 1966 but the new badges were not produced until 1985.

clerical duties, cleaning and sterilizing dental equipment, taking and processing radiographs (x-rays) and ordering supplies. The badge is a spatula on a mixing slab. In 1956 the trade went from Group 1 to Group 2 only. This trade was renamed Dental Clinical Assistant in 1966.

The trade of Dental Technician Clinical, which did dental work at the Group 3-4 level, was new in 1956. Their job was the prevention of dental decay and diseases. They removed tartar, cleaned and polished teeth, and instructed in oral hygiene. They also had to be able to run the clinic and take X-rays. To qualify for this trade, a prospective member had to be a Group 2 Dental Assistant of at least Sergeant rank. They then had to take a 24-week course. The Group 4 level of this trade was more advanced. In addition to the Group 3 requirements, their duties included instruction in nutrition and pharmacology (the study of drugs and their reactions) and pathology (the study of diseases). In 1963 the Group 3 and Group 4 levels of this trade were combined and the Group 4 was eliminated. (This trade would be known today as a dental hygienist.) [5]

In 1963, when the Dental Tech Clinical was reduced to Group 3 only, a new trade called Technical Dental Therapist was created. This trade worked at the Group 4 level only. Former Group 4 Dental Tech Clinical personnel could remuster to this new trade. Further recruiting came from the Dental Tech Clinical Group 3 personnel when they were ready for advancement. The Dental Technical Therapist did some of the work that was previously done only by the dental officer. They inspected teeth for needed treatment, inserted fillings into cavities that were made by the dental officer, polished fillings, applied medication for gingivitis, removed sutures, made dental impressions for false teeth, inserted and removed temporary crowns and bridges and selected shades of teeth for dentures.

Dental Clinical Assistant 722   Black   1-4
renamed Dental Tech 738 (00335-01)

The Dental Assistant had been renamed the Dental Clinical Assistant in 1966. Upon unification, this trade was upgraded to four levels of expertise instead of the previous two. In 1985, the badge was redesigned to a triangle. In 2003 the trade was renamed Dental Tech because they perform many dental duties on their own, and not just assist the dentist. Note that there used to be a trade called "Dental Tech" in 1956, later renamed Dental Lab Tech, who manufactured and repaired false teeth. As of 2000, one must be a certified dental tech before joining the military. The military used to provide training for this trade but no longer.

The triangle on the badge represents the Greek letter "D", called "Delta". [6]

                                    Khaki   1-4
Two different trades wore this badge in 1956.
Dental Equipment Repairer Group 1-3
Dental Tech   Group 1-3 (before 1954)
                           Group 1-4 (1954-)

The badge is a wax spatula and a bunsen burner. The Dental Tech worked on dentures. They had to create or repair partial and full sets of dentures, as well as bridges and crowns. Partial plates and dentures could be made from acrylic or metal. They created and repaired plates, bridges and crowns using gold, silver, copper alloys, mercury, acid, gypsum, shellac, abrasives, wax, ceramic, rubber, rouge, whiting and modelling clay. They had to know the proper method of mixing and storing all of these substances and how to solder with the precious metals. At the Group 4 level, they also had to instruct junior tradesmen in their duties.

The Dental Equipment Repairer worked on dental equipment. He had to be able to repair any of the instruments used by the dental officer, the Dental Tech, the Dental Technician Clinical or the Technical Dental Therapist. At the Group 2 level, they had to install dental drills and other equipment used at the dental chair including airline and gas line fittings. At the Group 3 level they also installed and repaired dental X-ray equipment.

Neither of these trades could advance to Group 4 until, in 1954, the Dental Tech was upgraded to Groups 1-4.

Over the years both of these trades had their name changed slightly as follows:

1957	Dental Tech	renamed Dental Tech Laboratory
1964	Dental Equipment Repairer	renamed Dental Equipment Technician
1966	Dental Equipment Tech	renamed Dental Equipment Maintenance Tech
	Dental Tech Laboratory	renamed Dental Laboratory Tech

In 1985 each trade got its own badge as shown below.

Dental Lab Tech 723 Black 2-4

This technician manufactured and repaired dentures, crowns and bridges. The badge is a combination of the dental triangle and the bunsen burner from the old Dental Tech badge above. No direct entry. This trade started at the QL5 level. Potential members for the trade were selected from the Dental Clinical Assistant trade. The trade is obsolete as of 2000, and is now done by civilians. This trade existed only at the third and fourth levels but the badge was also produced for the second level of expertise. It was never used.

Dental Equipment Tech 724 Black 2-4
                              Green 2-4

This technician repaired dental equipment. Note that the name was changed in 1968. The word "Maintenance" has been dropped, changing it back to Dental Equipment Tech as it was in 1964. No direct entry. This trade started at the QL5 level. Potential members for the trade were selected from the Dental Clinical Assistant trade. The trade is obsolete as of 2000. This job is now done by the Biomedical Electronics Tech which repairs both medical and dental equipment. Members of this trade had the option to remuster to the BE Tech or take their release. (See medical section.)

Like the Dental Lab Tech above, the trade existed only at the third and fourth levels but badge was also produced for the second level. It was never used.

Dental Therapist
Dental Hygienist 725 (00335-02) Black 4 only
                                     Green 4 only

The Dental Therapist was a combination of the Dental Technician Clinical and the Technical Dental Therapist. If you have not already done so, you should read about their duties at the beginning of the dental section. These two trades were in reality, the third and fourth levels of expertise of the Dental Assistant trade. Upon unification all trades were eligible to advance up to the fourth level of expertise in their own trade, therefore the Dental Assistant (renamed Dental Clinical Assistant in 1966) was upgraded to four levels and these two trades were combined to create the new trade of Dental Therapist.

As stated above, all trades, after unification, could advance to the fourth level. However, not all trades existed at the lower levels. The Dental Therapist trade existed at the fourth level only. (Reminder: As stated earlier in the book, I refer to the four badges as levels rather than use their proper name because the proper name kept changing. Originally called groups, they changed to pay levels, then trade qualification levels, then qualification levels. To keep it simple, I refer to them throughout the book as the four levels of expertise.)

As oral hygiene was the main duty of this trade, the name was later changed to Dental Hygienist. They provide oral hygiene including scaling, polishing, radiographs and fluoride treatments. They also update patient dental records, perform sterilisation and disinfection and maintenance of dental equipment. (Major repairs of dental equipment are sent to the Biomedical Electronics Tech, which is not a dental trade. The dental branch no longer does repairs to dental equipment.) No direct entry. Potential members for the trade are selected from the Dental Tech (formerly Dental Clinical Assistant) trade. The Dental Hygienist exists at the QL6 level only.

OTHER TRADES

The Dental Corps also had the following trades before unification:
Clerk Administrative Group 1-3
Storeman Clerk Group 1-3

Flash!

Just before going to press the existence of a Dental Hygienist badge at the first level has been discovered. This book shows only badges that are known to exist. There is a theory that all CF and garrison dress badges were produced at all four levels. If the Hygienist badge exists at the first level, it seems probable that the 2nd and 3rd levels exist also. The same applies for a few other badges. I will not change the book based on speculation, but it is possible that badges other than those listed in the book do indeed exist. If new discoveries are made, they will be noted in a future edition of the book. Badge courtesy of the W.E. Storey Collection.

In addition to the dental trades there were personnel from the Clerk Administrative and Storeman Clerk trades in the Dental Corps. If you read about the Storeman Clerk in the clerk section, you will find that he was more of an accountant than a storeman. A new trade was created in the Dental Corps for their Storeman Clerk personnel.

Dental Storeman   Group 1-3   new in 1960

Storeman Clerks in the Royal Canadian Dental Corps remustered to this new trade in 1960. Their job was to maintain, order, and account for all dental supplies. The Storeman Clerk and the Dental Storeman wore the accounting badge. Both of these trades became obsolete in 1966 and were replaced by the new trade of Supply Tech. See clerk and supply sections for more information.

THE ROYAL CANADIAN DENTAL CORPS

The RCDC is believed to be the oldest military dental service in the world. It was formed in May 1915.

DRIVERS

Driver Mechanical Transport Khaki 1 and 2 only
                                Red 1 and 2 only

In spite of the name, this person was not a mechanic (for mechanics, see Vehicle Tech). This trade was formerly called the Driver Mechanic Wheeled. After 1954 that name was used only in the RCAC. His duties were to drive and maintain unit vehicles and do minor repairs and maintenance such as grease jobs and oil changes. At the Group 2 level he also had to instruct in driving and vehicle maintenance. Drivers of tracked vehicles also wore this badge, except for tank drivers which had their own distinctive badge (see Armoured section). It does not include the RCASC driver after 1957 when they became a separate trade with their own badge, shown below. This badge was worn by the Infantry Driver, Driver RCA, Driver RCA Tracked, and Driver Mechanical Transport (all other Corps). Nor was this badge worn by the Driver Operator. The Driver Operator also had to be qualified in the operation of radio equipment (see Communications section).

These drivers were very good at making necessary repairs to their vehicles. No doubt some were highly skilled and others no so skilled. Repairs that were beyond their abilities were sent to the RCEME Vehicle Techs. The trade is now obsolete. Today most soldiers are qualified to drive several different vehicles, and many are qualified to drive tracked vehicles.

Do not confuse this trade, or any other driver trade, with the term "driver wheeled." Driver wheeled is simply a course to learn to drive. It has never been a trade. Soldiers of any corps cold take a driver wheeled course. For example, an Operator Wireless and Line could take a driver wheeled course to learn to drive his radio vehicle. This would make him a qualified driver, but not a driver by trade. There was a trade called Driver Mechanic Wheeled but not "driver wheeled."

Trade progression for this tradesman varied by corps as follows:

In RCE the Driver Mechanical Transport Group 1 could progress to Group 2 or to Mechanic RCE. The Mechanic RCE could eventually become a Mechanist Machinery Group 4.

In the Signal Corps he could progress to Group 2 or become a Signals Electrician (formerly called Driver Electrician) or a DR. The Signals Electrician could then advance to Group 3.

In RCEME and RCASC the Driver Mechanical Transport Group 2 could become an Assistant Instructor Group 3.

In all other corps he could progress only to Driver Mechanical Transport Group 2. There was no Group 3 level in this trade.

By 1964 this trade existed in only in RCE, RCOC and RCEME.

Reminder: This and some other trade badges were also produced in red for the rifle regiments.

Transport Operator   Group 1-3   Khaki 1-4
Chief Transport Op   Group 4 only 1957-1966
Transportation Controller Group 4 only 1966-1968

This is the professional driver of the RCASC. This badge was not among the original group issued in 1956. After a ten-year campaign with Army HQ the Transport Op finally became a separate trade in 1957. Keep in mind that many of the trades mentioned in this part of the book began before 1956. That was simply the year that the badges were first produced. The Driver Mechanical Transport had been a trade long before they had a badge. This was the trade that the RCASC drivers were included with originally. They began asking to form a separate trade in 1947.

The wagon wheel represents ground transportation. The superimposed wings represent the RCASC's increasing role in air supply. The trade of Despatcher Air Supply was discontinued and the job included with this new trade. (See parachute trades.)[7]

At the Group 1-3 levels, the trade was called "Transport Operator." They were required to operate and maintain all types of vehicles including both wheeled and tracked vehicles and motorcycles. They had to be skilled at loading and unloading supplies into and from both fixed and rotary wing aircraft. They also had to do the paperwork to account for their stores.

The Transport Op could be employed in two different environments. As a base employee, he would drive all types and sizes of vehicles including staff cars, large trucks, motorcycles, buses, ambulances, fuel tankers and tractor trailers. If posted to a field unit, he would belong to a Transport Company which consisted of four platoons of 20 2½ ton cargo trucks each and a workshop platoon and a composite platoon. The Transport Platoons had the task of delivering supplies to the troops in the field, usually at night. The workshop had their own RCASC vehicle mechanics until 1964 when all mechanics had to be RCEME. The composite platoon consisted of Butchers, Clerks RCASC, Storeman RCASC and others who were responsible for record keeping and getting the loads onto the correct truck to go to the unit that ordered the supplies.

The Group 4 was called a "Chief Transport Operator" (a Staff Sgt). He was responsible for the coordination and direction of RCASC transport both in the field and in static positions. To become a Chief Tpt Op, a Group 3 Tpt Op had to be qualified to drive motorcycles as well as all types of land vehicles including tracked vehicles. They also had to be qualified as an instructor and in air supply including the rigging of stores for aerial delivery. They instructed corps personnel in operations in both peace and war, and other general military training. This trade took the place (in the RCASC) of Instructor Air Supply and Assistant Instructor RCASC which then become obsolete. Instructor Air Supply continued to exist in other corps until 1964. (See parachute trades and instructors.)[8] In 1966 the Chief Transport Operator was renamed Transportation Controller.

Although approved in 1957, the RCASC drivers had to take many courses to learn and master their new obligations. Some of them had been driving for years but knew little about air supply. Others were experts on air supply but could not drive large vehicles. The process took several years to convert all of them to this new trade.

Photo by author

Mobile Support Equipment Operator 932
Transportation Controller 934
Black   1-4
Green   1-4

After unification, the Transport Operator was renamed the Mobile Support Equipment Operator. The Transportation Controller remained as a separate trade. They became more than just the fourth level of the Transport Op. This trade was now in addition to the four levels of MSE Op and not in place of the fourth level. It was non direct entry trade. To be accepted as a Transportation Controller, one had to be at the fourth level of expertise of either a MSE Op or a Traffic Tech. The Transportation Controller encompassed all aspects of these two trades at the supervisory level. One of their main duties was to accept or reject requests. If a unit requested a vehicle and driver for a certain period of time, the Transportation Controller would grant or deny the request based on availability of vehicles and drivers and other priorities. (In larger units this job is done by an Transport Officer). The Transportation Controller would be a Chief Warrant Officer and would therefore not wear a trade badge. (See Traffic Tech for related info).

Mobile Support Equipment Operator
935 (00171-01)

Sometime in the 1970s (I don't know the exact year) the MSE Op 932 and the Tn Controller 934 were merged to become a MSE Op 935. The air supply duties were eliminated and the Tn Controller was merged with the Group 4 MSE Op.

A new badge was designed (the eight-spoked wheel) for the MSE OP in 1985. This trade is no longer involved with air supply and therefore the wings have been removed from the trade badge. Note that the old Transport Op badge (8-spoked wheel with wings) is now the new Traffic Tech badge. The MSE Op is employed at the Base Transport Section where their duties include snow and ice removal from the roads in winter and road grading in the summer. The Base Transport Section includes both MSE Ops and civilian equipment operators.

OTHER DRIVERS

Driver Operator - see Communications, Artillery and Field Engineers

Driver Mechanic Tracked - see Armoured Section
Driver Mechanic Wheeled - see Armoured Section
Driver RCA - see Artillery section
Infantry Driver - see Infantry section
Despatch Rider - see Communications
Driver Radio Op - see Communications, Field Engineers and RCEME
Driver Electrician - see Communications

FIELD ENGINEERS

Field Engineer 041   Khaki   1-4
                         Black   1-4
                         Green   1-4

The job of the Field Engineer was to build bridges, roads, and airfields. They are also trained in mine warfare, water supply and demolitions. Until 1954 the trade existed only in the Group 2-4 levels. Group 1 was a different trade known as the Pioneer RCE who assisted the infantry with engineer tasks. In 1954 the Pioneer RCE was abolished and the Field Engineer upgraded to Groups 1-4. The infantry had created their own pioneer trade in 1950. In 2003 this was reversed (see Infantry Pioneer and Combat Engineer).

Operator Special Engineering Equipment
                                   Group 1-3
Operator Engineer Equipment   Group 1-3
Field Engineer Equipment Operator 042
                         Black   1-4
                         Green   1-4

This tradesman had to be able to drive and operate heavy engineering equipment such as bridge layers, cranes, bulldozers, excavators, graders and tractor-trailers. The military has always seemed unsure where to include this trade. In 1956 they were called Operator Special Engineering Equipment but wore the machinist badge and were included in a group with the Fitters, Machinists and Toolmakers (see Materials Tech). In 1966 the name was shortened to Operator Engineer Equipment. In 1974 the trade was abolished. The personnel who were employed as Operator Engineer Equipment were sent to work with the base Mobile

Support Equipment Operators (see Drivers). No new personnel were admitted into the trade and the operators who were employed with the MSE Ops were gradually phased out upon retirement. In 1986 the trade was resurrected with the new name of Field Engineer Equipment Operator and new members were recruited from the Field Engineer trade. A new badge was designed featuring a bridge layer. There was no direct entry for this trade. Potential members had to be at least a QL4 with two years as a Field Engineer. He could then switch to this trade at the first level. In 2003, the trade was abolished once again and the members merged with the Field Engineers. The combined trades are now known as a Combat Engineer.

Crane, bridge laying equipment, and road laying equipment. Photos by author.

Mechanic RCE

This trade was created in 1950 to make repairs to the special engineering equipment. This trade was abolished in 1966 and the personnel were remustered to other trades. (Probably RCEME Vehicle Techs).

Combat Engineer 043 (00339-01)

In 2003, the Field Engineer and the Field Engineer Equipment Operator were combined to create the Combat Engineer. The badge is the same as the previous Field Engineer badge. The Combat Engineer, as the name suggests, provides close engineering support to the combat arms. The Infantry Pioneer was abolished and we have now come full circle, back to the Engineers providing pioneer support to the infantry when required instead of the pioneer being a member of the infantry. This was the situation prior to 1950.

A Combat Engineer could be employed in one of two roles. Combat Engineer Regiments are no longer involved with building roads, airfields and bridges. They are employed only on combat related duties such as working with demolitions and minefields. They may be called upon to build or demolish vehicle or tank obstacles. They are also required to built temporary bridges in a combat zone. Construction of permanent roads, airfields and bridges are now the responsibility of the Engineer Support Regiment. Members of this unit are of the same trade, but are involved with non combat engineering duties.

OTHER TRADES

The Royal Canadian Engineers also had the following trades before unification:

Clerk Administrative   Group 1-3
The Clerk Administrative had the option of changing to an Engineer Accountant at the Group 2 or 3 level if they wished.

Driver Operator   Group 1 only
Renamed Driver Radio Operator Group 1-2 in 1958, then changed to Group 2 only in 1963. (See Communications.)

FIRE SERVICE

Fire Fighter   No badge 1-3 obsolete 1960
Fire Safety Inspector   Khaki   2 and 3 only

When the modern army trade badges were first introduced in 1956, there were still a few trades that did not have one. According to dress regulations of 1956, trades that did not have a trade badge were to continue to wear the "T" badge until one was designed for their trade. The army firefighter was one of these. However, contrary to regulations, the army firefighter wore the trade badge of the Field Engineers while waiting for their own trade badge to be approved. Both Field Engineer and the Firefighter were RCE trades. No badge was ever approved and the army firefighter was phased out in 1960 and replaced by civilians of the DND fire department.[1]

A new trade was created called "Fire Safety Inspector" whose job was to inspect, test, and report on unit fire safety measures and equipment. He also planned and conducted fire safety training. He could act as station fire chief or a firefighter if required. This trade started at the Group 2 level. Group 1 could be any trade or corps but were mostly RCE. The trade became obsolete in 1966. The job is now done by a mixture of civilians and air force personnel, mostly civilians on army bases.

*Shilo Fire Hall and army fire trucks.
Photos courtesy of firehouse651.com*

GEOMATICS

Geomatics is the name for the people involved with map making. These trades did not have their own trade badge but shared it with several other trades. See Artillery Surveyor for a picture.

Cartographer Group 1-4   survey badge

A Cartographer produced standard road maps. They produced colour plates for the production of regular and topographical maps. They also revised existing colour plates and negatives. They could add colour tints to lithographic plates to produce roads in different colours. They received their data from the Photogrammetrist and the Photographer Cartographic. This trade was formerly called the Draughtsman Cartographic whose job was to produce standard maps on paper. In 1946 the trade was combined with the Draughtsman Lithographic (who prepared the map onto the lithographic plate for printing) and the Photo Writer (who edited negatives) to create the Cartographer. (You can read about the old draughting trades and the Photo Writer in Part Two, and the Photographer Cartographic in this part of the book.)

Lithographer Group 1-4   survey badge

The Lithographer operates printing equipment. Once the Cartographer had produced one copy of a map, the Lithographer could print many copies by printing from the lithographic plates. The plates would be made of zinc or aluminum. They were very thin and flexible. The Lithographer used an oil based ink which adhered only to the image and not to the blank areas of the plate. The plate was coated with a photosensitive material that was oleophilic which means that it attracted oil. The blank area was hydrophilic which means that it attracted water and repelled oil. Printing was not done directly from the metal plate. The data was transferred to a rubber roller which in turn transferred the image to paper.

Photogrammetrist   Group 2-4   survey badge

The Photogrammetrist produces input for map production from aerial photography. Using a stereoscope, he would view two overlapping photographs of the same area, taken from two different aerial locations. With this equipment, heights and distances can be obtained. To determine the scale a ground survey is required, but photogrammetry reduced the ground work by 90 per cent. Using the heights and distances of the ground survey given to him by the Surveyor Topographical, the Photogrammetrist can then compute all other heights and distances. He then produces a planimetric map which can be used by the Cartographer to produce a topographical map. This trade did not exist at the Group 1 level as it was a non direct entry trade. The Photogrammetrist was recruited from the Group 1 Surveyor Topographical trade (see CE section trades).

In 1966, the above three trades were combined into one under the name of Cartographer.

Draughtsman Graphic Arts
        Group 1-4   draughting badge

This tradesman made any required graphics for the group such as the box of map symbols that can be found in the corner of any map. They did not work only on maps. They produced a wide variety of art work including paintings, drawings, posters, murals, signs and labels. They had to have knowledge of many types of media including crayons, charcoal, tracing paper, ink, water and oil colours. Obsolete 1959.

Draughtsman Topographical
        Group 1-2   draughting badge

This tradesman had the job of drawing and designing topographical maps. He received input from the Surveyor Topographical. He had to produce maps from any data, such as surveyor's notes, aerial photographs or standard maps. He also had to enlarge or reduce a map. He could make corrections on lithographic plates. Obsolete 1959.

Training Aids Artist Group 1-4 draughting badge
renamed Graphic Artist 1966

This trade was created in Feb 1959 by combining the above two Draughtsman trades. Their job was to produce signs, diagrams, charts, maps, and overlays. In 1966 this trade was renamed to Graphic Artist.

Map Reproduction Tech 151   Black 1-4
                                           Green 1-4

Approximately 1969, the Cartographer and the Graphic Artist were combined into one trade called the Map Reproduction Tech. The badge however, was not produced until 1985. They use the data collected by the surveyor to create and produce topographical maps. An Engineer Trade. It was a non direct entry trade with some exceptions. Reserve force recruits could join directly into this trade at the first level and occasionally some civilians were recruited, but most new members came from other trades of the CF. Now obsolete.

Geomatics Tech 142 (00238-01)   Black 2-4

In 1998 the Map Reproduction Tech was merged with the Topographical Surveyor to become the Geomatics Tech. They provide global geospacial information and services. In other words, they are responsible for the acquisition, production and distribution of digital and graphic geometric products. Map making now uses high technology equipment such as the Global Positioning System and digital cameras and Geographic Information System software to produce the end product. A member of this trade must be able to create, add to, and interrogate the Geographic Information System databases, and conduct terrain analysis studies (survey) of man-made and natural topographical features. They produce and revise maps and charts using remote-sensing imagery, aerial photography and a wide variety of other sources. They must be able to print the results using automated cartographic reproduction equipment and a lithographic printing press. Geomatic teams can also work on the battlefield to produce on the spot data for the task force commander. Small scale maps can be produced within 24 hours and typical topographical 1:250000 scale maps within seven days.

If you have read the job descriptions of the many geomatics, survey and printing trades mentioned in previous parts of this book, you will know that this is a highly skilled individual who is a combination of all of the previous related trades.

In addition to their map making duties, they also operate the Geomatics depot for the distribution of both hard copy and digital geospatial data for the Canadian Forces. This is a non-direct entry trade.

Applicants from any other trade can enter this trade at the QL4 level after passing the required course, which explains the absence of a first level badge.

All of the trades discussed in the Geomatics section were/are Engineer trades.

INFANTRY

Khaki 1-3	Red 1-3
Green RWR 1-3	Black 1-4
	Green 1-4

Leading Infantryman
Master Infantryman (1963-1966)
Infantryman 031 (00010-01)

The infantry's job is to close with and destroy the enemy. They use weapons such as rifles, explosives, mortars, machine-guns, grenades, etc. They also use communications equipment and drive both wheeled and tracked vehicles. In 1956 the name of the specialty was Leading Infantryman. When ready to advance to Group 2, he could become a Group 2 Leading Infantryman or a Group 2 in any of the other infantry specialties shown below. The same applies at the Group 3 level. There was no Group 4 infantry trade but he could become a Group 4 instructor. In 1963 the name Leading Infantryman was shortened to simply Infantryman.

Also in 1963, the Group 4 instructor was replaced with a Master Infantryman Group 4. His job was to assist in the tactical deployment and administration of a rifle company or other sub unit in the battalion. He also had to do the job of the instructor that he replaced. To reach the Group 4 Master Infantryman level, the soldier had to be a Group 3 Infantryman plus be able to drive all unit vehicles, plus be familiar with communication voice procedure plus be qualified in any three of the other four infantry specialties. Not many soldiers made it to Master Infantryman and no badge was ever made for the Group 4 level that I could find. A Master Infantryman would probably be a WO and would therefore not wear a trade badge.

In 1966 the Master Infantryman was replaced with a Group 4 Infantryman.

An infantry battalion is divided into companies. There are normally three or four rifle companies plus a support company and an administration company. The companies are further divided into platoons. The rifle companies are divided into three rifle platoons. Support Company was divided into platoons that specialized in specific weapons. There was a mortar platoon, an anti-tank platoon, a machine gun platoon and a pioneer platoon. These were specialties within the Infantry, each with their own distinctive badge. The newer badges, issued in 1985, (shown below) exist in levels two to four (QL4 to 6) only, as all infantrymen start out wearing the basic infantry badge (shown above,) before going to one of the specialty trades at level two (QL4). The older, 1956 badges, existed in groups one to three only. In those days they did not have to take the Group 1 Leading Infantryman course first, and there was no Group 4 level. This organization no longer applies. The Infantry has lost their pioneers to the Combat Engineers and the heavy mortars have gone to the artillery. The infantry still has machine guns and light mortars but these are weapons that can be used by any infantryman and not limited to use by a certain platoon. (See SORD at the end of Part Three.)

Infantry Anti-Tank Gunner   Khaki 1-3
                                                  Red   1-3

This soldier was trained in anti-tank weapons such as the 106 mm Anti-tank gun.

Black 2-4

In 1985 the Anti-Tank badge was re-designed. They now have more sophisticated weapons such as the TOW missile.

Infantry Machine Gunner   Khaki 1-3
                                                  Red   1-3

This soldier was trained to fire medium and heavy machine guns such as the 7.62 calibre and the 50 calibre machine gun.

Black 2-4
Green 2-4

In 1985 the badge was re-designed. This speciality was discontinued in the late 1980's.

SKILL AT ARMS

Infantry Motarman Khaki 1-3 Red 1-3
　　　　　　　　　　　Black 2-4 Green 2-4

This soldier fires mortar weapons in two sizes, the 60mm and the 81mm. The 1985 version of the badge remains unchanged from the original 1956 design.

In 2002, the task of firing the larger 81mm was moved to the artillery. The infantry still uses the smaller 60mm but they have done away with the mortar platoon. The 60mm mortar is now just another weapon for the basic infantryman.

Infantry Pioneer Khaki 1-3 Red 1-3
　　　　　　　　　　Black 2-4 Green 2-4

The Pioneer performs minor Engineering tasks in an infantry unit. They lay minefields, minor bridging, demolitions, create obstacles, do carpentry work and prepare defensive positions. The 1985 version of the badge remains unchanged from the original 1956 design.

In 2002 this specialty was abolished. The Combat Engineers now provide this service for the infantry. (See Combat Engineer for details.)

Infantry Sniper Khaki 1 only Red 1 only
　　　　　　　　　Black 2-4 Green 2-4

In 1956 the sniper existed at the Group 1 level only. The 1985 version of the badge remains unchanged from the original 1956 design.

Notes on infantry specialties

1. In 1956 the Leading Infantryman (later renamed simply Infantryman) progressed from Group 1 up to Group 3. At the Group 4 level he could become an instructor or, from 1963 to 1966, a Master Infantryman. Since 1966 the trade progresses through all four levels without the necessity of changing trades at the fourth level.
2. All of the other infantry specialties with the exception of the Sniper advanced as follows:
    a. In order to advance to Group 2 they had to become qualified as a Leading Infantryman Group 1 and also pass a driver wheeled course.
    b. To reach Group 3 they had to be a senior NCO and be a qualified Infantry Signaller Group 1.
    c. There was no Group 4 in their trade until 1966. They could become an instructor. The Instructor was replaced by the Master Infantryman from 1963-1966.
3. The Sniper could not advance past Group 1 as a Sniper. He could advance to Group 2 as a Leading Infantryman.
4. All of the Infantry specialties except Leading Infantryman became obsolete in 1963. After 1963 the jobs and the badges continued to be used, but the trade of all these soldiers was Infantryman. This brought about the unique case of badges without a trade. A soldier who wore the machine gunner badge in the 1980's would be a Infantryman by trade, not a machine gunner. The same applies for the other infantry specialties. Since 1963 there has been only one trade in the infantry, and that is Infantryman. Some of the badges were redesigned in 1985.

Infantry Stretcher Bearer Khaki 1 only
　　　　　　　　　　　　　　Red 1 only

This badge is often thought to belong to one of the medical trades. It is an infantry badge, not medical. This infantryman's job was to carry wounded soldiers off of the battlefield. They were well trained in basic first aid but they were not qualified medics. They would administer sufficient emergency first aid to stop any bleeding, and try to get the patient to a medical facility in time to prevent his condition from getting worse. Although a member of the infantry, the Infantry Stretcher Bearer was not a combat trade and had no relationship to the other infantry specialties discussed above. The Infantry Stretcher Bearer was a trade and not a specialty like the other members of the infantry unit. This trade existed at the Group 1 level only. In order to advance to Group 2 he would have to remuster to another trade or specialty. This trade is now obsolete (since 1963) and there is no 1985 version of the badge. Today any soldier in a field unit can be a stretcher-bearer. There is no special trade for this job.

Infantry Reconnaissance   Black   2-4
                              Green   2-4

The word reconnaissance is seldom used in the military. It is always referred to by its abbreviation of "recce". The job of the recce is to go out ahead of the main body of troops and observe the enemy. They try not to come into contact with the enemy, but must be prepared if that happens. Their goal is to observe the enemy and report their findings so that the main body of troops will be better prepared to deal with them This badge was new in 1985 and did not exist in the battledress version. Like other infantry duties, this remains a job and not a trade. The only trade in the infantry is Infantryman. The armoured units also have a recce squadron who does the same job for their unit. (See Armoured Recce.)

Infantry Driver   Khaki   1 and 2 only

No badge is shown because it is the same as that worn by other drivers (see Driver Mechanical Transport). His duties at the Group 1 level were to drive both wheeled and tracked vehicles used by an Infantry unit, and to do light maintenance. In order to advance to Group 2, he must also be familiar with the duties of a Leading Infantryman Group 1. He could not advance past Group 2 in this trade, therefore he would have to remuster in order to progress further. He had the option to become a Signaller. As an Infantry Signaller he could then advance to Group 3 Infantry Anti-Tank or Pioneer. He could become an instructor at the Group 4 level. (See Artillery driver for a similar trade.) Obsolete 1963

Infantry Signaller   Khaki   1 and 2 only

No badge is shown because it is the same as that worn by other signallers. At the Group 3 level he could become a Anti-Tank Gunner or a Pioneer. See Comms section for details. Obsolete 1963.

The Infantry Driver and the Infantry Signaller are no longer required. In the modern army, all infantrymen are trained to drive and use communication equipment. Both of these jobs were specialties and not trades. The only trades in the infantry before unification were Stretcher Bearer and Assistant Instructor.

Assistant Instructor Infantry   Khaki Group 4 only

The infantry instructor wore the same badge as other instructors. (See Instructors below.) Any infantry specialty Group 3 could become an instructor. In 1963 this trade was replaced by the Group 4 Master Infantryman. (See Infantryman.)

OTHER TRADES

In addition to the above trades and specialties, there were Bandsman, Clerk Administrative, Instructor Para, and Stewards in the infantry.

INSTRUCTORS

Assistant Instructors   Khaki   3 and 4 only
                          Red   3 and 4 only

In 1956 most instructors were renamed "Assistant Instructors". The Assistant Instructor was a soldier who became an instructor at a certain point in his career, but did not necessarily remain an instructor permanently. See the Armoured and Artillery trade progression charts for examples. They were called "Assistant Instructors" because "Instructors" were either officers or soldiers who went out from the regular force to teach the reserve forces. (See instructors in Part One for more information on this.) Assistant Instructors worked at Corps schools. If you compare the list of Assistant Instructors in 1956 to the list in Part Two of the book, you would see that the list has become shorter. Some of the instructor trades were obsolete by 1956 and all of them were obsolete by 1968.

This badge was worn by Assistant Instructors except the Physical Training Instructor, the Parachute Instructor, and the Artillery Instructor. These trades had their own distinctive badges. The badge for the PTI can be seen in this section. The Para Instructor and the Artillery Instructor badges can be seen in their respective sections in this part of the book. Note that some instructors were Group 2 but the badge was produced for only the Group 3 and 4 levels. The Assistant Instructors that were still in use in 1956 were:

Assistant Instructor AA Artillery	RCA	Group 3-4
Assistant Instructor Field Artillery	RCA	Group 3-4
Assistant Instructor HD Artillery	RCA	Group 3-4
(Replaced by Chief Gunnery Assistant in 1963)		
Assistant Instructor Infantry	Infantry	Group 4 only
Assistant Instructor RCAC	RCAC	Group 4 only
(Replaced by Master Crewman in 1963)		
Assistant Instructor RCAMC	RCAMC	Group 3-4
Assistant Instructor RCEME	RCEME	Group 3 only
Assistant Instructor RCOC	RCOC	Group 3-4
Assistant Instructor RC SIGS	RC Sigs	Group 3-4
Instructor Airportability	any corps	Group 2 only
Instructor Air Supply RCA, RCE, RC SIGS, RCASC, RCAMC		Group 2-3
(Replaced in RCASC in 1958 by Chief Transport Op)		
Instructor Arctic Training	any corps	Group 2 only
Instructor Driver Mechanic Tracked	RCA	Group 2 only
Instructor Driver Mechanic Wheeled		
RCA, RCE, RC Sigs, RCASC, RCOC, C Pro C		Group 2 only
Instructor Regimental Communications	RCA & RCEME	Group 2 only
Instructor RCASC	RCASC	Group 2 only
(Replaced in 1958 by Chief Transport Op)		
Senior Instructor RCASC	RCASC	Group 3 only
(Replaced in 1958 by Chief Transport Op)		
Instructor C Pro C	C Pro C	Group 2-3
(Replaced in 1956 by Service Policeman Group 3 which was previously Group 1-2 only.)		

Military Instructor   Any corps   Group 3-4

By 1966 most of the instructor trades had become obsolete. Those that remained were combined into a single trade. This was a short-lived trade and became obsolete after unification. Since unification, instructing is a job and not a trade.

Assistant Instructor Physical Training Khaki 1-4

The Assistant Instructor Physical Training personnel got their own distinctive trade badge in 1956. They could be a member of any corps. This was similar to musicians and clerks at that time. The group levels kept changing over the years as follows:

Before 1953 it was Group 1-2 only.
In 1953 it changed to Group 2 only.
This meant that it was a non-direct entry trade.
In 1954 the Group 3 was added.

The AIPT spent most of their working hours in gym clothing, therefore a crest with their trade badge was worn on their singlet. The soldier on the right is Cpl Willy Weiler who was a Group two. The other two solders are Cpl Gerry Lindner (on the left) and S/Sgt Ken MacDonald who are both Group three. My thanks to Ken MacDonald for this photo taken in 1959.

In 1963 the Assistant Instructor Physical Training was split into two new trades, one for the infantry and one for the remainder of the army as follows:

Physical Training and Recreation Specialist
Group 2-4 infantry only

Physical Training Instructor
Group 1-2 all corps except infantry

Also in 1963 the Physical Training Staff was created. They had their own shoulder titles and hat badge. Members of the Assistant Instructor Physical Training (now known as Physical Training and Recreation Specialist) trade were moved to this cadre. Previously they could have been a member of any corps such as Signals, Artillery, etc. This cadre was a part of the infantry corps.[9] The Physical Training Instructor did not become a part of this new staff. They remained as unit PT instructors and were members of their particular corps (except infantry). Just because members of this cadre were part of the infantry corps does not mean that they worked only with infantry units. They were sent to most army bases to assist the PTI with the physical training of their troops.

Physical Education and Recreation Instructor 851
      Black   1-4
      Green   1-4

In 1966, the unit Physical Training Instructor was abolished as a trade. It existed only from 1963 to 1966. The Physical Training and Recreation Specialist was renamed Physical Education and Recreation Instructor or PERI for short. After unification they became members of the Administration Branch of the CF. In December 1980 they left the Admin Branch and formed their own branch of the Canadian Forces called the Physical Education and Recreation Branch[10]. A new badge was designed in 1985. The trade became obsolete in March 1997. Each unit must now provides their own physical training instructors who perform this duty as a part time job in addition to the regular duties of their trade.

Also see Instructor Parachute Training under parachute trades. You can find more information about some of these instructors in their own corps section.

INTELLIGENCE

               Khaki   1-4
Intelligence Investigator   Group 1-3
Chief Intelligence Investigator Group 4

Their job description in 1956 was to investigate potential or actual enemy hostile activities and neutralize them or reduce their effectiveness. Basically, they gathered intelligence about the enemy. The badge shows the true and magnetic north. This trade existed only at the Group 1-3 levels until the Chief Int Investigator Group 4 was added approximately 1960.

Plotter Air Photo
Assistant Photo Interpreter   Group 1-3
Chief Assistant Photo Interpreter Group 4

The Assistant Photo Interpreter was known as the Plotter Air Photo before 1956. Their job was to gather intelligence from aerial photographs. They also plotted detail onto aerial photographs and determined the scale of measures from photographs. They also assisted in the preparation of intelligence reports. This trade existed only at the Group 1-3 levels until the Chief Assistant Photo Interpreter Group 4 was added approximately 1960. C Int C.

Intelligence Collator   Group 1-3

The job of the Intelligence Collator was to collect, collate and disseminate information on enemy forces. This was a new trade in 1960. After Group 2, he could progress either to Group 3 in his own trade or switch to a Group 3 Radio Intelligence Collator. There was no Group 4 in this trade. The only way to get to Group 4 was to first switch to Radio Intelligence Collator at the Group 3 level.

Radio Intelligence Collator   Group 3 only
Chief Radio Intelligence Collator Group 4 only

The Radio Intelligence Collator's job was to intercept and translate enemy radio transmissions to obtain information of intelligence value. This was a new trade in 1960. It did not exist at the Group 1-2 level. Members of this trade had to be an Intelligence Collator Group 2. They had to be fluent in at least one foreign language. This trade existed at the Group 3 level only until the Chief Radio Intelligence Collator Group 4 was added approximately 1960.

Intelligence Operator 111 (00099-01)
(Black 1-4
Green 1-4

In 1966 all of the above trades except the Radio Int Collator were combined into one which was named the Intelligence Operator. The Radio Int Collator and the Chief Radio Int Collator became part of the new Communicator Research trade (see Communications). The Canadian Intelligence Corps was merged with the Military Police from 1968 to 1982, when it became a separate branch of the army once again. There is no direct entry for this trade in the regular force, so the badge is used in the 2 to 4 levels only. The first level of the badge is used in the reserve forces where direct entry is possible. The badge shows the north star. Intelligence Branch.

The Corps of Guides

Before the formation of the Canadian Intelligence Corps, some intelligence work was done by The Corps of Guides. The hat badge of the Canadian Intelligence Corps was obviously derived from that of the Corps of Guides. The Corps of Guides was absorbed by the Royal Canadian Corps of Signals in 1929. You can read about them in part one of the book under Communications.

	Khaki 1-3
Intelligence Linguist	
renamed Linguist	(1956)
renamed Linguist Russian	Group 1-3 (1958)
Interpreter Russian	Group 4

The Intelligence Linguist was renamed simply Linguist in 1956. They were not members of the C Int C. The Linguists were a group of soldiers who could speak languages other than English. Basically, they were translators, to be called upon when needed. In 1958 all languages other than Russian were eliminated and the name was changed to Linguist Russian. Their job was to translate Russian to English. They had to pass a test annually to retain their trades pay. The Group 4 level was called the Interpreter Russian. In spite of the name and the job, this person was not necessarily a member of the Intelligence Corps. They could be of any corps, but C Int C was responsible for their training. Obsolete 1966.

Note that the Linguist badge is listed as existing only at Groups 1-3 but the Interpreter Russian worked at the Group 4 level. This book lists confirmed existing badges only. It is possible that a Group 4 linguist badge and other badges not listed in this book do indeed exist. Is so, they were produced in tiny quantities and are unknown to me. I discovered the existence of the Group 4 Meteorological badge during the writing of this book. If you have a badge that is not listed in this book please contact the author.

The Canadian Intelligence Corps
Formed October 1942

LAUNDRY

Laundry and Bath Operator Group 1-2 badge ?

A new trade in 1950, this tradesman's job was to set up, operate and service mobile laundry and bath equipment in the field. The army had laundry and bath equipment during the Second World War but the operators were not deemed to be tradesmen until 1950. In Nov 1964 the trade was reduced to Group 1 only. There was no progress to other trades. In order to advance past Group 2, this tradesman would have to remuster to another trade.

Like the Firefighter, the Laundry and Bath Operator did not receive a trade badge when all the new badges were produced in 1956. It is unknown what badge they wore. If you know, please contact the author. They were members of the RCOC. This trade became obsolete in 1966. The job is done today by members of the Supply Tech Trade.

Trade Badges 1956 to Date

Photo courtesy of the Cdn Forces (taken April 1945)

MATERIALS

                Khaki   1-3

This badge was worn by four trades

Leather and Textile Worker   Group 1-2
Shoemaker   Group 2-3
Shoe Repairer   Group 1 only
Tailor   Group 1-3

The Leather and Textile Worker repaired, modified, manufactured, and preserved tents, tarpaulins, vehicle covers, stretchers, instrument cases, flags and other leather and textile items. They also upholstered furniture and vehicle seats. This trade was employed at RCOC depots. The Shoe Repairer trade operated at the Group 1 level only, while the Shoemaker worked at the Group 2 & 3 levels. The Shoemaker spent most of his time making repairs but was qualified to design shoes (and boots) from scratch. The badge is an awl and threaded needle. An awl is an instrument used to make holes. The tailor would use it to make button holes and the leather worker would use it to make holes in canvas for tie-downs. The holes would be reenforced by sewing or adding a metal ring. All of these trades except the Leather and Textile Worker became obsolete approximately 1960. The Leather and Textile Worker's became obsolete in 1966. All were RCOC trades.

Machinists   Khaki   1-4

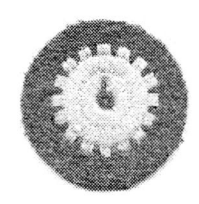

In 1956 the machinist badge was worn by six trades that were involved with manufacturing and repairing vehicle parts, tools, and other items of metal. It was also worn by the Operator Special Engineering Equipment who was a heavy equipment driver.

Fitter RCE   Group 1-3

This machinist made repairs to heavy engineering equipment. An RCE trade. After Group 3 he could become a Mechanist Machinery Group 4. The trade was made obsolete in May 1957 and the job taken over by the Mechanic RCE. (See Field Engineers.)

Mechanic RCE   Group 2-3

As a Group 1, this person would have been a Driver Mechanical Transport or an Operator Special Engineering Equipment. His job was to repair heavy engineer equipment (see Field Engineers) and other RCE vehicles. After 1957 he also took over the job of the Fitter RCE when that trade became obsolete. He could become a Mechanist Machinery group 4.

Operator Special Engineering Equipment
                                Group 1-3

This tradesman was not a machinist like the others in this group. They operated all types of heavy engineering equipment. They made repairs to their equipment but were not as skilled as a machinist. They had the option to become a Mechanic RCE when ready to proceed to Group 2 or they could remain in this trade as far as Group 3, then possibly become a Mechanist Machinery if they could meet the requirements. (See Field Engineers for information about this trade after unification.)

Mechanist Machinery   Group 4

This was an RCE trade that worked at the Group 4 level only. He was in charge of installation and maintenance of all mechanical equipment used by the RCE. His job was to inspect, test and supervise the operation, maintenance and repair of water supply equipment, sewage disposal equipment, heating and plumbing systems, mechanical engineer equipment, stationary or mobile power plants, pumps and refrigeration plants. He also supervised the repair of heavy engineering equipment. The Mechanist Machinery was a highly skilled individual. He had to have a working knowledge of mathematics, draughting, internal combustion engines, heating with water or steam, ignition systems, carburetors, fuel injection, pumps, steam boilers, refrigeration, fuels and lubricants, water purification, hydraulics, soldering, welding, electricity, field bakeries, laundries, steam and oil cooking equipment, disinfectors, earth moving machinery and distillation plants. He also had to destroy heavy equipment with demolitions to stop it from falling into enemy hands if this situation were to arise. The Operator Special Engineering Equipment, the Mechanic RCE and the Fitter RCE could all aspire to became a Mechanist Machinery. Those three trades could only advance as far as Group 3.

Machinist Fitter   Group 1-3

Formerly called the Machinist Metal before 1953, these tradesmen were involved with the manufacture and repair of metal parts for tools and machinery. They set up and operated machines for sharpening, planing, slotting and milling. They also had to oil and maintain the machinery and be able to work from blueprints. This trade became obsolete in 1966. The duties of this trade are now included with that of the Materials Tech.

Toolmaker   Group 1-3

This tradesman worked on a variety of things including drilling out broken studs (getting bolts out when the head is broken off) and cutting screw threads (putting threads on a smooth bolt). And as the name implies, they made tools. They could make precision tools such as jigs, dies and cutting tools. They also forged tools using forge and anvil and had to know the proper cutting lubricants for each metal. They sharpened drill bits and other cutting tools. They also made keys and keyways (locks). This required great skill with measuring devices such as micrometers and calipers. They had to have a knowledge of the effects of heat on different types of metal, as well as geometry and trigonometry and be good at reading blueprints. A RCEME trade, they had no possibility to advance to Group 4. Obsolete 1961.

Moulder   Group 1-2

This badge was also worn, according to dress regulations of 1956, by the Moulder. However, the trade had been at nil strength since 1949, and existed on paper only. A RCEME trade, it became obsolete about 1961. See Part One for a job description.

Note: There were several other types of fitters that were obsolete by 1956. See Parts One and Two of the book.

All of the above trades except the Operator Special Engineering Equipment were obsolete in the Army by 1966. This type of work was being done after 1966 only by the Metals Tech which was an Air Force trade. The Air Force Metals Tech also included the duties of the former army trades of Body Repairman and Welder which became obsolete in 1966. This remained the case until the creation of the Materials Tech in 1985. (See Field Engineers to find out what happened to the Operator Special Engineering Equipment.)

Materials Tech 441 (00134) Black 1-4
                                          Green 1-4

In January 1985 a land element version of the Metals Tech was created called a Materials Tech. The army Materials Tech worked with more than just metal. They manufacture and repair items from metal, fibreglass, leather, textiles and rubber. They also do welding and autobody work and make repairs to air conditioning equipment. It is an EME trade.

MEDICAL

                                          Khaki   1-4

In 1956 the medical badge was worn by several different trades:

Medical Assistant

Group 1-2 until 1956, 1-3 starting 1956

The duties of the Medical Assistant have not changed over the years. His primary job is the care of the wounded during wartime. They work in medical units and field and static hospitals during peacetime. The name of the trade changed a couple of times. See Nursing Orderly and Nursing Assistant in Part One and Two. They are known as "medics" to other trades. He could became a instructor at the Group 3 level or an Op Room Assistant at the Group 3 or 4 level.

Senior Medical Assistant Group 3 only

This person was a medic who worked at the Group 3 level. This trade became obsolete in 1956 and the Medical Assistant trade was increased to work at the Group 3 level instead of only the first two levels of expertise.

Nursing Assistant Group 1-3

This trade was the female equivalent of the Medical Assistant. Formerly a CWAC trade, it became a RCAMC trade when the CWAC was abolished in 1964. They did the same work as the Medical Assistant but only in static hospitals. They could not be employed in a field environment. (Note that the Medical Assistant was once called the Nursing Assistant. See Part One and Two.) This trade was merged with the Medical Assistant upon unification but were not employed in field units unit after 1987. (The author worked in a Field Ambulance in the mid 1980's and there were no females in the unit at that time.)

Laboratory Assistant Group 1-4

The name of this trade was changed to Lab Tech approximately 1960. See below for job description.

Technical Assistant Medical Group 4 only

The Technical Assistant Medical was basically a chemist. He did the same type of work as the Lab Assistant but on a higher level. He had to have a university degree or equivalent civilian experience on the job. The trade was at nil strength since 1949. Before 1947 he could have been employed as a chemist in a chemical warfare plant. (See Part Two for details.) This trade became obsolete approximately 1960.

Radiographer Group 1-3 until 1956,
Group 1-4 starting 1956

The name of this trade was changed to X-ray Tech approximately 1960. See below for job description.

Master Radiographer Group 4 only

The Master Radiographer was simply the Group 4 level of the Radiographer trade. This trade became obsolete in 1956 and the Radiographer trade was increased to Group 1-4.

Operating Room Assistant Group 3-4

The Operating Room Assistant would have been a medic at the Group 1-2 levels. See below for job description.

Physio-Occupational Therapy Aide Group 3 only
Occupational Therapy Aide Group 2 only

In 1956 the Group 2 level of the Physic-Occupational Therapy Aide was deleted and replaced by a new trade called the Occupation Therapy Aide. The new trade took over the work at the Group 2 level, while the older trade became Group 3 only. They would have been a Medical Assistant at the Group 1 level. These tradesmen were tasked with helping soldiers to recovery from injuries and operations. They taught patients how to exercise damaged joints and muscles. There was no opportunity for advancement to Group 4. Both became obsolete approximately 1960. The job is now done by civilians with an officer supervisor.

Pharmacist Group 4 only

A Pharmacist dispenses prescription drugs. He would have been a Medical Assistant at the Group 1-3 levels. Obsolete approximately 1960. This job is now done by a solider of officer rank.

Hygiene Assistant Group 1-3
Hygiene Tech Group 3-4

The name of this trade was changed from Hygiene Assistant to Hygiene Tech in the early 1960s. The Group 1 level was dropped and a Group 4 level added. About 1980 the name was changed again to Preventive Medicine Tech. (The name of this trade changed several times. Look it up in Part One under the name of Sanitary Assistant.) Their job was the prevention of diseases. See Part One and further down in this section for more information. They could become an instructor at the Group 3 level or go to Group 3 in their own trade.

Instrument Mechanic Surgical Group 1-3

This tradesman repaired medical equipment. This trade became obsolete approximately 1960. See Biomedical Electronics Tech below for more information.

Optician Group 3 only

The Optician made and repaired eye glasses.

This trade became obsolete approximately 1960. The job has been done since then by civilian contractors.

Optometrist   Group 4 only

The Optometrist tested soldier's eyes to find out if they need glasses. He would then write a prescription that would be taken to the Optician to have the glasses made. This trade became obsolete approximately 1960. Since then, a civilian optometrist would look after soldiers in need of an eye test.

Biosciences Tech   Group 3-4

The Biosciences Tech assisted medical and specialist officers in research, development and training in the field of applied physiology with the special reference to variations in environmental pressure, thermal stress, acceleration and vibration, human engineering and survival. This was a new trade in the early 1960s and became obsolete in the army approximately 1980. (A similar trade still exists in the air element.)

The Royal Canadian Army medical Corps was founded in 1909

OTHER TRADES

The Royal Canadian Army Medical Corps also had the following non-medical tradesmen:

Steward   Group 1-2
Storeman Medical   Group 1-3

The Storeman Medical kept stock of medical supplies. (Obsolete early 1960s).

Clerk Accounting RCAMC   Group 2-3 (obsolete early 1960s)
Clerk Administrative   Group 1-3
Clerk Stenographer   Group 2-3

In the RCAMC the Clerk Administrative had the option to switch to a Clerk Accounting RCAMC or a Clerk Stenographer when he was ready to advance to Group 2. This would be his only opportunity to do so. All three of these clerk trades could advance to the Group 3 level but they could not change trades after reaching Group 2. The Clerk Accounting RCAMC and the Clerk Stenographer did not exist at the Group 1 level.

Assistant Instructor RCAMC Khaki 3-4

In 1956 three medical trades were eligible to become an Assistant Instructor at the Group 3 level. These trades were Hygiene Assistant, Storeman Medical, and Medical Assistant. These trades could advance after Group 2 to Assistant Instructor Group 3 or go to Group 3 in their own trade. If they chose to go to Group 3 in their own trade, the Hygiene Assistant and the Storeman Medical could not get to Group 4. The Medical Assistant, if he chose not to become an instructor could become an Operation Room Assistant Group 4. The Assistant Instructor RCAMC taught classes in medical procedures, hygiene, and handling of medical stores. Getting to be an instructor was not easy. The qualifications for Group 3 instructor were:

The Medical Assistant Group 2 also needed Hygiene Group 1 and Storeman Group 1
The Hygiene Assistant Group 2 also needed Medical Assistant Group 1 and Storeman Group 1
The Storeman Medical Group 2 also needed Medical Assistant Group 1 and Hygiene Group 1

To get to be a Group 4 instructor, one needed to be a Group 3 instructor plus one of the following:

The Medical Assistant Group 3 also needed Hygiene Group 2 and Storeman Group 1
The Hygiene Assistant Group 3 also needed Medical Assistant Group 2 and Storeman Group 1
The Storeman Medical Group 3 also needed Medical Assistant Group 2 and Hygiene Group 1

All corps Assistant Instructor trades were abolished by 1966 and replaced by a single trade.

This is a photograph of 1 Field Ambulance deployed on exercise. The Field Ambulance has doctors and a fleet of ambulances and other medical personnel. Patients that cannot be returned to active service are sent back to a hospital. Photo by author.

The above trades were part of the Royal Canadian Army Medical Corps before unification. Following are the post unification Medical Branch trades.

Medical Assistant 711   Black 1-4
renamed Medical Tech 737 (00334-01) Green 1-4

By 1985 some of the medical trades discussed above were obsolete or merged together. The new badge is the same as the old medical badge except for a small letter superimposed on the "Rod of Aesculapius". In the case of the Medical Tech badge, it has the letter "M" on it. The main job of the medic is to provide medical aid to soldiers who are wounded in combat. In peacetime, they provide medical aid for accidents and illnesses that occur during training exercises. To become a medic, a recruit must have a high school diploma with courses in biology and either chemistry or physics. The trade was renamed from Medical Assistant to Medical Tech in 2003.

Physician Assistant 732 (00334-02)   no badge

The Physician Assistant is a highly skilled medical practitioner whose job is to extend the hand of the physician to remote locations. They provide medical service without the direct supervision of a doctor, although they would be in contact with a doctor for advice by radio or some other means of communication. The physician is responsible for the Physical Assistant's actions. They are also authorized to write prescriptions for military personal.

There are 124 members of this trade but most of them are employed with the navy. There is a Physician Assistant on each frigate and submarine. In the land element of the CF (army), they could be employed in Alert (a remote site on northern Ellesmere Island in the arctic) or any other remote location. They are also employed with United Nations peacekeeping forces and with infantry units on exercise within Canada. Navy personal are also employed on army bases.

This is a new trade approximately 2000, although the job existed before that as a nine month course for a senior Medical Assistant 711. The trade has existed for over 40 years in the navy. Qualification for this trade is now a two year course. Candidates would be Sgt Medical Techs. Subjects covered on the course include internal medicine, trauma, general surgery, urology, orthopaedics, pediatrics, psychiatry, anaesthesia, obstetrics and gynaecology.

It was made a separate trade so that they could qualify for specialist pay. The Medical Tech trade does not receive this extra pay.

Upon graduation, candidates would be promoted to WO, therefore there is no trade badge for this trade as they are not worn by WOs.

Operating Room Assistant 713   Black   1-4
Operating Room Tech 713 (00334-03) Green   1-4

The job of the Operating Room Assistant, as the name implies, is to assist the surgeon during operations. They also maintain and sterilize operating room equipment and prepare the room before surgery. They also apply plaster casts. See information below about entry into this trade. The name was changed to Operating Room Tech approximately 2000. The badge is the same as the Medical Tech except with letter "O" superimposed.

Preventive Medicine Tech 716 (00334-04)
Black   1-4
Green   1-4

The Hygiene Tech was renamed the Preventive Medicine Tech sometime in the 1970s or early '80s. I was unable to find the exact year. Members of this trade are engaged in the prevention of diseases. They inspect latrines, food, cooking areas and water for health hazards. In addition to the usual military operations, they inspect conditions at some of the buildings on base such as day care facilities, restaurants and gymnasiums. The Pre Med Tech, as they are know, also monitors communicable disease control programs and pest control. They even check for damage to one's ears from excessive noise. See information below about entry into this trade. The badge has the letter "P" on it.

Aeromedical Tech (00334-05)

This trade replaced the Biosciences Tech. It is an air element trade and does not exist in the army.

The Medical Tech is a normal trade in the sense that one joins as a recruit, learns the trade and becomes a QL3 and then progresses upward through the next three levels over the span of their career. The other trades mentioned above do not begin at the QL3 level. There are two possible ways that a person could enter these trades. They would have been a Medical Tech before remustering to one of the 00334 trades at the QL5 level. Or they might join as civilians who are already trained in their trade before joining the military. The trade badges for these trades were produced in all four levels but are normally only worn at the third and fourth levels. New members of this trade would normally be a QL5 and would therefore never wear the first level of the badge. Some new members might start with the third level badge depending on the trade and their qualifications.

Lab Tech 714   Black 1-4
Medical Lab Tech 714 (00152-01) Green 1-4

The Lab Tech does an analysis of biological specimens (blood, urine, stool, etc). To join this trade, one must be a registered lab tech before joining the forces. There is no longer a military course to learn this trade. The name was changed approximately 1980 from Lab Tech to Medical Lab Tech so as not to be confused with the Dental Lab Tech. Ironically, the Dental Lab Tech is now obsolete. The badge has the letter "L" on it.

X-ray Tech 715   Black 1-4
Medical Radiation Technologist 715 (00153-01)
                                                 Green 1-4

Members of this trade operate X-ray equipment. To join the forces in this trade, one must be a certified medical radiation tech. There is no military course. The badge has letter "R" on it.

In 2003 the X-Ray Tech was renamed Medical Radiation Technologist. (The abbreviation "Tech" stands for technician throughout this book. Technologist will be spelled out in full).

Biomedical Electronics Technologist 718 (00155)
                               Black1-4

The job of the Biomedical Electronics Technologist is to repair both medical and dental equipment. The trade was new in 1997. Dental equipment was previously repaired by the Dental Equipment Tech and medical equipment, since the Instrument Mechanic Surgical became obsolete, was repaired by medics after passing a special two year training course in the USA. The Dental Equipment Tech is now obsolete and medics no longer repair medical equipment. Only dental equipment that is used in the field in the dental van is repaired by members of this trade. Dental equipment at the base dental clinic is repaired by civilians. One must have a biomedical engineering technologist diploma in order to join the military in this trade. There are only 21 members of this trade in the CF. The badge was not produced until 2003 and has the letter "B" on it.

Health Services Technical Manager 719 no badge

This trade existed only from 1995 to 2000 approximately. All medical trade CWOs became members of this trade upon reaching that rank. The idea behind it was that CWOs are mainly supervisors and no longer workers in their trade. Therefore, members of this trade concentrated on management instead of their former job. The idea was abandoned and all members returned to their previous trade. No army trade badge was ever made because trade badges are not worn by CWOs.

Preventive Medicine Tech Jr 733 (00334-06)
Medical Lab Tech Jr. 734 (00152-02)
Medical Radiation Technologist Jr. 735 (00153-02)
Biomedical Electronics
Technologist Jr. 736 (00155-02)

These are temporary trades for new members. Personal would remain in these trades only until meeting all of the requirements to be considered fully trained. This could take from one to four years depending on the trade and when the required training and courses can be completed.

For example, a Preventive Medicine Tech Jr 733 would previously be a Medical Tech OL5 before remustering to this trade. They would wear the same trade badge as the Preventive Medicine Tech except for the level. A QL5 would wear the second level of the badge with symbol and wreath. Upon completion of training and their QL6 course, they would advance to Preventive Medicine Tech 716 with the third level of the badge. The other three Jr trades are similar. Some trades now accept civilians who have enough qualifications and experience. The badges were produced in all four levels but were never used at the first level.

No badges are shown for the Jr trades because they are no different than those worn by the senior branch except for the level. See the individual trades in this section.

(Because the Medical Tech 737 no longer includes training for Physician Assistant at the senior levels, a QL5 will wear the third level badge with crown instead of the second level badge with wreath. This means that new members coming into the Jr trades might be wearing the third level badge instead of the second. A QL6 will have both crown and wreath.)

Field Medical Tech 720   no badge
Base Medical Tech 721   no badge

These two trades never really existed except on paper. They are basically the same except that one would be employed in a field unit and the other in base unit. They would have basic first aid training only. The Field Medical Tech could be employed as a stretcher bearer. The Base Medical Tech could be employed at any required duties in a static medical facility. There are no personnel in these trades and there is no badge. They would be only be recruited in time of mobilization for war.

Big Changes in the Medical Trades.

Until recently, the army medical trades looked after all the medical needs of the soldiers on a 24 hour basis. All large army bases had hospitals, some larger than others. A main hospital for serious cases was located in Ottawa. There was no excuse for a soldier not to go to work, even if he was ill or injured, because that was where they had to go to get medical attention. The soldiers had no medical coverage to go to a civilian doctor or hospital.

In recent years, the base hospitals have been gradually closing down. The bases now have a medical clinic that provides services during working hours only. If a member of the military needs medical attention after normal working hours, they go to the civilian hospital. Medical staff are sometimes employed in civilian hospitals in order for them to get the necessary training that they need for overseas duties.

Patients being loaded into a helicopter at the Field Ambulance. Photo by author.

MILITARY POLICE
Khaki 1-3

Service Policeman   Group 1-3

Although the official name was Service Policeman, they were more commonly referred to as either "Provost" (the name of the corps) or "MP" (for Military Police). Their job was law enforcement, crime investigation, security services, Prisoner Of War management and traffic control. Before 1956 this trade existed at the Group 1-2 level only. In 1956 the Instructor C Pro C was replaced with a Service Policeman Group 3. The trade did not progress past Group 3.

A Canadian Service Policeman directing traffic in Hanover Germany in 1966.

Photo courtesy of George Hennecke.

Fingerprint Classifier
Group 2-3

Fingerprint Tech   Group 2-3

The Provost badge was also worn by a trade called the "Fingerprint Classifier". His job was to take photographs and fingerprints of prisoners and suspects. He was also tasked with producing identification cards for the base personnel. He had to be a MP Group 1 before becoming a Fingerprint Classifier Group 2. In 1964 the name was changed to Fingerprint Tech. This trade became obsolete in 1966.

Special Investigator C Pro C   Group 4 only

This was a new trade in March 1958. He took over the job of investigating crime from the Service Policeman, leaving him for regular police duties. His job was to solve crimes involving military personnel. They carried out raids and surveillance. To qualify for this trade, he had to be qualified Service Policeman Group 3 plus Fingerprint Classifier Group 2. There was no trade badge for the Group 4 level so members of this trade made their own badge by cutting the crown off of a group three badge and sewing it above a group two badge. There were so few members of this trade that a group four badge was never produced.

renamed Military Policeman 811   Black 1-4
renamed Military Police 811 (00161-01   Green 1-4

In 1966 the name of Service Policeman was changed to Military Policeman. The above three trades were combined into this one new trade. In February 1968 the Provost Corps merged with the Canadian Intelligence Corps to became the Security Branch of the Canadian Forces. In 1982, the Intelligence trade broke away from the MP's to form their own branch once again. The badge remains the same as the Provost badge except for the colour to match the new uniform. Potential recruits for the military police trade must have a two year law and security diploma. The base MP's wear a black uniform which is different from other members of the Armed Forces. MP's who are employed with a field unit, wear the same combat uniform as other soldiers. In the early 1980's the name was shortened from Military Policeman to Military Police. In 1999 the name of the branch was changed to Security and Military Police Branch.

Disciplinarian C Pro C Khaki 2-3

The job of this soldier was the supervision of prisoners. The badge depicts a rampant lion. Potential members could be a Group 1 of any army trade, not necessarily a Service Policeman, but the vast majority of new members were former MP's. They guarded prisoners of all three services (Army, RCAF and RCN). This was a new trade in 1956. Before that date, prisoners were guarded by members of the Service Policeman trade. This was a C Pro C trade.

The Disciplinarian was a short-lived trade and became obsolete in the trade restructuring of 1966. The task of guarding prisoners is once again combined with the duties of the Military Police trade.

The Canadian Military Police Corps was formed in September 1917 and disbanded in December 1920. It was formed again in June 1940 with the name of Canadian Provost Corps. This corps became the Security Branch of the CF after unification.

MUSICIANS

Khaki 1-4
Red 1-4

Bandsman Group 1-3 (obsolete 1958)

The role of the band is to provide music for military functions. In 1956 there were only two band trades, that of the Bandsman and the Bandmaster. The Bandsman was any member of the band who played any instrument. A Bandsman had to play a brass, woodwind, or percussion instrument in keys of not more than two sharps or five flats. They had to play different kinds of music including light concert, sacred (hymns) and military marches. They had to be able to play while on the march. They had to have a through knowledge of most major scales and of musical terms and signs and the care and maintenance of their instrument. The badge is a lyre. Although the badge was produced in four levels, the Bandsman could advance only as far as Group 3 unless he became a Bandmaster and there was only one Bandmaster per band. The Group 4 badge was not used by the Bandsman until 1966. See "Musician" below.

Bandmaster Group 4   Khaki 4
Red 4
Metal 4

The Bandmaster had to take complete charge of all aspects of the band from practice to marching. He had to conduct rehearsals and give instruction. He was in command of the band when on parade. The badge is a lyre with crown above and maple leaves to the lower right and left. The badge was made in metal for scarlet tunics used on ceremonial occasions, and also khaki for use on battledress and red for battledress in rifle regiments. The metal version is shown. There were originally three maples leaves on each side of the lyre. In the cloth version this was increased in the 1940s to five leaves on each side, but the metal version remained at three. There would be only one Bandmaster per band. The Bandmaster badge was a combination of trade badge and rank badge. A Bandmaster would be a WO1 (Chief Warrant Officer) but the normal badge for this rank would not be worn.

The British version of this badge is the same except that it has oak leaves while the Canadian version has maple leaves.

Trade Badges 1956 to Date

Note the bandmaster badge on this soldier. Note that no other rank or trade badge is worn. The badge is the cloth version not shown here, but is shown in Part Two of the book. He was the Bandmaster of the Esquimalt Garrison Band. (Unfortunately his name is not known to me.) Photo from Bennett collection.

Drummer and Fifer	Khaki and Red	1 only
Bugler	Khaki and Red	1-2
Trumpeter	Khaki	1-2
Piper	Khaki	1-3

The 1956 dress regulations state that these badges were not for use by regular army bands. They must have been produced for use by the militia only. CAO 269-1 states that the regular army had only one band trade (other than Bandmaster) in 1956 and that was "Bandsman."

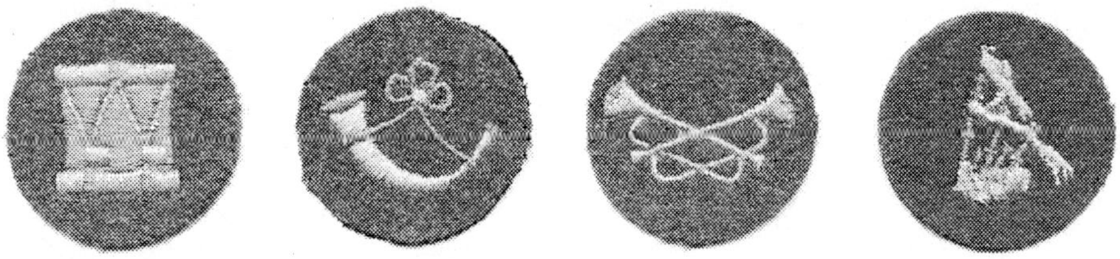

The list above shows badges that I know to exist. It is possible that there are other levels and colours that are not listed here.

In 1958 the Bandsman trade was deleted and replaced by a separate trade for each instrument as follows:

Bandsman Bass Bass Clef	Group 1-3
Bandsman Bass Treble Clef	Group 1-3
Bandsman Bassoon	Group 1-3
Bandsman Clarinet	Group 1-3
Bandsman Cornet or Trumpet	Group 1-3
Bandsman Euphonium Bass Clef	Group 1-3
Bandsman Euphonium Treble Clef	Group 1-3
Bandsman Flute and Piccolo	Group 1-3
Bandsman French Horn	Group 1-3
Bandsman Oboe or English Horn	Group 1-3
Bandsman Percussion	Group 1-3
Bandsman Saxophone	Group 1-3
Bandsman Trombone Bass Clef	Group 1-3
Bandsman Trombone Treble Clef	Group 1-3
Piper	Group 1-3
Bandsman Baritone	Group 1-3
Bandsman Tenor Horn	Group 1-3
Drummer	Group 1-2
Drum Major	Group 3 only
Bell Lyrist	Group 1 only
Bugler or Trumpeter	Group 1-2
Fifer	Group 1-2
Master Bandsman Bass	Group 4 only
Master Bandsman Clarinet	Group 4 only
Master Bandsman Cornet or Trumpet	Group 4 only
Master Bandsman Bassoon	Group 4 only
Master Bandsman Euphonium	Group 4 only
Master Bandsman Oboe & English Horn	Group 4 only
Master Bandsman Percussion	Group 4 only

Prior to unification there was no specific corps for bands. Several corps had their own band. Most had at least a drummer and a bugler or trumpeter. They wore the hat badge of their respective corps. Shown is the band of the Royal Canadian Corps of Signals. It was formed 22 Jan 1952. The years following unification were not kind to military bands. Five of the Nine corps bands were disbanded. In 1968, The RC SIGS band was merged with the RCD band and became the Vimy Band of Ottawa. It 1970 it became the Air Transport Command Band. In 1974 it was renamed the Vimy Band and moved back to Kingston. It was disbanded 12 Jun 1994. Photo courtesy of the Communications and Electronics Museum.

In 1956, the following band badges were also produced.

Master Bandsman Flute and Piccolo	Group 4 only
Master Bandsman French Horn	Group 4 only
Master Bandsman Trombone	Group 4 only
Master Bandsman Baritone	Group 4 only
Master Bandsman Tenor Horn	Group 4 only
Master Bandsman Saxophone	Group 4 only
Pipe Major	Group 4 only

Perhaps after 1958 band members began to wear the drummer, bugler, trumpeter and piper badges instead of the bandsman badge, when they became separate trades. I have not been able to find any evidence to confirm or disprove this possibility.

The Trumpeter played solo trumpet or bugle calls and was not the same trade as the person that played a trumpet in the band. There was a trade for "Bugler or Trumpeter" and a separate trade for "Bandsman Cornet or Trumpet"

The Fifer, the Bell Lyrist and the Bugler or Trumpeter had no chance of progress past Group 2 unless they learned to play another instrument and remustered to that trade, each instrument being a separate trade. The Fifer also played the cymbals as there was no separate trade for a cymbal player.

The Drum Major instructed the Drum section of the band, which also included the Fifers. Note that the Drum Major was a Group 3 trade, while the Pipe Major was a Group 4 trade. A potential Pipe Major had to be qualified Piper Group 3 plus Drummer Group 1. He could direct a pipe band on parade. There could be only one Drum Major or Pipe Major per band.

There was no change in the trade of Bandmaster.

MASTER BANDSMAN

Starting in 1958, all of the above trades had the chance to advance to Master Bandsman at the Group 4 level without the requirement of being a Bandmaster. The restriction of only one Bandmaster per band remained. Previously a Bandsman could advance only to Group 3 unless he became a Bandmaster.

The Master Bandsman would be a Warrant Officer. The badge was similar to the Bandmaster badge in that it was a combination of rank and trade badges but did not include any maple leaves. No other rank or trade badges were worn. Both the Bandmaster badge and the Master Bandsman badge were worn on the lower sleeve in the manor of all other Warrant Officers. (The information that I have about this badge is undocumented.)[11]

Although, officially, each instrument was a separate trade from 1958 to 1966, most units did not put this into use. For purposes of nominal rolls, etc., all band members continued to be treated as if they were all members of the same trade. Also, apparently the Master Bandsman badge was not widely used.

Musician 871 (00166-01)   Black   1-4
                               Green   1-4

All of the above trades lasted only from 1958 to 1966 when they were all combined into a single trade once again with the new name of Musician. This new trade included the Master Bandsman and the Bandmaster who became Group 4 Musicians. If a Group 4 was not a Warrant Officer, he would wear the Group 4 Bandsman badge with the lyre as shown at the beginning of this section.

The Bandmaster was still the Bandmaster. He still did the same job as previously and still wore the same badge. The difference is that he would no longer be a Bandmaster by trade. He would be a Group 4 Musician, but would not wear the Group 4 trade badge.

Piper   Group 1-3

The only exception to the above was the Piper which remained a separate trade. They probably wore the piper trade badge but I have not found any photographic evidence of this.

As a result of unification in 1968, all regimental and corps bands were encompassed into the Band Branch of the CF. At this time the Piper was also absorbed into the Musician trade. No trade badges were worn from 1968 until 1985. The new badges are of the same design as the old Bandsman badge first issued in 1956.

The army used to conduct a two year program of individual and ensemble instrumental instruction, but since the closure of the School of Music in 1994, the CF recruits only trained musicians.

Since 1966, the positions of Drum-Major, Pipe-Major and Bugle-Major have been appointments and not a separate trade. The Bandmaster has been replaced by a person called the Director of Music who is of officer rank.

Drum-Major

The Drum-Major fills the role of the Bandmaster. The Bandmaster has been obsolete as a trade since 1966 and no longer exists even as an appointment. (See Bandmaster at the beginning of this section.)

The duties of the Drum-Major include:
- Leading the band on parade
- Band administration
- Dress and deportment of the band
- Stopping and starting the band on parade.

This includes stopping/starting music and/or starting/stopping marching. This is done with either voice commands or signals with the mace.
- Training for drummers

The Drum-Major would previously have been the lead drummer of the band.

The current DEU version of the badge has the drum on top of the four stripes. Older versions of the badge were in two separate parts with the drum being above the stripes and not on top of them. The rank badge is currently worn above the Drum-Major badge. Before unification, no rank badge was worn with the Drum-Major badge if he/she was a Sgt or lower. Since unification, both appointment and rank badges are worn. A Sgt Drum-Major would have four stripes on the lower arm pointed up and three stripes on the upper arm pointed down. Currently a Drum-Major would be a WO or higher which avoids this problem.

Some units now wear the current badge on the DEU uniform (with drum and stripes as one piece) and the older version (with the drum above the stripes) on their ceremonial uniform.

There can be more than one Drum-Major per band. It is not necessary that the Drum-Major be a musician. Since the cutback on unit bands in the 1970s many units have bands that consist of a mixture of several trades and civilians. The Vimy Band in Kingston still exists but is not officially part of the military and has many civilian members. In the Calgary Highlanders, the Pipe-Major is a civilian. In the Ceremonial Guards of Ottawa, the Drum-Major is an Infantryman.

Drum Major Robert F. Zubkowski P. P. C. L. I. U. N. tour of Cyprus.

Photo courtesy of: Robert F. Zubkowski

Pipe-Major

The Pipe-Major is an appointment, not a rank or trade. It does not exist in the regular force as there are no longer any regular force pipe bands. Many militia units have Pipe-Majors. This includes the Calgary Highlanders, the 48th Highlanders, the Black Watch and others. The main duties of the Pipe-Major are training the pipers in the band and selecting the music to be played.

The Pipe-Major is senior to the Drum-Major and would be in charge of the band when off parade. On parade, the Drum-Major is in charge and the Pipe-Major would march on his right flank. Keep in mind that only bands with pipers have Pipe-Majors.

Bugle-Major
Trumpet-Major

This badge could be for a Bugle-Major or a Trumpet Major. The same badge is worn by both. These are appointments, not a rank or a trade. Neither the Bugle-Major nor the Trumpet-Major exist in the regular forces. Most militia bands do not use these positions either. They would fill the position of the Drum-Major in a bugle or trumpet band, but the military no longer has such bands. The only one that I could find is a Bugle-Major with the Queen's Own Rifles.

The Band Branch

The bands of the Canadian army used to belong to the individual army corps. The Signal Corps band were members of the Signal Corps, The Artillery Band were members of the Royal Canadian Artillery, and so on. In 1969, the bands were taken away from the army crops and they became members of the CF Band Branch.

The situation has almost come complete circle. All the military bands of today have some type of affiliation with one particular Branch or element of the Canadian Forces. The Artillery Band wears the artillery hat badge, title flashes and other accoutrements, even though they are not members of the Artillery Branch. Another band wears air element hat badges.

This brings about the strange situation where all the members of a branch of the CF are wearing hat badges of other branches of which they are not members. No band wears the Band Branch hat badge.

PARACHUTE TRADES

Instructor Parachute Training Khaki 2 and 3 only
Assistant Instructor Parachute Training

This trade was an instructor for parachutist courses. They could be of any trade but were mostly infantry. The trade was renamed in 1956 from Instructor Parachute Training to Assistant Instructor Parachute Training as were most instructor trades at that time. The chief instructor was an officer. This trade became obsolete in 1963. Parachute instruction is now a temporary job, not a trade.

FLASH
Just before going to print a Group 1 Para Instructor Badge has been discovered.
See A9 in Part Four.

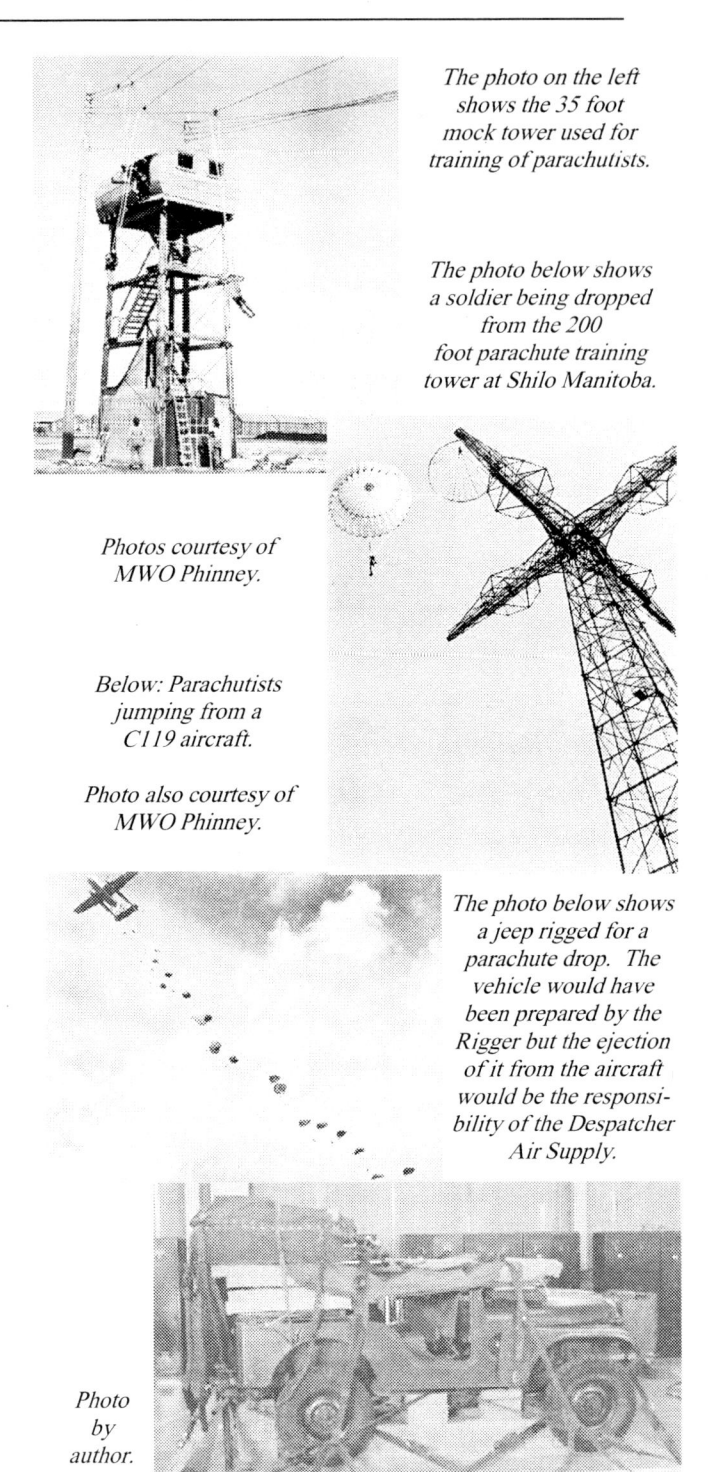

The photo on the left shows the 35 foot mock tower used for training of parachutists.

The photo below shows a soldier being dropped from the 200 foot parachute training tower at Shilo Manitoba.

Photos courtesy of MWO Phinney.

Below: Parachutists jumping from a C119 aircraft.

Photo also courtesy of MWO Phinney.

The photo below shows a jeep rigged for a parachute drop. The vehicle would have been prepared by the Rigger but the ejection of it from the aircraft would be the responsibility of the Despatcher Air Supply.

Photo by author.

Parachute Rigger   Khaki 1-3

The rigger's job is to pack parachutes for the parachute drop of cargo or paratroopers. They also inspect and repair parachutes and air-drop containers. Riggers must be parachute qualified, and must occasionally make a jump using one of the parachutes that they have packed, picked at random by their supervisor. They had to be proficient with sewing machines and knot tying. They also had to know the proper method of drying and storage of parachutes. The trade became obsolete in 1966. This is now a temporary job, not a trade. Riggers now wear a specialist badge like the paratrooper. They would wear the trade badge of their individual trade, such as infantry, etc. See Part Four of this book for a picture of the current badge. Before progressing to Group 3, the Rigger must have had an air supply course. A RCOC trade.

Despatcher Air Supply Khaki 1 only

The Despatcher Air Supply is trained in the ejection of cargo from an aircraft in flight. He is also responsible for packing the cargo onto a wooden pallet and attaching the parachute. (The exception to this is for ammunition, ordnance stores, and vehicles, which would be packed by personnel of the RCOC.) Large cargo parachutes are used, not the same ones as used by paratroopers. For very heavy loads such as vehicles, more than one cargo parachute could be attached. There are two main methods of ejecting the cargo from the aircraft. The first method is to use a small extraction parachute. This small parachute would pull the load out of the aircraft and then pull open the large cargo parachutes. The second method is to eject the cargo manually by simply pushing it out of the aircraft. A static line would be fastened to a ring in the floor of the aircraft which would pull open the parachute. For heavy loads, the pallet could be placed on rollers and untied (or cut) when ready to push it out. This was a RCASC trade, now obsolete.[12]

This trade was new in 1954. As this trade had no opportunity to advance past Group 1, personnel could become an Instructor Air Supply (Group 2-3.) They would then wear the Assistant Instructor badge. The Instructor Air Supply would supervise the Despatcher Air Supply as well as instruct new candidates for that trade.

When the new trade of Transport Op came into being in 1957, Despatcher Air Supply and Instructor Air Supply personnel were gradually remustered into this new trade. The Instructor Air Supply became obsolete in 1958 and the Despatcher Air Supply in 1961.

Today this job is done by two different people. First the rigger ties the cargo onto a platform and attaches the parachute. This rigger can be someone of any trade who has successfully completed the appropriate course. It is not the same person as the parachute rigger in Part Four who packs parachutes. When ready, the cargo would be ejected from the aircraft by the Loadmaster, which is an air element trade.

PHOTOGRAPHY
Khaki 1-4

Photographer	Group 1-4
Photographer Cinematographic	Group 1-3
Photographer Cartographic	Group 1-4
Photo-Mechanical Tech	Group 1-4
Photographic Tech	Group 1-4

In 1956 there were three photography trades: the regular Photographer who made still images, the Photographer Cartographic, and the Photographer Cinematographic. The Photographer had to be skilled in all aspects of photography including projection equipment, processing film, printing and making enlargements. He had to be able to photograph fingerprints and maps.

The Photographer Cinematographic was involved in the production of documentary movies. The movies were used for newsreels and training films.

The Photographer Cartographic took pictures that assisted the Cartographer in his job of map production. The Cartographer would produce a map on a metal plate. The metal plate could then be used for printing the map, or the plate could come back to the Photographer Cartographic who could make a negative from it. The Photographer Cartographic could also transfer an image onto a lithographic plate using chemicals. The metal plate could be processed much like developing a negative. (For more information on lithographic plates see the Geomatics section.) In 1962 this trade was renamed to Photo Mechanical Tech.

In 1966 all of these trades were combined into a single trade called the Photographic Tech. They were all members of the Royal Canadian

Engineers. Upon unification, the Photographic Tech became an air element trade, and no longer exists in the army.

POSTAL

Postal Clerk 881 (00167-01)   Khaki 1-3

You may remember from the previous part of this book that the Postal Clerk was reduced to nil strength in 1949 as it was thought that they would not be required in peacetime as domestic mail service was provided by Canada Post. The Postal Clerk was revived for the Korean war and has been with us ever since. In 1956 the badge consisted of the letter "P" on a postal bag and the trade was only Group 1-3.   RCPC.

Black   1-4   Green   1-4

In 1985 the badge was re-designed. They provide postal services at CF bases overseas and other locations such as Alert in the Canadian Arctic. The horn is an old postal symbol. Most European countries use the horn as a symbol of their post office. In days gone by, the mailman would blow his horn when the mail cart arrived in the village. The old RCPC hat badge depicted a postal horn. This trade became part of the Administration Branch upon unification but became a separate branch of the CF in 1986. In 1999 it was moved to the Logistics Branch.

PRINTING

The printing trades of Printer Machine Minder and Printer Compositor became obsolete in 1956. The Lithographer has been moved to the Geomatics section.

PUBLIC RELATIONS

Public Relations Assistant   Khaki 2 and 3 only

This was a very short lived trade, being new in 1960 and obsolete in 1966. There was no direct entry. The new applicant could be a Group 1 in any trade. Their job was to deal with the public and the media on military matters. The trade is now officer rank only. The badge shows a scroll superimposed with a feather and a microphone. The badge reappeared in 1985, slightly modified, as the new badge of the Administration Clerk.

RCEME

RCEME was formed in February 1944. Before that, electrical and mechanical repairs were done by the RCOC Engineering Branch. Also, several corps such as RC SIGS and RCASC had their own vehicle mechanics and electricians until 1964.

After unification (1 Feb 1968) RCEME was renamed Land Ordnance Engineering (LORE). On 15 May 1984 it was renamed Land Electrical Mechanical Engineers (LEME). In 1990 it was renamed yet again. The word "land" was dropped and the new name was simply Electrical Mechanical Engineers (EME).

The former RCEME trades can be found throughout this part of the book under their respective job sections as follows:

The **communications equipment trades** can be found in the Communications section.

The **Vehicle Mechanics** can be found in their own section. They include the **Welder.**

The **Weapons Techs** can be found in their own section. This includes the **Instrument Repair** trades, **Watchmaker, Typewriter Mechanic** and the **Fire Control System Techs,**

Listed under **Woodworking** are the now obsolete woodworking trades.

After placing all the RCEME trades in their appropriate sections, there were a couple left over that did not fit into any particular section, so they are placed here. All of them are now obsolete.

Draughtsman Electrical and Mechanical
Group   1-4

This draughtsman made drawings of electrical diagrams and items that needed to be repaired or manufactured. They had to produce complete diagrams of machines or parts, including cross-sections. They wore the draughting badge. See the CE section for picture. Obsolete 1966.

Electrical Mechanic	Group 1-3
Electrical Artificer	Group 4
Electrical Tech	Group 1-3
Master Electrical Tech	Group 4

The Electrical Mechanic could advance to the Electrical Artificer at the Group 4 level.

These tradesmen made repairs to electrical components of generators and weapons electronics. They wore the same trade badge as the electrician (see CE section). In 1964 these two trades were renamed Electrical Tech and Master Electrical Tech respectively. The Master Electrical Tech made electrical repairs to AFVs and infra red equipment in addition to the equipment worked on by the Electrical Tech.

Electro-Mechanical Tech 431

In 1966 these two trades were combined into one and renamed the Electro-Mechanical Tech. This trade became obsolete approximately 2000. The weapons system repairs are now done by the Fire Control System Tech (see Weapons Tech section). The generator repair portion of this trade is now done by the Electrical Generating Systems Tech (an air element trade).

Projectionist Clerk   Group 1-2

This tradesman used to be called the Projector Mechanic, which was a more appropriate name for this job. In 1956 it was renamed Projectionist Clerk which is strange. He was not a clerk. He did repairs to movie projectors and similar equipment. The Projectionist Clerk wore the electrical badge. (See CE section for picture.) Obsolete 1966.

Driver Operator   Group 1 only
Driver Radio Operator   Group 1-2

RCEME had soldiers who were members of the Driver Operator trade. This trade was renamed Driver Radio Operator in 1958. This trade became obsolete in RCEME in 1963. See Communications section for more information on this trade.

SUPPLY
Khaki   1-3

The main job of the storeman was to order and store supplies and drive vehicles up to ten tons and fork lifts. They also had to do stock record keeping. The duties varied depending on which corps the storeman belonged to. In some cases they also had to prepare items for shipping. All storemen were trained at the RCOC school regardless of corps affiliation. There used to be about 15 different Storeman but they were all obsolete by 1950 except the three mentioned here.

Storeman Medical   Group 1-3

This storeman worked in medical units and kept stock of medical supplies. This trade became obsolete in 1964. Thereafter, medical supplies were accounted for by a member of the Medical Assistant trade.

Storeman RCOC   Group 1-3

The Storeman RCOC kept stock of ordnance stores (clothing, furniture, tents, cleaning supplies, vehicles and parts, tools, weapons) and ammunition at division corps and army level. The Storeman RCOC had the option to became an Ammo Tech at the Group 2 level.

Storeman Supplies RCASC   Group 1-2

The Storeman Supplies RCASC looked after rations, fuel and ammunition (at brigade and lower level) and when the army used to move on horseback: fodder.

There was also a trade called the Storeman Clerk, who could be of any corps. He was actually an accountant and not a storeman in spite of the name. He wore the accounting trade badge and not the storeman badge. See Clerks. See the Dental section for information about the Dental Storeman.

renamed Supply Tech 911 (00168-01)
Black   1-4   Green   1-4

The above three storemen were combined into one Logistics trade after unification. The badge remains the same.

The Logistics Branch

The purpose of the Logistics Branch, originally, was to provide transportation, supply and financial services. The new branch was made up of members of the RCOC, the RCASC, the RCAPC and their equivalent trades in the former Air Force and Navy. As the trades that make up the branch were changed over the years, the role of the Logistics Branch has changed with them. For example, with the demise of the Administration branch in 1998, administrative duties were added to the Logistics Branch.

In 1978, the Logistics Branch consisted of the following trades:

Finance Clerk (Called Accounting and Finance Clerk
 for a short while after unification).
Steward   (Formerly Admin Branch)
Cook   (Formerly Admin Branch)
Supply Tech   Traffic Tech
MSE OP   Ammo Tech (Formerly EME)

The Transportation Controller had been a Logistics trade but became obsolete in the 1970s.

In 1999 the Steward became a Navy trade as they are now employed almost exclusively on Navy bases and ships.

The Finance Clerk no longer exists. See RMS Clerk.

TRAFFIC TECH

Traffic Tech 933 (00170-01) Black 1-4 Green 1-4

This was a new trade in 1970. It was previously an air force only trade. Their job is to plan and execute the movement of personnel and material by road, rail, air and water. They also prepare, load, secure, and off-load cargo and move personal furniture and effects. The badge is the old RCASC driver badge. It was adopted by the Traffic Tech trade in 1985 because they have taken over the duties of air transport from the MSE Op, and some of the duties of the Transportation Controller. A Traffic Tech could become a Transportation Controller until that trade became obsolete in the 1970's. This is Logistics Branch trade. (See Transport Op and Transportation Controller in the Drivers section for related information.)

VEHICLE TECH
Khaki 1-4

Originally six different RCEME trades wore this badge.
Body Repairman   Group 1-3
Tire Repairman   Group 1-3
Welder   Group 1-3

The above three trades had no progression past Group 3.
Vehicle Mechanic Tracked   Group 1-3
Vehicle Mechanic Wheeled   Group 1-3
Vehicle Artificer   Group 4

The Vehicle Mechanics could advance to Vehicle Artificer Group 4

All of these trades were involved with vehicle repair of some type. One of them worked on tracked vehicles only, another repaired tires, one did body work and one was a welder. The Vehicle Mechanics were also responsible for vehicle recovery. There was once a separate trade for vehicle recovery but it became obsolete in 1955. The Tire Repairman became obsolete in the early 1960's.

Metals Tech   Group 1-3

The Welder and Body Repairman were combined in 1964 to create the Metals Tech. This trade lasted only from 1966 to 1968. It became an air element trade after unification. In 1985 it was created in the army once again and renamed Materials Tech (see Materials Tech).

The Welder became obsolete in RCEME in 1964 but continued to exist until 1966 in RCE. This job is now included with that of the Mat Tech.

Some corps, such as RC SIGS and RCASC had their own vehicle mechanics until 1964.

Master Vehicle Tech   Group 4

In 1963 the Vehicle Artificer was renamed the Master Vehicle Tech.

Vehicle Tech 411 (00129-01) Black 1-4 Green 1-4

In 1966 the Vehicle Mechanic Tracked, the Vehicle Mechanic Wheeled and the Master Vehicle Tech were all combined into a single trade named simply Vehicle Tech. There was no change in the badge except for colour. An EME trade.

WEAPONS TECH
Khaki 1-4

In 1956 this badge was worn by four different Weapons Techs and two FCS Techs.

Armourer   Group 1-3

The Armourer made repairs to small arms such as rifles and machine guns, and adjusted them for accuracy. They also adjusted range finders for accuracy. According to old records of their job description, they also got saddled with repairing just about anything that needed repair other than vehicles, including bicycles, helmets and respirators. (The Pushcycle Repairer became obsolete in 1946.) Obsolete 1966 and included with the new trade of Weapons Tech Land.

Small Arms Artificer   Group 4

The Small Arms Artificer made complicated repairs to rifles and machine guns that were beyond the abilities of the Armourer. Obsolete 1960.

Gun Mechanic   Group 1-3

The Gun Mechanic worked under supervision of the Armament Artificer, doing much the same work such as overhauling breech mechanisms. They did the less technical jobs such as lubrication and drilling out broken studs. A Group 3 Gun Mechanic could aspire to become an Armament Artificer if he gained the necessary skill and rank. (This trade was called Fitter before 1953.) Obsolete 1960.

Armament Artificer   Group 4

The Armament Artificer AA and the Armament Artificer Field were combined in 1956 to create the Armament Artificer. They made repairs to large weapons such as field and anti-aircraft artillery and tanks. They could disassemble and overhaul breech mechanisms, buffers, recuperators, sights, elevating and traversing gears and hydraulic jacks. They would ensure correct clearances and tolerance using micrometers, calipers and height and pressure gauges. The sometimes repaired other types of equipment such as flame throwers, field stoves and machinery. They would have the rank of Staff Sgt or Warrant Officer. Obsolete 1960.

Fire Control System Tech Anti-Aircraft
                                                    Group 1-3
Fire Control System Artificer Anti-Aircraft
                                                    Group 4
Master Fire Control System Tech   Group 4

The Fire Control System Tech (FCS) made repairs to weapon electronic systems. In 1956 they wore the same badge as the weapon repair trades. In 1963 the Fire Control System Artificer was renamed the Master Fire Control System Tech. In 1964 both of these trades became obsolete and the job was included with that of the Weapons Tech. It exists today as a separate trade once again.

Weapons Tech   Group 1-3
Weapons Artificer   Group 4

In 1960 the Gun Mechanic became known as a Weapons Tech. This trade existed only at the Group 1-3 levels. The Small Arms Artificer and the Armament Artificer were combined to create the Weapons Artificer. These combined trades repaired all types and sizes of weapons ranging in size from pistols to tanks and artillery. The Armourer continued to exist as a separate trade until 1966.

Master Weapons Tech   Group 4

In 1964 the Weapons Artificer was renamed the Master Weapons Tech.

All Weapons Techs and FCS Techs were RCEME trades.

Weapons Tech Land 421 (00130-01)   Black 1-4
                                        Green 1-4

In 1966 the Weapons Tech, the Master Weapons Tech and the Armourer were combined to create the new trade of Weapons Tech Land. The Master Weapons Tech became the Group 4 Weapons Tech Land. All four levels of expertise are included in a single trade. (There was a trade in the Air Force called Weapons Tech Air.) The badge remained the same except for the colours. Starting in 1964 this trade also included the duties of the Fire Control System Tech and the Instrument Tech which became obsolete in that year. An EME trade.

                    Khaki 1-4

The instrument repair badge was worn by the following trades.

Instrument Mechanic Electrical   Group 1-3
Instrument Mechanic Optical   Group 1-3
Instrument Artificer AA   Group 4 only
Instrument Artificer HD   Group 4 only
Instrument Artificer Field   Group 4 only

The mechanics worked at the first three levels of expertise while the artificers worked at the Group 4 level. They were engaged in the repair of mechanical and optical instruments such as sights on anti-aircraft guns, etc. They also repaired items such as compasses, telescopes, binoculars, clinometers, directors, theodolites and range finders.

Instrument Mechanic HD & AA   Group 3 only

In 1956 the Instrument Mechanic Electrical was renamed Instrument Mechanic HD & AA and the level of expertise was changed to be Group 3 only.

Instrument Artificer HD & AA   Group 4 only

In 1956 the Instrument Artificer HD and the Instrument Artificer AA were were combined into a single trade.

Instrument Tech   Group 1-3
Instrument Artificer   Group 4

In 1958 all of the above Instrument Mechanics were combined and named the Instrument Tech. The two different types of artificers were combined and named the Instrument Artificer.

Master Instrument Tech   Group 4 only

In 1963 the Instrument Artificer was renamed the Master Instrument Tech.

All of the Instrument Tech trades became obsolete in 1964. Their job was included with that of the Weapons Tech.

The following two trades did not have anything to do with weapon repairs but they are included in this section because they wore the same badge as the instrument repair trades.

Typewriter Mechanic   Group 1-2

The Typewriter Mechanic made repairs to adding machines, calculators, duplicating machines, and other office equipment in addition to typewriters. Calculators were manual devices in those days with a crank on the side to crank up the total, not the small electronic disposable calculators that we have today. This trade became obsolete in 1966. After that date, there was no special trade to repair typewriters. Repairs were made by various trades including Vehicle Techs, Mat Techs and Radio Techs. If repair was not possible, then the equipment would be sent to a civilian repair facility. Typewriters remained in use until the 1990's when they were gradually replaced by computers.

Watchmaker   Group 1-3

The Watchmaker did not make watches; he repaired them. He also repaired clocks, chronometers, voltmeters, ammeters and barometers. This trade became obsolete in 1966. Watches were still issued to some soldiers who required them in their duties (such as Radio Operators). A watch was an expensive item at one time, as so justified the expense of having someone to repair them. By 1966 a simple wrist watch had become an inexpensive disposable item. Damaged watches were simply thrown away and replaced with a new one.

All of the above trades were RCEME trades.

Black 1-4   Green 1-4
Fire Control Systems Tech Electronic 432
Fire Control Systems Tech Optronic 433
Fire Control Systems Tech Land 435

In 1978 it was decided that combining the Instrument Techs and the FCS Techs wth the Weapons Tech was a mistake and they were made separate trades once again with the name of Fire Control Systems Tech. Three types of FCS Techs were created as listed above. They repair and maintain electrical and optical equipment such as battle tank electronics, tow missile electronics, artillery sights and mounts, laser systems, thermal observation systems, miscellaneous electrical and optical equipment and generators up to 30kw. This was all the duties of the several different FSC Techs and Instrument Techs combined. Basically the FCS Techs and the Instrument Techs were combined with the Weapons Tech from 1964 until 1978 when they were separated again but this time the duties of the Instrument Tech was included with that of the FCS Tech.

Fire Control Systems Tech 434 (00327-01)

About 2000 the three types of FCS Techs were combined into a single trade. The Electro-Mechanical Tech was also made obsolete and the weapons system part of that trade is included with the new FCS Tech. The generator repair part of the Electro-Mechanical Tech is now included with the Electrical Generating Systems Tech. (See RCEME for more information about he Electro-Mechanical Tech.) An EME trade.

WOODWORKING

Pattern Maker   Khaki 1-3
Machinist Wood

The Pattern Maker made wooden patterns of items that would later be made of metal. He made patterns of such items as pulleys, bearings, pistons, pinion wheels, etc. The patterns would then go to one of the machinist trades (see Materials Tech) to be copied in metal. This trade originally existed in both RCEME and RCE but was eliminated in RCE after the second world war. It became obsolete in 1961.

The dress regulations of 1956 state that this badge was also worn by the Machinist Wood. This was a woodworking trade that was similar to that of the Carpenter. The Carpenter worked mostly on buildings, while the Machinist Wood built furniture and other wooden articles. He had to build articles from blueprints, or of his own design. The badge was never worn by the Machinist Wood as this trade had been reduced to nil strength in 1950. In 1956 it was still officially listed as an army trade but in reality there were no people in it. It became obsolete in 1958. A RCEME trade.

Trades at Nil Strength in 1956

The following trades existed in the army in 1956 but had been reduced to nil strength. They existed on paper only, and all were obsolete by 1965.

Machinist Wood (RCEME)
Printer Machine Minder (RCOC)
Moulder (RCEME)   **Quarryman** (RCE)
Operator Special (RC SIGS)
Sawyer (RCE)   **Optician** (RCAMC)
Technical Assistant Medical (RCAMC)
Optometrist (RCAMC)
Leading Assault Trooper (RCAC)
Printer Compositor (RCOC)

ARMY TECHNICAL WARRANT OFFICER

In the 21st century, the use of new technology will have a major impact on warfare. A challenge for the military will be to use the new technology to its best advantage. This will require NCO's who not only understand the technology they command, but have the ability to apply it effectively.

Previously the Master Gunner filled this position, but with technology advancing at an ever accelerating pace, the need for a more technical course was required. The course must also be broad based and not applicable to the Artillery only. The Army Technical Warrant Officer (ATWO) course will fill this need. The Master Gunner course was taught at the Combat Training Centre in Gagetown, New Brunswick. This course will no longer be taught. The ATWO course will be a ten month course at the Royal Military College in Kingston, Ontario. Unlike the Master Gunner course which was for artillery personnel only, the ATWO course will be open to all arms. The first course had students from the Infantry, Armoured, Artillery, Signals, Electrical Mechanical Engineers and Combat Engineers. The student will be of the rank of Warrant Officer.

The course will cover the following topics:

- Mathematics, Calculus and Algebra.
- Electricity and Electronics.
- Physics.
- Probability and Statistics.
  This involves problem solving using logic, probability and random variables.
- Thermodynamics and Fluid Dynamics.
  This theory is used in the hydraulics and mechanics of weapons.
- Applied Human Factors Engineering.
  Covers human/machine interaction, human capabilities, stress and performance.
- Nuclear, Biological and Chemical Defence.
- Military Communications and Information Systems.
  Covers radio, cryptography, satellite, computers and electronic warfare.
- Weapon Technology and Guided Systems.
  Covers rocket and missile propulsion for ballistic and non-ballistic weapons.
- Military Vehicles.
  Covers the designing of military vehicles and their survival during wartime.
- Intelligence and Surveillance.
  Covers surveillance from ground, air and space.
- Defence Management.
  Provides the necessary skills for evaluation and acquisition of military equipment.
- Trials and Evaluations.
  Design, conduct and analyse the results of equipment trails.

As you can see, this a very intense and difficult course. I have only used a few words to describe each topic when actually a whole paragraph is needed to properly explain them.

The successful graduate of the course will be awarded the qualification of "Army Technical Warrant Officer" and the title of "Master Gunner". The badge is the same as the old Master Gunner badge.

The ATWO course was approved in Feb 2000.

SORD

SORD stands for Strategic Operations and Resource Direction. So what does that mean? It means there will be a big transformation in army units over the next couple of years as described below:

1. First, the infantry battalions will lose their mortar, pioneer, and anti-tank platoons. The infantry will consist only of rifle companies. These rifle companies will still have light mortar and anti-tank weapons.

The infantry battalions will lose these weapons but the army will not. They will be moved to other units. Anti-armour will consist of TOW mounted on LAVs. These LAVs and their crew will be members of the LSDH(RC) which is an armoured unit, not infantry. The crew will be PPCLI. Yes, you read correctly. Infantrymen in an armoured unit. They will wear the black beret with the PPCLI hat badge. They will be called the Long Range Anti Armour Weapon Company of the LDSH(RC).

2. ADATS vehicle and crew will also be moved to the LDSH manned by soldiers of the Artillery Air Defence trade.

3. The following changes will be made to LDSH(RC):
- Assault Troops will be eliminated
- The recce sqn will be the same as recce sqns in RCD and 12 RBC.
- The Leopard tank will be replaced with the Stryker, an eight-wheeled vehicle with a 105 mm gun.

4. The following changes will be made to infantry units:
- Rifle companies will be increased using personnel from the former anti-armour and motor and pioneer platoons as not all of these soldiers will be needed in the LDSH.
- Infantry recce platoons will convert from coyote to LUVW. The coyotes will go to LDSH(RC)
- Mortars (81mm) will be transferred to the artillery.

5. The following changes will be made to Air Defence units:
- The 35mm skyguard will be removed from service as of 21 April 2005
- The Javelin MANPADS will be removed from service.
- Some of the ADATS will be moved to the LDSH(RC).

The new LDSH will be a combined arms Direct Fire Unit instead of a tank unit. On 15 April 2005 the members of PPCLI that were posted to LDSH were marched over to their new home led by their drum line. The remainder of SORD will be implemented over the next few years with completion by 2010.

See infantry Pioneer and Infantry Mortarman for more info on these jobs.

references 1. *The Maple Leaf 7 July 2004*

WOMEN IN THE CANADIAN ARMY

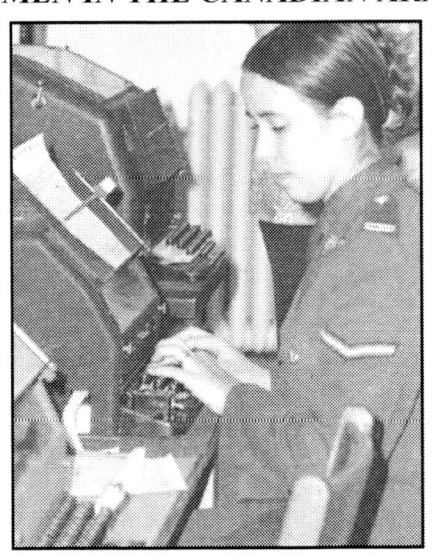

Photo courtesy of the Museum of the Regiments

The photo above shows a female Teletype Operator in the Royal Canadian Corps of Signals. The only time that women were members of the army corps were from 1964 to 1968. Before 1964 women were recruited only as members of the Canadian Women's Army Corp (with the exception of the Nursing Sisters in the Medical Corps). In 1968 the Army, Navy and Air Force ceased to exist and the women, like the men, became members of the Canadian Armed Forces.

Starting in 1964, women could join the regular army corps but not in any unit that was required to spend time in the field. They were employed only in static positions. Trades that were open to women gradually increased over the years. In 1974 women could join 60 percent of the army trades. By 1985 this had increased to 75 percent but still only in static positions. The author was a member of 1 Field Ambulance from 1985 to 1987 and there were no women in the unit. In 1987 most field positions were opened to women and today they make up about 50 percent of the members in 1 Field Ambulance. The percentage is much lower in other units, such as infantry. In March 2001 the final restriction on women was lifted (service on submarines) and today women can work in any trade or unit of the military.

Part Four

Parachute Badges

CANADIAN PARACHUTE BADGES

This part of the book will illustrate and explain the more than 140 different parachute badges worn by the Canadian Armed Forces since the first Canadian paratroopers were trained in 1942.

This is not intended to be a complete history of the Canadian Airborne forces, but a brief history is included in order to explain the evolution of the badges.

Badges are of the following types:
regular – Normal machine embroidered badges made of rayon. Usually issued free to the soldiers.
bullion – Made of metallic thread at member's cost for their best uniform. Often hand embroidered.
mylar – A bullion-like badge but made of mylar instead of metallic. (Mylar is a shiny material, sometimes called J-metallic.)
Metal – Made of metal instead of cloth
Mess Dress – Miniature wings for formal mess uniforms.
Subdued - Badges made of olive green for wear on jump smocks or combat uniforms.

The badges are numbered for reference purposes. The scans are 75 per cent of original size.

CANADIAN ARMY 1942-1971

Canada formed two battalions of paratroopers in 1942. The First Canadian Parachute Battalion was first authorized by cabinet on 1 July 1942. In the summer of 1942 some officers and men were trained at Ringway England. Subsequent training was done at Fort Benning Georgia, U.S.A. In April of 1943 1 Can Para Bn was incorporated into the British 6th Airborne Division. The Battalion was disbanded 30 Sep 1945.

The Second Canadian Parachute Battalion was raised in 1942 to serve as the Canadian contingent of the joint Canadian/American First Special Service Force, based in Helena Montana. In May 1943, the Second Canadian Parachute Battalion was renamed as the First Canadian Special Service Battalion. The FSSF was disbanded 5 December 1944. The First Canadian Special Service Battalion was disbanded one month later on 5 January 1945.

No Canadian paratroopers served with Canadian formations during the Second World War.

Eighty-five personnel who qualified as parachutist in England were awarded the British wings (Second World War pattern shown.) All others were qualified in U.S.A. and wore the U.S. wings. Canadian wings were designed and made available in 1943. The First Special Service Force, both American and Canadian personal, wore the American wings throughout the war.

A1

Canadian Army (1st type) 1943 - 1953

The Canadian Parachute Training Centre opened in 1943 in Shilo, Manitoba. Training ceased in 1945 when the two parachute units were disbanded. In 1947, the Parachute Training Centre was renamed the Joint Air School and moved to Rivers, Manitoba and training was resumed as a joint army/air force unit. More on this unit later. (The dates for this wing are approximate. See A4 and A5 for more information.)

A2

Bullion type 1

This is an example of an early bullion parachute wing. Bullion badges are hand embroidered of metal thread and are quite attractive. They were not issued to the soldiers, but had to be purchased at their own cost. Most parachutists wanted to have one of these badges for their best battledress.

Canadian Special Air Service Company 1947-1949

In 1947, a Canadian Special Air Service Company was formed, but it was short-lived and was disbanded in 1949. No special badges were produced for this unit.

Mobile Striking Force 1949-1958

At this time, it was decided that each infantry regiment would train a battalion of airborne/air transportable troops. As the infantry regiments had been reduced to just one battalion each after the war, this meant the entire infantry corps was to be airborne or air transportable. The SAS company was dissolved and its members employed as parachute instructors in their respective battalions or in the Parachute Training Centre. The PPCLI was trained in 1949, the RCR in 1950 and the R22R in 1951. These troops are often referred to as "parachute battalions". In reality, only one company consisted of paratroopers. The remainder of the battalion was trained in air transportable operations but not necessarily as paratroopers. These three battalions together were called the "Mobile Striking Force". Airborne exercises were conducted in 1949 and 1950 but no further airborne exercises took place until 1968. (Unit airborne exercises occurred during this period, but none involving the three battalions of the Mobile Striking Force working together.) The three airborne battalions were intended to form an airborne brigade, but it never functioned as such and there was no brigade headquarters.

A3

Korean War 1950-1953.

During the Korean war, the regiments were increased to three battalions each, and the "jump battalion" was the 1st battalion of each regiment. When the 2nd battalion of each regiment came home, the 1st battalion replaced them in Korea. The 2nd battalion then had to be parachute qualified to fulfill its role in the MSF. Thereafter, the parachute battalion was the one of the three that was not in Korea or Germany at any given time.

These wings were made in Japan during the Korean War for Canadian soldiers on leave from Korea for wear on their best battledress. They are silver bullion on a light green background. As the jump battalions were rotated, many of the troops fighting in Korea were paratroopers. Bullion wings are an optional item at the soldiers expense. There are a few minor varieties of this wing. (See additional photo in this section.)

Infantry Reorganization

With the Korean war over, the PPCLI and the RCR were reduced to two battalions each. The R22eR remained at three battalions. Two new regiments of two battalions each were added to the regular force infantry. These were the Black Watch (formerly the 1st and 2nd Cdn Highland Bns reserve units) and the Queen's Own Rifles (formerly the 1st and 2nd Canadian Rifle Bns reserve units). Another new regiment, the Canadian Guards, had four battalions (formerly 3RCR, 3PPCLI and the 1st and 2nd Infantry Bns which were new units created for the Korean war and for service in Europe with NATO in 1951 and 1952.)

The Canadian Joint Air Training Centre

In 1949 the Joint Air School was renamed the Canadian Joint Air Training Centre, a tri-service unit.
Royal Canadian Navy personnel became involved in August 1948. The role of the CJATC was as follows:
- Training and research in airportability of army personnel and equipment.
- Air force training in tactical support of land operations.
- Testing of new airborne equipment, especially in winter conditions.
- Training of paratroopers. These were mostly army personnel but some RCAF and RCN personnel were also trained. New candidates for the Para Rescue course were trained at RCAF Station Edmonton, not at Rivers. You can see the Air Force and Navy wings further in this section.
- Training of army pilots for gliders, light aircraft and helicopters.
- Training of an Air Cadet squadron.

Defence of Canada Force 1958-1968

As the infantry battalions were rotated to Korea and Germany, the role of "jump battalion" was also rotated. If the first battalion went to Germany, for example, the second battalion would assume the airborne role. Because of these rotations and a lack of resources (aircraft and training time) and instructors it became impossible to maintain an airborne/air transportable battalion in each regiment. In 1958, the "jump battalions" were reduced to "jump companies" and this airborne force was renamed the "Defence of Canada Force". It never really existed as a "force", only as individual unit jump companies. The idea was that they could be deployed together if they were ever needed.

A4

Canadian Army (2nd type) 1953 - 1957

The dates for this badge are approximate. There is no way to determine an exact year that a badge was made. However, one can tell that it was made sometime between A1 and A5 by the following attributes:

- It has upswept corners. Early wings (see A1) did not.
- It has thick shroud lines like A1. Newer wings (see A5) have thin lines.
- It is slightly scalloped. Older wings are round at the bottom; newer badges are quite heavily scalloped.
- It has the original style of maple leaf like A1, except with a longer stem. Newer badges (see A5) have a more realistic shape maple leaf.

A5

Canadian Army (3nd type) 1957-1971.

Approximately 1957, the design of the parachute wing was modified again. The scalloping on the lower edge is more pronounced. The shroud lines were made thinner, and the maple leaf is more realistic. There are several other minor varieties of A1, A4 and A5 but the differences are slight. The battledress uniform on which these wings were worn was replaced by the Canadian Forces uniform starting in 1968. This was a gradual process and some soldiers wore the old uniform as late as 1971.

A6

Bullion Wings type 2

Bullion wings were available for best battledress and dress blues. These wings were made with metal thread and are quite attractive. These wings were modelled on the third type of para wing (A5) used in the 1960's. There are several different minor varieties.

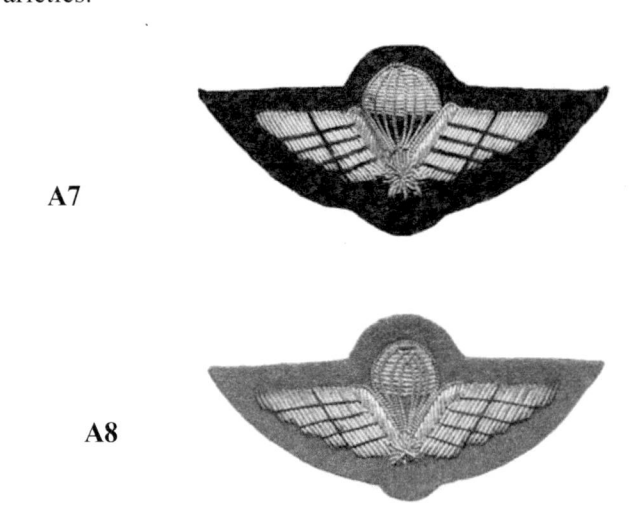

A7

A8

Army Mess Dress in blue and scarlet

These small wings were made for army mess kit in blue and scarlet. The mess kit is worn for mess diners and other very formal occasions. A7 appears to be black in photographs but it is actually a very dark blue. Note the "bump" on the bottom of mess wings from this period.

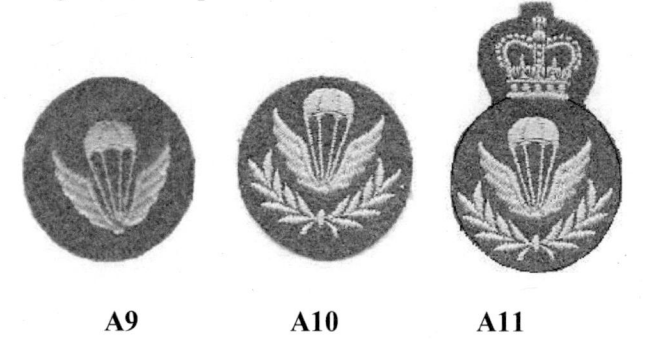

A9   A10   A11

Assistant Instructor
Parachute Training 1947-1963

These trade badges were worn on the lower right sleeve of the battledress and TW uniforms by instructors at the Parachute Training Centre. This was a trade from 1947 until 1963. There were parachute instructors before 1947 and there are parachute instructors today, but it was only during these years that instructing was a trade. Before 1947 and after 1963 being an instructor was a temporary job and not a trade. The badges were first produced about 1958. (See parachute trades in part three for more information on this trade.)

Flash! A9

Just before going to press the existence of a Group one Para Instructor badge has been discovered. This is the third new badge to be discovered during the writing of this book. There may be others. If you know of a trade badge that is not shown in this book please contact the author so that it can be included in a future edition of the book.
Badge courtesy of Louis Grimshaw.

Evolution of a Badge

The Canadian Army parachutist badge was in continuous use from 1943 until 1971. I was probably one of the last to wear this badge as I did not receive my Canadian Forces uniform until mid 1971.

The photographs on this page will show how the badge evolved over the years. The first picture is the original badge as issued in 1943.

The colour of the wings on all these badges are identical. They appear to be different due to age, wear and different scanning processes.

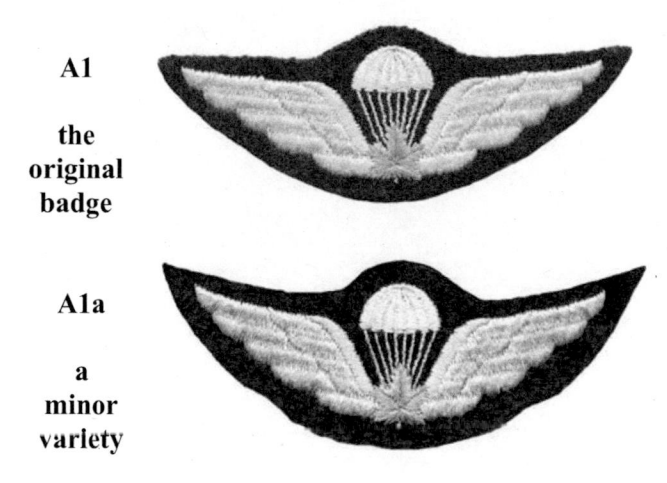

A1 the original badge

A1a a minor variety

There are several minor varieties of this badge. In this book I have limited the numbering to three major types. This one falls between the first and second type in the evolutionary process of this badge. Note that the bottom edge is slightly scalloped; more than the original badge but not as much as the second type.

A4 type two

The is the second type badge in use from about 1953 to 1957. Dates are approximate as there is no way to determine the exact year of issue for these badges. Note the upswept corners and scalloped bottom which are the main differences. It also has a larger stem on the maple leaf.

A5 type three

The final version of the badge was in use from about 1957 until its demise with the issue of the new CF uniform. Note the heavily scalloped bottom, the thin shroud lines, and the redesigned maple leaf with the stem pointing to the left.

There are several other minor varieties, not shown, that fall between those shown here.

Blue Wings

A12

First of all, I must say that I have found no documentation for the existence of these blue wings. I have come to the conclusion that they were worn by Air Force personnel mostly by the process of elimination.

It has been reported in more than one publication that these wings were worn by the PPCLI when they were in the Korean War. Hence the UN blue colour. I interviewed a large number of Korea War Vets and also placed a notice in their newsletter. None of the them were familiar with these wings. I also talked with a former member of the Canadian SAS and got the same results. None of these people had seen these blue wings before.

A couple of long retired soldiers who were posted at Rivers in the 1950's said they remember some RCAF personnel taking jump courses. I believe they these wings were locally made, probably by the base tailor in Rivers, and were unofficially sanctioned for wear at the Canadian Joint Air Training Centre. No documentation could be found to confirm this; probably because they were never approved by Ottawa. I was unable to find a RCAF parachutist to confirm my theory but neither was I able to find any other plausible explanation for the existence of this badge.

A13

Like the RCAF wings, I found no documentation to explain the existence of these dark blue wings. There were Navy personnel working at the CJATC so it seems logical that if some Air Force personnel got on a jump course, that a few Navy personnel managed to find their way onto one of these courses also. The base tailor was probably asked to come up with a suitable wing for a Navy uniform.

Or perhaps they were made for the Army dress blue uniform.

If any reader can confirm my theory on these blue wings with some type of documentation or photograph or personal experience, I would love to hear from you. On the other hand, if someone has another theory, I would like to hear about that also. You can contact me through my website. (See back of book.)

Varieties 1943-1968

AV1

This is a fake copy of A1. It is pure white. The original badge is more of a cream colour. The fake is also much poorer in workmanship, especially the maple leaf.

Parachute Badges

AV2a,b,c

Three different varieties of green wings. All of which I believe to be fake. Genuine green wings were made during the Korean war. I have seen them only in bullion. I have never seen a genuine embroidered version. If it looks like brand new, it probably is. Most of these wings are poorly designed. Especially the maple leaf.

AV3a **AV3b** **AV3c**

Several different varieties of mess kit wings exist. As both the badges and the uniforms were private purchase, the soldiers felt no obligation to follow standard army pattern wings. Badges were probably all the same within any given unit. The black on red wings are no doubt for rifle regiments. AV3a is similar to the regulation pattern. There is no explanation for the drastic changes made in AV3c. No doubt there are other varieties in addition to these three.

Korean War

The photo above shows the green-backed para wings (A3) worn on a uniform of the Queens Own Rifles. This is a different version than the one shown in the text. This one looks more like A1. The background colour doesn't show well in the photo, but it is a bullion wing on a green background.

Photos by author.
Uniforms courtesy of the Provincial Museum of Alberta

First Canadian Special Service Battalion

The First Special Service Force was disbanded 5 December 1944. All members of this elite force, both American and Canadian, wore U.S. Army uniforms. The Canadian members of the FSSF, known as the First Canadian Special Service Battalion, changed back into their Canadian uniforms at this time. The First Canadian Special Service Battalion had no badges or accoutrements of their own so members continued to wear FSSF insignia on their Canadian battledress while waiting for a posting to a new unit. The crossed arrows (the FSSF collar badge) served as a hat badge. The USA/Canada spearhead was used as a unit patch and the FSSF lanyard was worn as shown in the photo above. American para wings were replaced with Canadian ones. Some of these men transferred to the First Canadian Parachute Battalion, and some went to other units. The First Canadian Special Service Battalion was disbanded on 5 Jan 1945.

UNIFICATION 1968-1985

In 1968, the Canadian Army, Navy, and Air Force were unified into one force. A new uniform and a completely new set of badges were issued. Most documentation states that this change was made in 1968. On paper this is true, but it took a few years for complete implementation. I took my jump course in Rivers in January 1970 and was awarded the old 1943 style wings which I wore until 1971.

C1

Canadian Armed Forces 1968-1985
Canadian Airborne Regiment 1968-1975

Also in 1968, the Defence of Canada Force was dissolved and the Canadian Airborne Regiment was formed. At first, the wings worn by members of the Canadian Airborne Regiment were the same as other jumpers in the Canadian Armed Forces. The background appears to be black in photographs, but it was in fact a very dark green colour called "rifle green". It is not very noticeable in the pictures but the wings of this era were slightly scalloped. All CF wings from this date on are padded. Previous wings were flat. The regiment was formed in Edmonton Alberta, and in 1970 the jump school also moved to Edmonton and became the Parachute Training Wing of the new Canadian Airborne Centre.[1]

At this time, The Black Watch, The Queens Own Rifles and the Canadian Guards were removed from the order of battle and the remaining three regiments were increased to three battalions each. The Black Watch and the Queens Own became reserve force units. The Cdn Guards were disbanded (the 3rd and 4th Bns had been disbanded in 1957).

C2

Canadian Airborne Regiment 1975-1985

In 1975 a silver metal maple leaf was added to distinguish members of the Canadian Airborne Regiment from other parachutist in the Canadian Armed Forces. This badge is identical to C1 except for the addition of the metal pin placed over the red maple leaf. Personnel who were jump qualified but never a member of an active jump unit continued to wear wings with a red maple leaf. Ex-members of the Airborne Regiment were also allowed to wear the silver maple leaf. This also included parachutists of the MSF, Cdn SAS, Defence of Canada Force, CFPMD and any others who had served in an operational jump unit.

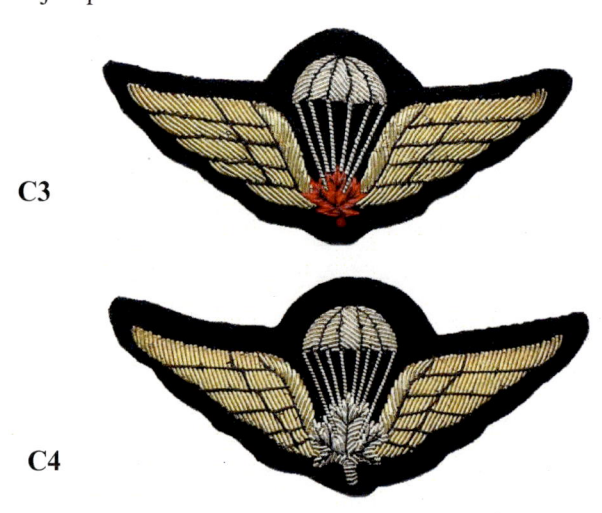

C3

C4

Bullion Wings

Bullion wings were made available for a fee. The silver maple leaf was metallic embroidery, not a metal pin. Note that wings of this era have gold wings with a red or silver maple leaf. Previous badges had cream colour wings with a gold maple leaf. There are several varieties, some of which are illustrated in this section.

C5   **C6**

Metal

In 1975, metal wings were issued for wear on the CF short-sleeved shirt when not wearing a tunic. These wings are still in use. For the Airborne wings, the maple leaf is white instead of the usual silver. The remainder of the Armed Forces wore the version with the red leaf.

On newer wings the veins in the maple leaf

Parachute Badges

are more noticeable; on the original badge the veins were quite faint.

C7

Dual Qualification Wings

Dual Qualification wings are parachutist badges that are intended for wear by a member of the forces who is already wearing some other qualification or hazardous skill badge such as a pilot or diver. If the space on the uniform normally used for the wearing of a parachutist badge is already occupied by another badge, then the dual qualification wing would be worn on the pocket below the other badge.

The original Dual Qualification wing was introduced in 1975. It is not a very attractive badge. The maple leaf, which looks more like a star than a maple leaf, is made from a separate piece of metal and superimposed on the badge making the maple leaf twice the thickness of the remainder of the badge. This badge was not available with a white maple leaf.

C8

Combat Wing 1975

This all green wing was made for the combat uniform on a trail basis. They were issued to some members of the Airborne Regiment. Apparently only a few hundred of these badges were made and many of them were given out to British paratroopers who happened to be on a training exercise with the Airborne Regiment at the time. After the trail period, no more badges for the combat uniform were ever produced. Most of the badges were worn and eventually discarded. Very few were saved.

C9

C10

Smock Wings

First issued in 1976, these wings were produced for wear on the jump smock and later, the SSF camouflage smock. They were made with a white maple leaf for the Airborne regiment and ex-airborne personnel, and a red leaf for jumpers who were never in the airborne. They exist in several minor varieties, some with borders and others without a border.

Without repeating myself over and over, henceforth the "Airborne Regiment" wings with the white or silver maple leaf is deemed to include all operationally tasked parachutists, and former members of those units (see C2); not only those in the Airborne Regiment

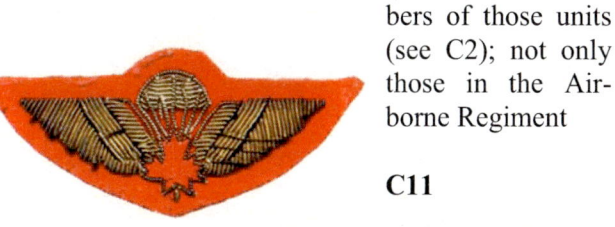

C11

C12

Mess Dress 1975-1985

Like the other wings of this era, the mess kit wings were produced with both silver and red maple leaves. There are several differences between these and previous mess kit wings. The "bump" from the bottom of the badge has been removed. The wings are gold coloured; previous badges had silver wings. The maple leaf is either silver or red; previous badges had a gold leaf.

CV1a

Varieties 1968-1985

There are several varieties of bullion wings and about ten different varieties of mess kit wings from this period. Two varieties of bullion wings with red leaves and one of mess kit are shown. Badges from this period had gold wings with a red or silver maple leaf. Previous badges had silver wings with a gold leaf.

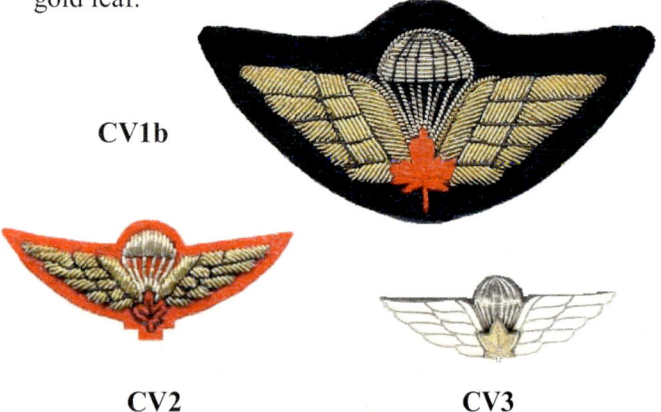

CV1b

CV2   **CV3**

(Thanks to Louis Grimshaw for the photo and information on this badge).

Dual Qualification Wings

The QM issue version of the dual qualification wings is shown at C7. As mentioned there, it was not a very attractive badge. Therefore some soldiers purchased this private made badge at their own expense. It was worn mostly by army pilots who were also qualified as parachutists. The badge is made of silver and was manufactured by Birks jewellers (they are stamped "Birks" on the back).

DISTINCTIVE ENVIRONMENTAL UNIFORM (DEU)
First Issue 1985-1990

D1

D2

In 1985, the air, sea and land elements of the Canadian Armed Forces were once again issued with three separate uniforms called Distinctive Environmental Uniforms (DEU.) New badges were also issued. There is not too much difference between the DEU and the CF wings. They are the same gold colour; and for the Airborne Regiment, a silver metal maple leaf was added. There were two differences. The scalloping is more pronounced, but the main difference is the background colour. The CF wings have a dark green background; the DEU wings have a black background. The difference is not very noticeable until you look at one of each type side by side.

D3

D4

Mylar Wings

Since shortly after the Second World War, Canadian soldiers have been paying to have bullion versions made of their parachute wings. The mylar wings were an attempt to fill that need without the expense of the bullion wings. Bullion badges are hand embroidered with metal thread, making them fairly expensive. The mylar wings were machine embroidered like the normal rayon wings. Mylar, being a shiny material, made a reasonable imitation of a bullion wing. (Mylar is sometimes called J-Metalic.) Soldiers had the option of wearing the normal rayon wings or the mylar badges. In the same manner as the regular wings, a metal maple leaf was added to the wings worn by members and ex-members of the Airborne Regiment.

Personally, I prefer the regular rayon wings. The photos do not show how shiny these mylar wings were. In my opinion, they are too shiny and look a bit like plastic.

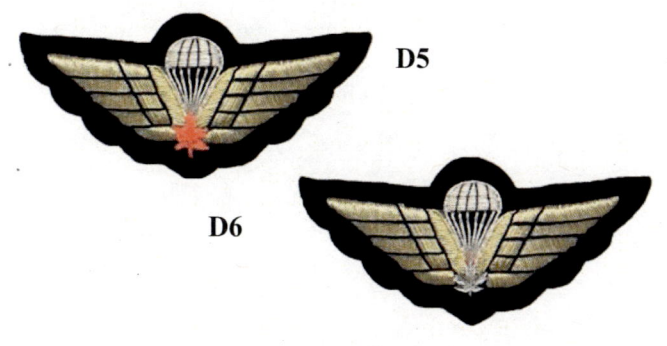

Parachute Badges

Mess Dress Wings
Mess dress wings were available for those who owned a mess uniform. They are miniature replicas of the mylar wings, including a miniature metal maple leaf for members of the Airborne Regiment.

Garrison Dress

Garrison Dress 1985-1998
These wings were issued for the short-lived Garrison Dress, with red and white maple leaves for non-airborne and Airborne Regiment soldiers. Garrison Dress wings are flat, DEU wings are padded.

Airborne!

Photo by author

DISTINCTIVE ENVIRONMENTAL UNIFORM
(DEU2) Second Issue 1991 to date

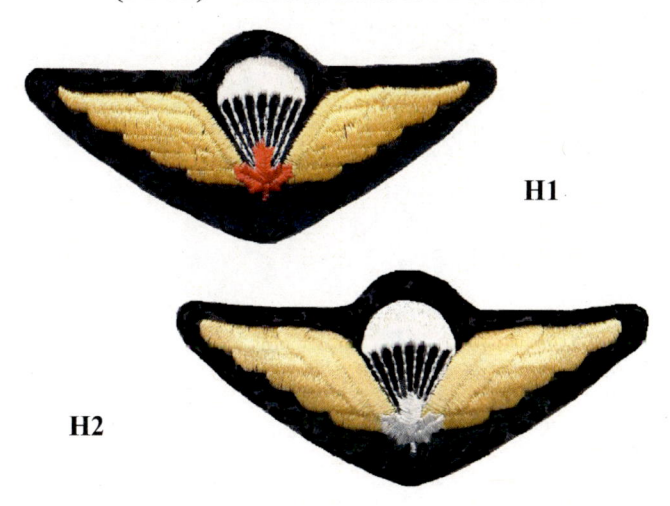

In 1991, a new set of wings were issued. The silver metal maple leaf was replaced with a white embroidered maple leaf for members and ex-members of the Airborne Regiment. The red leaf continued to be issued for soldiers who had a jump course but were never members of the a jump unit. The bottom edge is now straight instead of scalloped.

Mylar type 2
A new set of Mylar Bullion wings were also produced. Although still an imitation bullion, they are much nicer than the original Mylar wings. Like the new rayon wings, the metal leaf was replaced with a white embroidered leaf and the scalloped edge was replaced with a straight edge. Also, the black lines have been removed from the parachute.

Canadian Airborne Regiment Disbanded 1995
In 1995, the Canadian Airborne Regiment

was disbanded and Canada returned to the jump companies of the 1950's. The white maple leaf now represents someone who has served in an active jump unit which could be the Airborne Regiment, or since 1995, a jump company. The red maple leaf still represents someone who has had a jump course but never served in an active jump unit.

In 1996 the Canadian Airborne Centre was moved to Trenton Ontario and renamed the Canadian Parachute Centre. It is also the home of the "Sky Hawks", the Canadian Forces parachute display team. In 1998, the Canadian Forces Parachute Maintenance Depot followed and was amalgamated with the CPC. The centre is responsible for packing and maintenance of all parachutes, as well as conducting jump courses. Also taught at the CPC are free-fall parachute courses, aerial delivery of equipment, rappelling, patrol pathfinder and rigger courses.

What has also returned from the 1950's is the attitude of neglect for our parachute capability. No airborne exercises were conducted from 1951 to 1968.[2] No airborne exercise with all three jump companies have occurred since the Airborne Regiment was disbanded in 1995. The jump companies have difficulty getting aircraft for their jumps and mostly jump from helicopters.[3] There is a difficulty obtaining Hercules aircraft for several reasons: the expense, the age and amount of maintenance required on the aircraft, the distances involved getting the troops to the the airfield, non-airborne commitments, waning numbers of qualified aircrew and lack of interest from those above. Also, three widely dispersed jump companies from different units would not have near as much influence or operational capabilities as the Airborne Regiment had.

H5

H6

Hand Embroidered Bullion
In 1999 these wings became available for optional purchase. They are hand embroidered and very attractive. They are part of a series of new wings that include the mess kit wings shown later in this section and others that you will see in this part of the book. Like previous bullion wings, they are available at extra cost and not issued free in the QM stores.

H7   H8

Metal Dual Qualification Wings
In 2001 the old dual qualification badge was replaced with a new version that is a miniature of the regular metal parachutist wings. They are available with either a red or a white maple leaf. These small wings have vein makings on the maple leaf and therefore might be confused with the miniature RCR wings (see M9 and M10.) The vein lines are the only thing in common with the RCR wings. Otherwise they are exactly like the full size CF metal wings. They are also smaller than the RCR wings being under four centimetres in legth. (The miniature RCR wings are 4.3 cm in length.)

Apparently these small wings are also being used as mess kit wings in lieu of the cloth versions although this was not their intended purpose. The CF dress regulations of 1992 state that army mess dress badges are to be of cloth.

These same dress regulations state that army and air force personnel shall wear a maximum of two flying or specialist skill badges. Navy personnel may wear only one such badge.

H9

H10

H11

H12

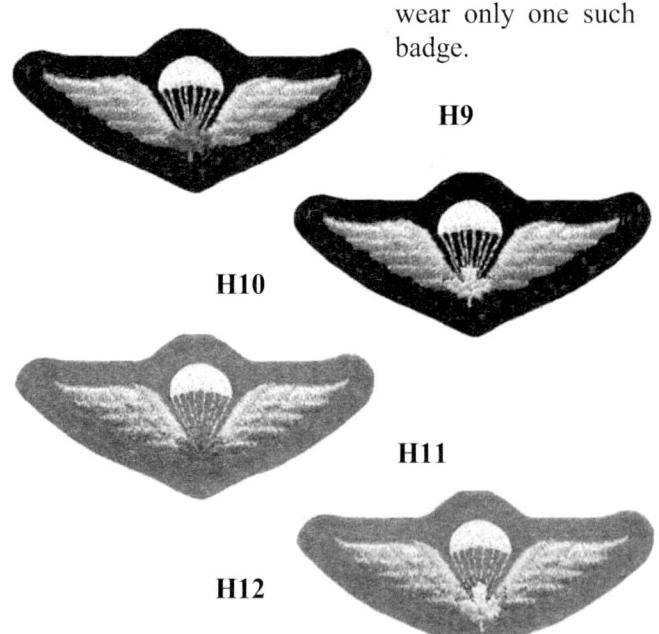

230

Parachute Badges

DEU2 Mess Dress Wings

Mess dress wings were available in black and scarlet for both airborne and other jumpers. These wings were made of mylar, but were not exact copies of the full size mylar wings. The black lines that make the full size version so attractive are missing from these smaller wings.

H13

H14

H15

H16

Hand Embroidered Mess Dress Wings

These mess kit wings were the first of the new hand embroidered series to appear in 1994. They are available in black or scarlet, each with a red or silver maple leaf.

H17

H18

PPCLI Mess Dress Wings

Another new type of mess dress wings made their appearance recently. They are being sold at PPCLI kit shops (and possibly others but that is where I first noticed them).

H19

H20

Queen's Own Rifles Mess Dress Wings

The Queen's Own Rifles is the only militia unit with a jump company. They wear the same parachute badge on their DEU as the rest of the Canadian Forces, but they have a unique black on red badge for their mess dress uniform.

MISCELLANEOUS WINGS

The following wings are an assortment of badges that do not fit into any of the previous categories. Some of them are authorized for issue and others are not.

M1

M2

RMC Wings

These wings were produced for wear on the Royal Military College cadet uniform. They would only be worn if a cadet had a jump course before going to RMC (or one of the other two military colleges before they were closed.) This could happen only if a soldier goes to RMC after already being in the military for a while. Militia or cadet personnel could have had a jump course while serving in the reserve forces.

M3

M4

Unofficial Metal Wings Type One

There are several different types of the metal wings other than the official QM issued version. This first type are made in China for an American company. They are sold on American army bases and by mail. There are several differences between these wings and the genuine Canadian wings as follows:

1. The maple leaf is a different shape than the genuine wings. Compare them to C5 and C6.
2. The areas to the left and right of the parachute lines are raised. On the genuine wings, these areas are indented.
3. The area behind the parachute lines is speckled. On the genuine wings, this area is unmarked.
4. These wings have only two clasps on the back. Genuine wings have three posts.

These wings are supposedly sold for American soldiers who have jumped with the Canadian forces. Wings with the white maple leaf would never be given to foreign troops as they are reserved for wear by active Canadian jump units and former members of these units. Foreign troops could wear the badge with the red maple leaf it they have jumped with the Canadian Forces.

M5　　　　**M6**

Unofficial Metal Wings Type Two

A second type of unofficial metal badge is being sold in Canadian kit shops (stores on military bases). They are the same as the official badge with the following exceptions:

1. The colour is different. They are dull yellowish gold, rather than the bright gold of the official wings.
2. The maple leaf is solid white or red. The official wings have veins on the leaves.
3. There are only two pins on the back instead of the regulation three pins.
4. They feel almost flat to the touch. All other versions of this badge have raised and indented parts.

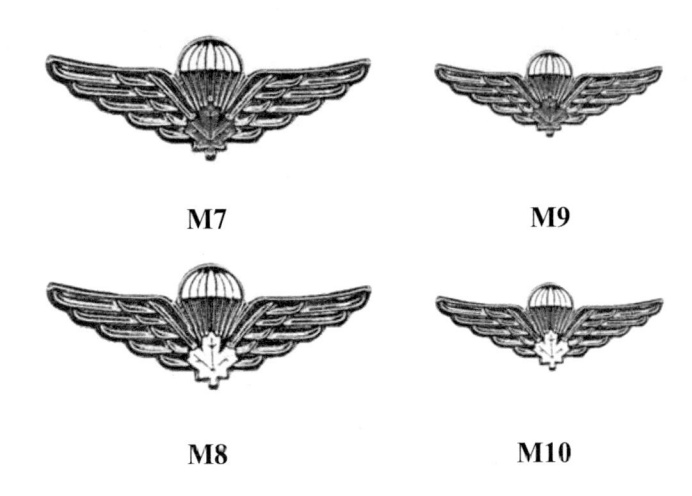

M7　　　　**M9**

M8　　　　**M10**

RCR Wings

For reasons that no one has been able to explain to me, the RCR's have been producing their own version of the metal parachute wings since 1993. They are different from either the regular CF wings or the unofficial version in the following ways:

1. They are much shinier than either the CF or unofficial versions.
2. The white portion of the parachute is indented. On both the CF and unofficial versions the parachute and the gold lines are of equal height.
3. The area behind the shroud lines is speckled like the unofficial wings. The CF wings are plain in this area.
4. The wings of both the unofficial and CF version are marked to resemble feathers and are relatively flat. Each feather of the RCR wings is indented with a single line inside.
5. The area to the left and right of the parachute lines is indented with a single line inside in the manner of all other feathers.
6. The maple leaf has gold coloured vein markings. The CF wings have faint veins on the maple leaf and the unofficial versions have none.
7. These badges have three pins on the back, the same as the CF version. The unofficial wings have only two pins.
8. Miniature versions were produced for mess kit. These wings are identical to the larger version with one exception. The maple leaf is made from a separate piece of metal and then applied

Parachute Badges

on top of the wing, making the maple leaf double the thickness of the remainder of the badge. Regulations state that mess dress wings are to be of cloth.

M11

M12

M13

M14  **M15**

Army and Air Cadets

These badges were produced for Army and Air Cadet uniforms. The yellow badge (M14) was for the Army Cadet uniform and the blue/grey badge (M15) for Air Cadets. They were in use until from 1981 to 1988. Cadets were not allowed to parachute for a time. Now, regular CF badges are worn by cadets.

M16a  **M16b**

Mock Tower Badges

Part of the parachutist course is to jump from the 35 foot high mock tower before jumping from an aircraft. The exit from the tower is the same as jumping from an aircraft, except that no parachute is used. The jumper wears a parachute harness that is hooked to a line. After jumping, the soldier would slide down the line to a mound of dirt where they can get unhooked. Army and Air Cadets sometimes made jumps from the mock tower but never went on to make an actual jump from an aircraft. Two different versions of mock tower wings are shown. These badges were never worn by the regular or reserve forces.

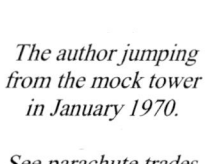

Foreign Troops

These wings were supposedly made for wear on the uniforms of foreign troops when they jump with the Canadian Forces and qualify for Canadian Jump wings. They are designed for the uniforms of the following countries:

M11   U.S.A.
M12   U.K.
M13   Germany (1960's)

I know, from conversations with several U.S. army personnel, that M11 is being used by U.S. soldiers on their fatigue uniforms. I have no proof that the British or German versions were ever actually worn by soldiers of those countries.

The author jumping from the mock tower in January 1970.

See parachute trades in part three for another photo of the mock tower.

SKILL AT ARMS

M17

M18

Reproduction Smock Wings

These are modern reproductions of the 1976 smock wings. Compare them to C9 and C10.

PATROL PATHFINDER

Pathfinders parachute into an area one or more days in advance of the main body of paratroopers to secure the Drop Zone (DZ) and guide the main force to the objective. When the main group of paratroopers arrive, the pathfinder will brief them and guide them to their objectives. They must be prepared to clear the DZ of enemy forces if necessary, but they would prefer to remain hidden and avoid enemy contact. In addition to securing a DZ, pathfinders could be tasked to secure remote airstrips or beachheads.

After insertion, the pathfinders need time to gather intelligence about the area and find routes from the DZ to the objective. When the main force arrives, the pathfinders will provide the commander with an accurate up-to-date report of conditions, enemy activity and a choice of routes.

Although reconnaissance is their main role, pathfinder could be inserted on an independent mission. They could be tasked to ambush the enemy and prevent them from carrying out certain activities, or they could parachute behind enemy lines to conduct sabotage such as destroying bridges.

The course is a difficult one of two and half months in length. Some of the subjects on the course include knots and lashings, building a rope bridge, climbing, improvised harnesses, water crossings techniques, rugged terrain operations, map reading, use of GPS, photo imagery, basic survival techniques, weapon training including all current Canadian weapons and also foreign weapons, communication equipment, communication security, antennae construction, demolitions, mines and booby-traps and first aid including use of morphine and IV. They must be qualified in freefall as well as static line parachuting.

The Pathfinder badge was first issued in 1976 by the Canadian Airborne Regiment. They did not receive approval from NDHQ and it was withdrawn later the same year. In spite of the rejection, the badge re-appeared in the early 1980's in drab, rayon, mylar and metal. No explanation was ever given as to why a previously rejected design was now ok. It was finally authorized for wear in the dress regulations of 1991.

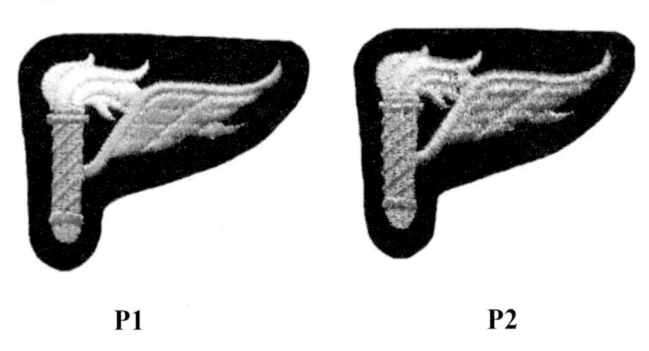

P1   **P2**

The pathfinder badge for the dress uniform became available in both rayon (P1) and mylar (P2). The rayon badge is gold, whereas the mylar badge is more of a yellow colour and is shiny in appearance. The rayon badge was first issued in 1982; the mylar version came out in 1991. Neither of these badges were ever worn on the CF uniform. They were produced because of a CF policy that all skill badges be produced in all formats. All ex-pathfinders that I spoke with said that they wore only the metal badge on the CF uniform.

P3   **P4**

Parachute Badges

Metal

The metal Pathfinder badge is worn on the left breast pocket, below the regular parachutist wings. There are two versions. The first, P3, was issued by the Canadian Airborne Regiment. It was eventually replaced in the early 1990's by P4, a CF issue. There are several differences as follows:

- The CF version is slightly larger than the Airborne version. It measures 4cm across the top vs 3.8 for the Airborne issue.
- The CF version has three pins on the back; the Airborne version only two.
- The flames on the Airborne badge are speckled with gold. The wings on the CF badge are pure white.
- The bottom of the Airborne badge is flat; the CF version is rounded.
- The gold on the Airborne badge is a combination of feathered and smooth metal. There are no smooth sections on the CF version.

Fake copies of the airborne badge exist. See PV3.

Before the Canadian pathfinder badge was approved, the American pathfinder badge was worn on the CF uniform. Occasionally, soldiers wearing this badge were told to take if off, as it was not authorized. They took them down for a while but soon began to wear them again. This went on until the Canadian badge was issued in the early 1990's.

P5

Dual Qualification

In the early 1990's it became CF policy that all skill badges were to be produced in all formats. Therefore, if a miniature metal parachutist wing was to be issued as a dual qualification badge, then a miniature pathfinder, rigger and SAR Tech badge would also be produced. Although this became the policy in 1991, the badges were not produced until 2001, starting with the new version of the miniature parachutist wing (see H7 and H8.) This policy has caused some confusion. There has never been a requirement for a miniature dual qualification pathfinder badge. Dual qualification badges are worn on the left breast pocket. This is were the full size metal pathfinder badge was already being worn. Other skill badges are worn above the pocket.

This badge is often labelled as a mess dress wing. Dress regulations state that mess dress wings are to be of cloth.

P6    P7

Smock Wings

The Pathfinder badge with the grey flames (P6) was the original Pathfinder badge issued by the Airborne Regiment in 1976. Apparently only 300 were made. The design was rejected by NDHQ and they were withdrawn from use the same year. NDHQ had two complaints about the badge. The first being that there was no maple leaf included in the design. The second complaint was that if worn on the right sleeve the flames went toward the front of the uniform, which gave it the appearance of being sewn on backwards.

The badges reappeared in 1982, this time with a white flame. While no maple leaf was ever incorporated into the design, the problem of the flames flying to the front was solved by wearing it on the left sleeve only. It was to be worn on the left sleeve of the smock and on the left breast pocket of the CF tunic. (Only the metal version was worn on the CF uniform.)

SKILL AT ARMS

This photo shows the white flame pathfinder badge being worn on the left sleeve of the jump smock. On the dress uniform, the metal version of the badge was worn on the breast pocket and not on the sleeve.

Photo courtesy of Don Collier

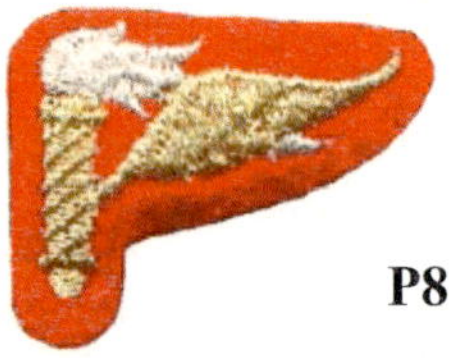

P8

P9

P10

Mess Dress

For many years the miniature mylar badge on a scarlet background was the only Patrol Pathfinder badge available for the mess dress uniform (P8). Then, in 1999, small hand embroidered versions became available with black or scarlet backgrounds.

P11

P12

Garrison Dress 1885-1998

There were two distinct forms of the Pathfinder badge for the short-lived Garrison Dress; one with a white flame and one with a gold flame. Both are on a green background.

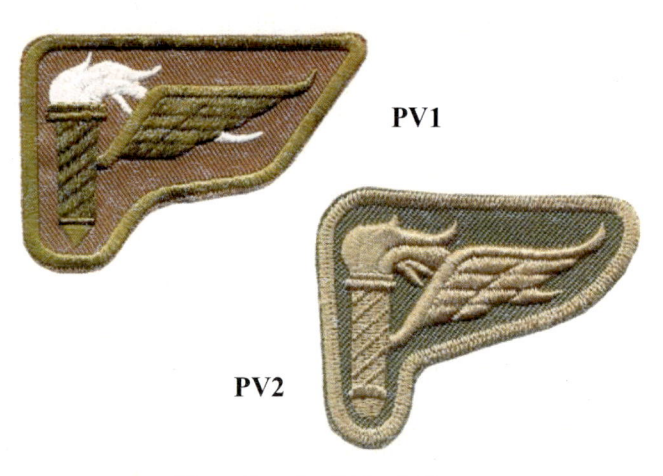

PV1

PV2

Unauthorized Varieties

The are two unofficial varieties of Patrol Pathfinder wings. The first one, PV1, is different from all other pathfinder badges in that it has a brown background. It is also slightly larger than any other pathfinder badge. The second, PV2, is all green, including the flame, and has a rubberized backing. It is believed that these are unauthorized badges made as novelty items to sell to badge collectors.

PV3

This is a modern copy of P3. It is quite well made but there are a couple of differences. The flames are pure white; the original has speckled flames. The colour is a shiny gold whereas the original is a bit yellowish. This second feature is difficult to notice unless you see the two of them together.

RIGGER

Riggers pack and maintain parachutes. They must be jump qualified in order to work in this role. They must occasionally jump using a parachute that they have packed, picked at random by their supervisor.

R1

R2

R3

236

Army 1956 - 1970

These are army trade badges used from 1956 to 1970. For more information on these badges see Parachute trades in Part Three. The Rigger is no longer a trade. After unification it was changed to a specialty. Like the parachutist, a rigger could be any trade.

R4

R5

R6

Navy 1950-1970

The term "rigger" was not used in the Royal Canadian Navy (it was used in the US Navy). They were originally called "Safety Equipment Technicians". This was changed in 1968 to "Safety Systems Technician".

The Safety Equipment Tech was responsible for the maintenance, inspection and repair of parachutes, life rafts, mae-wests and other types of life jackets, helmets, flying suits, immersion suits, oxygen masks, survival equipment and ejection seats. They were not necessarily parachute qualified.

They were employed on HMCS Shearwater, HMCS Magnificent and HMCS Bonaventure.

The badge was produced in three colours for wear on the three different Navy uniforms of the day as follows:

- Gold on navy blue for wear on the #1 dress uniform
- Red on navy blue for wear on the winter uniform
- Blue on white for wear on the summer uniform

In all examples that I have seen, the white badge is much larger than the blue background badges. The edges of the white badges were folded under before sewing on to create a nice edge. The measurements are as follows:

- White background 78 x 110 mm
- Blue background 68 x 80 mm

Any of the above navy badges might be found with a metal crown pinned on top of the maple leaf. This would indicate that the wearer is an instructor.

R7   R8

These badges are identical to the previous ones except in size. The larger badges were worn on the arm by Petty Officers and below. The smaller versions were worn on the collar by Chief Petty Officers. They measure 50 x 60 mm. The small badges were produced in gold on blue, and red on blue only. None were produced with the white background.

R9

SKILL AT ARMS

R10

CF 1985-

With the unification of the forces in 1968, all of the above badges became obsolete. The position of packer/rigger became a job (specialty) and not a trade, like a parachutist. The previous rigger badges were trade badges. New CF badges were not introduced until 1996, with the exception of the smock version. The Rigger badges, above, were produced in the usual rayon (R9) and mylar (R10.)

R11

R12

Bullion

In 1996 the Rigger wings were produced in a very attractive hand embroidered bullion version in both black and scarlet.

R13

Metal

A full size metal Rigger badge was produced for wear on the shirt when not wearing a tunic.

R14

The miniature metal Rigger badge is intended for wear on the pocket of the DEU as a dual qualification badge. In the early 1990's it became CF policy that all skill badges were to be produced in all formats. Therefore, if a miniature metal parachutist badge was to be issued as a dual qualification badge, then a miniature pathfinder, rigger and SAR Tech badge would also be produced. Although this became the policy in 1991, the badges were not produced until 2001, starting with the new version of the parachutist wing (see H7 and H8).

Dual qualification badges are worn on the left breast pocket. The member's main or first badge would be worn in the full-sized version above the pocket. A maximum of two skill badges is allowed.

The badge was not intended to be a mess dress badge. The dress regulations of 1992 state that mess dress badges were to be made of cloth.

R15

R16

Smock

This was the first Rigger badge. An unofficial badge, it was produced in 1978 by the riggers at the CF Parachute Maintenance Depot for wear on the

R17

238

jump smock. About 1985, a maple leaf was added to the design

Note that the previous two badges were in English only. In the late 1980's a bilingual version in olive drab was produced.

R18

R19

Mess Dress

The original mess dress wings were produced in mylar only.

R20

R21

These wings, first produced in 1996, are miniature versions of the hand embroidered Rigger wings. They are fairly large for mess dress, being about 2/3 the size of the full size wings.

R22

Garrison Dress 1985-1998

Like other skill badges, a Rigger badge was produced for the now obsolete Garrison dress.

SEARCH AND RESCUE

The Search and Rescue Technicians of the Canadian Armed Forces are always standing by to assist people in distress. Their job is to find and rescue survivors of aircraft crashes, ships in trouble at sea or others who need assistance in remote or hard-to-reach locations.

SAR Techs, as they are known, are trained in advanced life support, parachuting into any terrain including water or forest or mountains, diving and underwater rescue, mountain climbing and repelling. They are trained in survival on land or at sea or under all Canadian climatic conditions.

In order to become a SAR Tech today, a potential candidate must have four years of service in the Armed Forces in any other trade. This was not the case with the original courses in the 1940's and 1950's.[4]

S1 **S2**

*S2 is the bullion version of this badge.
(Photo courtesy of Pierre Rodriguc)*

Para Rescue 1945-1954

The trade was not always known as SAR Tech, and it was not always a trade. It began in 1945 under the name of Para Rescue. Like a regular parachutist, Para Rescue was a specialty, not a trade. The original candidates for Para Rescue were members of the RCAF trades of Air Frame Mechanic and Air Engine Mechanic. These trades were selected because, in addition to their new Para Rescue duties, they could determine if an aircraft, or any specific parts of it, were salvageable. By the time of the third course in 1947, this was changed to Air Frame Mechanic and Safety Equipment Tech.

By 1950 it was decided that more medical experience was required by the Para Rescue teams. Therefore, the next two courses consisted mainly of candidates who were RCAF Medical Officers, Medial Assistants, and Nursing Sisters. By 1953, the requirement to have Air Frame Mechanics on the team was dropped. The strength of the Para Rescue organization in 1953 consisted of five Medical Officers, seven Nursing Sisters, 17 Medical Assistants and 24 Safety Equipment Techs.

On 19 Dec 1950, two Para Rescuemen made history by being the first Canadians to parachute from a helicopter.

The badge was worn on the upper left arm above the rank badge, except for Flight Sergeants (equal to an army Staff Sergeant) who wore the badge on the lower left arm. This was necessary because Flight Sergeants had a crown above their stripes and therefore had no room for the badge in its normal location. The badge was not worn by officers.

Photo courtesy Para Rescue Association of Canada.

This photo was taken at the time the first Para Rescue badge was replaced with a new design in 1954. Sgt Ted Braidner, wearing the old style badge on his sleeve, points to the new badge, which is worn above the left pocket by F/S Del Wright. The last course to be awarded the old badge was conducted in 1952, and the first one to be awarded the new badge took place in 1954. (There were no courses in 1953.) The badge was changed due to the fact that the old badge could not be worn by officers and was worn by Flight Sergeants in a different position than other ranks. The new badge could be worn, in the same position, by all Para Rescue qualified personnel, including Flight Sergeants, Officers and Nursing Sisters.

The Para Rescue badge was the first hazardous skill badge to be awarded to a female. A joint exercise with the USAF in 1955 caused some surprise as it was the first time the Americans had seen a female military parachutist.

S3   S4   S5

1954-1971

The redesigned badge made its appearance in June of 1954. It had gold coloured wings instead of the wine coloured leaves that surrounded the parachute on the original badge. Also, the word "RESCUE" was eliminated, and the letters "RCAF" were moved to be above the parachute. The badge was given the nickname of "butterfly" by the personnel who wore it.

The badge was issued in two versions as shown above. S3 has eleven feathers while S4 has eight. Also, on S3 there is a small indent on either side of the crown. The change from S3 to S4 was made in the late 1960's. I don't have the exact year.

By 1956 there were no longer any Medical Officers or Nursing Sisters in the Para Rescue organization. Although it seemed to be a good idea in theory, it was very difficult for these personnel to maintain their professional skills while employed with Para Rescue. It was decided to employ only Medical Assistants and Safety Equipment Techs from then on.

In 1959 personnel from the RCAF Munitions and Weapons Tech were recruited into the Para Rescue organization. This was done because American aircraft flying over Canadian territory might be carrying nuclear weapons. What could Canada do if one of these aircraft were to crash on Canadian soil? The Munitions and Weapons Techs could make safe any type of weapons found at a crash site including conventional, nuclear, biological or chemical weapons. They had to ensure that the aircraft was safe for other Para Rescue personnel to administer to the wounded and to rescue them. The Munitions and Weapons Techs would then guard the weapons until they could be removed.

Due to unification of the three military services, the Para Rescue badge had to be changed again. The last course to be awarded the RCAF Butterfly was conducted in 1969.

Bullion

S5 is the wire bullion version of this badge. It was intended for wear on mess dress. There are a few different varieties of this wing, some are more like S2 and S3 in appearance than the one shown.

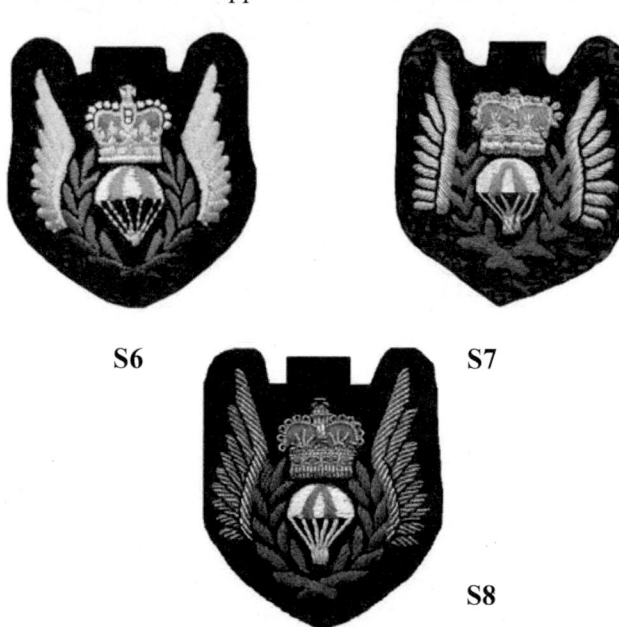

S6   S7

S8

Rescue Specialist Type I 1972-1977
(short wings, 9 feathers)

No courses were conducted, and therefore no badges awarded, during 1970 or 1971. In 1972 the name of the specialty (still not a trade) was changed to Rescue Specialist to more accurately reflect the duties of the speciality. A new badge was designed that included both the laurel leaves and the wings of the two previous designs. The letters RCAF are no longer used.

The 1972 course received the new badge upon graduation but graduated under the old name of Para Rescue. The name was changed after completion of this course. No further courses were conducted until 1976.

After unification Rescue Specialist personnel could be members of any trade or element of the Canadian Armed Forces. Recruits came from the infantry, the air element and many other parts of the military. Upon successful completion of the course, Rescue Specialist personnel would still retain their previous trade. They would be awarded the new Rescue Specialist badge, but like the regular parachutist or the rigger, this was a specialty course only and did not change their trade. The 1972 course was the first one to be open to any trade in the CF.

In 1975, diving was added to the list of skills that were required by a Rescue Specialist. This was due to the increasing number of responses involving marine accidents. From then on, all Rescue Specialists were required to take the diving course in addition to the regular course for the specialty.

The Rescue Specialists wanted to have their own distinctive colour beret, like the airborne maroon beret. The 1976 course was the first to graduate wearing the new Rescue Specialist scarlet beret.

Mylar & Bullion

S6 is the normal rayon badge. S7 is the mylar version of this badge and S8 is the wire bullion version.

Metal

No metal version of this wing was ever produced that I have seen.

Combat

At the same time as a combat version of the parachutist wing was issued (about 1975) a Rescue Specialist badge for the combat uniform was produced. (See badge C8.) Like the parachutist badge, this one was never issued after the trial period.

S9

Mess Dress

A small mess dress version of this badge was produced in mylar.

S10

S11 (Green)   S12 (Black)

Rescue Specialist Type II 1977-1981
(long wings, 15 feathers)

Approximately 1977 the Rescue Specialist badge was modified. The wings on either side of the badge were increased from nine to 15 feathers. Also, the bottom of the badge was rounded. The previous versions were somewhat pointed at the bottom. You cannot tell the difference in these photos but S11 has a dark green background while S12 has a black background.

In September 1979 the Rescue Specialist specialty was made a trade. It was renamed Search and Rescue Technician. All current Rescue Specialist personnel were offered the opportunity to remuster to SAR Tech or return to their previous duties. All personnel accepted the remuster. For some, this meant a change of uniform and hat badge as the new trade was part of the air element. Once again, the badge had to be redesigned but this was to take a couple more years. Three more courses were conducted in 1980, '81 and '82 that still received the Rescue Specialist badge after it was renamed to Search and Rescue Tech, but before the new badge was available.

S13 (Green)   S14 (Black)

Mylar

These are the mylar (J-metallic) versions of S11 and S12 above. Besides the difference in background colour, note that the tip of the wings on S14 are pointed while S13 is rounded.

S15 I have never seen a bullion version of this wing but the number S15 has been set aside for it.

S16 Metal 
A small metal version of this badge was produced for wear on shirts when not wearing a tunic.

S17   S18

Mess Dress

The mess dress version was produced with black and scarlet backgrounds.

S19 (Green)

S20 (Black)

Search and Rescue Technician 131
(00101-01) 1983-

This trade was new in 1979 but the badge was not produced until 1983. It originally had a green background for the CF uniform. The background was changed to black in 1985 for the DEU.

Parachute Badges

Like all the parachute badges in this book, it is difficult to see the difference between the green and black backgrounds until you see them side by side.

S21

Mylar

This is the mylar (aka J-metallic) version of the badge.

S22

Bullion

This is the wire bullion version of the badge. It exists in a few different minor varieties. This one has red markings on the parachute. I have one that is slightly smaller in size and has orange markings on the parachute.

S23

Metal

This metal SAR badge is for wear on the shirt when not wearing a tunic.

S24

The miniature metal SAR badge is intended to be a dual qualification badge. I'm not sure if it was ever used for that purpose. All of the miniature metal para badges were produced as dual qualification badges but I keep getting reports that they are being worn as a mess dress badge.

This badge is not identical to the full size metal badge. The full size badge has a black wreath whereas on the miniature the wreath is wine coloured.

S25

Mess Dress

This cloth mess dress wing is made of mylar and has red markings on the parachute. There are probably other minor varieties.

S26

Garrison Dress 1985-1998

This is the Garrison Dress version of the SAR badge.

S27 (black)   **S28 (grey/green)**

Cadets

To qualify for the Cadet Rescue Specialist badge, a cadet had to have a basic para course plus a junior level first aid course. S27 first appeared in 1974 and has a black background with no border.

SKILL AT ARMS

This was changed in 1977 to S28 which has a grey/green coloured background and a border of the same colour. No equivalent of the current SAR badge was ever produced for the cadet uniform. The para course that they took could be from a civilian parachute school and not necessarily military.

Varieties

This is a variety of the 1954 Para Rescue badge. It is all black and white with the exception of some colour in the crown. The reason for its existence is unknown to me.

SV1

SV2   **SV3**

These are prototypes for the new Rescue Specialist badge when it came out in 1972. SV2 has a very tiny parachute and SV3 has a gold coloured parachute. Neither of these were adopted as official badges. It is unknown how many copies of each were produced.

SV4 is a variety of the Rescue Specialist Type 1 badge. This one has seven pearls on each side of the crown instead of the usual six.

SV4

SV5

This is a version of S21. The difference is the red gores on the parachute instead of the normal orange.

SV6

This SAR Badge has yellow wings instead of the ususal gold colour. The markings on the parachute are red instead of the usual orange. It is probably a private made badge. Its origins are unknown. Like AV1, I classify these badges under the heading of "fake".

SV7

This is a subdued version of the SAR wing. I have seen no evidence that it was ever worn on any uniform. I have seen photos of SAR Techs in their orange flight suits wearing the normal CF rayon badge.

Chevrons, Wound Stripes, Corps Insignia and other Badges

Part Five

**Service Cheverons
General Service Badges
Good Conduct Badges
Wound Stripes
Corps Insignia**

SERVICE CHEVRONS

First World War

Service Chevrons are small stripes, pointing upwards, that show the number of years that a soldier has served. They were originally authorized in 1918 for overseas service during the First World War. For Canadians, this would include service in the United Kingdom, but for British soldiers, it meant service in other parts of Europe. For Canadians, this did not include U.S.A.

Although first authorized in 1918, they were intended to show overseas service since the declaration of war in 1914. The total period during which these badges could be earned was 5 August 1914 to 1 May 1920. [1]

They were worn on the right forearm with the apex of the lowest stripe four inches from the bottom of the sleeve.

Each chevron was supposed to represent one year of overseas service; however, this is misleading. The first chevron was awarded after only one day of overseas service. The second was awarded after twelve months service. Therefore, three chevrons would mean two full years service, plus some more which could be anything from one day to 365 days.

Time that was spent in detention, AWOL or in a hospital did not count toward earning one of these stripes. Up to one month leave was allowed in the time counted.

Service chevrons earned on or before 31 December 1914 were red; those earned on or after 1 January 1915 were blue.

Chevrons illustrated here are:
above left, top four blue and bottom one red
Above right: four blue
Below right: two blue

Using the above criteria, the badge on the left represents more than four years of overseas service starting in 1914 and ending in 1918. The badge on the right represents more than three years of overseas service starting after 1914. The badge below on the right represents more than one year of overseas service starting sometime after 1914.

Service chevrons were not worn on the greatcoat. [2]

The chevrons were produced in strips of red or blue and were cut into sections of the required number of strips. Badges with both the red and the blue stripes on a single badge were private made and not from ordnance stores.

Wearing more chevrons than entitled was punishable by a fine of $100 or three months in prison. [3]

No service chevrons were awarded after 1920. Soldiers who had them were allowed to continue wearing them until they were prohibited from wear in October 1941. (Except for members of the Veterans Guard of Canada who were allowed to continue wearing them until 31 January 1943.) [4]

Other references [5]

Second World War

The wearing of service chevrons was authorized again on 3 December 1942.[6] This time a full completed year of service was required in order to earn one chevron. Total service counted, not necessarily overseas.

The colour of the stripes for Second World War service was originally black, but was later changed to red. Time counted to earn the first chevron could start 10 September 1939 or any date thereafter. In addition to any black stripes, a silver stripe was awarded if the soldier enlisted on or before 10 September 1940. Therefore, the first black chevron could be earned on 10 September 1940 or for any completed year after that date. The method of wear was also changed. They were to be worn 5 ½ inches from the bottom of the left sleeve or above any good conduct badges or above a Warrant Officer rank badge.

Like the previous set of service chevrons, they were not to be worn on the greatcoat. Unlike the First World War badges they were not to be worn while serving overseas. [7]

Like the previous badges, the silver stripe was produced separately and would be sewn below the black strips to create the appearance of being a single badge.

Using the above criteria, both of the above badges would be awarded for three full years of service. The badge on the left shows service starting sometime on or before 10 September 1940. This could be as little as three years and one day. The badge on the right would represent three years of service starting sometime after 10 September 1940

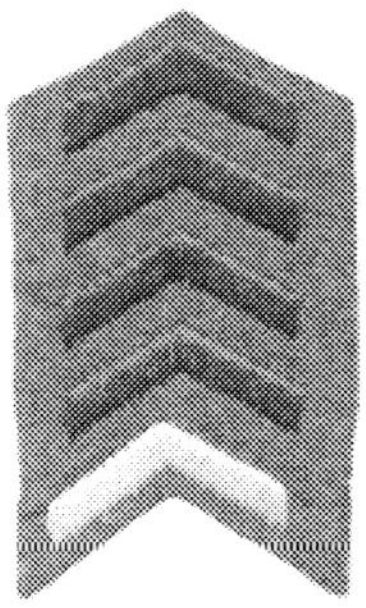

On the first of March 1944 the rules regarding service chevrons changed dramatically. The most obvious change was the colour and size. They changed from black to red and were narrower. The silver chevron was no longer given in addition to any others, but counted as the first full year. Previously, the silver stripe showed only that the soldier had enlisted on or before 10 September 1940 and could represent any amount of service, even a single day, as long as it was before the qualifying date. [8]

Also, the position of wear was changed from the left forearm to the right, and the distance was changed from 5 ½ inches above the cuff, to four inches. The red service chevrons were allowed to be worn while serving overseas.

Using these new criteria, the badge on the left represents five full years of service staring on or before 10 September 1939. The badge on the right would represent three full years of service starting sometime after 10 September 1939.

Service in the CWAC starting 13 Aug. 1941 was eligible for service chevrons.

The end of the qualification period for service chevrons was 31 December 1945. [9]

Post war

The wearing of service chevrons was once again discontinued after the war. However, they were revived again in 1956 (authorized Feb. 1955). These new service chevrons were worn by the militia only and were never worn by the regular force. Even in the militia they were not always worn. The wearing of these badges was not compulsory and apparently not very popular.

This time the colours of the stripes were french grey on a khaki background. They were made in individual badges with one to five stripes instead of a long strip with the number of required stripes to be cut off, as in previous issues. Each stripe represented two full years of service. These new service chevrons represented years of service anywhere, not necessarily overseas. A silver maple leaf was worn above the fifth stripe, but not if less than five stripes had been earned. Five chevrons represented ten years of service. If the soldier was awarded the Canadian Forces Decoration (a medal), all chevrons would be removed. Part of the criteria to earn the Canadian Forces Decoration is 12 years of service. These badges were discontinued with the introduction of the new CF uniform (1968).

The badge above with four chevrons represents eight years of service. The badge on the right represents the maximum of ten years of service. The maple leaf shows that the soldier has somewhere between ten and 12 years in. The maple leaf badges were produced with stems pointing to the left, as in this example, and to the right. There was no

SKILL AT ARMS

special significance to this.

Note that unlike all previous service chevrons, these badges were worn point downwards. They were worn on the right sleeve 6 ½ inches from the cuff to the lowest point of the badge when no other badges are worn on the lower sleeve. If another badge was worn on the forearm, such as an MWO rank badge, then the service chevrons would be worn one half inch below this badge.

References [10]

GENERAL SERVICE BADGE

The General Service Badge was introduced during the Second World War to distinguish volunteer soldiers from those who had been conscripted. To qualify, a soldier had to volunteer to serve anywhere, including overseas, for the duration of the war.

The badge was to be worn in Canada only. It had to be removed when proceeding overseas. It was to be worn on the left arm, 5 ½ inches from the bottom, or above any other badges. It measured about one inch across. [11]

The badge was no longer worn once the soldier qualified for the Canadian Volunteer Service Medal. (18 months voluntary service in Canada or 6 months outside Canada).

THE TRAINED SOLDIER BADGE

The Trained Soldier Badge is also known as the Mars Badge. This is because the badge depicts the zodiac sign of Mars, the god of war. Another Second World War badge, it was awarded to fully trained privates after successful completion of their basic training and trades training and after qualifying for their second pay increase.

It was worn 4 ½ inches from the bottom of the right sleeve, but above any other badges. It was not to be worn overseas. The badge measures 1 3/4 inches across. [12]

GOOD CONDUCT BADGES

Good conduct badges were awarded to soldiers who did not get themselves into serious trouble for a period of at least two years (Fines of $25.00 or less and other minor punishment did not count.) They look like rank badges but were worn point upward. They were worn by privates and L/Cpls only, and have been in use since before the First World War.

They were worn 6.5 inches from the bottom of the left sleeve. Later this was changed to seven inches. The measurement was made from the bottom of the sleeve to the bottom of the inverted point in the centre of the badge.

During the First World War, each good conduct stripe represented four years, to a maximum of four stripes.

By the Second World War the time required to earn the first stripe had been changed to two years of good conduct. Additional stripes could be awarded as follows:

5 years	2 stripes
12 years	3 stripes
18 years	4 stripes
23 years	5 stripes
28 years	6 stripes

If the soldier had no offences whatsoever (not even minor ones) for 14 years, the time required for the 4th, 5th and 6th stripes could be shortened to 16, 21 and 26 years respectively.

After the war the time required to earn a good conduct stripe was changed again. The first stripe could be earned after one year, a second stripe after 5 years, and a third stripe after nine years of good conduct.

A soldier would lose one good conduct stripe

for each occurrence of an offence that resulted in a fine of over $25.00 or a more serious punishment.

The badges were issued in the same colours as the rank badges to match the different coloured uniforms.

The use of good conduct badges was discontinued upon unification. References [13]

WOUND STRIPES

First World War

During the First World War soldiers who were wounded received a badge with a gold coloured stripe to indicate that they had been wounded in battle. They were available in metal or cloth. If a soldier was wounded more than once, then more than one wound stripe could be worn.

They were worn vertically on the left forearm with the lower end of the stripe being four inches from the cuff. They were not worn on greatcoats. [14]

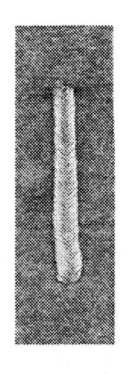

The photos show the cloth version on the left and metal on the right. The metal one clamps on with a pin at each end.

Second World War

The gold wound stripes issued during the First World War were prohibited from being worn after 1941. (Veterans Guard members continued to wear them until 1942.) A red stripe was made available for soldiers who had been wounded prior to the Second World War. Gold stripes then indicated that the soldier had been wounded during the current conflict. As in the First World War, soldiers were allowed to wear one gold stripe for each time they were wounded in battle. However, they could wear only one red stripe, regardless of the number of times they were wounded, to indicate wounds that occurred before the Second World War started.

The Second World War wound stripes were of cloth only. The wearing of wound stripes was discontinued after the war.

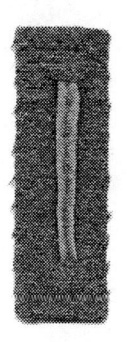

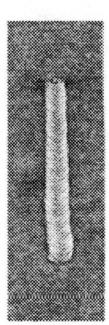

The red stripe on left represented one or more wounds received before the outbreak of the Second World War. Gold stripes on right indicated one wound received in the current war. The metal stripe was discontinued.

Post War

In 1956 wound stripes made an appearance for a third time. This time they were authorized for wear by the militia only. (The wear of service chevrons and wound stripes was authorized in Feb 1955 but did not get issued until early 1956. See post war service chevrons.) Like previous wound stripes, these badges were to be gold in colour and worn on the left forearm. They could represent wounds from enemy action in either the Second World War or the Korean War. Red stripes were once again authorized for wounds received prior to the Second World War. These badges were intended for wear by the militia only and were not to be worn by soldiers of the regular army. The wearing of these badges was discontinued when the battledress uniform was replaced by the CF uniform in 1968-70.

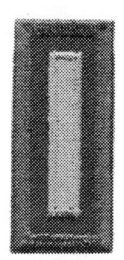

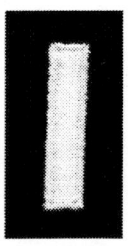

Current Issue

The wearing of wound stripes was authorized for a fourth time approximately 1996. The Canadian military has not been involved in a war since the 1950's, but there are a few soldiers who had been wounded while engaged in peacekeeping forces in Bosnia. The badges were a little shorter, at 1 1/4 inches, than the previous three issues which were 1 ½ inches in length. They are also about twice as wide. These stripes were produced in gold on black for the DEU and on green for the garrison dress.

According to current dress regulations, to qualify for the wound badge a soldier must receive a physical injury during an operation. Injuries sustained during training exercises do not count.
References [15]

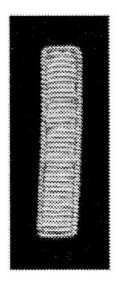

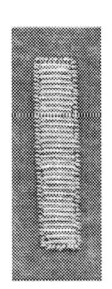

Wound stripes recently became available in bullion for mess dress uniforms in black and red.

CORPS INSIGNIA

Before the Canadian Forces uniform was brought into service with unification in 1968, senior NCO's in some corps wore their corp insignia above their rank badges.

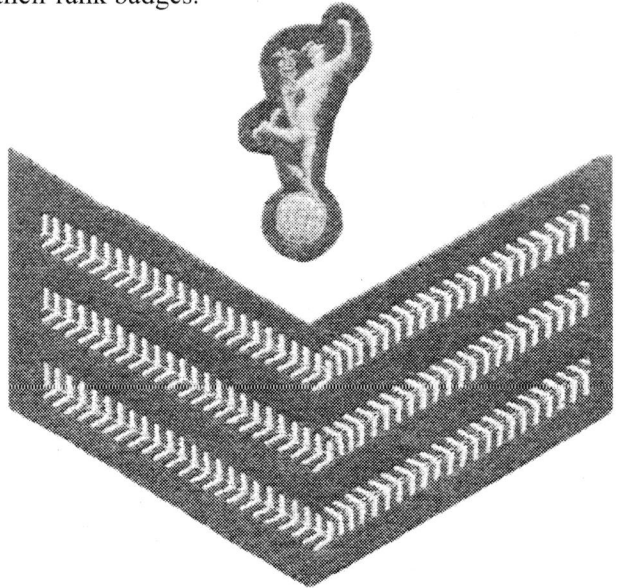

The photo above shows the rank badge of a sergeant in the Royal Canadian Corps of Signals. The insignia, known affectionately by members of the corps as "jimmy", was originally produced in metal in the 1950's. It was changed to cloth in the 1960's.

Corps insignia were worn only by Sergeants and Staff Sergeants (not Lance Sergeants).

When there is insufficient space for the corps insignia, it could be placed directly on top of the rank badge.

Chevrons, Wound Stripes, Corps Insignia and other Badges

CORPS INSIGNIA

Royal Canadian Engineers
This badge can be easily confused with the WWI trade badge of Infantry Bomber. The bomber badge has seven flames; the Engineer grenade has nine flames.

Photo courtesy of Randall Parker.

Royal Canadian Signals
The Signals "Jimmy" badge was available in left and right versions for each arm. The right facing Jimmy is shown on the previous page.
The cloth and metal versions were not worn simultaneously. The metal badge was worn in the 1950s and it was changed to cloth in the 1960s.

Royal Canadian Artillery
The Artillery badge is the same badge as that worn by the Master Gunner. It was available in left and right versions for senior NCO's. When worn by a Master Gunner, it was worn only on the right arm only, near the cuff. (See Master Gunner in Artillery section.)
A metal version was worn on the TW uniform.

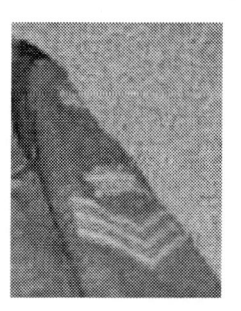

Physical Training Staff

The metal crossed flags was worn on the TW uniform and a cloth version on the bush uniform. Unlike the other badges, this one was worn by all ranks. (Pte in PPCLI on the right and Sgt with RCIC flashes on the left.)

Photos courtesy of Ken MacDonald.

MARKSMANSHIP BADGES

As mentioned in the very first section of this book, the crossed rifles was in use early in the 1900's as a skill-at-arms badge for marksmanship. It was produced in both cloth and metal before the First World War, but only in cloth since the war. When worn on the upper arm, it represented an instructor at the school of musketry. It is the only skill-at-arms badge that is still in use today; therefore, I thought it appropriate to end the book with this badge.

Sometime after the Second World War, a second badge, the crossed rifles with crown, was introduced. This became the new marksman badge and the crossed rifles without a crown was reduced to a lower standard called "First Class Shot".

The following crossed rifle badges are known to exist:

- The regular crossed rifles in worsted drab as shown at the beginning of this article.
- The regular crossed rifles in metal.
- Crossed rifles with tudor crown as shown above.
- The regular crossed rifles in black on red for most rifle regiments.
- Crossed rifles with tudor crown in black on red.
- The regular crossed rifles in black on green for the Royal Winnipeg Rifles.
- Crossed rifles with tudor crown in black on green.
- After the accession of Queen Elizabeth to the throne in 1952, the tudor crown was replaced with the St Edward's Crown. These were produced in drab, black on red and black on green.
- Some of the above badges may have been produced at the soldiers expense in bullion.
- In recent years the crossed rifles and crossed rifles with crown were produced in gold on black for the current army uniform.
- These two badges were also produced in gold on green for the now obsolete garrison dress.
- The current CF badges were also produced in mylar.

first class shot

marksman

Pictures above are the current versions of the crossed rifles badge. The current dress regulations refer to them as the "first class shot" and the "marksman" badges respectively. To qualify for the marksman badge a soldier needs to obtain a score of 46 hits out of 55 shots.

The minimum needed to qualify on the annual PWT (personnel weapon training) is 33 out of 55. One would therefore assume that the first class shot badge would represent something between the minimum of 33 and the marksman standard of 46. This is not the case. Neither the manual that gives the instructions for the PWT nor the dress regulations set any specific score needed to obtain the first class shot badge. Several soldiers that I spoke with told me they needed only the minimum score of 33 to qualify for the first class shot badge. There seems to be no difference between the minimum score needed to pass and the first class designation.[16]

Appendix A
Acronyms, Abbreviations & Definations

AA	Anti-Aircraft
ADATS	Air Defence Anti-Tank System
Admin	Administration
AFV	Armoured Fighting Vehicle
AHQ	Army Headquarters
AI	Assistant Instructor
AIG	Assistant Instructor in Gunnery
AIPT	Assistant Instructor Parachute Training
AKA	Also Known As
Ammo	Ammunition
APC	Armoured Personnel Carrier
Artificer	A highly skilled tradesman who works at the highest trade level.
AWOL	Absent Without Leave
Bn	Battalion
CAC	Canadian Armoured Corps
CD	Coastal Defence Artillery
CDC	Canadian Dental Corps
CE	Construction Engineers
CEF	Canadian Expeditionary Force (overseas forces in WWI)
CF	Canadian Forces
CFPMD	Canadian Forces Parachute Maintenance Depot
C Int C	Canadian Intelligence Corps
CJATC	Canadian Joint Air Training Centre
Comm	Communications
Corps	A Branch of the Army before unification, now called Branches
Coy	Company (part of an infantry battalion)
Cpl	Corporal
CPC	Canadian Parachute Centre
CPC	Canadian Postal Corps
CPO	Chief Petty Officer (a navy rank equal to WO)
C Pro C	Canadian Provost Corps
CSC	Canadian Signalling Corps
CWAC	Canadian Woman's Army Corps
CWO	Chief Warrant Officer
Det	Detachment
DEU	Distinctive Environment Uniform (the current uniform of the land, air and sea elements of the CF)
DND	Department of National Defence
DR	Despatch Rider
DZ	Drop Zone (a landing place for parachutists)
EME	Electrical Mechanical Engineers
Eqpt	Equipment
FCS	Fire Control Systems
Fin	Financial
F of S	Foreman of Signals
F of W	Foreman of Works
FSSF	First Special Service Force
HD	Harbour Defence Artillery
IC	Instructional Cadre
IC	Internal Combustion engine
IC	person In Charge
Int	Intelligence
JAG	Judge Advocate General (military legal section)
Lab	Laboratory
LAV	Light Armoured Vehicle
LCF	Line Chief Foreman
LCIS	Land Communications and Information Systems Tech (radio and other communications equipment tech)
LCpl	Lance Corporal
LDSH(RC)	Lord Strathcona's Horse (Royal Canadians)
LER	Loyal Edmonton Regiment
LSgt	Lance Sergeant
LT	Line Telegraphy
LUVW	Light Utility Vehicle Wheeled
Mech	Mechanic
Met	Meteorological
Misc	Miscellaneous
MO	Medical Officer
MP	Military Police
MSE Op	Mobile Support Equipment Operator
MSF	Mobile Striking Force
MT	Motor Transport
MV	Motor Vehicle
NCO	Non Commissioned Officer
NDHQ	National Defence Headquarters
OC	Officer in Charge
Op	Operator
OWL	Operator Wireless and Line
PERI	Physical Education and Recreation Instructor

PA	Physician Assistant	RMC	Royal Military College
PO	Petty Officer (a navy rank equal to sergeant)	RMS	Resource Management Support Clerk
		RSM	Regimental Sergeant Major
POL	Petrol, Oil and Lubrication	SAA	Skill-At-Arms
PPCLI	Princes Patricia's Canadian Light Infantry	SAR	Seach and Rescue
		SAS	Special Air Service
Provost	an old name for military police	SB	Stretcher Bearer
PT	Physical Training	Sgt	Sergeant
Pte	Private	Sig	Sigalman (A member of the Signal Corps)
PTI	Physical Training Instructor		
QL	Qualification Level	Signaller	Someone who is employed in communications but is not a member of the Signal Corps.
QM	Quartermaster (the place where stores of uniforms and equipment are kept)		
QMSgt (or QMS)	Quartermaster Sergeant	Sigs	Unofficial, but commonly used abbreviation for RC Sigs
RBC	Regiment Blinde du Canada		
RCA	Royal Canadian Artillery	SSF	Special Service Force
RCAC	Royal Canadian Armoured Corps	S/Sgt	Staff Sergeant
RCAF	Royal Canadian Air Force	Steno	Stenographer
RCAMC	Royal Canadian Army Medical Corps	Tech	Technician
RCAPC	Royal Canadian Army Pay Corps	TOW	Tube-Launched, Optically-Tracked, Wire Guided (a missile)
RCASC	Royal Canadian Army Service Corps		
RCCS	Royal Canadian Corps of Signals (later changed to RC SIGS)	Tpt	Transport
		TQ	Trade Qualification level
RCD	Royal Canadian Dragoons	TW	Tropical Worsted (a summer dress uniform before unification)
RCDC	Royal Canadian Dental Corps		
RCE	Royal Canadian Engineers	veh	Vehicle
RCEME	Royal Canadian Corps of Electrical and Mechanical Engineers	VT	Visual telegraphy
		WO	Warrant Officer (ranks between sergeant and lieutenant)
RCIC	Royal Canadian Infantry Corps		
RCN	Royal Canadian Navy	WO1	Warrant Officer first class
RCOC	Royal Canadian Ordnance Corps	WO2	Warrant Officer second class
RCR	Royal Canadian Regiment	WO3	Warrant Officer third class
RC SIGS	Royal Canadian Corps of Signals	Works Company	The former name of CE
Recce	Reconnaissance	wpm	words per minute
Regt	Regiment	Wpn	Weapon
Remuster	To change trades	WT	Wireless Telegraphy

APPENDIX B

Bibliography

Army Employment, Civilian Jobs, DND 1945
Canadian Army Courses Manual 1955
Canadian Army Journal
Canadian Army Manual of Trades and Specialties
Canadian Forces Dress Instructions
Canadian Ordnance Catalogue 1958
CAROs
CAO 269-1
Dorosh, Micheal, Dressed to Kill, Service Publications 2001
Edwards, Denis & Langley, David, British Army Proficiency Badges, Sherwood Press 1984

Financial Regulations and Instructions 1940
Granatstein, J.L., Canada's Army, University of Toronto Press 2002
Grimshaw, Louis, The Badges and Insignia of the Canadian Airborne Forces 1981
History of the Royal Canadian Corps of Signals, Corps Committee 1962
Horn, Lt-Col Bernd, Bastard Sons, Vanwell Publishing 2001
It's Your Army 1954
Johnston, Col Murray, Canada's Craftsmen, Lore Association 1984
King's Regulations and Orders 1939
Law, Clive M., Khaki, Service Publications 1997
Love, David W, A Call to Arms, Bunker to Bunker Books 1999
Murray, Gil, The Invisible War, Dundurn Group 2001
Murray, J.D., The Last Wagon
Nicholson, G.W.L., The Gunners of Canada, Imprimerie L'eclaireur 1972
Orders and Instructions for Dress of the Canadian Army 15 Oct 1953, amended 1956
Otter, Lt Col W.D., The Guide, Copp Clark Co. 1894
Otter, Lt Col W.D., The Guide, Copp Clark Co. 1914
Overseas Military Forces of Canada 1918.
Pugh, Harry & Clark, Thomas Canadian Airborne Insignia C&D Enterprises 1994
McKean VC, GB, Scouting Thrills, CEF Books 2003
Signalling 1916
That Others May Live, Para Rescue Association
To the Thunderer His Armys, W.F. Rannie 1984
Trades in the Canadian Armed Forces, DND undated.
Tradesmans Tests 1937

APPENDIX C
Notes
Part One

1. CARO 1311 1941
2. Dress Regulations CEF
3. Regulations and Instructions for the Clothing of the NPAM 1926
4. CARO 5131, Amend 16 to War Dress Regs 1943
5. The Gunners of Canada by G.W.L. Nicholson
6. MO 158 1929
7. Pay Chart RC Sigs trades 1928
8. Financial Regulations and Instructions 1940
9. Signalling 1916
10. The Guide 1914
11. The Guide 1894
12. CAJ Vol IX No 2 Apr 1955.

Part Two

1. CARO 2370 1942
2. CAO 330 24 Sep 1942.
3. War Dress Regs 1943
4. CARO 2533 1942.
5. CARO 2704 1942.
6. CARO 3066 1943
7. Amend 16 1944 to War Dress Regs 1943
8. CARO 4865 1944

SKILL AT ARMS

9. CARO 4749 1944
10. The Invisible War by G.S. Murray and conversation with the author.
11. The Gunners of Canada by G.W.L. Nicholson
12. CARO 6579 1946
13. CAO 269-1 April 1947

Part Three

1. Several people have told me that the army Fire Fighter trade never existed but the trade is listed in "Orders and Instructions for Dress" amend 7 dated 12 Mar 1956 and also in the Canadian Army Courses Manual 1955 and also in the Canadian Army Manual of Trades annex E Part 3, list of RCE trades. It was made obsolete with AL30.
2. This badge is often listed as an Artillery Signaller badge. Indeed the barrel does appear to be an old artillery gun barrel. This is probably an error in the design of the badge. The badge is listed in the 1956 dress manual as that of a Gunner-Signaller which was an RCAC specialty. To confirm this I have checked with three retired soldiers who were Artillery Signallers in the 1960s and they had never seen this badge. They wore the regular crossed flags badge of the Driver Operator.
3. The duties of the gun crew was obtained from several different manuals for several different guns dating back to the First World War. It is not an exact job description for any particular gun or time period but is intended to be a brief explanation in layman's terms of the duties of the crew.
4. C and E newsletter vol 35
5. CAJ vol XIII #2 Apr 1959.
6. From conversation with dental personnel and not from official docs.
7. CAJ vol XII #2 Apr 1958
8. RCASC in the Field
9. CFAO 2-10 1980
10. A-PD-050-058/PT-001 PERI Branch Handbook
11. The master bandsman badge was confirmed by verbal converstions only. I found no documented proof of the use of this badge by Canadians.
12. RCASC in the Field.

Part Four

1. The CABC also included CFPMD, TALS, ALSTW and ATES
2. By airborne exercise I mean an exercise involving all the jump companies. Small parachute exercises were arranged by single jump companies.
3. At least this is true for soldiers that I interviewed at CFB Edmonton. I did not interview soldiers in the other jump companies (2003).
4. Names and dates for the para rescue/SAR badges come from the book "That Others May Live" by the Para Rescue Association.

Part Five

1. CEFRO 508, 2394 and 1695
2. CEFRO 1107/1918
3. CEFRO 732/1918
4. CARO 1376/1941, 2697/1942 and 2865/1943
5. AO 4/18, 132/18, 286/18, 361/18, 57/20
6. CARO 1376/1941, 2670/1942, 2697/1942 and 2865/1942.
7. CARO 2681, 2670, 3079 and 3524 1943
8. CARO 4110 1944
9. CARO 6284 1945
10. CAO 82-24, CAO 84-28 and CAJ vol X No 1 Jan 1956.
11. CARO 2671 1942
12. CARO 2767 1943
13. GO 165 1940, CARO 635/1940, 1311/1941 and CAO 84-26
14. CEFRO 281 1918
15. CARO 1376/1941, 2697/1942, 4649/1944 and CAJ vol X No 1 Jan 1956.
16. B-GL-382-001/PT-001 (shoot to live) and also dress regs as in #15 above.

INDEX

PARTS

Part One (before 1942)	9
Part Two (1942 to 1945)	73
Part Two (1946 to 1955)	95
Part Three (1956 to date)	125
Part Four (parachute badges)	219
Part Five (miscellaneous badges)	245

SKILL-AT-ARMS BADGES

DM (driver mechanic)	12
G (tank gunner)	12
G (artillery gunner)	13
H (height taker)	12
L (layer)	10
LG (lewis gunner)	12
MG (machine gunner)	12
MT	71
O (observer)	11
P (plotter)	11
R (rangetaker)	11
Crossed Cannon	14
Crossed Flags	14
Crossed Rifles	14
Star	14

SECTIONS

Aircraft Tech	130
Artificers and Armourers	20, 76, 97
Ammunition	20, 76, 97, 131
Armoured	22, 77, 97, 131
Artillery	22, 78, 98, 139
Chemicals	78, 99
Clerks	23, 79, 99, 154
Communications	25, 79, 101, 161
Construction Engineers	103, 176
Cooks	36, 81, 105, 181
Dental	37, 82, 106, 181
Drivers	37, 82, 106, 187
Electrical and Mechanical	38
Equestrian	41, 82, 107
Field Engineers	42, 82, 107, 189
Fire Service	108, 190
Forestry	42, 82, 108
Fortress Company	44, 83
Geomatics	49, 85, 108, 191
Gliders	108
Infantry	49, 86, 109, 193
Instructors	110, 195
Intelligence	86, 113, 197
Laundry	113, 198
Materials	52, 86, 114, 199
Medical	53, 87, 114, 200
Military Police	57, 88, 115, 205
Musicians	57, 88, 116, 206
Non-Tradesmen	70
Parachute Trades	88, 116, 210
Photography	61, 89, 116, 211
Postal	89, 117, 212
Printing and Publishing	62, 89, 117, 212
Public Relations	212
Railway	63, 90, 117
RCEME	90, 117, 212
Supply	66, 92, 119, 213
T Badges	124
Traffic Tech	214
Unknown Trades	70, 95
Vehicle Mechanics	67, 92, 119, 214
Water Transport	68, 94, 120
Weapons Tech	121, 214
Woodworking	70, 95, 121, 216

INSTRUCTORS Pre 1942

Instructors (various types)	16, 17

TRADES

Accountant Signals	79, 99
Accounting and Finance Clerk	156
Administrative Clerk	155
Aeromedical Tech	203
Aircraft Techs	130
Ammunition Examiner	20, 76, 97, 131
Armament Artificer AFV	77, 120
Armament Artificer Anti-Aircraft	77, 121, 215
Armament Artificer Coast Defence	121
Armament Artificer Electrical	77, 118
Armament Artificer Field	77, 121, 215
Armament Artificer Fitter	20, 76
Armament Artificer Vehicle	120
Armament Artificer Instruments	20, 76, 121
Armament Artificer MV	77, 120
Armament Artificer Radar	77, 102
Armament Artificer Wireless	21, 76, 102
Armourer	21, 77, 121, 214
Armourer IC RCOC Workshop	21, 77
Army Technical Warrant Officer	217
Artificer RCA	21, 77
Artillery Air Defence	143
Artilleryman	141
Assistant Foreman Departmental	67, 92
Assistant Instructor Anti-Aircraft Artillery	147
Assistant Instructor Field Artillery	147
Assistant Instructor Harbour Defence	147
Assistant Instructor Infantry	195
Assistant Instructor In Gunnery	148
Assistant Instructor In Gunnery Air Defence	148
Assistant Instructor Parachute Training	210
Assistant Instructor Physical Training	111, 196
Assistant Instructors (various types)	195
Assistant Instructor RCAC	133
Assistant Instructor RCAMC	202
Assistant Photo Interpreter	197
Artillery Locator	146
Artillery Surveyor	146
Baker	36, 82, 105, 181
Bandmaster	58, 88, 116, 206

Bandsman	57, 88, 116, 206	Communication Tech	167
Base Medical Tech	204	Communicator Research	169
Battery Surveyor	23, 78	Computer Progammer	156
Biomedical Electronics Technologist	204	Computer Trigonometrical	49, 86
Biosciences Tech	202	Concretor	45, 83, 103, 176
Blacksmith	44, 83, 103, 176	Concrete Worker	45
Blockman	63, 90, 117	Construction Tech	178
Boilermaker	44, 83, 103	Construction Engineer Tech	178
Body Builder Metal	67, 92	Construction Engineer Procedures Tech	179
Body Repairman	119, 214	Construction and Maintenance Tech	179
Bomber	49	Cook	36, 82, 105, 181
Brakeman and Shunter	63, 90, 117	Cook Hospital	37, 82, 105
Bricklayer	44, 83, 103, 176	Coppersmith	38, 90
Bugler	59, 88, 207	Court Reporter	25, 79, 100, 154, 157
Bugle-Major	209	Crew Commander RCAC	133
Butcher	36, 82, 105, 181	Crewman	132, 134
Cable Joiner	26	Crewman Recce	133
Cable Splicer	26, 79, 101, 161	Cyclist	71
Cabinet Maker	44	Cryptographer	162, 166
Cabinet Maker Signals	26	Cymbal Player	59, 88
Carpenter	45, 83, 103, 176, 177	Data Processor	156
Carpenter and Joiner	45, 83	Dental Assistant	37, 82, 106, 181
Carpenter and Wheeler	45	Dental Chair Assistant	37
Carpenter Signals	26	Dental Clinical Assistant	185
Carriage Smith	41	Dental Equipment Repairer	106, 185, 186
Carriage and Wagon Repairer	63, 90, 117	Dental Lab Tech	186
Cartographer	108, 191	Dental Tech	37, 82, 106, 185
CE Superintendent	180	Dental Tech Clinical	181
Checker Number Taker	63, 90, 117	Dental Instrument Repairer	37, 82
Chemical Tech	78, 99	Dental Hygienist	186
Chief Artilleryman	146	Dental Therapist	186
Chief Assistant Photo Interpreter	197	Despatcher Air Supply	116, 211
Chief Cryptographer	162, 166	Despatch Rider	26, 79, 101, 165
Chief Gunnery Assistant	148	Disciplinarian	206
Chief Intelligence Investigator	197	Diver	45, 83, 103
Chief Locating Assistant	145	Draughtsman Architectural	45, 83
Chief Locator	146	Draughtsman Architectural and Engineering	83, 103, 176-178
Chief Meteorological Assistant	147	Draughtsman Cartographic	86, 108
Chief Punch Card Equipment Op	154	Draughtsman Engineering	45, 83
Chief Radio and Telegraph Op	162, 167	Draughtsman Electrical and Mechanical	117, 178, 212
Chief Radio Intelligence Collator	197	Draughtsman Graphic Arts	86, 108, 178, 192
Chief Teletype and Cipher Op	166, 167	Draughtsman Lithographer	89, 117
Chief Transport Op	188	Draughtsman Mechanical	38, 90, 117
Chiropodist	87, 114	Draughtsman Railway Construction	64, 90
Cipher Operator	80, 162, 166	Draughtsman RC Signals	27, 79, 101, 163
Cleaner Locomotive	64, 90, 117	Draughtsman Topographical	45, 83, 103, 178, 192
Clerk	24, 79, 99	Driller	103
Clerks (various types)	23	Driller Diamond Setter	84, 103
Clerk Accounting (various types)	99, 155	Driller Diamond and Rotary	84, 103
Clerk Administrative	99, 154	Driver Electrician	101, 165
Clerk Departmental	25, 79	Driver IC (various types)	37
Clerk Engineer Accountant	79, 100, 155	Driver IC Tractor Forestry	42, 82, 108
Clerk Operations	99, 143	Driver Mechanic	37, 82, 106
Clerk Stenographer	79, 100, 154	Driver Mechanic Carrier	82, 106
Clerk Superintending	25, 79, 99	Driver Mechanic MV	82, 106
Clerk Typist	100	Driver Mechanical Transport	106, 165, 187
Coach Painter	67, 92, 119	Driver Mechanic Tracked	106, 132
Coach Trimmer	67, 92, 119	Driver MT RC Signals	27
Combat Engineer	190	Driver Mechanic Tank	82, 106
Communications Op	167	Driver Mechanic Wheeled	106, 132
Communication System Artificer	165, 166, 168	Driver Op	27, 79, 97, 99, 101, 107, 109, 119, 141, 170, 213
Communication System Tech	165, 166, 168		

Index

Driver Radio Op	170, 213	Fitter MV	67, 93
Driver RCA	106, 142	Fitter RCE	104, 199
Driver RCA Tracked	106, 142	Fitter Signals	28, 79, 101
Driver Steam Lorry and Steam Tractor	38	Fitter Special Engineering Equipment	82, 107
Driver Signals	166	Fitter Tractor Forestry	43, 83, 108
Driver Transportation Plant	38, 82, 107	Foreman Departmental	66, 92, 119
Drummer	59, 88, 207	Foreman Departmental Forestry	43, 83
Drum-Major	207, 209	Foreman Fore and Aft	94, 120
Edgerman Forestry	43, 82, 108	Foreman of Signals	28, 79, 101, 164, 167
Electrical Artificer	118, 212	Foreman of Works	46, 84, 104, 176
Electrical Distribution Tech	178	Foreman of Works Bush Forestry	43, 83, 108
Electrical Mechanic	117, 212	Foreman of Works Mill Forestry	43, 83, 108
Electrical Tech	212	Gas Fitter	46
Electrician	46, 83, 103, 176-178	Geomatics Tech	192
Electrician Control Equipment	117	Glider Pilot	108
Electrician Fitter	39, 90	Graphic Artist	192
Electrician MV	93	Grinder Precision	39, 91, 118
Electrician Radar	78, 98, 102	Gun Mechanic	121, 214
Electrician RCEME	90, 117	Gun Number Anti Aircraft	140
Electrician Signals	27, 79	Gun Number Harbour Defence	140
Electrician Vehicle and Plant	93, 119	Gun Number RCA	99, 139
Electrician Wireless	36, 81	Gunner-Driver Mechanic Tracked	98, 131
Electroplater	93, 119	Gunner-Driver Mechanic Wheeled	98, 131
Electro-Mechanical Tech	213	Gunner Operator	77, 97
Engine Artificer	21, 77	Gunner RCAC	131
Engine Artificer Forestry	43, 82	Gunner Signaller	97, 131
Engine Driver IC	38	Hammerman	44
Engine Driver Railway	90, 117	Hatch Tender	94, 120
Engine Driver Steam	38	Health Services Technical Manager	204
Engine Fitter IC and Pump	83, 103	Helicopter Tech	130
Engine Fitter Steam Reciprocating	84, 105	Helioworker	62, 89
Engine Hand IC	38, 84, 103	Helioworker and Litho Prover	89, 117
Engineer Accountant	100, 155	Helper Engineers	48
Engineer Store Accountant	23	Hospital Sergeant	56
Engineer Water Transport Diesel	94, 120	Hygiene Assistant	115, 201
Engineer Water Transport Gasoline	94, 120	Infantry Anti-Tank Gunner	109, 193
Engineer Water Transport Steam	69, 94	Infantry Driver	106, 110, 195
Engineer Works Foreman	46, 84	Infantry Machine Gunner	110, 193
Equipment Mechanic	104	Infantry Mortarman	109, 194
Equipment Repairer	52, 86, 114	Infantry Pioneer	109, 194
Farrier	41, 82, 107	Infantry Reconnaissance	195
Field Engineer	107, 189	Infantry Signaller	109, 195
Field Engineer Equipment Operator	189	Infantry Sniper	109, 194
Field Medical Tech	204	Infantry Stretcher Bearer	109, 194
Fifer	59, 88, 207	Infantryman	193
Finance Clerk	156	Institute Bookkeeper	155
Fingerprint Classifier	115, 205	Instructors (various types)	110, 195
Fire Control System Artificer Anti-Aircraft	121, 215	Instrument Artificer	215
Fire Control System Tech	121, 215, 216	Instrument Artificer HD and AA	215
Fire Fighter	108, 190	Instrument Artificer Anti-Aircraft	121, 215
Fire Safety Inspector	190	Instrument Artificer Coast Defence	121
Fireman	46	Instrument Artificer Field	121, 215
Fireman Locomotive	64, 90, 117	Instrument Artificer Harbour Defence	121, 215
Fireman Stationary Engine	38	Instrument Maker	39
Fitter	39, 91, 97, 98, 101, 104, 118	Instrument Maker WT and LT	28
		Instrument Mechanic	39, 91, 121
Fitter AFV	93	Instrument Mechanic Electrical	121, 215
Fitter Gun	22, 78, 98	Instrument Mechanic Field	91, 118
Fitter IC Tank	22, 77	Instrument Mechanic Field Survey	91, 118
Fitter Locomotive Diesel	64, 90, 117	Instrument Mechanic Heavy Anti-Aircraft	91, 118
Fitter Locomotive Steam	64, 90, 117	Instrument Mechanic HD and AA	215
		Instrument Mechanic Light Anti-Aircraft	91, 118

Instrument Mechanic Optical	121. 215	Materials Tech	200
Instrument Mechanic RCE	46, 84	Meat Cutter	105
Instrument Mechanic Signals	28, 79, 102	Mechanic MT RC Signals	30
Instrument Mechanic Surgical	53, 87, 114, 201	Mechanic RCE	107, 190, 199
Instrument Mechanic Typewriter and Cipher	91, 118	Mechanic Refrigeration Plant	84, 104
Instrument Repairer	46	Mechanic Special Engineering Equipment	107
Instrument Repairer Dental	82, 106	Mechanic Stationary Engine	103
Instrument Tech	215	Mechanic Tire Maintenance	94, 120
Intelligence Collator	197	Mechanic X-Ray	88, 115
Intelligence Linguist	113, 198	Mechanical Systems Tech	179
Intelligence Investigator	113, 197	Mechanist	39, 91, 118
Intelligence Operator	198	Mechanist Coxswain	69, 94, 120
Intelligence Specialist	113	Mechanist Electrical	46, 84, 104, 178
Interpreter Russian	198	Mechanist Electrician	46
Investigator Intelligence	113	Mechanist Fitter	200
Laboratory Assistant	53, 87, 114, 201	Mechanist Instrument Repairer	46
Laboratory Tech	87, 114, 204	Mechanist Machinery	46, 84, 104, 199
Land Communication and Information System Tech	169	Medical Assistant	114, 200, 202
Laundry Operator	113	Medical Orderly	55
Laundry and Bath Operator	113, 198	Medical Radiation Technologist	204
Leading Assault Trooper	98, 134	Medium Machine Gunner	110
Leading Infantryman	109, 193	Metals Tech	214
Leather and Canvas Worker	114	Meteorological Observer	78, 98, 147
Leather and Textile Worker	114, 199	Military Instructor	196
Line Construction Foreman	161, 167	Military Police	115, 205
Lineman	27, 79, 101, 161	Military Staff Clerk	25
Lineman Field	28, 101, 161	Millwright	39, 91, 118
Lineman Mechanic	29, 80, 103, 164	Miner	47, 84, 104, 176, 177
Lineman Permanent Line	29, 101, 161	Minor Diamond Setter	47, 84
Linguist	113, 198	Minor Mechanic or Driller	47, 84
Lithographer	62, 89, 117, 191	Mobile Support Equipment Operator	189
Lithographer Draughtsman	62, 89	Motor Assembler	67, 93
Lithographer Machine Minder	62, 89, 117	Motor Mechanic	67, 93
Lithographer Prover	62, 89	Motor Mechanic Forestry	43, 83
Loftman	29, 80, 101	Motorcycle Mechanic	93
Log Canter Forestry	43, 83, 108	Moulder	40, 91, 118, 200
Machinist Fitter	118, 200	Musician	208
Machinist Metal	39, 91, 118	Nursing Assistant	114, 201
Machinist Signals	28	Nursing Orderly	87, 114
Machinist Wood	70, 95, 121, 216	Nursing Orderly Mental	95
Map Reproduction Tech	192	Occupational Therapy Aide	201
Mason	46, 84, 104, 177	Operating Room Assistant	53, 87, 115, 201, 203
Masseur	53, 87, 114	Operator Airways RC Signals	35
Master Aircraft Tech	130	Operator B2 Signals	36, 70
Master Bandsman	208	Operator CAC	78, 97
Master Cook	105, 181	Operator Chemical Plant	79, 99
Master Crewman	133	Operator Cipher	80, 101, 162
Master Electrical Tech	212	Operator Fire Control AA	98
Master FCS Tech	215	Operator Fire Control Coast Artillery	98
Master Gunner	22, 78, 98, 149, 217	Operator Fire Direction Coast	98
Master Infantryman	193	Operator Fire Director Harbour Defence	99, 143
Master Instrument Tech	215	Operator Fixed Wireless Station	80, 101, 163
Master Medical Assistant	115	Operator Keyboard	35, 81, 102, 162
Master Radio Equipment Tech	164, 167, 168	Operator Kine Theodolite	78, 98, 145
Master Radiographer	115, 201	Operator Light and Power Plant	84, 104
Master Seaman	121	Operator Monitor Signals	80, 101
Master Sig	170	Operator Predictor	99, 143
Master Teletype and Cipher Equipment Tech	164, 167, 168	Operator Punch Card Tabulating Machine	79, 100
Master Terminal Equipment Tech	164, 167, 168	Operator Punched Card Machines	100, 154
Master Vehicle Tech	214	Operator Radar	78, 99
Master Weapons Tech	215	Operator Radar AA	99, 143
Mate Water Transport 1st Class	94, 120	Operator Radar Coast	99

Index

Operator Radar Harbour Defence	99, 143	Radar Tech	102, 165, 168
Operator Radio RC Signals	31	Radio Artificer	102, 165, 168
Operator RCAC	97	Radio Equipment Tech	163, 168
Operator RC Signals	30	Radio Intelligence Collator	197
Operator Searchlight	99, 143	Radio Mechanic	102, 103, 163
Operator Special Engineering Equipment	42, 82, 107, 189, 199	Radio Operator	167
Operator Special Signals	81, 101, 163	Radio Tech	102, 165, 168
Operator Steam Power Plant	85, 105	Radio and Telegraph Operator	161
Operator Switchboard	81, 102, 162	Radiographer	54, 88, 115, 201
Operator Teletype	102	Railway Engine Driver	64, 90
Operator Wireless and Line	31, 81, 102, 161	Recovery Mechanic	120
Optician	87, 115, 201	Refrigeration and Mechanical Tech	179
Optometrist	87, 115, 202	Resource Management Support Clerk	156
Painter	47, 85, 104, 176, 177	Rigger	48, 85, 104
Painter and Decorator	47, 85, 104	Riveter	48, 85, 104
Panel Beater	67, 92, 119	Roofer	48
Paperhanger	47	Rough Rider	41
Parachute Packer	88, 116	Saddle and Harness Maker	52
Parachute Rigger	89, 116, 210	Saddle Tree Maker	52, 86, 114
Parachute and Safety Equipment Worker	116	Saddler	52, 86, 114
Pattern Maker	70, 95, 121, 216	Safety Equipment Tech	116
Pay Clerk	155	Sanitary Assistant	54, 88, 115
Pharmacist	115, 201	Sanitary Inspector	88, 115
Pharmacist and Dispenser	54, 88, 115	Sawdoctor	43, 83, 108
Photogrammetrist	86, 108, 191	Sawfiler Forestry	44, 83, 108
Photographer	89, 116, 211	Sawyer	48, 85, 105, 176
Photographer Cartographic	117, 211	Sawyer Forestry	44, 83, 108
Photographer Cinematographic	89, 116, 211	Scout	51
Photographer Dry Plate	61, 89	Scrutineer	24
Photographer Wet Plate	61, 89	Seaman	120
Photo-Mechanical Tech	211	Senior Medical Assistant	114, 201
Photowriter	62, 90, 117	Senior Projectionist	91, 118
Physical Education and Recreation Instructor	197	Service Policeman	115, 205
Physical Training and Recreation Specialist	196	Sheet Metal Worker	85, 105, 118, 176, 177
Physical Training Instructor	196	Shipwright	69, 94, 120
Physician Assistant	203	Shoe Repairer	114, 199
Physio Therapy Aide	114	Shoeing Smith	41
Physio-Occupational Therapy Aide	114, 201	Shoemaker	52, 87, 114, 199
Pioneer	50, 86, 109	Shoemaker Orthopaedic	87, 115
Pioneer RCE	48, 85, 107	Side-Runner	94, 120
Pipe-Major	208, 209	Signal Op	169
Piper	207, 208	Signals Electricain	165
Plasterer	48	Signaller	32
Platelayer	64, 90, 117	Signaller Artillery	32, 81, 99, 101, 141
Plotter Air Photo	113, 197	Signaller Infantry	32, 81, 101, 109
Plumber	48, 104, 176, 177	Signaller-Driver Mechanic Tracked	98, 132
Plumber Gas Fitter	177	Signaller-Driver Mechanic Wheeled	98, 132
Plumber and Pipe Fitter	48, 85, 104	Signaller RCAC	97, 132
Plumbing and Heating Tech	177	Skipper Water Transport 1st Class	94, 121
Postal Clerk	117, 212	Small Arms Artificer	121, 214
Postal Sorter	89, 117	Special Investigator C Pro C	205
Postal Supervisor	89, 117	Specialist RCAC	98, 133
Preventive Medicine Tech	203, 204	Stationary Engineer	105
Printer Compositor	63, 90, 117	Steamfitter	48, 85, 105
Printer Machine Minder	62, 90, 117	Stenographer	154
Projector Mechanic	118, 213	Sterotyper	63, 90
Public Relations Assistant	212	Stevedore	69, 95
Punch Card Equipment Op	154	Steward	100, 155, 157
Push Cycle Repairer	93, 120	Stoker Fireman	69, 95
Quarryman	48, 85, 104, 176	Stoker Stationary Engine	48, 85, 105
Radar Artificer	102, 165, 168	Storeholder	92, 119
Radar Mechanic	102	Storeholder MV	92, 119

SKILL - AT - ARMS

Storeholder RCOC	66, 92
Storeman (various types)	119
Storeman Departmental	66
Storeman Clerk	119, 155
Storeman Medical	119, 213
Storeman RCASC	119, 213
Storeman RCOC	119, 213
Storeman Technical (various)	66
Storeman Technical Forestry	44
Storeman Technical and Departmental	92, 119
Strategic and Information Systems Tech	169
Stretcher Bearer	55
Structural Steel Worker	104, 176
Structures Tech	177
Supply Tech	213
Surveyor Cadastral and Engineering	49, 86
Surveyor Engineering	48, 85, 105, 176, 177, 179
Surveyor Ordnance	70
Surveyor RCA	22, 78, 98, 145
Surveyor RCA Flash Spotting	98, 145
Surveyor RCA Radar	98, 145
Surveyor RCA Sound Ranging	98, 145
Surveyor Railway	65, 90
Surveyor Topographical	49, 85, 105, 176, 177, 179
Surveyor Trigonometrical	49, 86
Switchboard Installer	29
Switchboard Operator	36
Tailor	52, 87, 114, 199
Technical Assistant (various types)	99, 142
Technical Assistant Medical	114, 201
Technical Assistant Survey	98
Technical Supervisor Radio	95
Technician Dental Therapist	181
Telecommunication Artificer	102
Telecommunication Mechanic (various types)	81, 102, 165
Telegraph Mechanic	103, 164
Teletype and Cipher Equipment Tech	164, 168
Teletype and Cipher Op	166
Teletype Operator	102, 162, 166
Terminal Equipment Tech	164, 168
Textile Refitter	52, 86, 114
Tinsmith	40, 91, 118
Tinsmith and Whitesmith	40, 92
Tire Repairman	120, 214
Toolmaker	40, 92, 118, 200
Topographical Surveyor	179
Traffic Operator Railway	65, 90, 117
Traffic Tech	214
Training Aids Artist	192
Transport Operator	188
Transportation Controller	188, 189
Trumpet-Major	209
Trumpeter	61, 88, 207
Turner	40, 92, 118
Typewriter Mechanic	40, 92, 118, 216
Unknown trades	70, 95
Upholsterer	67
Vehicle Artificer	120, 214
Vehicle Mechanic AFV	93, 119
Vehicle Mechanic MV	93, 119
Vehicle Mechanic	119
Vehicle Mechanic Tracked	119, 214
Vehicle Mechanic Wheeled	119, 214
Vehicle Tech	214
Veterinary	42
Vulcanizer	68, 94
Wardmaster	54, 88, 115
Watchmaker	40, 92, 118, 216
Waterman Boatman	69, 95, 120
Weapons Artificer	215
Weapons Tech	215
Wellborer	49, 85, 105
Welder	105, 118, 177, 214
Welder Acetylene	41, 92, 118
Welder Electric	41, 92
Welder Gas and Electric	92, 118
Wheeler	68, 94, 120
Winchman	95, 121
Wireless Intelligence Linguist	86, 113
Wireless Mechanic	36, 81
Woodworker	70
Wood Turner and Machinist	70, 95
Workshop Foreman Field Hygiene	88, 115
Workshop Supervisor	53, 87, 114
X-Ray Tech	54, 88, 204

PARACHUTE BADGES

Parachutist	220
Pathfinder	234
Rigger	236
Search and Rescue	239

MISCELLANEOUS

Administration Branch	157
Armoured Regiment	135
Army Technical Warrant Officer	217
Artillery Schools	148
Artillery Survey	146
Band Branch	210
Corps Insignia	251
CWAC	74, 96
Flags	31
General Service Badges	248
Good Conduct Badges	248
Infantry Specialties	194
Logistics Branch	213
Marksmanship Badges	252
Medical Branch	205
Rank names	13
Service Chevrons	246
Signaller Qualification	34
SORD	217
Trades at nil strength	216
Trained Soldier Badge	248
Women	97, 128, 218
Wound Stripes	249

For comments on errors, omissions, or additions to the book contact the author via his website:

www.skill-at-arms.ca